Things Fall Apart

Things Fall Apart

A history of the STATE BANK of SOUTH AUSTRALIA

Greg McCarthy

Australian Scholarly
PUBLISHING

Melbourne

This publication was supported by the South Australian Government through the History Trust of South Australia.

© Greg McCarthy 2002

First published in 2002 by
Australian Scholarly Publishing Pty Ltd
PO Box 299, Kew, Victoria 3101
102/282 Collins Street, Melbourne 3000
Tel: (03) 9654 0250   Fax: (03) 9817 6431

National Library of Australia
Cataloguing-in-Publication data has been requested.

ISBN: 1 875606 96 3

Cover by Green Poles Design
Printed by Mercury Printeam

CONTENTS

Acknowledgments	vi
Introduction	vii
Part I A TALE OF TWO BANKS	1
1 Modern banking for a modern colony	3
2 Modernising through thrift, planning and housing	21
3 Inward-looking modernism	57
4 Don Dunstan's plan for modernisation	96
Part II TELLING TIMES	123
5 Open for business: the new destroys the old	125
6 From a thrift to an entrepreneurial bank: what went wrong?	149
7 Who's looking after the shop?	169
8 Keeping up appearances	195
9 Welcome to the circus	213
A eulogy to public banking	225
Notes	227
Bibliography	258
Index	264

Acknowledgments

Given that this is both a theoretical and an empirical study, there are two categories of acknowledgment that should be made in thanking those who have aided its realisation. In regard to the broader theory under-pinning this book, I would like to acknowledge my colleagues in the Politics Department at the University of Adelaide who have either shared or encouraged my interest in culural theory and the politics of finance. In particular, I wish to thank Doug McEachern, Clem Macintyre, Carol Bacchi, Peter Mayer, Pal Ahluwalia, Paul Nursery-Bray, John Playford and Jenny Stock. Mention should also go to my colleagues in History and Law, notably Hugh Stretton, Wilfred Prest, John Keeler, Kerrie Round and Robert Dare who offered assistance either in reading parts of the manuscript or in helping with the process of its publication.

For help with my empirical research I would like to thank Michael Sullivan of the Politics Department, Royal Commissioner Samuel Jacobs AO, QC for permitting me access to the Royal Commission transcripts, and Auditor-General Ken MacPherson for his help in my investigation. Particular thanks must also go to the University of Adelaide for a grant which enabled me to purchase transcripts of the Royal Commission and the published Auditor-General's reports, as well as granting me a period of special study leave to write up my findings.

I was granted access to the records of the Savings Bank of South Australia and the old State Bank of South Australia by the South Australian Asset Management Corporation, and wish here to express my thanks to that organisation. Likewise, I am obliged to the librarians and archivists (notably Jane Thinke) at the South Australian State Records, who were generous with their time and expertise in difficult circumstances. I thank John Bannon for his willingness to be interviewed and for permitting his views to be used in this book.

Special thanks should go to the administrative staff of the Politics Department, to Tina Esca for her perseverance with the multiple drafts and to Chris McElhinney for her assistance. A particular mention must be made of the History Trust of South Australia for their timely assistance in the publication of this book.

I would like to thank Jude Adams, and our children Brer, Finn and Morris for their forbearance in living with this book over eight years and for re-organising many a plan, big and small, to fit in to its production. I would especially like to thank Jude for helping me unravel some of the complexities of cultural theory which lay in the text. For the shortcomings which still exist in the text after hers and many other wise counsels, I take full responsibility.

INTRODUCTION

This is a tale about two public banks, the Savings Bank of South Australia and the State Bank of South Australia. It is told in two parts. The first part deals with the formation and progression of these two banks, the Savings Bank of South Australia (1848) and the State Bank of South Australia (1896) from their inception last century to their merger in 1984 to form the new State Bank of South Australia (SBSA). The tale is told through historic records and loan books which depict the respective cultures of the banks and outlines the relationships they had with their customers. The second part of the book tells the story of the merger of the two banks to form the State Bank of South Australia and how the new bank underwent a cultural transformation. The past was discarded and the SBSA was plunged into a high risk strategy of rapid growth based on the pursuit of corporate clients. In the end the SBSA had borrowed so much money, to lend so unwisely to risk-taking entrepreneurs, that it had to be rescued by the taxpayers. It was subsequently sold to Advance Bank, therein ending 150 years of public banking in South Australia.

The tale begins outside of South Australia with the idea of creating a savings bank for both practical and moral reasons. The notion of such a savings bank came from the experience in Scotland, where in 1810 the first savings bank was founded in Edinburgh, with the aim of instilling frugality into the working people. This concept was incorporated in the plans for the colony of South Australia by the Colonial Office. Governor Hindmarsh was instructed to form a savings bank upon his arrival in the new world. There was a dual aim behind this instruction, the first was to inculcate into the 'working classes' the Protestant Ethic of thrift and to tie them to the fledgling colony. It was soon discovered that the working classes would not deposit their savings in such an institution unless it was backed by the governor and their savings were treated with some equity. After one false start the Savings Bank of South Australia was formed on 11 March 1848 with the Lieutenant Governor F H Robe as President of the Trustees.

Once given a guarantee the Savings Bank of South Australia soon had an excess of funds and it was then decided to lend a proportion of these reserves to those with adequate security. The Trustees acted with due diligence in their evaluation of loans, taking an ultra-cautious approach to lending. As a result, the Savings Bank had practically no bad loans, rather, as the security requirements were so high, the bank built up a large reserve of funds. By 1860 the Savings Bank had accumulated such substantial reserves that it decided to lend to the government for infrastructure development, notably railway lines.

In the case of the State Bank of South Australia its origins were internal to the colony and stemmed from the financial crises of the 1880s. The bank crashes of the 1880s and early 1890s led to a loss of confidence in private banking and a call for a public bank which would serve the people by both stabilising the money markets and providing safe loans to farmers and the working classes. It was the Kingston government in 1894 which took up this concept and moved, in the first instance, to turn the Savings Bank into a public bank proper. When this attempt was defeated, Treasurer Holder steered a bill through the parliament which saw the passing of a State Advance Act in late 1895 and the formation of the State Bank on 1 February 1896. The State Bank used the then novel idea of credit foncier loans (instalment loans where the capital was paid back from the commencement of the loan) to lend capital to farmers and for home loans.

Part I of the book follows the progress of these two banks from their inception through Federation to their merger in 1984. The tale follows their expansion in the first two decades of the twentieth century. The story covers the trauma of the Great Depression where both banks had to protect their reserves and carefully manage accounts in arrears. The attitude of the banks to those behind in their payments was a mixture of moral superiority mixed with a sense of 'there but for the grace of God, go you or I'. Having weathered the dark years of the Depression both banks were caught up in the prosperity of the war years where savings rose and rationing had the effect of deferring demand. The banks set about planning for peace. The State Bank had the experience of the 1,000 Homes Scheme in Colonel Light Gardens to use for its housing plans. The Savings Bank too began to copy the ideas of the State Bank with credit foncier loans and the purchase of land for its own real estate ventures, notably in the Daw Park and Edwardstown area.

The post-World War II period began with the two banks seeking to modernise their operations. The Savings Bank turned to mechanisation as a means of efficiently operating their savings accounts. Equally, the Savings Bank prepared the way for the future by building up its home lending services with an architects department and a set of plans for modern homes. Likewise the State Bank had its own plans for building homes using modern mass-produced products and building techniques. In this push for modernisation the banks eased out the women employees who had replaced the men during the war, in keeping with their belief that banking was a man's world.

The banks' plans for modernisation, nevertheless, were retarded from the outside by the restrictions placed on their lending. When the Menzies government made its arrangements with the trading banks giving them protection in the local market and the ability to offer credit through their financial subsidiaries, the State Bank and the Savings Bank were placed at a disadvantage. Both banks sought from the Playford government the power and resources to offer credit facilities to their customers, notably cheque accounts and then overdraft facilities but both moves were blocked, preventing the banks from becoming proper market players. The Playford government preference for the Bank of Adelaide as the dominant trading bank in South Australia meant that the State Bank and the Savings Bank were not able to compete effectively or gain knowledge of the changing commercial lending market. This was an inadequacy which was to reinforce their inward looking culture and peculiar concepts of modernisation, which excluded women and clung to a conservative past of Empire and paternalism. These inadequacies were the basis from which the merged banks would be colonised by a private sector culture some twenty years later.

It was both the government and the banks which were at fault. Governments became too cosy with local and multinational capital behind the high tariff wall. The banks themselves became stultified and complacent in their respective niche markets. The State Bank saw its functions as looking after the rural sector, offering concessional home loans and as a conduit for government acts. These functions were hamstrung, however, by the State Bank being continually starved of funds. By 1965, the State Bank board began to look to a merger with the Savings Bank so that it could have the funds to use the lending powers contained in its Act. Notwithstanding the financial logic of the request such a move was opposed by both the Playford government and by the Savings Bank Board of Trustees.

Throughout the 1960s, the Savings Bank came to live out a paradox. On one level the bank was comfortable in its closed culture; where women were obliged to resign upon marriage, where deference to superiors was the *sine qua non* of service and where the visit of the Governor for lunch was deemed the highlight of any year. Yet, at another level, the Savings Bank was continually losing customers to the trading banks who advertised their services in terms of doing 'all your banking under one roof', and many managers resented the top down conservative culture of head office. The Trustees repeatedly had to badger respective governments, both Liberal and Labor, for an extension of the Savings Bank's power to offer services (notably competitive overdraft facilities) so as to match its opponents.

It was Premier Dunstan who offered the obvious answer to the paradox. Upon his re-election on 2 June 1970, Dunstan began to assert his legal authority over the banks and pushed them to merge so that the State Bank's trading structure could be founded on the Savings Bank's large deposit base. His ultimate aim was to merge the two public banks so they could modernise and thereby meet the new banking challenges. He sought to shake the banks out of their complacency by asserting his Ministerial power over them and through his appointments to their boards. At that time the Australian banking system was beginning to feel the first shock waves of the deregulation of the international monetary system, symbolised by President Nixon ending the Bretton Woods Agreement in 1971. It was this volatility which indirectly led to the floating of the Australian currency in 1983 and the subsequent deregulation of the Australian financial markets at the very time the new State Bank was being launched.

The political pressure from Dunstan, combined with the global changes, had the initial effect of reinforcing the two banks' conservatism. The Savings Bank Trustees vehemently opposed Dunstan's efforts at bringing the bank under his control, and by 1976 the Trustees had turned to the Liberal opposition for support. This resulted in a motion of no-confidence in the Premier which, after much acrimony in and outside the parliament, was defeated on the floor of the House of Assembly. Premier Dunstan retreated from his plan to merge the banks and sought to bring them together through joint appointments to their boards. The no-confidence motion against Dunstan was nevertheless to leave a strong impression on the rising Australian Labor Party politician John Bannon and as a consequence affected his approach to the Savings Bank and the State Bank. He was determined that his government would be seen to be at 'arm's length' from the banks.

In the mid-1970s, however, the Savings Bank tended to carry on as before, simply making incremental changes to its policies. In contrast, the State Bank became more aggressive in its pursuit of local corporate business. It was the collapse of the Bank of Adelaide in 1979 which both revealed the dangers of the new financial climate and presented an opportunity for a new corporate bank in South Australia. The fall of the Bank of Adelaide, due to property speculation outside of South Australia (mainly by its financial subsidiary Finance Corporation of Australia in Sydney and Perth), shocked the local banking community. It was the catalyst for the Savings Bank Trustees to begin earnest discussions with the State Bank over a merger.

By 1982 the two banks jointly approached the Tonkin government requesting a merger and the commercialisation of its business. The thinking by the respective bank boards was that the new bank would be more commercial than its predecessors so as to serve the business community in South Australia. The Tonkin government procrastinated on the joint request and it was left to John Bannon to bring the banks together. In fact, Bannon had independently begun to canvass the idea of a bank merger and had included this concept in his election campaign of 1982.

Upon being elected Premier, Bannon facilitated the merger of the two public banks. But, being ever cognisant of the political problems Dunstan had encountered, he ensured that the terms for the merger were those recommended by the banks. The appointment by the two boards of Tim Marcus Clark as Managing Director of the new bank, was meant as a signal to the local business sector that the State Bank of South Australia (SBSA) was to be both a more commercial entity and independent from the government. From the outset Clark was very keen to commercialise the SBSA along private banking lines and to promote it as autonomous from the government.

Part II of the book outlines how the SBSA was captured by a private sector entrepreneurial culture which destroyed public banking in this State. The narrative highlights how the culture within the SBSA was transformed from that of a public institution serving the State in niche local markets to that of a private bank, which became integrated into global financial markets. The original idea behind the merger was to link the past to the present, to relate retail banking to wholesale banking. What happened almost overnight was that the past was obliterated by the present which rapidly placed in danger the whole future of the SBSA. Wholesale banking, especially loans on commercial property and finance, swamped the retail side of the new bank. By 1986, the SBSA's lending was out of control.

Any opposition to this change within and outside the bank was dismissed as being 'out of date' thinking in the new era of deregulation. Managing Director Clark said his aim was to 'put a new broom' through the old retail banking culture and this he effectively did. Clark regarded the old banks' history as outmoded and preferred the new text book philosophical dictum that 'one man's disadvantage was another man's opportunity' as the basis for constructing the SBSA's business strategy. To match this philosophy Clark recruited (mainly) men, many with limited banking experience (the 'whizz kids', as they colloquially were called within the bank) or promoted those who were loyal to his philosophy of 'doing the deal'. In contrast, those bankers who questioned the new direction were categorised as 'out of date' and soon subjected to Clark's 'autocratic' style.

The old culture honed in the years of conservatism was structured on the basis of home loans and simple accounting methods, using retained profits as the basis for lending. Soon this elementary system of prudential controls was having to deal with borrowing on the international money market and making complex calculations on loans to corporate clients on minimal margins. The SBSA could obtain funds from the global money markets because it had a government guarantee. Concomitantly, there was a steady stream of customers coming to the bank, as the corporate sector had shifted to debt financing. Moreover, with high inflation there was an unholy scramble for assets rising faster than the rate of inflation, such as commercial property, racehorses, works of art, etc. The dilemma for the SBSA was how to minimise the risks and make a profit from these commercial loans.

It became evident as early as 1986 that the bank could readily borrow funds and equally find customers lining up to take out a loan, but that there was difficulty in knowing if the bank was making a safe profit from its transactions. That is, as early as 1986 there were some in the senior management who questioned whether the institution could safely expand at its current rate given the failings in the bank's prudential system. These concerns were brushed aside by Clark and his followers. The bank grew even faster and the rudimentary system of checks and balances fell even further behind. Rather than slow down the lending to allow the system to catch up, and for the staff to be recruited and trained in risk management, Clark and his management team audaciously accelerated the pace of growth.

The reason why the management was reluctant to reduce its lending was that it went against self interest. Expressed bluntly, the bankers who made the corporate loans were subject to a remuneration system which had a concord with the bank's asset growth. A culture of greed had been inculcated into the institution and had taken over its lending and prudential controls. The remuneration packages of the managers were subjectively determined by the Managing Director and were broadly based upon the growth in the assets. These remuneration packages rose at an exaggerated rate and were way out of kilter with not only the old banks but with that of the public sector in South Australia. The salaries began to match those of the big private banks in the Eastern States – a salary scale built mainly upon loans written and growth of assets not profitability (the ratio between profit and assets).

The changes in the corporate culture inside the SBSA were in tune with the corporate thinking outside of it, where the motto of the time was 'greed is good'. Moreover, financial deregulation had changed the banking rules and introduced foreign competition into the Australian banking market. There was a fierce contest for corporate clients and an accompanying fall in prudential standards. Without a system for evaluating the profit margins of a deal the SBSA priced its loans at what it estimated was the market rate. The bank, as the Auditor-General discovered to his alarm, never knew what its overall assets and liabilities were at any one moment, nor what its exposure to any one client group was at any time. It was in effect lending without due knowledge of the risks involved and in doing so placing at high risk the taxpayers' money. In short, it never had an effective risk management system in place.

This gamble could not last forever and what was remarkable was that it lasted as long as it did. The most disturbing aspect of the bank's lending was that after the share market crash of October 1987, and then the property market collapse of 1990, the SBSA's lending did not slow down, rather it was lending at record rates. It assumed that because it was stealing clients from the big banks it was achieving its desire of being a major player in Australian banking. The illusion of success was shattered when on a quiet Sunday afternoon on 10 February 1991, Premier Bannon announced that the taxpayers would have to rescue the SBSA. The initial indemnity was $970 million, rising eventually to $3 billion. When the government bailed out the bank it set in place an inquiry, headed by the Auditor-General Ken MacPherson, who, under the State Bank Act, was charged with the responsibility of investigating the causes of the debts. This inquiry was to be conducted in private and to report to the parliament. However, under pressure from the opposition and the media, Premier Bannon was obliged to hold a Royal Commission into the bank.

As a consequence, the government decided that the Auditor-General was to report to the Royal Commission as well as the parliament. The Royal Commission was to take into consideration the Auditor-General's analysis of the causes of the debts in its deliberation on who was responsible for the SBSA crisis. The Royal Commission was held in the public (the media's) gaze, headed by retired Supreme Court Judge Samuel Jacobs, whose terms of reference were basically set at examining relations between the SBSA and the government.

Both inquiries concluded that the SBSA grew too fast. In short, the two inquiries agreed that it was accelerated growth which killed the bank. Nevertheless, there was quite a different construction on who caused that growth and who was responsible for the debts. Justice Jacobs constructed his inquiry as a 'whodunit', and found Premier Bannon guilty of not controlling the bank's irresponsible growth and therefore considered that the Premier was legally responsible for the losses. Expressed in the terms used by Commissioner Jacobs it was Premier Bannon 'whodunit' because he should have exercised more control over the SBSA and concomitantly should have intervened less in the SBSA on political issues, such as interest rates at election time.

In contrast, Auditor General MacPherson placed the cause of the SBSA's debts squarely on the bank's management and Board of Directors. Additionally, MacPherson singled out Tim Marcus Clark for his most damaging criticism for being the 'hormone' in the bank's rapid growth and for the imprudent management of the bank's lending and its negligent asset management. These failings caused the SBSA to make so many loans which should not have been made and which resulted in the loss of millions of dollars of taxpayer money. He was also critical of the board for lacking 'commonsense' in its overseeing of the bank. Finally, he was critical of the respective external auditors (Peat, Marwick, Mitchell & Co (later KPMG Peat, Marwick) for SBSA and Price Waterhouse for BFC) for certain inadequacies in carrying out their responsibilities.

What this book reveals is that the SBSA was brought down by a combination of self-interest and mismanagement, in an era where the past had lost its meaning. That is, it was an acquisitive culture which drove the bankers to make so many loans. It was mismanagement which resulted in inadequate prudential checks and balances on the loans, which failed dismally when faced with the incessant pressure to sign up corporate business and for the managers to make a bonus in the process. This all happened in a period where the old regulations were abolished and the past was swamped by the intensity of the present.

But this is only part of the picture. The SBSA fell because of the combination of its desire to be a player on the national and international financial scene, and because it had to create symbols to match this desire. Having decided to live out its desire and be a major player the bank had to live up to its global image. In this process, the bank became dislocated from its past and caught up in a frantic pace of lending but with limited understanding of where it was going. For the bank the sign of success was corporate loans. The media depicted the bank group as being the fifth largest in Australia. For the government the sign of success was rising flows of funds to the Treasury. No one body or institution was adequately looking at the risks taken in doing the deals.

Once the SBSA decided to be a global bank it was propelled into the international financial market, but at a substantial disadvantage as it had almost no experience of the national banking market, let alone the global world of high finance. As the first part of the book shows, the collective experience of the merged banks was one of inward looking, stultified modernism. Without any historic base the SBSA copied the other banks and adopted the cultural banking norm of the day. It constructed as its own symbols of success a new headquarters that towered over Adelaide, with an exclusive executive sanctum at its apex. The bank at its height had branches in London and New York, and tax havens in the Cayman Islands, financing such ventures as the new Myer complex, the renovation of Wembley Stadium, mezzanine financing of apartments in New York, office blocks in Sydney and Melbourne, as well as holiday resorts on the Gold Coast.

To build these symbols of success the SBSA managers readily acquiesced to the demands of the corporate clients for loans. The managers were lauded for beating the competition to a deal, yet the deals were often made without effective research efforts. Many were unsecured or with minimum security, or faulty security such as 'negative pledges' (promises against the sale of share or property) or on the clients' security (shares or property), but not on the borrower and the borrower's income. According to the Auditor-General, the board showed complicity in this process as individual directors readily approved many large loans on 'round robin' phone calls where loans were not adequately assessed or properly evaluated against the security offered.

Having signed up the loan the managers were rewarded with generous remuneration packages which only propelled them onward to make more loans and gain further rewards. Moreover, wherever the bank looked it appeared as if everyone else was doing the same, tying salaries to growth and basing its growth upon the shaving of margins on corporate loans. Making the deal had become the universal sign of success. Responsibility for prudential standards or checks and balances on the loans were regarded by the bank's managers as someone else's business – someone else was supposedly looking after the shop. However, there was effectively no one else who was given the power and resources to evaluate the loans. Instead, against sound banking practice, the lenders sat on the committees agreeing to the very loans under their responsibility or that their departments had recommended. Equally, as the bank expanded, most of the directors were earning extra income from being on the board of the many bank subsidiaries and were thereby caught up in the hurly burly of lending.

A clear illustration of how making the deal became the sign of success was the volume of business the bank wrote in the period after the share market crash of October 1987, when the value of stocks fell by over 40 per cent. In 1988 the bank grew by 39.5 per cent, nearly double the rate of asset increases of other Australian banks, its assets rising from $7.8 billion to $11 billion. In 1989 the SBSA's assets rose by another 36.6 per cent, mainly for commercial property, at the time when that sector of the property market was over-heated. In 1990 when property values were tumbling and the economy was slipping into recession, the bank's assets rose by 40.7 per cent (four times the rate of consolidated bank growth in 1990) to be $21.1 billion.

The drive to take on corporate business had become a dangerous obsession. The SBSA management was so out of control that it could not restrain its lending in a climate of such high risk that the loans could best be described as imprudent. Yet the bank saw itself in a successful light as the fifth largest banking group in Australia. By 1990 the bank was totally over-exposed to commercial property, which was in large part due to Beneficial Finance Corporation, whose exposure to real estate was 56.4 per cent of its risk assets based on the illusion that property was safe. When the property market crashed by over 50 per cent this belief was exposed as folly, at the expense of the taxpayers. The recklessness of the loans and the lack of security now became the problem for the taxpayers of South Australia.

In sum, the onset of the 1990 recession revealed the danger of desire. The bank had to be rescued from itself. The bank was then divided in two. The bad loans were transferred to a public authority, the Group Asset Management Division, appropriately called the 'bad bank'. Concomitantly, the 'good bank' was dressed up for sale. The State Bank of South Australia had its name changed in 1994 to that of Bank SA, a name it retained when the Brown government sold it to the Advance Bank (which in turn became a part of the St George group) for $730 million in June 1995. At its sale the bank had returned to its pre-1984 days of concentrating on the South Australian housing and small business market and recorded a profit of $90 million for the financial year – a clear case of the privatisation of profit and the socialisation of debt. This is a telling tale about one culture based on thrift, conversation, paternalism, Empire and regionalism, giving way to another characterised by debt financing, precipitance, fraternalism and globalism.

Part I

A Tale of Two Banks

1

Modern banking for a modern colony

Carrying the Protestant Ethic to the colony
South Australia was born modern. By this I mean it was built on the idea that the principles of the Enlightenment could be transferred from Britain to colonial South Australia. This idea had its expression in the acceptance of the British class system and the ambiguous civilising mission of Empire. The colony began with a plan to import the British class system with its sense of cultural superiority to South Australia. Yet the class system was to be improved; the old barriers to upward mobility, the church and hierarchy nobility, were to be replaced by the principle of wealth as the basis for progress. It was to be an English settlement borrowing from the mother country but it was to be with a new beginning with more religious and political freedom than to be found in England. The colony's progressiveness, nevertheless, was based on the dispossession of the local Aboriginals. Such dispossession was justified in terms of the primitiveness of the 'natives' and of the civilising mission of the colonists, the burden of the coloniser. Dispossession was seen as essential because wealth was deemed to emanate from the land.

From the outset there was to be a unity in the exchange between the so-called superior class and the working classes and an absence of unity in the exchange between the colonialists and the Aboriginals. The unity in the exchange between the classes was based on the Protestant belief of progress through delayed gratification.[1] So a specific institution was deemed necessary to instil in the working classes the belief in the link between work, thrift and material progress. The ideological and practical expression of this schema was in the Wakefield plan, whereby land was to be sold at a price that would exclude the working classes from property. In exchange they were offered assisted passage to fill their social place as the labourers and domestic servants of the propertied classes. The collective work of the lower classes would provide the basis for saving and personal advancement. The role of women was to act as the moral guardians of thrift and instil in the menfolk the husbandry of their money.

The initial funding of the colony was to be principally from private capital shipped from Britain. The South Australian Company was the major agency for channelling this capital into land sales. The Bank of South Australia, established in 1837 under Royal charter, was the funding arm of the South Australian Company, and the initial bank of the superior classes. It had competition from the Bank of Australasia and the colonial banks from the other colonies, the most prominent of these being the Bank of New South Wales and the National Bank of Australia.

Nevertheless, the Bank of South Australia remained the dominant financial institution in South Australia until the financial crises of the 1880s when it was taken over by the Union Bank in 1892.

Implanting a thrift bank into a modern colony

The first Resident Commissioner, James Hurtle Fisher, was given the task of implementing the savings bank provision of the Bill passed by the House of Lords on 14 August 1834. The Colonisation Act instructed Fisher, who sailed with Governor Hindmarsh, to oversee the creation of a savings bank to promote thrift among the working people and to act as a deterrent against the labouring people moving to other colonies. The Ordinance stated that the governor was to establish a savings bank because it was:

> The economical institution which seemed best calculated to promote habits of frugality and industry, and to bind the working classes to the Colony by ties of interest, is a savings bank, founded on the principle that no deposits shall be withdrawn except in cases of death, until after a residence of some fixed period, say three years, in the colony.[2]

On 21 January 1841 James Hurtle Fisher called a General Meeting of Immigrants in the Council Room of the Corporation of Adelaide with the intention of forming a savings bank. The enthusiasm for such an institution was evident in the 101 men who were nominated to be directors. Governor Gawler was made patron with six vice-patrons. With such an unworkable number of directors, a new meeting was called the following week to appoint a more appropriate board of directors. The directors then set a series of rules over deposits and loans which sought to institutionalise the link in the Act between savings and the stability of the colony, principally by restricting the eligibility for withdrawals to a minimum deposit time of three years.[3]

The working classes, for whom the directors saw their philanthropic efforts being directed, were reluctant to deposit their savings in a bank which had such a three year restriction on withdrawals. The bank was, moreover, dependent on the trading banks for interest on its money and the trading banks were keen to protect their position by marginalising any savings bank. Additionally, the 1840s was a period of economic recession and of disputation between the colonial Governor and the Colonial Office over the viability of the South Australian experiment. When the Colonial Office dishonoured the bills of Governor Gawler and replaced him with Governor Grey, the future of the fledgling South Australian Savings Bank became tenuous. The bank, in 1847, had only 100 active accounts out of a population of 15,000 and total deposits were but £1,100. The Governor was still, however, committed to fulfilling the instructions of the Act and made plans for a new savings bank that would be more attractive for deposits.

On the 22 September 1847 Lieutenant Governor Robe made an edict declaring that he was intending to establish a thrift bank to be called the Savings Bank of South Australia –

> ... for the encouragement of frugality and the persons possessing small sums of money beyond what they require for the supply of their immediate wants, should be afforded an opportunity of depositing the same on good security to accumulate at interest.[4]

The emphasis had shifted to that of a safe bank for working peoples' savings and not a bank to tie the labourers to the colony. This shift was to prove decisive in the consolidation of the savings bank. The bank provided more open exchange between the classes, based on work, frugality, and self-denial by the working classes to acquire savings to buy property. The propertied classes were to use this savings as a source for loans to acquire more property, thereby keeping one step ahead of the frugal workers.[5] When the Ordinance became public the fate of the South Australian Savings Bank was sealed and it was left to its diligent manager Mr Wotherspoon to wind up the bank, which he did at a public meeting of directors on 27 December 1847.

The Savings Bank of South Australia opens for business

The new bank, titled the Savings Bank of South Australia, opened for business on 11 March 1848, in a small room in Gawler Place, with the specific mandate to be a safe bank for thrifty small depositors. For the depositors the Savings Bank was an improvement on its predecessor in that withdrawals could be made with only one month's notice required for funds under £50 and three months for funds over £50, although interest was only paid if deposits were maintained for a year. To ensure that the bank was not in direct competition with the private trading banks the Act placed a limit of £30 on deposits in any one year and a maximum deposit balance of £200. The hours of business were also an indication of its inferior status; the bank was open for deposits between 12 and 2 pm and from 7 to 9 pm, withdrawals were to be made only on Wednesdays from 12 to 2 pm.

The Governor's support for the Savings Bank was symbolised through the appointment of Lieutenant Governor, F H Robe, as the bank's first president, with the Colonial Secretary, A M Mundy being vice president, giving the impression of government backing for the institution. At its foundation 11 prominent men of the colony were publicly elected as trustees, they were: B T Finniss (later to become the State's first premier in 1857), S Davenport, P Cumming, W Allen, Captain J Watts, Captain W L O' Halloran, Captain G F Dashwood, W Peacock, C Flaxman, F S Dutton, and J Montefiore. The Trustees were prohibited from borrowing from the bank or from being directors of other banks.[6]

The Trustees were given the authority to employ an officer and, following an open advertisement, appointed John Hector as the bank's first manager/employee. Hector had defeated Mr Wotherspoon for the position and there was strong feelings by those who had dealings with the South Australian Savings Bank that an injustice had occurred.[7] Wotherspoon had, however, upset some of the less scrupulous propertied men of Adelaide by criticising their practice of acquiring both the land and the instalments when the payments of working people fell in arrears. He called for an institutional means by which small land holders could be protected from this double loss, saying that:

> ... the purchaser made a small weekly payment and if the whole was not paid within a certain time the instalments paid were forfeited. Now, in numerous instances, the plan adopted is to lodge the title deeds with the Savings Bank, to pay the instalments into that bank in the joint names of the seller and the purchaser, and upon the money being paid in full, it is paid over with interest to the seller, and the purchaser gets his title deed ... Hundreds, perhaps thousands of pounds, have been lost by poor men through forfeiture of deposits and instalments, and the sooner such an unjust system is put to an end to, the better.[8]

For his part, Hector had sound business connections and was a successful mine owner. At the time he was the director of the Union Mining Company and it was in this office that the bank began its business. He was also a property developer who owned land at Glenelg and standing on a portion of it was the old gum tree where it is assumed Governor Hindmarsh had proclaimed the colony of South Australia on 28 December 1836. Hector donated this land to the Crown as a recognition of self-government in 1857. To assist Hector in running the bank the Trustees instituted a roster system to take deposits and pay withdrawals. The first deposit of £29 was from an Afghan shepherd Croppo Sing[h] who was employed by William Fowler of Lake Victoria.[9]

With the steady rise in deposits the bank placed advertisements in the press seeking applications for loans, to a ceiling of £500, on the conditions that mortgages were up to the value of 50 per cent of the property, with 10 per cent interest accruing immediately and the principal to be repaid in full at the end of the loan. By the end of 1848, out of deposit funds of £5,313 the Trustees had lent £3,100 on mortgages.[10] At the close of the bank's first financial year depositor balance was £6,000. The first loan was for £500 to John Colton on 5 June 1848. Colton held two acres near the parklands (section 256) with a seven room stone cottage of which he wrote that 'the whole of which has been built since November 1847 at a cost of £1,100 including land and fencing' and this he placed as security on his loan.[11] The loan was for a term of five years but could be paid off or called in with six months notice. John Colton was to be appointed a Trustee of the bank in 1875.

The second loan was to Mr Reynell for £300. The third loan went to C Wilson for £100 on 17 acres at Reed Beds. The fourth loan was to John Herbert who had a two storey brick house and half an acre of gardens at 21 North Terrace, as security for his £100 loan. These loans were typical of the bank's lending in its formative period and became the pattern of lending until Federation. A critical factor in the bank's lending was its stress on a high level of security. As such, the loans were principally offered to men from the propertied classes. Examples of the Savings Bank's loans in this period are: John Hombrook who used as security for a loan of £250 on his city property in Rundle Street of 210 feet by 50 feet on acre 41, which he mentioned in his application had in occupation Mr Soward, Builder and Timber Merchant who was paying a yearly rent of £25. John Horgan had properties in Gouger Street, which he listed as nine dwelling houses – yielding a rental of £160 per year and a well of good water as security for a loan of £500. John Maxwell who had three acres at Glen Osmond, in seeking to borrow £30 to £50 to complete two, two room, cottages which he said he wanted to let to the miners of Glen Osmond. George Buckhurst borrowed £100, for one year, on a freehold property on Stephens terrace at Walkerville, with half an acre of crop and a large well built substantial residence. William Bickford the chemist borrowed £500 for 16 acres on section 170 at Glen Osmond using his pharmacy shop in Hindley Street and his home at Glen Osmond, including a cottage of four rooms with a large attic, dairy and an acre of garden and fruit trees, as security. Similarly, Thomas Playford borrowed £300 on an acre of land in Hindley Street where the bank's assessor said in supporting the loan that the land being so valuable it is thought it was unnecessary to specify any buildings. In his application for a loan of £500, Charles Bonney placed on mortgage, fifteen acres at Norwood, valued at £40 an acre, with the value of the house being £400 and the fencing £50, for a total of £1050. He defended his valuation saying that land at the time in Norwood was selling for £70 per acre.

The lending also reflected the spread of the settlement of South Australia and the diversity of agricultural production. For instance, E Homeshaw of the Exchange borrowed £250, on 515 acres as collateral in the areas of Onkaparinga, Yatala, Strathalbyn and Yankallilla, on which he was obtaining £108 and 16 shillings in annual rent. John Alsop in his application for a loan placed as security 240 acres at Encounter Bay. Richard Bell borrowed £350 on his 230 acres at McLaren Vale. Alexander Brodie borrowed £100 on 80 acres of wheat farming at Noarlunga. Daniel Brady applied for a loan on his property of 303 acres 'near the dry creek'. Robert Burns borrowed on land at 'Chain of Ponds'. Robert Cock had security of 200 acres at Balhannah; Charles Carleton 48 acres at old Brighton; John Clezy 160 acres at Nairne; William Gilbert had 434 acres at Rapid Bay; John Hillman 171 acres adjoining Nairne; William Holland on a loan of £200 placed 65 acres as security at Dulwich; Archibald Jaffrey placed 560 acres 'on the Sturt' as security on a loan; William Ledger placed 160 acres near the Chain of Ponds and 238 acres at Western part of Mitcham. John Warren borrowed £300 on 880 acres in the Barossa which included farming land and vine yards. William Gilbert borrowed on 434 acres at Rapid Bay. John Brundy borrowed on land 'near Kapunda'. Joseph Gilbert borrowed on a house and land at Pewsey Vale. Edward Giles borrowed on vineyards at Willunga.[12]

Alexander Brodie in his application for a loan of £100 described his 80 acre wheat farm at Morphett Vale, the Hundred of Noarlunga, numbered 649, in the following terms: 'the section is completely fenced with a post and rail fence, is clear of trees, which have all been grubbed out and is now under a wheat crop. There is not one unavailable acre in the whole allotment section and the land is of first rate quality for agricultural purposes ... the section as it now stands cost the proprietor upward of £300.' Alexander Murray, in applying for a £200 loan, spoke of his 112 acres at Coromandel Valley as being in three lots, one of 29 acres with a wooden house of three rooms, with four acres with fruit trees and vines and a river running through the property, a 10 acre allotment, and '83 acres which was well wooded, good water, and partly fenced let at £16/12 shillings per annum with right of purchase at £2 per acre in 11 years. Tenants bound not to cut any Timber'.[13]

While there were few single women of means in the colony who were able to borrow from the bank, there were, however, some exceptions who did make calls on the bank. For instance, there was Miss Bathgate who borrowed on the security of a 12 room house at the corner of Pulteney Street and Rundle Street and seven acres at Brighton and an inn and house at Thebarton. There was also Madam J Bristow who borrowed £200 for the security of seven acres at Brighton with a six room 'pise house', stables and a stone school house and another pise house with stone kitchen and stables to be erected and to be leased for 14 years at £40 per annum, and finally an allotment at Thebarton with a 'pise public house' to be leased for £31 per annum. Similarly, Catherine Hussey borrowed £200 on the security of a property on the corner of Ward and O'Connell streets, North Adelaide. As well, Jane Campbell borrowed £250 on land called the 'Pinery' near North Adelaide, lot '358', with a 'stone cottage thatched with outside and dividing fence. The premises are let to Michael Lee at £30 per annum, Tenancy expires January 1852'.[14]

The bank's attitude concerning women, however, matched that of the time in that they were regarded upon marriage as absolutely subordinate to their husbands in money matters. For instance, the Savings Bank's first *Handbook for Bank Tellers* instructed the tellers that: 'If a woman has a credit balance in a bank, and her husband have an overdraft, the bank may retain the wife's balance in liquidation of the husband's debt unless the wife's balance be proved to consist of money which are her separate property.' Moreover, in regard to married women the tellers were ordered to 'Never open one (a Married Women's Account) without the husband's consent … When a single woman has an account in a bank, and afterwards marries, get her husband's consent before paying her cheques. A husband has the right to know the state of his wife's account under any circumstances'.[15]

Exchange between classes: from working men/women to men of property
In brief, those who saved with the Savings Bank were working men and women, and those who predominantly borrowed from the Savings Bank were gentlemen of property. Moreover, there was a second exchange operating between the working and propertied classes facilitated by the Savings Bank. The working classes, not having sufficient security to purchase property, were obliged to rent, which provided the basis for further borrowing and class solidification. This exchange between the classes can be read in the following example. In his application for a loan W Holland used 65 acres at Dulwich as security which he noted had two cottages on it, one of which was let for £30 per annum. Similarly, Mr P Clisby borrowed £500 on an acre in King William Street which included the City Arms Inn with a double-fronted shop and three cottages and seven roomed house rented for £410 per annum. R L Milne borrowed £500 on land at Le Fevre Terrace, supporting his application by noting he was renting acres at £16 per annum and selling water at 2 shillings and 6 pence per ton. Henry Heard borrowed £100 on a two storey dwelling and shop in Currie Street leased at 35 shillings per week. W Williams borrowed £500 on a series of properties at North Adelaide, which he listed as nine houses which were let for £26 per annum and five houses at £40 per annum and 1 house at £44 per annum.[16]

Of course, there were other forms of exchange going on between classes. For instance, the Savings Bank loan book records a range of applications for loans where a public house was used as security. For example, there was Miss Bathgate who borrowed on an Inn at Thebarton. The scope of lending gives some credence to the adage that Adelaide was the city of both churches and pubs. William Bradshaw borrowed on the security of a hotel and shop in North Adelaide. Thomas Biddles borrowed on land and a hotel at Mount Barker. John Cousins borrowed £200 on the She-Oak Log on North Road. W A Hughes borrowed £500 on a hotel and four lots at Angaston; later he was to borrow another £500 on his property at

Palmer Place North Adelaide. Robert Haysman borrowed £1,000 on the Ship Inn at Port Adelaide which he valued at £1,800 and said he received rent of £200 per annum. James Johnston borrowed on the security on land and a hotel at Woodside; Joseph Ind on the Paradise Bridge Hotel; Edward Morris on the Commercial Inn in Tynte Street North Adelaide; Patrick McCarron on the Forresters and Squatters Arms at Thebarton. Similarly, Henry Simpson borrowed £1,500 using the Albert Hotel at Port Adelaide as security.[17]

Exchange between the private and public sectors

In general, loans made by the Savings Bank grew steadily but the high security test for loans saw the bank accumulate a surplus of funds. Additionally, in 1852 with the Victorian gold rush, the Trustees were faced with the problem of rising bad debts and few borrowers. There re-emerged the problem prevalent in the early days of the bank of borrowers doing a 'bolter' to the other colonies, in this case to the gold fields to try their luck. The Trustees having few private calls for loans and holding £13,082 for loans decided to take up the provisions in the Act to invest in government securities.

On 1 February 1853, the Trustees instructed the accountant to write to the Colonial Secretary requesting that the large amount of unemployed funds be made available to the government in the form of securities. While these negotiations were underway the Trustees decided in 1854 to invest £11,600 worth of South Australian government railways bonds at 6 per cent which were then used to build the railway line from Port Adelaide to Adelaide.[18] This loan was to be the forerunner of many more and set in place the final form of exchange, that being between the bank and to the government for modernising projects.

A symbiosis was established where the government looked to the Savings Bank to offset its debt and to help with building the State's infrastructure. From the formation of self-government in 1856 onward, one third of the bank's loans went to government sources (as securities, as loans to statutory authorities or as a response to direct government requests for specific public purposes). With the formation of self-government a close relationship was also formed between the Board of Trustees and the government of the day, but perhaps never as close as in 1857 with the first Premier of South Australia, B T Finniss, who had been Vice President of the Savings Bank of South Australia Board of Trustees. The first President of the Legislative Council (from 1849 to 1855), J H Fisher, was the bank's solicitor at that time. The Savings Bank looked to the government as a safe source for investment and for protection against the power of the trading banks.

The government looked to the Savings Bank as a source of funds, and as such was prepared to protect its niche market while ensuring that the trading banks remained dominant. In 1872 the Savings Bank was given the legislative power to lend to municipal corporations, and this became another regular source for loans.

During the boom years of the 1860s, banking expanded in South Australia with the formation of what was to become the major local trading bank, the Bank of Adelaide, which opened for business in 1865. The trading banks, being concerned over the success of the Savings Bank, placed pressure on the government to restrict its lending, notably on mortgages. The government, however, now having commenced a program of major infrastructure expenditure, principally on railroads, found the Savings Bank a useful source of funds.

By 1868 the Savings Bank deposits stood at £312,728 of which £187,255 was lent on mortgages, £105,000 on fixed deposits and £25,000 on government securities. By 1872 deposits in the bank had reached £500,000 with 15,955 depositors with an average balance of £35. Government securities were £141,900 in 1872, rising to £316,000 by 1874, before nearly doubling again to £604,306 in 1880. By 1880 the bank was able to celebrate its first million pounds of deposits with government securities becoming equal to lending on mortgages which were around £635,965 in 1884. From the 1890s government securities rose to be larger than those of mortgage loans. By 1900 the Savings Bank was one of the largest holders of public debt, holding at that time 21per cent of the government inscribed stock and 9 per cent of the total bonds.[19]

Modernisation derailed by speculation
The 1870s was a period of economic boom and urban expansion in South Australia.[20] The mood was one of optimism with no forewarning of the financial crisis which was to unfold. Prince Alfred, The Duke of Edinburgh, had just visited South Australia in 1867, laying the foundation stone for the General Post Office in King William Street, and Prince Alfred College was named after him. The telegraph cable was completed to Darwin, enabling South Australia to be the first colony to have telegraph communication to the outside world. Compulsory education was introduced in 1872 (although it was not free until 1892) and this was reflected in the proportion of depositers who signed their names in their deposit books rather than leaving a 'mark'.[21] In 1887, 18 people per 1,000 in South Australia were depositors in the Savings Bank of South Australia, rising to 29 in every 1,000 by 1897.[22] The export market for wheat was buoyant, stimulating an expansion of farming beyond Goyder's line. There was government expenditure on long line railways, promoting a boom in property purchases in the hills. There was also the expansion of the Adelaide tramway system encompassing such suburbs as Kensington, Mitcham, Unley, Goodwood and Hindmarsh. Finally, there was a bulge in the age profile of the population (18 years to 34 years) placing pressure on the property market.[23] The boom, moreover, had followed a period where land had been tightly controlled and there had been pent up demand due to high savings. The banks and building societies were flush with funds and there were limited avenues for investment.[24] As the land market opened up, land brokers were quick to see the opportunities and began to market sub-divisions, only adding more fuel to a speculative fire. The share market was chasing the next bonanza after Broken Hill and there was speculation on mines at Silverton and in the Northern Territory.[25] The success of the early speculators encouraged others to abandon the Protestant ethic and to pursue get rich quick schemes. Those with inside information in the State or Local government or from within the banks were not adverse to using this knowledge for speculation on their own behalf.

However, just as the speculative boom began in earnest, the colony was hit by poor harvests in 1881 and 1882 which reduced rural incomes and left the farmers on marginal land exposed; many had to walk off the land carrying their debts with them. With the economic centrality of Adelaide in the colony, the rural downturn had a flow on effect in the city with the first fall coming in commercial property, followed by a decline in the prices for urban land.[26] The financial sector began to feel the effects of the decline in property values and this in turn exposed the unscrupulous activities of some of the fund managers. There were a number of embezzlements of small building societies, and their managers were not averse to taking passage on the first available ship leaving the colony. Nonetheless these seemed isolated incidents in what had been a remarkable progress for the colony.

Celebrating the Jubilee

At the time of the colony's Jubilee, in January 1886, there was a feeling of achievement and celebration around the theme that the settlers had civilised a 'wilderness'. The newspapers recorded the success of the colony's progress in terms of acres under cultivation and of the exportation of wheat, wool and minerals. The prominent parliamentarian and Savings Bank Trustee, Sir Samuel Davenport lauded the colonists for 'their intelligence, energy, and perseverance, hardy daring and untiring labours, which had effected that greatest conquest of a savage land'.[27] The *Advertiser* measured the progress in terms of rail and road construction, telegraphic communication, public works, charitable, religious and philanthropic institutions, gas lit city streets, and the magnificence of North Terrace as the boulevard of culture; concluding with the observation that 'the colony with the adoption of all the appliances of advanced civilisation seem to assume dimensions that are truly wonderful'.[28]

The Commercial Bank of South Australia falls

The colonists' sense of self satisfaction was shattered when, on 24 February 1886, one of the colony's prominent banks, the Commercial Bank of South Australia closed its doors. It came to light that the managers had been embezzling money for speculating on silver mining stocks and had been allowing the clients of the bank too much credit for speculative purposes.[29] The Commercial Bank was managed by a Mr Alexander Crooks, who had previously worked at the Bank of South Australia and who was held in high regard by the local financial community. On 6 April Crooks pleaded guilty to embezzlement and was sentenced to eight years hard labour. His assistant, Wilson, received a six year sentence. There was much talk about what the directors knew or were doing to control the bank but they escaped any legal charges. If justice in this case was selective it was at least swift. This did not satisfy some of the shareholders who considered that the directors had, at least, showed a lack of due diligence, complaining that the banking laws were far too lenient.[30]

The collapse of the Commercial Bank of South Australia led to a good degree of moral rumination in the colony with the press calling for a return to the settler spirit of the early colonists and the clergy setting aside a day of prayer to restore morality to business. But this was of little avail as the adverse effects of the speculative land boom had not yet flowed fully through the system. The next bank to get into trouble was the Town and Country. It had commenced business in 1881 at the height of the boom and was immediately engaged in lending on land speculation. Rumours spread rapidly in June 1886 that the bank was heavily overexposed on speculative land ventures. The bank was chaired by a prominent merchant, immediate past President of the Chamber of Commerce and Member of Parliament, S D Glyde, who tried to calm shareholder criticisms of the bank's lending before he had to admit the bank could no longer trade. In November 1886 the Town and Country was liquidated with over 40 per cent of its lending accruing losses. It was absorbed into the Commercial Bank of Australia which in turn was caught up in land speculation in Victoria and was the first bank to run into trouble in that State's banking crash of 1893.[31]

In February 1886 the Savings Bank reported that it was in a sound financial position with its total funds of £1.6 million, £375,000 in cash, £659,000 in mortgage loans, £533,465 in State Government Bonds. There were also loans to local government including the City of Adelaide which had taken out bonds worth £33,150, and Kensington and Norwood which had bonds of £3,000. The bank's premises were valued at £8,000. This confidence was challenged when, following the Commercial Bank crisis, there was a run on the Savings Bank. In response, Sir Henry Ayers, chair of the Trustees, called a Special Board meeting to plan a defensive strategy. The Trustees met at 10.30 am on Friday 16 April 1886. At the meeting Ayers told the other Trustees, Sir William Milne, John Colton, A Hardy, D Murray and P Basedow, that on Wednesday 14 April 1886 withdrawals had totalled £15,000 and the next day £36,000.[32] It was decided that the best way of quelling the panic was for the bank to hold its nerve and to not make any departure from its ordinary routine of the bank so as to present an image of stability; this procedure was effective.

In July 1886, there was another run on the Savings Bank. In response Henry Ayers again called a special meeting of the Trustees to discuss how to stem the outflow. He reported that in the first two weeks of July withdrawals were over £37,536 and that over 50 per cent had been of amounts over £100. Ayers said that the outflow was a direct result of the Bank of Adelaide offering 6 per cent interest rates as compared to the Savings Bank's 4½ per cent, and this was attracting large depositors.[33] The Trustees decided that the bank had little option but to match the interest rates of their competitor. It was also reported that a large loan to Adelaide Land Investment Company was at risk and that, in an effort to stave off liquidation, the bank re-scheduled the loan.

In late 1886 there was turmoil within the National Bank of Australia which also related to loans to the Adelaide Land Investment Company. The bank's Melbourne head office discovered that two of its Adelaide directors, both parliamentarians, William Everard and Henry Scott, had a conflict of interest. Everard, a prominent financier who was a director of the failing Adelaide Land Investment Company, had, against the directive of the Melbourne National Bank manager, taken out a large loan on his deeply troubled land speculation company and Scott had made a substantial commission on the loan.[34] The company went into liquidation, taking with it the Savings Bank's loan.

The financial crisis in the National Bank had a flow-on effect to other banks. The better off depositors began to look for a safe place for their finances. The crisis saw a flood of large deposits into the Savings Bank, as it was seen as having the backing of the government. In 1882 the Savings Bank had 27,684 accounts totalling £1,568,712 of which £512,412 was lent on mortgages, £538,848 on fixed deposits and £482,392 was in government securities. In 1886 deposits rose to £1,653,080 rising again to £1,896,248 in 1889. The most notable rise in deposits was from accounts with deposits over £250 which were 262,550 in 1887 but rose to 360,667 in 1889. Nevertheless, the Savings Bank deposits still remained dominated by those from the 'working classes'. In 1898 there were 45,995 accounts under £20 compared to 7,515, accounts between £20 and £50. There were 4,549 accounts between £50 and £100, and 1,320 accounts from £150 and £200 and 1,145 accounts between £200 and £250, and 1,300 accounts exceeding £250.[35]

First State Bank Royal Commission 1888
The failure of the Commercial Bank of South Australia in 1886 raised concerns as to the financial security of other private banks. This anxiety was echoed in the parliament which prompted a debate on the public provision of banking services, expecially to the rural community. What followed was the establishment of a Royal Commission into banking and the issue of a local mint.

The Royal Commission was charged with investigating the issue of whether a state bank could provide cheap loans for rural producers. Also the Royal Commission was requested by the parliament to investigate the issue of whether the state needed its own Royal Mint to control note issue. Evidence was taken from around Australia and overseas on different forms of credit advances and note issue banks. The Royal Commission canvassed the then novel idea of credit foncier lending, first raised by Robert Torrens in 1858 in regard to his Real Property Act and propagated by Carl Pinsch, Consul for Austria–Hungary in Victoria.

The Commission was perplexed over the concept of credit foncier lending. The practice used in Europe, particularly in Austria, had the perceived benefit over traditional loans in that principal and interest could be paid off both from the outset of the loan and also in instalment form. This meant that a borrower did not have to have the capital saved separately to pay off the loan on the day of termination. For a bank, such a system had the advantage of reducing its reserves as the principal was being repaid on a regular basis. Notwithstanding the symmetry of the scheme there was at that time no theoretical model of the multiplier effect of deposits on loans. Moreover, the immediate problem of unpredictable runs on the banks made them collectively wary of such an approach to lending. The submissions from the banking community to the Royal Commission all considered the system too risky. Equally, the Commissioners were personally wary of credit foncier lending and they became divided on whether a public institution should be formed to carry out this role or whether the existing private banks should be allowed to address this issue. There was strong opposition from some of the Commissioners to the Savings Bank playing such a role.

The Royal Commission concluded with a guarded finding against a state bank.[36] When the findings of the Royal Commission were presented to the legislature it became apparent that the parliament was divided over whether there was the need for a public bank. The dispute turned on whether the existing private banks could provide loans for small farmers and working people. It was suggested that the Savings Bank could fulfil this role, but there was strong opposition from sections of the legislature to the Savings Bank becoming a lender to working men or small farmers. The voices of support for the equity loans began to promote the idea that the Savings Bank could be a state bank proper.

From market failure comes a public bank
The banking crisis of the early 1890s became the stimulus for the government to establish a public bank. The first major bank to run into difficulties was the Bank of

South Australia (1835) which had been the financial arm of the South Australian Company with its head office in London. In the 1880s the bank had lent freely to land speculators in Victoria, coming into the Victorian property market near the end of the boom, only to be one of the first to fall in the bust. The management had been producing misleading profit reports and had tried to disguise the extent of the bank's exposure to the property market.[37] In 1893 rumours began to spread that the Bank of South Australia was over-exposed in Victorian property where it had lent £92,000 to the Imperial Banking Company, which went into liquidation in July 1891 and brought that bank down with it. The rumours were denied by the Bank of South Australia. However, disquiet persisted, and the directors attempted to bluff it out. This move did not stem the fall in share price, obliging the directors to resign before the bank was taken over by the Union Bank.[38]

The bank crashes of 1893 had their origins in land speculation in Victoria and were soon felt in South Australia. In 1893, 13 banks closed their doors and restructured their capital base. Shareholders were called upon to make good the losses and depositors became reluctant shareholders. Alongside the fall of the Bank of South Australia in 1891, the restructuring of the National Bank of Australia was the most significant crash to affect South Australian shareholders and depositers adversely. There were 71,000 shares held in the National Bank within South Australia by 2,160 shareholders, of whom many were established and respected families.[39] The extent of the hardship on those affected by the National Bank can be seen in the Lord Mayor opening a relief fund for the victims. In brief, the bank crisis of the early 1890s saw the banks reconstruct to their benefit and to the detriment of the shareholders and depositors, which in turn led to a general distrust of private banks.

From private disaster comes a public bank
The financial crisis of the 1880s and of 1893, combined with the realisation of the vulnerability of the South Australian economy, reinforced the commitment of a group of parliamentarians, headed by the progressive liberal Charles Kingston, to expand the role of the state including the area of banking. Under Kingston the public sector was expanded into arbitration, tariff protection, progressive taxation and into health (with a protracted battle with the Royal Adelaide Hospital).[40] In 1894 the Kingston government extended the vote to women. In that year Treasurer Holder introduced a bill to create a credit system for farmers akin to the continental European model of credit foncier, where credit would be more freely available and repaid on more flexible terms. The vehicle for the scheme was to be the Savings Bank of South Australia.

Round one: nationalising the Savings Bank of South Australia
The bill proposed that the Savings Bank would be given a full guarantee by the government for credit foncier loans but in return would be obliged to lend to rural producers. The Treasurer argued that, despite what people believed, the Savings Bank was not guaranteed by the government. Yet it was this false perception which had saved it from the crashes of 1893. He said 'when there had been runs on other banks, in nineteen cases out of twenty, depositors had refrained from rushing the Savings Bank because they believed in some way or other that the government guarantee was behind the bank'.[41] Holder added that the Savings Bank survival

had been more by luck than good management. He pointed out that it had transferred its uninvested funds to the Bank of New South Wales and that fortunately that bank was not affected by the crashes but, if it had been, then 'the depositors would have had reason to know to their cost that the Savings Bank was not a Government institution'. In supporting the conversion of the Savings Bank to a State bank proper, Treasurer Holder noted that the public sector in South Australia was involved in many activities and that in a time of agricultural crisis the establishment of a public bank was a logical extension of the state's ambit:

> at one time it was necessary to argue that the railway should belong to and be under the control of the State, but today in this colony with the exception of one short line the whole of the railways were in the hands of the Government. We have also in this colony assumed control, not merely of the ordinary branches of the postal department but also the telegraphic and telephonic departments which in some parts of the world were in the hands of private companies. We had taken charge of public education system and the result had been that a better education at a lower total cost to the people, both collectively and individually, had been secured. We had for some time advanced money for mining companies, and although all the money would not be returned, yet the State had the advantage of a considerable amount of information regarding our mineral resources.[42]

Treasurer Holder then turned to agriculture loans and defended credit foncier lending by saying that:

> The Parliament was characterised by a desire to help the producers, and one way of doing that was to provide the producers, if not with cheaper money, at least with money on such terms as would best retain him [sic] on the soil and permit him to make a living for himself and his family. It was necessary for the Government to step in and do what private capitalists had not shown their willingness to do, but the Government would not lend on securities that would not be accepted by other people. Private capitalists would not take their principal back in half yearly instalments on the terms that the Government proposed to do.[43]

The nationalisation of the Savings Bank was, according to Holder, but an extension of the public role of the bank. He added that in 1893 the previous Downer government had announced its intention (although never proceeded with) to place the Savings Bank more directly under government control and the bill was in keeping with that purpose. He hoped that these would be support from all in the parliament for the change.

The Savings Bank versus the Kingston government
The bill became a focal point for attacking the Kingston government in general, and as such, the intention of one piece of legislation became lost in the political campaign to keep the government's hands off all banks. This campaign was supported by the Savings Bank and orchestrated by parliamentarians, led by John William Castine and Clement Giles, who were both Trustees of the Savings

Bank. Giles and Castine's campaign was given secret backing by the Savings Bank Board. The Trustees met on Friday 23 November 1894 to go through, clause by clause, the government State Advances Bill and 'to consider certain propositions from the chairman Sir Henry Ayers'. It was decided that 'no minutes be recorded on the debate or the proposals'.[44] At the meeting were Sir Henry Ayers, Sir W Milne, Sir E T Smith, Sir J Colton and T Graves, A Hardy and W Gilbert and the members of Parliament A Campbell, J O'Loghlin, J Castine and C Giles.[45]

What followed from the secret deliberations was a political campaign led by John Castine and Clement Giles, who both barnstormed the countryside, spreading disquiet over the alleged government intention regarding the deposits of the Savings Bank. In the parliament, the leader of the opposition, Sir John Downer, came out strongly against the bill and used it as a vehicle to attack the reforms of the Kingston government. The campaign against the Holder bill was based on the claim that the government was only interested in nationalising the Savings Bank of South Australia for the purpose of getting hold of its deposits. The conservative paper, the *Register* (whose owner Joseph Fisher had close links with the Bank of Adelaide) opposed a public bank saying that it was not an issue of private banking failure but of the lack of security by the borrowers that prevented loans from going to the rural producers.[46] The *Register* went on to argue that a credit foncier system might be all right for France but was inappropriate for a British colony.[47] It added that the Savings Bank already had ample reserve funds to lend to the farmers, if they had sufficient security, and argued there could only be a hidden and sinister motive behind the bill and this was to get control over the deposits of the Savings Bank for political purposes. In contrast, the progressive paper of the day, the *Advertiser*, supported a credit foncier system but was not convinced that the Savings Bank was the best vehicle for such a system.[48]

Savings Bank versus the State Bank
In the face of this opposition, the bill was defeated in the last sitting of the 1894 parliament. This did not deter Treasurer Holder, who on 11 July 1895 introduced a State Advances Bill to establish a government guaranteed bank with the primary intention of establishing a credit foncier system to help the farmers. The idea was that the government would establish a bank which would directly compete with the Savings Bank and would focus on the provision of credit on an instalment basis to both small farmers and those farmers who rented land but who had a sufficient level of cash-flow as backing for a loan application.

The Savings Bank moved quickly to block such an occurrence. A special meeting of the Savings Bank Trustees was called on 9 August 1895, when Castine moved that the Savings Bank usurp the agenda of the government by adopting the credit foncier system itself and to liberalise the bank's lending policies to leaseholders.[49] The Trustees decided not to accept the motion but to allow it to lay on the table while the bank conducted a political campaign against the State Advances Bill. Sir Edwin Smith proposed that the bank use the petition it had organised amongst the depositors and staff, which had gathered 5,600 signatures, as the basis for stimulating opposition to the bill.[50]

The Second Reading debate on the State Advances Bill commenced on 8 October 1895. In an attempt to pre-empt debate, Castine sought to move that a committee be set up to approach the Savings Bank to ascertain whether the bank could fulfil the credit foncier role suggested by the Treasurer.[51] Holder derided Castine's motion by reminding him that the Trustees of the Savings Bank had run a campaign against that very scheme. He went on to mock Castine saying that the government 'had been told [in the previous debate] that the Savings Bank was such a good institution that there should be no alteration in its constitution or management. Arguments had been used, based on the alleged super excellence of the Savings Bank, to show that it was so perfect that it could not be improved, so that it was better to leave it severely alone'.[52] Holder said that as the Savings Bank had opposed the previous bill to make it a credit foncier bank there was no point in countenancing Castine's motion.

The parliamentary debate became divided on simple lines between those who supported the Savings Bank and those who wanted a State Bank. Those opposing the new bank praised the Savings Bank for its safe lending and claimed that a new bank was not necessary and only stemmed from government spite for failing to nationalise the Savings Bank. In contrast, supporters of the bill marshalled evidence to show that the Savings Bank had in tough times not been a friend of the small producers or the working man. William Archibald, for instance, said that the Savings Bank was keener to lend on 'palatial palaces rather than on a working man's house'.[53] Similarly, John Macpherson said that:

> It was not many years ago that if a man wanted to borrow £100 from the Savings Bank it was impossible to get it. Men desirous of improving their properties had made applications and had been absolutely refused. Was it now not true that the Savings Bank today had several hundred thousand pounds awaiting investment and yet there was never a time when the smaller producers were more in need of assistance than they were now.[54]

In his closing speech on the bill Treasurer Holder indicated that public banking would be an issue in the forthcoming election and accurately predicted that the bill 'did not offer something for everybody, and no supporter of the government had ever said it did, but if they could not help everyone that was no reason why they should help no one. Besides offering money on good terms they were establishing an institution whose scope would be ever extending'.[55] In his final remarks, Holder who had been the editor and proprietor of the *Burra Record*, could not resist the temptation to expose the contradictory positions held by some of those now opposing his bill. He commented that:

> ... government were exceedingly thankful to some members for their straightforward and constant support, but they had nothing to thank several other members for, who now spoke largely of their desire to establish the Credit Foncier system, though they once scoffed at the idea of the State lending money to farmers. Seeing that the scheme had caught on in the country these members were trying to hedge round, but the electors would be able to see through so thin a dodge.[56]

This was a clear reference to the Member for Gladstone, Alfred Catt who had supported credit foncier lending but in the final analysis voted against the bill.

Equally it was a final passing swipe at Castine who now called for credit foncier lending but only through the Savings Bank.[57] The bill passed through both houses of parliament and was proclaimed on 20 December 1895.[58]

The State Bank of South Australia begins operation

The State Bank commenced business on 1 February 1896. When the directors had their inaugural meeting on 11 February 1896, the first issue was to appoint an Inspector General to run the bank. The directors were H M Addison, who was elected chairman, J A Johnson, G Inglis, J B Spence and S Stanton. The directors requested the Treasurer supply the bank with £1,000 as an advance to begin the process of lending on mortgages.[59] The next item was to agree on a sitting fee, which was set at two guineas per board meeting. At the 20 February meeting it was decided that yearly railway tickets be provided for George Inglis from Georgetown and S Stanton from Strathalbyn.[60] The bank was offered one room in the Money Order Department to conduct its business and had £50,000 in mortgage bonds at 3.5 per cent interest as its loan capital. By March the board meetings began to develop a lending pattern which was to dominate board meetings for over 80 years. The board cautiously evaluated each loan while carefully monitoring the repayment schedules of each borrower.

The approach of the directors was one of extreme caution over lending public money to the small producers. The bank had limited financial resources as it relied on government advances, and so the trustees thoroughly evaluated each loan that passed through the bank. The first meeting of the directors which dealt with loans was held on 10 March 1896 where there were three applications for loans. S Pearce sought £500, offering 345 acres at the Hundred of Hanson as security. Similarly, C J Symons sought £300 pounds on land at Eba and Michael Cunningham sought £300 offering 103 acres at Port Adelaide as security. Finally, S Sheppard sought £1,000 using 398 acres at Willunga as security. The Trustees rejected the first three applications as not having sufficient security and sought an inspection and valuation of Sheppard's land. Professor Perkins was appointed to conduct the inspection and he described the property as having 'two, 6 roomed, houses, part brick and stone, a smiths shop, cart shed, underground tank, stone barn and stable, cow and sheep yards, orchards and fencing'. Following Perkins's evaluation the Trustee, on 17 March 1896, lent the full amount to Sheppard.[61]

The mortgage for Sheppard was made on terms of 42 years on half yearly instalments of £26/12/6 of which the principal being paid off was £4/2/6 with interest being £22/10/0. The loan was repaid on 30 March 1899 totalling £1,133/15/0. At the second meeting of the Trustees in 1896 loan applications were received from Uriah Smith for £550 on property at Laura and from J & S Atkinson for £850 on land at Yackamoorundie, finally from P O'Loughlin for £950 on land at Pekina. At the next meeting S Graham sought £1,000 on land at Macclesfield; W Gillard, £1,100 on property at Yatala; Margaret Paterson Graham sought £1,000 on land as security at Macclesfield and Strathalbyn which, upon inspection, was valued at between £2,000 and £3,000.[62]

In 1896 the government amended the Bank Act to allow the bank to lend on improvements to lessees who had added to the selling value of the land. The government also sought to permit the State Bank to lend on Crown land with good security to urban dwellers.[63] Holder, in presenting the amendments, noted that the State Bank had lent £123,880 in its first year, indicating that the change was but an improvement to a successful public bank.[64] Castine again attacked the bank by arguing that, as the State Bank had only lent around £100,000 in its first year, it had not proved any major advantage to farmers and (having it both ways) that if it did lend more money it was in danger of placing public money at risk.[65] Similarly, the pastoralist Edgar Warren argued that the question of lending on improvements could place the money at risk, as a number of farmers were fighting against 'nature'.[66] The amended Act enabled the Trustees to lend on homes and to people with a reliable income up to four-fifths of the purchase price to a maximum of £700. This became a basis for loans to urban citizens, especially to returned soldiers and was the foundation for the State Bank's lending for the garden city of Colonel Light Gardens.

The State Bank was set up on a foundation of State Advances so as to provide loans on credit foncier terms to farmers and the working classes. A sample of such borrowing can be seen in the following loans. Patrick Ryan a dairyman of Parkside received a £100 loan, using his stone brick house of five rooms and iron roof, and cow shed as security on his loan. Alfred Poppins a pianoforte tuner and vine grower of Magill obtained a £250 loan on security of ten acres with vines. George Blencowe the younger, a farmer of Carrieton borrowed £550 at 4H per cent on security of 527 acres, including a stone house with four rooms with veranda, stone dairy, men's stone house of two rooms, stone barn and two dams and two wells. Michael Burt, farmer, borrowed £100 on 387 acres with a five room house, and Fredrick Setters, gardener, of Summertown, borrowed £350 on 24 acres and a stone house of four rooms and dairy with stable and outbuildings. George and Janet Rosson borrowed £250 for a dairy and ten acres at Richmond. Florence Walsh, grazier and hotelier of Balaklava, borrowed £4,150 on 2,728 acres including five houses. William Osborne horticulturalist of Norton Summit, borrowed £80 on 14 acres including a stone house. Thomas Farrell, dairyman of Bowden borrowed £250 pounds with two houses as security; the District Council of Murray Bridge borrowed £100; Bridget O'Donnell dairy woman of Goodwood, borrowed £375 pounds using a five roomed house and wash house as security.[67]

From 1896 South Australia had two public banking institutions with distinct deposit and lending bases. The Savings Bank relied on its large deposit base for its lending. The restrictions on lending and its high security requirements meant that it had excess funds which it invested with the government. By 1897 the Savings Bank was investing more of its money in government securities than it was in mortgages. The State Bank relied principally on the government for its capital base and much of its lending was to the rural area. The State Bank also became the agent for government transfers to farmers through specific Acts, such as the Vermin Act for wire netting vermin proof fencing and for soldier settlement and housing for returned soldiers. With the advent of Federation the State Bank became the conduit for Commonwealth as well as State government acts and during the Depression the Savings Bank for fencing, vermin control, frost relief, and advances to settlers on Crown land.

The Savings Bank had established itself as a safe bank for depositors and a secure lender on housing to those with security and as a provider of funds for the government. The Savings Bank, nevertheless, fiercely protected its independence from the government and followed a conservative lending policy. The State Bank was caught between the dilemma of lending safely and thereby not carving out a niche that made it different from that of the Savings Bank, and on the other hand, of adhering to its charter of lending to small farmers and the needy. Up until the turn of the century it had followed the path of security, but following government initiatives, became more of an agency for government acts which saw it lend to those who could not obtain money elsewhere or who were deemed deserving, by the government, of special attention. These were principally farmers on marginal land, and returned servicemen.

2

Modernising through thrift, planning and housing

At the turn of the twentieth century there were two public banks in South Australia, the State Bank and the Savings Bank. However, they tended to operate in quite distinct and separate segments of the market. The Savings Bank was primarily an institution formed on the moral principle of thrift, and therefore concentrated upon encouraging people to deposit their savings into the bank. To this end the Savings Bank fostered the idea of 'Penny Banking' or school savings so as to instil in the working people the benefits of monetary self-denial. For its part, the State Bank was basically a conduit for government advances to the rural sector.

On 22 December 1911, the Fisher Federal government established the Commonwealth Bank, to compete against the private banks. The bank began full operations in 1913 with exclusive right to use post offices as surrogate branches. The advent of the Commonwealth Bank had the immediate and practical effect on the Savings Bank of losing post offices as deposit agencies. In preparation for the loss of these facilities, the Savings Bank sought and gained support from the Peake government to allow it to build a branch network throughout South Australia. The Peake government passed legislation in 1913 specifically aimed both at protecting the market position of the Savings Bank of South Australia and limiting the influence of the Commonwealth Bank.

The Savings Bank business in the post and telegraph offices throughout South Australia had been greatly facilitated by the appointment of Charles Todd to the Board of Trustees in 1867. In the board minutes it was recorded that Todd's 'help and influence were largely responsible for the united and harmonious working which led to a very large amount of business being transacted at the agencies'.[1] With the opening of branches, the bank had to train its officers and to appoint 'Local Accountants' to head the branches. The first branch was opened at Port Adelaide in 1906 and by 1928 there were 39 branches at Angaston, Balaklava, Clare, Eudunda, Gawler, Glenelg, Goodwood, Gouger Street, Hindmarsh, Jamestown, Kadina, Kapunda, Kooringa, Maitland, Mile End, Moonta, Mount Barker, Mount Gambier, Murray Bridge, North Adelaide, Norwood, Parkside, Peterborough, Port Adelaide, Port Augusta, Port Lincoln, Port Pirie, Prospect, Quorn, Riverton, Rundle Street, Semaphore, St Peters, Strathalbyn, Tanunda, Unley, Victor Harbour, Wallaroo and Woodville.[2] The total staff of the bank in 1928 was 229, which included 11 'ladies'.[3]

To further protect the Savings Bank from the Commonwealth Bank, the Peake government passed legislation to strengthen its guarantee over the bank. The amendment of 1911 to the Savings Bank Act said, in effect, that in the case of the bank running into difficulty the government 'may' come to the assistance of the depositors. This alteration complemented the 1903 and 1907 amendments to the Act which empowered the Trustees to invest in securities protected by the State or Commonwealth governments but still retained the legislative and operative distance between the bank and the government.

Thrift: a moral mission

From 1913 onward there were now three 'people's banks' operating in South Australia. The Commonwealth Bank was a challenge to both the Savings Bank and the State Bank, especially with the backing of the federal government. The Savings Bank met this challenge by reaching into the schools. Changes to the Savings Bank Act in 1907 permitted the Savings Bank to open thrift agencies in private and public schools. The Act empowered the teachers to open accounts for the students and collect 'pennies' (thus the name the Penny Bank) from them. The success of these agencies was dependent upon the willingness of the teachers to accept and spread the thrift philosophy and to act as agents for the Savings Bank. The bank's official history recorded its appreciation of their efforts, saying that:

> The marked success of School Banking is to a great extent due to the willing service gratuitously rendered by school teachers in influencing children to open accounts and in collecting deposits each week. The success attained is a tribute to their sincere and disinterested regard for the welfare of the rising generation, and proof of their realisation of the value of inculcating frugal habits in the minds of the children.[4]

As well as espousing the bank's philosophy, Penny Banking was a clever marketing strategy to develop a customer base from primary school upward. The legislation establishing school banking met with two forms of opposition. One form of criticism was that Penny Banking was moralistic and usurped the role of parents in money matters. Such a view was expressed forcefully by Sir John Downer saying that the bill for Penny Banking was 'a piece of morbid sentimentalism ... The idea of throwing upon the school teacher the invidious and unpleasant task of trying to get children to hoard their pennies was a degradation of office'.[5] The other criticism came from those concerned that it was diverting over-worked public school teachers from their task of teaching. The Chief Secretary in reply to the criticism pointed out that there was no obligation on teachers to be agents but that it was something that they would have to apply 'voluntarily' to do.[6]

Finally there was the claim that it was a plot to deprive working class children of a penny's worth of pleasure. On this point J P Wilson said that he 'would rather see a child spend every penny it had, because the child of the workers generally did not get too much of the pleasures of life'.[7] The legislation passed both Houses of parliament and allowed for deposits of not less than one penny to be collected at the school. By 1909 there were 4,607 accounts with the balance being £21,990. The success of the school banking scheme can be gauged from the figures that by 1927 there were 964 school agencies with 45,015 accounts and £74,969 in juvenile deposits.[8]

School banking was matched by the sending of Home Savings Boxes to every new born child in South Australia. By 1927 the Savings Bank was sending 1,000 boxes each month to new-born infants. The idea of home savings was seen by the Savings Bank as complementing its philosophy of delayed gratification. Such a life-cycle logic was given symmetry by its being linked to personal improvement through work and the husband's provision of security for the family in home ownership. The bank was to offer such security via its mortgage loans. In discussing its Mortgage Department, in 1927, the Savings Bank Trustees wrote that:

> Private enterprise in its various forms has been stimulated by means of loans on mortgage, and thousands of persons have been assisted in financing the purchase of homes. The bank, therefore, is not only a medium for the development of character which comes of the self-denial imposed by habits of thrift, but also greatly benefits the community by its investments, which indirectly provide employment for a large number of people, thus creating of itself a veritable wheel of fortune shedding its beneficent influence throughout its entire revolution.[9]

School banking philosophy matched the bank's official morality which was sober, patriarchal, paternalistic and authoritarian. The board regarded its staff in moral terms asserting its own views over the staff's morality. The bank insisted on assessing each pay rise per person on their performance and on their code of honour. Moreover, the board opposed incremental pay rises and, consistently resisted union involvement in issues of pay and conditions.[10] The rumour among staff was that to reach to the top of the bank, a manager had to espouse the principles of the Freemasons. This claim is supported by the fact that no Roman Catholic was employed in the bank until 1916.

Employment in banking was seen as a middle-class (male) world where the only place for women was as temporary typist and then as wives. In keeping with other banks, male bank officers were expected to be sober and of high moral standing. The Savings Bank required that male officers had to obtain permission to marry and were only granted consent if their salary reached a prescribed level (£200 pa in 1913) adequate to support a wife and family. It was assumed that if an officer did not reach that level then, in accordance with middle-class norms, he might be 'tempted' (like Adam was with Eve) to embezzle money from the bank. This paternalistic and authoritarian view was resented by many officers of the Savings Bank but this was dismissed by the board. It took a decision against the 'marriage ban' in a Scottish Court in 1938 to end the practice of male bank officers gaining consent from their respective boards to marry.[11]

The State Bank and the 1,000 Homes Scheme
The State Bank was under the same authoritarian and paternalistic culture as the Savings Bank. It was nevertheless much more closely tied to the prevailing rules and regulations of the public service. Moreover, the State Bank was heavily reliant on the state government for funds. The State Bank therefore tended to respond more readily to the philosophies of the government of the day. It was, moreover, the conduit for government provisions to farmers and concessional home owners. Such provisions were provided for via the Advances for Homes Act of 1910, the

Loans to Producers Act of 1917, Advances to Settlers on Crown Lands Act 1914 to 1916, the Vermin Act 1914, Loans for Fencing 1919, and various Crown Land Acts of 1915 for loans to block holders, and for rainsheds and tanks and for soldier settlers. The State Bank played an innovative role in lending for producers, in acquiring credit for land improvements and for the transfer of loans through local councils and boards for the control of vermin and for water preservation.

Under the Gunn Labor government in the 1920s, the State Bank became the financial base for an urban planning and social justice experiment which was to set a precedent for other banks to follow. The experiment also played a crucial role in the reconstitution of the bank as a home lender and as an urban planner. The stimulus for this change was the idea of building a garden city in South Australia. The political agent for the scheme was William Denny, who was Minister for Housing, and he linked the idea of rewards for ex-servicemen and concepts of social justice for families to that of a garden city, built at Colonel Light Gardens. It was this which saw the State Bank launch its boldest experiment, the 1,000 Homes Scheme.

The 1,000 Homes Scheme

The State Bank become the agency for Denny's scheme for Colonel Light Gardens. The idea was to create a healthy environment which would sponsor progress and not squalor. The houses were to be built to individual designs but built by the modernist method of mass production.[12] The 1,000 Homes Scheme gave returned soldiers and working families the chance to own a home and, concomitantly, presented an opportunity for the State Bank to become a home builder. The houses were to be provided on a long term credit foncier basis. The homes were to be priced on a social justice basis whereby they were to be no more than £700, with soldiers paying no deposit and 14/6 per week; civilians with fewer than two children under 16 years paid a deposit of £100, with instalments at 16/1 per week; civilians with two or more children under 16 years paid a deposit of £25 with instalments of 18/1 per week. The interest rate was set at 6 per cent.[13]

The Labor government and the State Bank board of management corresponded continually over the scheme and they generally reached accord over how the program was to be funded and administered but were at logger-heads over who should build the homes. Following the grand logic of mass production the government wanted one builder for all the homes and gave the tender to the lowest bidder Joseph Timms at a price of £636/15/6 per house.[14] The State Bank board considered Timms too inexperienced for such a large project and made their views known to Denny but, under the insistence of the minister, reluctantly agreed to accept the bid from Timms.

The board's misgivings over Timms' competence were accurate, as he continually let deadlines pass him by. The board acted decisively, placing him into receivership then appointing their original preferred bidder, Henry Freburg, as the chief builder.[15] Freburg had built houses for the State Bank in the past, particularly for returned soldiers, and was regarded by the board as reliable and honest. The Trustees' choice was a wise one and the houses were built to schedule and to the intent, if not the full ideal, of the original garden suburbs plan. However, the scheme had to be modified due to continual attack by the opposition in the parliament and by the press as a socialist plot against private enterprise.[16]

A full trading bank

By 1925 the Gunn Labor government had decided that if the State Bank was to fulfil its role of serving the rural producers and home buyers it needed to become a trading bank proper. To achieve this end John Gunn introduced a bill into the parliament in August 1925 to make the State Bank a trading bank. The parliamentary debate on the State Bank Bill was notable for its ideological overtones. The Liberal opposition, led by Sir Henry Barwell, asserted the bill was the 'thin edge of the wedge' in the 'nationalisation' of all banking as part of the Labor party's goal of socialism.[17] Henry Kneebone was quite ready to take up the ideological challenge, arguing the benefits of socialism and 'nationalised' banking against that of the opposition and private banking.[18] The Treasurer and Premier, Gunn, nevertheless argued that the bill was not ideological in its intent, but merely extended the role of the State Bank to provide 'long and short term credits' to the agricultural producers.[19] He argued that it was essential that the bank be able to 'receive money on deposit and current account' basis and therefore it needed to become a full trading bank.[20]

The Gunn Labor government was successful in changing the State Bank Act allowing the bank to conduct general banking business. The change was symbolically represented with an opening ceremony on 1 July 1926, with Premier Gunn becoming the first depositor. He was followed by his ministry who all opened their own deposit accounts. The transformed State Bank, nevertheless, still carried out the old administration responsibilities of the State Advances Act, the Advances for Homes Act, the Loans to Producers Act, Advances to Settlers on Crown Lands Act, Vermin Act, Loan for Fencing Act, Rainshed and Tanks to Settlers Act, but now it could receive deposits and lend on mortgages.

Another symbol of change was the contract signed, for a 'modern five-story building in Pirie Street', as the new bank's head office.[21] The State Bank then set about creating a branch network to service its rural clients. New branches were opened at Berri and Waikerie on 6 September 1926 and at Renmark on 21 October, 1926.[22] Branches soon followed on Yorke and Eyre Peninsulas. The branches' annual reports became barometers of the rural economy, giving the head office an annual check on the state of the whole rural economy of South Australia.

State Bank and the Great Depression

The 1,000 Homes Scheme had given the State Bank considerable prominence and kudos within the South Australian community. Nevertheless, the patriotic and egalitarian nature of the project was by no means sound banking practice. The bank's report on the Scheme in 1926 noted that 974 houses had been completed but that the bank had suffered a loss of £95,242/15/11d of which £30,000 had been written off.[23] The 1926 Annual Report noted that the State Bank between 1910 and 1926 had approved 20,666 housing loans. In 1926 alone, 1,605 homes were provided under the Homes Act.[24] The State Bank had advanced £10,875,565 under respective housing Acts with balance outstanding at £7,987,343.[25]

With the onset of the Great Depression, however, the State Bank curtailed lending on housing, with only 85 houses built in 1931 as a carry over from the previous year.[26] No houses were built in either 1933 or 1934 and only nine in total between 1932 and 1937.[27] In 1932 the Annual Report stated that 602 properties had reverted to the bank with a value of £384,768, with 4,832 accounts in arrears of between £50 to £250.[28]

The Depression adversely affected many of the State Bank's home loans, notably those of borrowers who had bought homes under the 1,000 Homes Scheme. The bank recorded that two-thirds of the mortgages on the 1,000 homes scheme were in arrears in 1933, and that 673 had been reverted to the bank, with 651 tenanted before they were re-sold.[29] Overall a total 1,400 of the State Bank's total of home loans were reverted to the State Bank between 1926 and 1942.[30] Ray Broomhill observes that as a consequence of eviction many families were forced to either live with relatives, or experience the vagaries of the private rental market (often in slum conditions), or to rely on charities.[31]

Additionally, the bank was carrying large losses on both State and Commonwealth homes for soldier schemes. The State Bank's financial position was exacerbated by the government's Financial Emergence Act which reduced interest rates on homes, resulting in the State Bank accruing ongoing losses on its home lending throughout the 1930s.

In its strident efforts to reduce its urban arrears, the State Bank fell foul of the opposition. In 1936 the bank was depicted in parliament as being a 'callous landlord'.[32] Attorney General Jeffries (who, as an aside, was a Trustee of the Savings Bank), was accused of treating members of parliament with 'scant regard', over his failure to 'come clean' over what he called 'hitches' in the government's policy on rental arrangements on State Bank homes.[33] The Leader of the opposition Mr Lacey said 'the lives of occupiers of State Bank homes were being made unhappy by constant demands made upon them'. Ernest Anthony (Liberal and Country League) agreed and spoke of the 'harassing tactics of the State Bank', adding, 'I think it is most callous thing for a landlord private or governmental to put out in the street a woman and children who have no hope of finding a home'.[34]

Robert Richards (Australian Labor Party) defended the bank, noting that concessions given to private (LCL) renters were not available to State Bank renters and this was discriminatory. He said that 'the State Bank had been very sympathetic in its treatment of home purchasers some of whom had not been altogether genuine in their attitude. It was curious, however, that the people who were indebted to the Crown were not receiving the same consideration as those who owed rents to private individuals.'[35] John McInnes (ALP), in defending the bank, said that 'no criticism whatever could be directed at the State Bank which had in some cases allowed arrears to amount to £300 before it took action'.[36] Attorney General Jeffries said he would 'give the matter consideration'.[37]

In its handling of rural loans the State Bank was obliged to adhere to legislation against its own profitability. For example, in 1932 the State Bank had to reduce its interest on home loan accounts to a flat rate of 5 per cent. Following the Commonwealth Financial Emergence Act interest rates on Commonwealth housing loans through the bank were dropped by 1 per cent.[38] The bank carried its farming loans through this period and had accrued £227,223 in losses on its loans to producers, with £79,481 in arrears in the Advances to Settlers.[39] The State Bank had in 1930 suspended payments for district councils and vermin boards. Interest had also been reduced under the Financial Emergence Extension Act of 1931 to farmers with the rate of interest dropping from 6 per cent to 5 per cent.[40] A similar arrangement was made for councils in regard to the Fencing and Water Piping Act. In terms of the Drought Relief Act the bank warned that as the Treasury had only provided the bank with £130,000, whereas settlers owed £160,000 pounds, the bank could only administer the scheme at an ever increasing loss.[41]

The Farmers Relief Act of 2 April 1931 allowed the bank to offer funds to farmers so they would remain on their property, with adequate capital so as to work their land. This legislation saw the State Bank inundated with requests. There were 4,267 in all, of which 1,339 were from the West Coast, 1,055 in the Murray Lands, 273 in the Upper North and 792 in the Mid-North. Of these there were 3,459 successful applications and the area cropped under the Act was 1,609,000 acres with the average area sown being 465 acres at a cost of £152,109.[42] The Act was extended on 9 December 1931 where there were 3,140 applications of which 2,968 were approved, amounting to £453,065.[43] As the scheme became more well known and the rural crisis intensified, the call on the relief funds rose dramatically. For instance, after July 1932 there were 10,000 applicants and advances were made to a total of £391,326.[44]

The Depression also saw the State Bank accruing debts on its loans to rural co-operatives and producers. The bank had lent to 24 co-operatives (five wineries, five cold stores, eight fruit packing sheds, four butter and cheese factories, one tobacco farm and one fruit and vegetable market) at a cost of £263 288.[45] It had also made loans for land clearance under the Loan to Producers Act, and in total had outstanding advances of £240,991 as of 30 June 1936.[46] The vermin-proof fencing debt was £56,8094 as compared to £28,288 in 1932. The State Bank was also having to recognise that the Advances to Boy Immigrants (1923) was a failure, with there being 59 applicants of which 26 had obtained assistance. However 16 had abandoned their holdings, with the bank having to dispose of the stock and plant left at prices far below the original cost.[47] The scheme was phased out over the next two years with only six settlers remaining on their holdings, with the bank carrying a loss of £1,380 in 1937 and with arrears of £2,310/12/6 out of an original (1923) outlay of £7,415/3/-.[48]

The social role of the State Bank was intensified during the Great Depression with its main role being to support farmers through the tough times. To this end it carried out its tasks with sensitivity and with an awareness, through its branch network, of the specific regional peculiarities, so that when the economy picked up at the outset of the Second World War, the State Bank was well placed to fund the farming boom.

In 1934 the bank brought to the attention of the Treasurer that, as it was obliged to reduce its interest rates to primary producers to 5 per cent while the rate at which the bank had obtained its capital was around 4½ per cent, that this was 'insufficient to cover the costs of administration' and the government should 'provide for the losses that might accrue'.[49] The Treasurer's response was to reduce the current interest rates on capital to the bank to 3¼ per cent. In addition the parliament extended the conditions of the Financial Emergency Extension Act of 1934 which extended the cover until the maturation of the stock or debenture.

During 1935 the Treasurer raised the capital of the State Bank by an injection of £1 million to provide funds for advances on first mortgages of freehold securities to an amount of £5,000 for a maximum period of 30 years.[50] By June 1936, there were 184 applications under the Act for the amount of £465,877 with the bank carefully evaluating each request and in the end approving 65 loans for £177,300.[51] The new board was pleased to report that the injection of capital had resulted in the bank making a net profit of £16,922/17/11.[52] Nevertheless the board said it was still concerned over farm debts in the Murray Mallee and on the Eyre Peninsula, where the bank was obliged to enter into share farming arrangements simply to protect its loan on properties. When the economy began to pick up many of these properties were put up for sale, often to the original owners. In its aim of consolidating its financial position, the board decided that no new branches were to be opened and the number remained at 17 and the accounts at head office were 6,239.[53]

From 1936 onward the State Bank carefully reduced its rural arrears, but was hampered in clearing its rural debts because of the Farmer Relief Acts 1931 and 1932 and the Primary Producers Debt Acts of 1935–36, which granted protection from creditors to the farmers. In 1939 the State Bank gained approval to foreclose on a range of loans it had made in the Murray Mallee and the West Coast in the mid-1920s and which it had carried, at a loss, through the Depression.[54]

In 1940 the board approached the government to deal with the long term problem of carrying housing and rural loans. The bank wanted to write off a number of loans but recognised that it would result in considerable losses mainly with advances made to farmers in the Murray Mallee areas of the State. The bank conducted an exhaustive review of its securities and sought to dispose of its bad loans, but was frustrated by the onset of the drought which seriously reduced the income of the farming clients and therefore made a wholesale sell-off undesirable. By the end of the year the Treasurer agreed to write off £37,000 of the State Bank's debts.[55]

In 1941 the government passed three acts, the State Bank Amendment Act, the Primary Producers' Debts Act and the Homes Act, which revived the fortunes of the State Bank. The first Act allowed the bank to write off repossessed land that it had acquired in regard to Crown agreements. The Act permitted the bank to reduce debts by surrendering 278 properties to the Crown to an amount of £71,252, covered in part by the government agreeing to write off £50,000, leaving the bank with a final loss of £23,307.[56] The board considered that by surrendering so many properties it had finally cut the 'dead wood' from its books and it could look ahead to more profitable years.[57] The bank floated a public loan of £500,000 and repaid a previous loan of £403,400. The number of branches was 17 and several were being run only by the managers as so many staff had enlisted in the military services.[58]

The 1941 Homes Act gave the State Bank the right to build concessional housing on credit foncier terms. The Advances to Homes Act allowed the State Bank to lend up to 90 per cent of the value of a house to the maximum loan of £1,000, repayable over 42 years for stone, brick or concrete constructions and 20 years for wood or iron constructions. The State Bank was also permitted to grant a loan to repay an existing mortgage on an applicant's home. The income limit for the concessional loan was set at £450 but was raised to £660 in 1942.[59] While this was advantageous to the bank, and far in advance of the Savings Bank, it was still not fully competitive with the conditions offered by the Commonwealth Mortgage Bank, which could lend up to £1,250 for a period of up to 35 years.[60] In 1943 the State Bank showed a profit of £24,122/8/10. In 1944 the profit was £29,600 and in 1945 the bank recorded its best year since its transformation in 1926, announcing a profit of £34,624.[61] The board had begun to expand its home building program under the 1944 Act with 143 dwellings being erected in 1944–45 as compared to 32 in 1943–44 and 26 in 1942–43.[62]

State Bank preparing for peace

The State Bank announced in February 1944 that its intention was to build 5,000 houses, at a cost of £4,250,000 in the first five years after the war. In supporting the program Premier Playford praised the State Bank, particularly for building homes in the country and outer city areas, saying that:

> The State Bank had been the greatest single factor in providing comfortable homes in this State. In all, 13,611 houses had been built by the bank while it had assisted in the purchase of another 10,883, making a total of 24,490 assisted to own their own homes. Altogether £14,000,000 had been advanced under the Advances for Homes Act and the balance outstanding was £4,500,000. After the last war the State Bank had a building program for some years rising to 2,000 a year, but from 1931 to 1937 only nine houses were built and normal progress had not been resumed when the present war had broken out.
>
> The plan for 5,000 houses has been based on the assumption that on the cessation of hostilities the bank will be inundated by prospective home buyers ... There is already a long waiting list. It seems that there will be a shortage of 25,000 houses in this State after the war.[63]

At the end of the war the State Bank launched a comprehensive home building program. In 1944–46 it erected 407 new homes to a value of £323,511 and in 1946–47, 458 homes were erected to a value of £365,410.[64] The State Bank bought land for subdivision and signed contracts for the erection of 122 houses, under a group scheme arrangement with preference given to ex-servicemen. New housing business for the bank totalled £635,503 for the year. The balance outstanding on homes was £4,027,664/11/10.[65]

Building modern homes for patriots

In offering its home services, the State Bank had in 1944 developed 33 basic ground plans with a wide selection of designs. All group homes had five rooms with most being triple fronted with stainless steel sinks in the kitchens. The bank said that these were but the beginning of its plan to build modern homes for sale and it was acquiring land in suitable locations for post war housing. The houses were described as being:

> ... a radical departure from standard construction ... For example, the windows had been made by the adoption of a newly patterned steel box framed window with the sashes suspended on steel cable to counter balance each other which automatically operated a disappearing fly screen, top and bottom ... terrazzo floors were in use in front verandahs and bathrooms, built-in casements, enamelled bath, a shower recess, flush-jointed ceilings and decorated panels and glass doors, and fire places in textured brick varied with stucco finish, the front fence being of brick fitted with a welded steel gate.[66]

In 1948 the bank conducted an evaluation of its housing program and noted that the housing shortage was acute and that the cost of materials, and the bottlenecks in material supplies, had increased the cost of erecting homes. In particular, the increased cost of materials and the 40 hour week pushed the price up in the group erected homes targeted for ex-servicemen and low income families.[67] A standard bank house in the group scheme was £900 in 1945, £1,117 in 1946, £1,212 in 1947 and £1,413 in 1948.[68] All the homes erected in the scheme were being allocated to ex-servicemen, and given the sense of patriotism which the State Bank felt for such men, it wanted to ensure that they contained features comparable to private sector homes. It was therefore loath to omit any modern conveniences, or reduce rooms, or lower the height of ceilings so as to bring down the final prices to the returned soldiers. The State Bank built in total 600 houses in 1949.[69] In the five years up to 1948 the bank had assisted 2,711 families into homes to a commitment of £704,000.[70] There were 314 new houses under construction and contracts were signed for 424 homes, 260 in group schemes and 164 private dwellings. Constructions of group houses were in the areas of East Glenelg, Hammersmith, Plympton, Underdale, Flinders Park and Broadway Estate and further groups were contemplated for Brayville and Brooklyn Park.[71]

In the 1950 Annual Report, Advances for Homes totalled £4.3 million, Advances for Settlers, £68,220, Loans for Vermin Proof Fencing £97,769, Loans for Producers, £321,263, Loans for Fencing and Water piping £53,744, Frost Relief, £7,926 and Loans for Water Conservation £180.[72] Despite all of its building activity the State Bank was falling behind other banks in total home building. In short, the State Bank's role as a lender for housing reached its peak in 1929 when it had some 37 per cent of all home loans during the Depression and World War II but fell to 10 per cent by 1956.[73] That is, by 1950 housing was still a major activity of the State Bank but had declined in importance compared to the other home lenders in South Australia.

Savings Bank and the Great Depression
During the 1920s boom the Savings Bank had recorded a substantial rise in its deposits. In 1915 total deposits were £9,017,061. In 1921 deposits had risen to £14,771,172, by 1924 they stood at £16,989,081 and by 1928 were £22,467,830, rising to £22,795,000 in 1929.[74] The bank, flush with funds, began to feel confident in its expanding role as a lender for housing.

Given that the Savings Bank had fostered the philosophy of savings as a family responsibility, and espoused the slogan of 'save for a rainy day', it felt obliged to lend from its high deposit base to worthy borrowers. However, with the onset of the Great Depression it quickly discovered the fragility of its deposit base when in 1930–31 there was an excess of £3,300,000 withdrawals over deposits.[75] The board was then obliged to turn to the money market to sell treasury deposits of £1,550,000, and government stocks of £1,050,000 at a cash loss of £68,928, and reduce its external holdings by £412,000 and mortgage loans by £190,000, just to cover the depositor withdrawals.[76]

Alarmed at the change in circumstances, the Board of Trustees established a special sub-committee to monitor deposits and oversee mortgages. The Committee was headed by the Chairman of the board, Sir W Herbert Phillipps, who had been a Trustee since 1900. Phillipps commissioned a series of reports into the bank's savings and lending position. From the report into deposits, it was discovered that the rise in funds during the 1920s was mainly brought about by wealthy individuals, who were 'parking' their money in the Savings Bank only to withdraw it when the downturn began.[77] That is, in 1915 the percentage of large deposits in the whole was 26 per cent. By 1922 this had risen to 36 per cent, in 1926 it was at 45 per cent and by 1928 it was 52 per cent and in 1930 it was 53 per cent.[78] The management inquiry into deposits also found that the rural prosperity in the 1920s hid the vulnerability of the rural sector to international prices.[79] Finally, the increase in the state's population (from 502,411 in 1921 to 580,500 in 1930) had contributed to the rise in savings and, consequently, to a feeling in the bank that the boom would be sustained by local demand.

The Trustees realised that the 1920s had caused not just a shift in the thinking of the wealthy depositors but that the poorer classes were now saving, not for buying productive property, but for home ownership. The Secretary of the Mortgage Securities Department, Tom Linn, noted this shift in the thinking of depositors, saying in a report to the Trustees that the Savings Bank was once but

> ... the guardian of the *whole* of the savings of the poorer citizens – an end in itself. Now they are becoming more and more a means to an end – a place for the temporary accumulation of savings, which will be used to acquire home ownership. Home ownership formerly not dreamed of by the working classes, is now reasonably possible to all, and there are thousands of houses in this State owned and partly owned by depositors who have used the bank to save until they had sufficient to pay the first deposit on their homes and the subsequent instalments as they become due. In short, the bank is no longer merely a custodian of savings, it is, in an ever widening sense, the People's bank.[80]

The Savings Bank was therefore faced with a dilemma. The savings of the wealthier depositors were less stable than those of the working class borrowers, but the latter had principally their homes as security. As of 30 June 1930, out of total deposits of £21,700,00, over £11,500,000 was held by 21,746 depositors with an average of £530 per depositor. It was these wealthy depositors, the report noted, who were most likely to invest their money in government securities, shares and debentures, and as they were 'investment wise' and tended not to allow their savings to accumulate in their accounts over time.[81] Moreover, it was the withdrawals from these well-off depositors which significantly contributed to the record outflow in 1930.

In contrast, the poorer depositors were having their homes placed at risk due to unemployment. In 1931 out of a population of 580,500 the number of unemployed was 20,440, and the bank calculated that this translated into a declined savings pool of 75,000 depositors.[82] In response to the dramatic rise in arrears on current loans in July, August and September of 1931 the Trustees decided to halt any new home lending. The effect of this move can be witnessed in the following home loan approval figures. In 1928 there were 1,772 new home loans, in 1929 there were 925 home loans, falling to 450 in 1930. In 1931 there were only 18 carry over loans with in effect no lending on housing that year.[83] In 1932 only nine new loans were made, while in 1933 there were 18 new loans for homes, rising to 40 in 1934. Following the easing of the Depression, lending began to rise from the 1929 figures with 1,209 new loans in 1935.[84]

In March of 1935 the Savings Bank Board again commissioned Linn to evaluate the bank's mortgage position. Linn calculated that there was £5,779,340 invested in mortgages to 8,901 mortgagees.[85] The proportion of Mortgage Securities to bank funds was 25.3 per cent compared to the State Bank of Victoria with 22 per cent. Of the 8,901 borrowers, 6,983 had been able to keep up with their payments. Of the 1,323 loans in arrears on interest, the total amount owing was £99,295, representing 14.8 per cent of all loans. Of these arrears, Linn noted that slightly more than 50 per cent of outstanding interest was owing on loans in country districts. In all, 1,452 mortgagees under the instalment payment system (introduced in 1910) had been in arrears in payments on principal totalling £79,785.[86] Under the Mortgage Relief Act the bank was unable to take action on rural borrowers who fell behind in their instalments on principal. One measure of gauging the effect of the Depression on borrowers can be seen in the figures that in 1930 on loans of £4,237,339 interest in arrears was £48,117. In 1931 interest in arrears was £72,010. By 1934 interest in arrears was £86,242 on total loans amounting to £3,793,848.[87]

Linn commented that the Savings Bank had 842 mortgages with loans amounting to £1,474,00 on the security of farming or grazing lands. 685 of these borrowers were able to meet their payments, and of the 157 who were in arrears their interest was £51,577 and they were in receipt of relief from the Farmers Assistance Board. In addition, 41 were in the South East with ten on the drainage scheme, while 27 in the Mallee district were in arrears including rates and taxes. This was of concern to the bank as it had to wait in queue behind the council and governments before obtaining any of the arrears money. Likewise, the Debt Adjustment Act of 1929 tied the hands of the bank as it empowered the Director of Debt Adjustment to place a stay of proceedings against the recovery of debt. The bank made unsuccessful deputation to the government, pointing out that it was being placed at considerable disadvantage in regard to its security, and had to often lend more money to the farmers for seed, superphosphate, etc. so that the crops could be sown and harvested.

Linn noted that as of 30 December 1934 the Savings Bank was collecting rent from 290 mortgage securities with total rent collected for the year being £12,517. He observed that many tenants were having great difficulty reducing their indebtedness:

> It is difficult to foresee how some can pay very much off their arrears as generally the rent is increased before they have any opportunity. However, if the current rental is met and a *genuine effort* is being made to reduce the arrears, it is doubtful whether anything can be gained by requesting them to vacate ... Until recently it was practically impossible to let some properties and it was deemed necessary, in order to avoid damage from vandals, to permit a tenant, though not paying rent regularly (if at all) to remain in occupation and look after the property until a paying tenant was in occupation.
>
> ... The great majority of mortgagors *deem it a privilege* to be a borrower from the bank and express themselves as well satisfied with the treatment received, but regret their inability, owing to reduced incomes, to meet the request for a reduction of the mortgage [emphasis added].[88]

Linn noted that the Savings Bank had shown leniency towards those in arrears but was always diligent in protecting its security.

In conclusion, Linn bemoaned the fact that the Crown Debtor's Act, which had the effect of covering the repayment rates on State Bank loans, would cause the thrifty borrowers to rely on government support and not personal endeavour.

The outer suburbs and a speculators' market

As of November 1933 the bank had 290 mortgage securities from which it was collecting rent at an annual income of £12,517. It had been nearly impossible to let out some of its properties. For instance, of the 165 properties offered for sale between 1931 and 1934 due to evictions, only 27 were sold at or following the auction. In respect of 10 of the 27, the Savings Bank had sustained a loss of £1,118.

In deciding whether a mortgagor should be evicted the bank had to weigh up the risk to the equity held in the property, and also what effect a forced sale might have on the depressed property market. Linn noted that often those houses for sale were 'the worst of the bank's securities', they were 'generally in a poor state of repair, largely due to the reduced earnings and unemployment of the mortgagors who therefore have been unable to effect any repairs, except where materials have been supplied by the bank'. He added that, of the properties offered at public auction, 'there has been so little demand for real estate, particularly where houses are lacking in modern conveniences and situated in isolated localities, that at almost every auction sale not even a bid was forthcoming'. To preserve its equity the Savings Bank took over the management of properties and obtained tenants for them. It was also noted that the properties in such isolated suburbs as Devon Park, Renown Park, Seaton Park, Findon, Cheltenham Gardens and Morphettville Park were extremely difficult to let or sell.[89]

In a 1936 report to branch managers, Mr Dignum from the Mortgage Department commented that 'many mortgagors vacated their homes to reside with relatives – a practice that became popular at about this time and was soon reflected in the rents obtained'.[90] Country properties were causing particular problems for the bank as they came under government acts (Drought Relief Act, Farmers Assistance Act 1933) which protected the farmers from eviction and from paying off the principal. Dignum noted that:

> Country loans have caused considerable anxiety. In certain cases the bank has had to enter into share-farming agreements, supply super, bags, etc. so that crops could be sown and harvested. Drought relief and other loans have been granted by the Government and unfairly made a charge on land prior to that of registered mortgage; conferences with the governmental and parliamentary bodies have been attended by the bank's officers, resulting in certain cases in some measure of relief being obtained.[91]

Arrears

From June 1930 the Arrears sub-committee of the Trustees oversaw loans in arrears. The sub-committee, headed by Chairman, Sir W Herbert Phillipps, met weekly to evaluate the recommendations of the six arrears officers. The procedure of the committee was generally to endorse the recommendations of its lending officers as to a particular course of action. There were three options for the Arrears Committee to consider, namely, whether a mortgagee should be allowed to remain in residence, despite arrears, secondly, whether the mortgagee should be evicted and the bank place tenants in their place or, finally, whether the property should be sold to recoup the loan.

The Committee took each case on its merit with the over-arching concern to protect the bank's money. Nevertheless, it was confronted with the human consequences of mass unemployment and was generally prepared to extend a loan where effort was being shown by the mortgagee. For instance, in 1931 E Harvey had arrears of £46 on a loan of £436 and he had a wife and five children, with only one daughter working in Terowie. The rest were living on rations and because he had sold furniture, valued at £100, to partly meet repayments, it was decided that arrears on the loan be deferred.[92] In contrast, J Bartle was given notice that the bank intended to sell his house as his arrears were £55 on a loan of £960 and his payments had been irregular.[93] G M Harrison of Norwood, who was an ex-tramway worker, had arrears of £30 on a loan of £634. Because illness had reduced his working capacity to part-time and he had 12 children, of whom ten were still at home, the Committee decided to allow him to remain in residence, but as a renter.[94]

By 1936 the bank hardened its position on arrears. The change in attitude can be seen in the following examples. J L Cavanagh of Brompton who had been a farmer but was now conducting a greengrocer business, was paying the bank 7/6 pw with arrears of £51 and owing rates of £41 on a house purchased for £323. He had earned the disapproval of the bank because he had 'two sons unemployed but would not allow them to work out corporation rates'. The sub-committee recommended the sale of the house. W McMillan of Rosewater had arrears of £53, rates unpaid £55, on a loan of £200, and was a bricklayer with only '4 months work in the last 8 years and had been on rations most of the time'. The sub-committee decided that unless 'satisfactory payment was made within 3 months he be required to vacate the property'.[95]

Similarly, G V and F J Gardiner of Morphett Road, Morphettville had a loan of £1,350 with arrears of £138 and unpaid rates of £60 with a property consisting of 12 acres used for tomato growing, vines and a wool scouring business. The Gardiner family was notified that unless arrears were 'substantially reduced within 3 months the bank would give notice of sale'. E M Reynolds of Cumberland Park with a loan of £233, arrears of £38 and unpaid rates of £10 was 'a bricklayer out of regular employment for the last 7 years, last year's earnings were £20, on rations'. The sub-committee recommended 'that unless mortgagor is able to resume payments to the bank within 6 months he be required to vacate in order that the bank may let'.

In regard to Mrs H Coley of Prospect North with a loan of £220 with arrears of £39, rates unpaid, it was noted that her 'husband was out of work, retrenched in 1927, only odd jobs since then, on rations for long periods'. It was 'recommended that notice of sale be given'. Mrs Roach of Brighton had a loan of £676, arrears of £67, rates paid, the value of property was £1,050 but now only worth £750. She was a widow with 'occasional earnings from nursing and private income of approximately £30 pa'. The sub-committee 'recommended that unless substantial payment was made on the account of arrears the bank would issue notice of sale'. W Williams of Welland South had a loan of £606, arrears of £39, rates paid. He was a 'brick maker, deaf mute, formerly unemployed and on rations for over 3 years, now employed in brickyard and is paying bank 25/– pw; bank paying rates and taxes'. In his case it was 'recommended [that] no action be taken while payments are maintained'.[96]

On the death of Sir W. Herbert Phillipps (who was a Trustee for 34 years) his place as Chairman of the Board was filled by J C Rundle, who followed his predecessor's role in chairing the Arrears Committee. The committee's minutes in 1936 still read as a continuing litany of the economic and social hardships of the Depression and of the individual and collective response of the people to the hardships. For instance, Mrs Fox of Torrensville who was recently divorced was an invalid pensioner with an income of 18/- p. w. and was able to pay her arrears due to 'help from her friends'. Mrs Beatton of Cheltenham was a widow with arrears of £35, who had an income of £1/8/7 as a cleaner at a school and 21/- from board from her two children, was prepared to pay £1 per week if the bank would pay rates and taxes. The bank agreed to pay the rates. Mr Fooks of Albert Park was a labourer, 'out of regular employment for 5 years, now at settlement near Kuitpo, earning practically nil'. The property was let at 22/6 pw and the house was in need of painting. Fooks offered to undertake this task if paint was supplied; this was agreed to by the bank. Mr Jackson was a labourer 'out of regular employment 4 years, worked for the Tramways but now in ill-health, received invalid pension of 19/-, one child was ill, wife and three children on rations, one other son paid £1 board'. The board had recommended that the mortgagor should vacate but they were then promised payment of 17/6 pw rising to 19/- pw next year. Jackson requested that the bank pay rates and taxes of £42/11/-. After consideration of the committee's suggestion, the board agreed to pay the rates and taxes.[97]

Similarly, the Arrears Committee minutes record the beginnings of industrial diversity in the South Australian economy and how new industries, as well as the old, were adversely affected by the Depression. For example, Mr Lewis of Maylands had £40 arrears, 'he was a motor mechanic out of regular work for 5 years, now employed on a country property, he was letting the property at 22/- pw' and he was slowly bringing down the debt. Similarly, Mr Jeffrey of Plympton Park was a 'motor mechanic with only small earnings'; his house was to be placed in the hands of his wife who would sell the property after renovation and repayment of arrears of £64.[98]

Likewise the Arrears Committee minutes reveal the hardship faced by those relying on state welfare, notably women. For instance, Mrs Blewitt of Woodville West was a widow without means, she had vacated her house; let at £1/1- pw with arrears of £7/1/9. The bank decided to pay the rates of £46/19/1. Similarly, Mrs Brown of Prospect West with a house purchased for £638, which was now valued by the bank at approximately £647, was obliged to sell. She was a widow and the house had been let since 1932 at 22/- pw; an accompanying letter from her solicitor recommended that she not be obliged to sell at that time as she had no equity in the property, and therefore would lose all the interest she had paid. Notwithstanding the request, the bank recommended the house be sold.[99]

By 1940 the Arrears Committee was hardening its position on evictions and forced sales. For instance, Mr Stanton of Brighton was a storekeeper with small earnings, the house was let at 15/- pw, but it was noted that the mortgagee had failed to pay interest and rates as arranged. While the local branch manager recommended the loan be continued the Arrears Committee recommended that notice be given.[100] Similarly, Mrs Orr had purchased a property at North Croydon for £693 but had arrears of £8/2/9. The value of the house stood at £1,025 in 1929 and she informed the bank that she had been trying to sell the house since for £800.

The bank valued the property in 1940 at only £702. Her husband was 'a commercial traveller out of work for long periods' who was now earning £2 pw and she was teaching music for 15/– pw. The bank had forced them to vacate the premises and was collecting rent at 27/6 pw but now sought to press the sale.[101]

Even by 1940 it was still difficult to sell some houses. For example, J Marshall of East Adelaide was a widow occupying a house purchased for £635, valued by the bank at £644 (but once was valued as high as £930) and she had been trying to sell the property since 1935 but had received no enquires.[102] Likewise, Mrs Anderson had purchased a property in Port Adelaide for $829 now valued at £908 with arrears of £77/11/3. She had offered the property for sale in November 1932 but no bids were received. The property was vacated in July 1935 and let for some time at 22/6 pw. The local manager reported that 'on account of the locality there is little likelihood of effecting a sale or securing a higher rental which pays little more than current charges'.[103]

Evictions

By 1938 the Savings Bank management considered that it had gained valuable intelligence, from its management, of arrears and properties. The head of the Mortgage Department, H M Caire, reported that since 1930 the bank had collected £100,000 in rent, £85,00 on mortgage accounts and £15,000 on foreclosed properties.[104] In recounting the bank's experience with evicting mortgagees he noted that in the country areas there were very few cases where the Savings Bank took 'legal possession'. This was in no small part due to the government protection of farmers.[105] In the urban areas, however, evictions were more common, and they were not without complications for the Mortgage Department. Caire offered the following case study to illustrate his point.

The incident involved a property which was 'very old and [in a] dilapidated condition in a poor locality which was sold after much trouble to a speculator at considerable loss to the bank'.[106] The tenant vacated the property but the bank then discovered that the tenant had sublet 'some underground rooms in it [the house] to an unemployed man with a wife and 7 children living on rations'. The unfortunate 'sub-tenant could not find another home',[107] Caire said, so the bank brought 'an action in the Supreme Court for unlawful occupation at a cost of about £10/10/- which would only have added to an already considerable loss. However, eventually, after pressure, the man and his family vacated shortly prior to settlement'.[108]

Empire

The Trustees during the 1930s still considered Australia as an outpost of the British Empire and treated as a moment of great importance the rare visits from respective Governors. The Trustees took a wide interest in matters in Britain and this can be seen in the minutes when in 1936 the Trustees wrote to Buckingham Palace offering their condolences to the Royal Family over 'the death of his Most Gracious Majesty King George V' and reaffirming 'their loyalty and devotion to the Throne'.[109] When King Edward VIII departed before his Coronation, on 11 December 1936, no letter was sent to the Palace but the board felt the need to record in the minutes the change in the monarchical line by noting 'the abdication of King Edward VIII' and that 'his Royal Highness the Duke of York would accede to the throne'.[110]

The Prime Minister visits the Bank

The belief of Australia's place in the British Empire was nevertheless tempered by its recognition of Australian national leadership. For example, the Bank board was most delighted when the Prime Minister accepted its offer to visit the bank. The board minutes recorded that at 3 pm on 15 December 1938 Prime Minister J A Lyons visited the Savings Bank, and the minutes record that he 'was entertained at afternoon tea by the Trustees ... Mr J C A Rundle in a brief speech of welcome spoke of the history and progress of the bank, and the Prime Minister in reply expressed thanks for the cordial reception, and congratulated the Trustees on the advancement of the Institution'.[111]

Learning the political game: Savings Bank versus the Commonwealth Bank

During the 1930s the Savings Bank board was drawn into the political realm, notably when the Commonwealth government began to assert its influence on the financial markets. The 1931 banking crisis in New South Wales, in part precipitated by Premier Lang, saw the government Savings Bank of New South Wales merged with the Commonwealth Bank. The federal government then began to canvas the idea of one big savings bank for Australia and sought the Savings Bank of South Australia's opinion on whether it would merge with the Commonwealth Bank.

Expressed colloquially, this offer was like the government waving a red rag to the Savings Bank Board bull. The Board of Trustees immediately contacted State Premier Butler to assist the bank in defending its position in South Australia. The Trustees mounted their defence on the grounds of State's rights but also on the basis of their loans to the State government:

> So far as the Savings Bank of South Australia is concerned the suggestion should be resisted by all who have the welfare of this State at heart ... On 31st December, 1931, of its total funds amounting to over £20,270,000, of which £7,279,000 was on loan to the State Government, £6,400,000 on mortgage of Freehold securities, £359,000 representing advances to Corporations and District Councils, and £2,164,000 was on deposit with various Trading Banks.[112]

The Savings Bank of South Australia added that should there be an amalgamation, the 'the main control would pass out of the State and that the bolstering of the large savings bank at the expense of the small savings banks was inimical to the interests of depositors of this bank ... The main mischief today is that in all the States competition has been created by the Commonwealth Bank and thus depleted the funds already available for use in each respective State, in addition to duplicating the tax on the depositors by the maintenance and expense of two Branches where one would have done'.[113]

With the help of Premier Butler, the board successfully blocked the merger with the Commonwealth Bank. The Commonwealth Bank however had absorbed the Western Australian Savings Bank and begun to expand its lending into mortgage loans.[114] The next challenge from the Commonwealth Bank to the Savings Bank of South Australia came in 1934 with the decision to establish a national mortgage bank. When the Commonwealth Bank again publicly raised the mortgage lending issue, the Savings Bank Trustees again sought support from Premier Butler to have the

Commonwealth Bank withdraw its Savings Bank facilities in South Australia.[115] Butler wrote to Claude Reading, Chairman of the Commonwealth Bank Board, saying that there was no need for a mortgage bank in South Australia as it was covered by the Savings Bank and the State Bank and perhaps the Commonwealth Bank should use the Savings Bank as its mortgage bank in South Australia. Reading (somewhat tongue in cheek) replied that the Commonwealth Savings Bank would be willing to hand over its proposed mortgage business in South Australia as long as the Savings Bank would in return hand its deposits over to the Commonwealth Bank.[116]

Throughout the 1930s the issue of a Commonwealth Mortgage Bank was one which greatly concerned the Savings Bank Trustees.[117] These fears were confirmed when in 1941 the Curtin government announced its intention to provide the legislative framework for a Commonwealth Mortgage Bank. In response to a request from Treasurer Chifley to discuss this matter, the Trustees sent the manager of the Mortgage Department, Mr Caire, to a conference in Canberra on 17 November 1941 to discuss the issue before the bill was presented to the parliament.[118] The bank's position was to try and prevent the bank from entering the housing market and to confine a Commonwealth Mortgage Bank to the rural areas.[119]

At the conference Caire argued that home lending was saturated in South Australia and that the Commonwealth Bank should limit its ambitions to a rural mortgage bank. Even here, he said, the peculiar conditions of rural lending in South Australia, which was guided by the Goyder line of rainfall, meant such a venture would be of high risk.[120] Caire noted that the recently passed Homes Act 1941 in South Australia made provisions for loans on credit foncier terms for up to 30 years on 90 per cent of value so that the Savings Bank would take up most home loans, leaving no room for the Commonwealth Bank.[121]

This position was rejected out of hand by the representatives from the Commonwealth Bank who argued that they would be competitive in any lending arena. Claude Reading said that Prime Minister Curtin's plan was for a more nationally co-ordinated effort on housing. For his part, Curtin made an appearance at the conference speaking of his desire for a national bank for home lending. At the conference, Premier Playford defended State's rights over a national scheme, and said his main concern was with interest rates, not the provider of mortgage loans, but that he saw a problem with interest rates fixed at 3½ per cent by a mortgage bank as it could undermine both private and State banks. He said that 'such interest rates would attract the existing business from existing institutions which were carrying [out] valuable services'.[122]

In response to the concerns over the Mortgage Bank, the commonwealth government established a Parliamentary Committee on 15 October 1942 to examine the issues and to bring down a finding no later than 11 November 1942 on the proposed Mortgage Bank.[123] The Parliamentary Committee supported the change and in March 1943 the bill was again presented to the Commonwealth parliament. Recognising that a Mortgage Bank was now inevitable, the Savings Bank Trustees turned their attention to the bill itself and were concerned that it permitted the new bank to offer a loan on a 40 year term (as opposed to their 30 years term). The Savings Bank, seeing that this placed their credit foncier loans at a disadvantage, approached Premier Playford to extend their lending terms to match those of the Mortgage Bank. But to the Trustees' disappointment he refused to change the Act to make the Savings Bank competitive with the Commonwealth Bank.[124] In 1933 the board had found a solid ally in Premier Butler but in their dealings with Premier Playford they discovered that this was a give and take game. They were soon to learn that Playford was prepared to alter the rules of the game to his advantage when it suited him. Moreover, they were to find that the Premier was willing to bully the bank into supporting his housing and industrialisation schemes.

From Depression to prosperity: World War II
The outset of the Second World War and the introduction of rationing and economic recovery saw a remarkable rise in the level of the Savings Bank's deposits. During the Great Depression deposits had remained static, being £22 million in 1928 and £23 million in 1938. In the next eight years deposits all but doubled to be £45.5 million. In 1947 deposit balance was £53.8 million and the total government securities were £42.4 million.[125]

This increase in activity was being conducted by fewer staff and by temporary officers due to enlistment in the armed forces. In all, 219 of the bank's permanent staff served in the fighting forces, 13 of whom 'made the supreme sacrifice', nine were wounded in action and three became prisoners of war.[126] The board overcame the staff shortage by employing male and female 'temporary clerks' under the supervision of the permanent staff,[127] a move which the board did not realise would have legal implications when the war came to an end. By 1942 the bank found itself so short of trained officers that the board decided to close the bank for a day to reconcile the books. On 26 June 1942 the bank placed notices in all the newspapers in South Australia saying that, 'owing to the acute shortage of experienced staff following the enlistment of nearly all eligible men in the fighting services it has been found necessary to close the bank for one day on 30 June 1942 so that essential balancing work can be performed'.[128] The practice of closing the bank at the end of each financial year continued throughout the war period.

Run on the Savings Bank
In 1942 the commonwealth government introduced war time regulations bringing all material resources under government control. An unintended consequence of this was a run on the Savings Bank that spread across most branches, especially those in wealthier suburbs. Between 17 and 21 February 1942 there were withdrawals of £227,244 from Currie Street alone, and from the other branches an amount of £273,244 was withdrawn.[129] Chairman Rundle sent a staccato like telegram to Prime Minister Curtin saying that 'we feel it necessary to draw attention – considerable public unrest locally – due to misunderstanding of Governments' proposed regulations. Rumour that banks are to be closed and/or deposits frozen gaining ground and disturbing certain classes'.[130] Following the telegram Curtin issued a press statement to the effect that 'the regulations would not impose any restrictions on Savings Bank deposits, and would not affect in any way the availability of these monies to depositors'.[131] The public statement quelled the depositor's fears and the situation soon returned to normal.

A new head office

When the new head office was opened by Governor Sir Charles Malcolm Barclay-Harvey on 2 February 1943, the ceremony was deliberately austere in view of the times. After his Excellency's speech, a short address was made by Chairman Rundle, then it was time for Premier Playford and Lord Mayor Lt Col A S Hawker to open the entrance doors.[132] The Trustees were proud of the building with its spacious banking hall and the glimmering surfaces reflecting the extensive use of Macclesfield marble, combined with granite from Murray Bridge in the public spaces. Behind the public areas were modern offices with an impressive wood panelled board room and this wood theme was carried through into the senior managers' offices. There was a large staff cafeteria, and for the leisure of the officers a billiards room and a squash court at the top of the building. During the war the Trustees allowed the Civil Defence Forces to rent the squash courts for accommodation at £150 per annum for the duration of hostilities. The armed forces were allowed to place search lights on the roof and a watching post was set up after the bombing of Darwin.

During 1942 the Trustees instructed the managers to take stock of the bank's holdings for defence purposes. Particular attention was given to the new bank head office as to its safety in the unlikely occurrence of aerial bombing. All contingencies were considered, even preparations to evacuate the bank's records to a secret place out of Adelaide proper if there was a Japanese invasion. A study was undertaken by the management to discover a safe place for the bank's records, and this led to the renting of a premise in Kapunda.

Modernising advertising – the cinema

In keeping with the bank's desire to be modern the Trustees set up a publicity department which then commissioned a movie documentary of the new building under the title, *The House that Thrift Built*, and this was screened in the local cinemas. The documentary marked a shift in advertising from billboards to the movie screen and to radio advertisements. In 1943 the Trustees decided to abandon the use of railway bill boards for advertising. These were referred to in terms of their 'obsolescence', and the preference was now for popular cinema advertising to promote the bank.[133] The advertising budget in 1942 for cinema advertisements celebrating the new head office was set at £3,559.[134]

Public housing: 'jerry-built' versus modern houses

In planning its housing program the Board of Trustees was cognisant of the recent confrontation it had had with Premier Playford over his own housing plans. In that instance, the bank's desire to build houses principally for the middle class ran counter to the Premier's idea of low-cost housing for working families. The history behind the Trustees' program was that of mortgage arrears during the Depression, where the highest risk loans were to working class families, especially in outer suburbs. The idea behind the Premier's scheme was to provide low-cost housing, near industrial estates, for the working class, so as to keep wage rates down, and thereby offset the disadvantage South Australia had in regard to transporting manufactured goods.[135] Naturally, in the class politics of the day, Playford's scheme was seen in suspicious terms. For example, the *Workers Weekly Herald* saw the plan as 'Another Silly Scheme for welshing the workers by having the workers work for a lifetime to pay off a jerry-built house, obtained on a low deposit. Better that the Housing Trust provided rental accommodation than a lifetime of dependence.'[136]

When the bank realised it was at odds with the Premier, the board insisted that their choice of houses was not negotiable as it was merely a commercial decision based on risk management.[137] Playford's response was to threaten the bank that if they did not enter into his housing scheme then he would deliberately weaken the bank. The Premier said he would extend the government guarantee for financial matters to the building societies. Moreover, he wrote to the Trustees saying he was considering an amendment to the Savings Bank Act whereby the Trustees would be obliged to make an annual payment to the State government on a percentage of income on stock.

Playford was to play this game of brinkmanship to the limit. He moved an amendment to section 15 of the Savings Bank Act whereby the bank would be obliged to pay an annual sum from interest earned to the Housing Trust of South Australia. The bank calculated that all the bank's reserves would be eaten up in the payment to the Housing Trust.[138] When Playford presented the bill to the parliament the Trustees decided that they had little option but to agree to his terms, that is, of offering loans to 90 per cent of the value of a house provided by the Housing Trust. Playford then withdrew his bill, saying it had been all a misunderstanding.[139] He did, however, as a means of placating the Trustees, incorporate into the Homes Act of 1941 the provision for the Savings Bank to purchase land.[140] This reform provided the foundations for the bank's plans for post-war home building. The Trustees, nevertheless, had to wait until the favourable progress of the war before moving to take advantage of its new rights.

Robbery, the Premier and privacy
The next confrontation between the Premier and the Trustees came in June 1943 when the Savings Bank refused to pass on information to the police over a depositor. This led to a meeting between Chairman Rundle, the bank's solicitor G C Ligertwood KC, and Premier Playford on Thursday 17 June 1943, in the Premier's office. Ligertwood outlined the Savings Bank's policy on depositor confidentiality, to which the Premier replied that 'this bank was the only one to refuse to disclose information regarding customers to the police'. Mr Ligertwood countered by explaining that 'the bank had a duty to its customers and in the absence of a very good reason for disclosing any information would render itself liable for damages'.[141]

Despite this history of altercation between the Trustees and the Premier, a month later Premier Playford felt no compunction in calling on the bank for a loan to bail out the state government. Faced with a lack of ready capital to pay the State's public servants Playford, on 28 July 1943, approached the bank for a loan. The government was technically bankrupt and Playford asked for a loan of £500,000 to support the August budget.[142] Rundle, as Chair of the Trustees, on 29 July telephoned the Premier saying that the bank would approve the Premier's request and the money was immediately forwarded to the Treasury.

In July 1943 the Trustees began to prepare the post-war contingencies, notably by developing a plan for housing. The board instructed the management to explore possible sites for housing estates near the city.[143] The scheme was given the literal term, 'Post-War Program for the Purchase of Land for Home Building'. At the same time the management sought to develop the necessary back-up facilities and personnel to match the real estate plan. The management advertised for a staff architect to oversee house designs and to offer a service for home buyers.[144] At the 9 December 1943 meeting the Trustees decided to set up a special board sub-committee to develop the post-war program of land purchases.[145]

Housing estates
In August 1943, the Trustees approved the hiring of Charles Sutton, licensed land broker, to investigate properties for the bank to purchase for redevelopment for its housing estates.[146] Sutton prepared a report on three properties: Devitts land, 25 acres (114 building allotments) at Wellington Road, Payneham; Ellerslie estate, 18 allotments at Magill Road, Corryton; Cudmore's land at Daws Road, Edwardstown, which was located 'just west of the Military Hospital, about one-third of a mile from the electric tram terminus, comprising 81 acres' and was a deceased estate.[147]

The Trustees then called in the City Valuer to price the land. Having received the price, the sub-committee considered each property in turn, evaluating that Devitt's property was on poor land for building with its eastern extremities in Magill and passing westward through Corryton, Newstead, Trinity Gardens and Evandale. In short, the advantage was its location but its disadvantage was that the land was over-priced at £12,000 and the seller refused to budge on price.[148] Ellerslie was regarded as even less suitable for housing as the land was prone to cracking, but at a minimum, sections could be purchased as it was near good transport. The Dan Cudmore property was highly attractive as it consisted of 81 acres nominally priced at £14,000, which could (after setting apart 5 acres for reserves) be divided into 300 building allotments at 50 x 150 costing on average £50 a block.[149] On 9 December 1943 Sutton was authorised by the Trustees to negotiate a price of around £10,000 for the Cudmore estate, which included a seven room, two storey house.[150]

On 17 December 1943, Sutton wrote to the Trustees informing them that the Bank of Adelaide was the mortgagee and that they already had received a conditional offer of £12,000 on the Cudmore land and would not sell to the Savings Bank for less than £14,700. He said if he was paid commission on the higher price he could negotiate more freely to bring the price down. The State Valuer, Colliver, was then approached to re-evaluate the Cudmore property. He estimated that given the size of the estate, the land was highly desirable as there seemed to be no better proposition offering in the metropolitan area, and that the net profit derived by the Bank of Adelaide as mortgagee, of £659/1/6, showed a return of 5 per cent on invested capital of £13,000. The State Valuer said that 'if there were no National Security Regulations it is not by any means unlikely that the Land Speculation Company which owns the land in the adjoining Northern subdivision would be desirous of securing Cudmore's land'.[151]

The Bank of Adelaide informed Sutton that it would separate the house and vineyard from the rest of the property and sell 76½ acres as a separate lot. Sutton was instructed to offer around £10,000 for the 76½ acres with the provision to go to £11,000. On 12 February 1944 the Bank of Adelaide accepted £9,750 for the allotment. Rundle informed the board that having purchased the land the bank was still under war-time restrictions, and that it could not sell the land unless a dwelling house had been erected on it, but that the bank was well placed for post-war housing construction.[152]

The Savings Bank began to seek out more suburban land so as to hold a strategic position in the expected home building boom following the cessation of the war. Land was purchased in both the urban and country areas, including around the Edwardstown allotments, Port Augusta, Findon, Henley, Grange, Findon, Cowandilla, Barmera, Tailem Bend, Woodville North, Underdale, Craigholme, Hayhurst, Colonel Light Gardens, Lower Mitcham, Redfern and Streaky Bay. Accompanying this scheme was the decision to appoint a consultant architect to plan modern homes and to offer services to home purchasers in the form of a book of housing designs for four, five or six room houses, and architectural advice supplied by the bank. On 29 June 1945 the board agreed to advertise for a legal officer for land conveyancing and property settlements.[153]

On 7 September 1945 it was announced that the bank had appointed W Richardson as its draftsman providing a service for home buyers.[154] On 14 September 1945 the bank appointed a building inspector to make inspections and reports on homes in the course of their construction as security for mortgage loans.[155] At the same time, the board established an Architects' Department to produce a book of plans for clients, to be hired out to them with a deposit of £1/1/-, which would be refunded in full when the book was returned.[156] The Architects' Department would charge at a rate of £1/10/– per £100 for standard plans and £3 per £100 for special plans.[157] In November 1945 the General Manager presented to the board '16 sketch designs prepared by the bank's Architect of 4, 5, and 6 roomed houses, the estimated costs of which ranged from £860 to £1,200 and recommended they be approved' – which they dutifully were.[158] On 21 December 1945, 11 further sketches were presented to the board for approval, bringing 'the total to 27 to be issued in a loose-leaf book for prospective borrowers'.[159]

In regard to the expected post-war housing market demand in South Australia, Assistant General Manager Mr Caire calculated that there was £54,500,000 in the bank and that there was £6,500,000 available for loan, and that this was not an adequate amount to meet the expected demand and compete with the State Bank and the Commonwealth Bank.[160] He noted that 'the amount to be paid in gratuities to members of the Forces in this State (running into several millions), the volume of notes in hiding ... the increase in civil employment ... the expansion in peace–time secondary industries, and given reasonable seasons and prices from primary products implied boom conditions'.[161] Caire estimated that the pent up demand for houses was in the order of 30,000 homes and that the Savings Bank would have to compete intensely for its share.[162]

Battle over bank nationalisation
In preparation for its housing estates the Trustees, in October 1943, wrote to the commonwealth government seeking permission to purchase land. The commonwealth government wrote back to the Savings Bank board stating wrongly (as was to become apparent) that as the Savings Bank was a state authority it did not need commonwealth approval to purchase land.[163] The commonwealth's assumption that the Savings Bank was a state statutory authority meant that it needed to avoid antagonising the Federal government.

Nevertheless, in 1944, the Savings Bank was prepared to oppose Prime Minister Curtin's 14 powers referendum. When in May 1944 the Curtin government sought to extend commonwealth power to deal with such matters as Aboriginal affairs, social welfare and finance, the Savings Bank Trustees became alarmed that this could threaten their very existence. The Trustees decided to produce a large batch of leaflets for all depositors and to conduct a media campaign against the referendum, claiming it would place at risk the state government protection of the 500,000 accounts and the £40,000,000 deposits.[164] Having printed the leaflets and drawn up the advertisement for the press the Trustees were advised by telephone by Warren Kerr, the Chairman of the Savings Bank of Victoria, that the most appropriate course of action was not to antagonise the commonwealth government and to remain neutral over the referendum. Having accepted this advice the Trustees then acted 'to rescind the motion of 3 August 1944' and decided that 'no statement be published in the Press nor distributed to depositors'.[165] The Trustees then instructed General Manager Pedler to write to Lloyd Dumas, Managing Director of the *Advertiser*, asking him not to publish their statement.[166] The board then delegated a manager to ensure that all the leaflets were burned. It was recorded that the task was conducted 'scrupulously'.[167]

Relinquishing the title of 'People's Bank'

The political battle over the 14 powers referendum raised the profile of the Commonwealth Bank at the expense of the Savings Bank. The Public Relations Department of the Savings Bank decided that the term 'People's Bank' had become too politicised and closely associated with the Commonwealth Bank, therefore they advised the board that as it was now 'synonymous with the Commonwealth Bank', the Savings Bank should 'quietly cease calling ourselves 'the People's Bank'.[168] George argued that as the bank's centenary was looming the Savings Bank would be advised to look to the future and not the past. As an aside, he commented that the *Advertiser* had come to the bank's aid over the referendum attributing this to both the amount of advertising the bank did with the paper and to the good relations it had with the *Advertiser*.[169]

Having being caught out over what political tactics to adopt in regards to the referendum, the Board of Trustees acted cautiously in regard to political campaigns. For instance, when, on 14 December 1944 the Adelaide Chamber of Commerce contacted the bank requesting co-operation in disseminating educative matters with regard to the proposed nationalisation of certain industries, including banking, it was decided that for the moment 'no action be taken'.[170] Nevertheless, by March 1945 the Trustees were in full defensive mode against Prime Minister Chifley's bank nationalisation bill.

1945 bank nationalisation

In March 1945 the commonwealth Labor government moved to bring banking under its control. In response the Savings Bank set up a special committee of the Trustees, Messrs Taylor, Hogben and Jeffries, to consider the bill. At the same time they commissioned Ligertwood KC, as adviser, to investigate the bank's legal status in regard to the commonwealth Bill.[171] Ligertwood reported that in his opinion the Savings Bank Act did not protect the bank from the commonwealth legislation as it was technically not carrying on state banking business. Ligertwood concluded his legal opinion with the strategic conundrum for the bank in that he said that the commonwealth government had, in regard to housing regulations and the purchase of land, considered that the Savings Bank was a state instrumentality, which would make it exempt from the federal law, but that in his opinion this was incorrect. He said that if the Savings Bank pushed for an exemption the commonwealth would soon discover the Savings Bank's precarious legal status. Ligertwood wrote with great sagacity that: 'The real question of policy involved here is whether it is better to leave undisturbed the present Canberra opinion that the bank is carrying on State Banking and to run the risk of the Treasurer forcing the bank's deposits to the Commonwealth Bank, which of course he may not attempt to do or by making a move for protection to reveal to Canberra its mistake'.[172]

While the Trustees were grappling with this legal conundrum the bank was confronted by the problem that Premier Playford was politicising the legislation, regarding it as both an ideological (anti-socialism/ALP) and a state's rights issue. On the morning of 16 March 1945 Premier Playford telephoned the bank saying that he was seeking permission from the Trustees to use the bank's precarious legal position in his campaign against the commonwealth banking laws. The Trustees, through the Acting General Manager, Neuenkirchen, replied that the board was reluctant to have the bank's position raised in a public meeting, particularly as the bank was still not sure of the commonwealth's attitude to the bank. They indicated to Playford that they were exploring the option with the commonwealth government of protecting the Savings Bank.[173]

The Trustees were then informed by the Acting General Manager that Premier Playford had not taken their response 'kindly' and said 'he would recall State parliament to pass legislation definitely making us a state banking institution. He seemed to be very determined about it, and the board's decision did not help matters'.[174] Playford had in any case gone ahead at Balaklava and cited the Savings Bank as an institution which was at risk under the commonwealth's legislation.

On hearing on the wireless of Playford's statement that the Savings Bank 'was not engaged in State banking', Ligertwood realised the commonwealth would recognise its error and he contacted the Trustees saying that this speech 'had radically altered the position upon which I advised you in my previous memorandum'.[175] Ligertwood advised the board that it could no longer procrastinate, it had to either formally seek an exemption from the Commonwealth bill or have the state government protect the bank. It was recommended that Ligertwood meet with the Crown Solicitor-General, Sir George Knowles, over the bank's position, as the Trustees were concerned that the Premier was hindering the Trustees in their efforts 'to preserve the rights and interests of the depositors'.[176]

The Crown Solicitor General concurred with Ligertwood's opinion that the Savings Bank was not a state institution, noting that 'the Savings Bank does not carry out State Banking on by or for the benefit of the State. The State Governor appoints the trustees and the State *may* make good the lawful claims of the depositors, but in no sense can the bank's operations be described as State banking'.[177] Mr Bean, the Parliamentary Draftsman, also concurred with Ligertwood that the Savings Bank was 'not a state instrumentality' and referred to the case of the Bank Officials Association of South Australia vs Savings Bank of South Australia, saying that the question of whether the Savings Bank came under the Crown was considered in some detail by the High Court in 1923, and the Savings Bank of South Australia was deemed not to be a state instrumentality but whose salaries were, nevertheless, fixed by the Crown.[178]

There was a certain irony in the position the board found itself in. It was caught between Chifley and Playford and between present and past legal precedents. Where its previous position was to protect its self-interest by revoking the officers' pay demands by arguing before the court that, as it was not a state instrumentality, it should not pay the state award, the bank was now claiming it was a state instrumentality and therefore should be protected from nationalisation. Ligertwood KC showed clear foresight throughout this crisis, advising the bank that he was concerned that it was not just a matter of whether the commonwealth government would make the Savings Bank exempt from its legislation, but how it would do it. He noted that it might copy the exemptions it was now offering to the Hobart and Launceston banks (in Clause 2 of the bill), which would in effect limit the banking functions of the Savings Bank to only those matters related to State Acts similar to these two small State banks. The Trustees instructed Ligertwood to prepare both an amendment for the Commonwealth Bill and for a minimum amendment to its own Act should the former fail.[179]

At the same time Trustee Murphy and the General Manager decided to travel by train to Canberra to make deputation to the Prime Minister, explaining how the Savings Bank was quite different from the State Banks in Hobart and Launceston and required its own exemption clause. The delegation met with acting Prime Minister Chifley on 11 June 1945 and he made it clear to them that 'the avowed policy and the determination of the present Commonwealth Ministry is to control all banking in Australia that could be controlled'.[180] On return the General Manager's report to the Trustees on the meeting with Chifley stated that:

> In confidence, Mr Chifley stated that he was not lacking in courage and would like, out of regard for the Institution, to submit our claim for exemption to Caucus, but such an act would be hopeless, and from his point of view dangerous to his own prestige with the Party. He further stated that even if the miracle of Caucus agreement did eventuate, the proposed amendment when before the House would, from the Members in the Opposition (particularly from Tasmania), be the means of argument that would seriously embarrass the Government.[181]

Looking inward to Playford

The Trustees regarded Chifley's position as intransigent and detrimental to the interests of the Savings Bank. The General Manager's report to the board noted that the Labor government would use the provisions of the Act to control interest rates and lending policies and that the controls were 'so far reaching in their effect on our bank as to hamstring the Trustees almost with impotence ... Our bank could gradually cease to exist as a State entity and become for all practical purposes a Savings Bank department of the Commonwealth Bank'.[182] On 14 June 1945 the Trustees decided that they had little choice but to come under State legislation, and they wrote to Premier Playford seeking protection for the bank. A letter was summarily sent to Playford stating that in the interest of depositors it would be best that the Savings Bank be included in Part II of the First Schedule of the state bill.[183]

On 9 October 1945, Playford introduced a Savings Bank bill into state parliament giving the bank full immunity from the Commonwealth Act, by placing it on a similar status to that of the State Bank. The bank was 'to hold real and personal property for and on account of the Crown, which in conjunction with the rest of the Act, will constitute the bank an organ of the State'.[184] The Premier added the rider that 'it is, however, not intended to bring the trustees and staff of the bank under the Public Service Act ... they will not be officers of the public service within the meaning of the Act'.[185]

The leader of the opposition, R S Richards, supported the bill and reminded the parliament that in 1924 and 1927, Treasurer Gunn had negotiated an amalgamation between the Savings Bank and the State Bank but was prevented from doing so because of what he said was 'the pressure of big business'.[186] He went on to argue that the State Bank was always hampered in its reliance on the Treasury for funds and that 'it had to impose charges to repay bank loans so that the State Bank began behind scratch – that its advances became dearer to primary producers and home builders than did money which was available from private institutions'.[187] Richards added that he preferred a course whereby the Savings Bank and the State Bank should 'merge so that they can render greater service to the community. The State Bank should not be dependent upon the good graces of the Government and the Loan Council'.[188]

Playford defended the existing structure of the Savings Bank and noted that the principal change in the Act was that the government shall be liable for any shortfalls. He said that the Savings Bank had provided the state government £750,000 at the height of the Depression when the Loan Council refused to give the State government any money and he added that during the war the Savings Bank had lent the government three loans of over £500,000 to meet deficiencies. He then said, without a hint of irony over his previous blackmail of the bank, that 'I am particularly pleased with the part the bank has played recently in financing housing. Under the Homes Act of 1941 it was one of the institutions for which provision was made with regard to guaranteeing advances for homes'.[189] The bill, he noted made it 'mandatory that the government guarantee the funds of the Savings Bank'.[190]

In the Legislative Council, on 20 November 1945, the LCL member of the Council, C R Cudmore, announced his intention to move an amendment to the bill which would oblige the Savings Bank, in lieu of taxation, to make an annual payment to the State Revenue of an amount equivalent to 5 shillings for every hundred pounds of the depositors' funds, calculated to be equivalent to £116,000 for 1946.[191] The bank board contacted the Premier to oppose the amendment and then launched a public campaign against the proposed change. While this campaign was under way the chair of the board, J Rundle, tactically approached the Premier raising the matter of the Savings Bank's previous loans to the government and of the possibility of a quid pro quo in return for the retention of its autonomy and the defeat of the Cudmore amendment.

Premier Playford met with Rundle on 31 October 1945 seeking long-term loan agreement to fund housing through the Housing Trust. At this meeting it was recorded that a 'gentleman's' agreement was reached between Chairman Rundle and Premier Playford. Rundle took the Premier's position to the 2 November board meeting where he gained approval for an immediate loan to the government for housing, noting that the 'the Premier's board should support proposals for Housing Improvements to the sum of £500,000 a year over the next eight years on the terminable annuity system for 42 years at a rate of interest of £1.10.0 % per annum'.[192] The Premier's proposal was noted and approved.

At the 6 November 1945 board meeting the General Manager, RJH Pedler, read a letter from the Treasurer advising that 'the Government accepts the bank's offer to advance the sum of £500,000 a year over the next eight years and appreciates very greatly the offer of the Trustees to make money available for housing at a low rate of interest'.[193] In the meantime the government and the media, notably the *Advertiser* and the *News*, responded to the Trustees' invocations and conducted a campaign against the Cudmore amendment.[194]

On 22 November, when he realised he had no government support for his position, Cudmore decided to withdraw the amendment. The bill was passed by both Houses of Parliament on 6 December 1945. The Savings Bank was saved from nationalisation but was now dependent upon the Playford government and the Premier was all too ready to remind the board of its need for his protection and to turn to the bank for funds for government projects and revenue – while in the same breath accusing the Labor party of having 'socialistic' intentions towards the Savings Bank.

In a comment to the Senior Officers on his retirement, Mr Pedler noted in regard to the Savings Bank Act 'that there are all sorts of forces at work – unfortunately, subterranean forces which do not always appear on the surface. Political forces have very great strength in these days. I thought perhaps to paraphrase the words of the immortal bard and say "to be or not to be *free* that is the question" – whether " 'tis better in the mind to dwell, or to take arms against absorption, and by opposing it"'.[195] Pedler here was clearly referring to the Chifley government, but it was a warning that could also be applied to Premier Playford. While Playford allowed the Savings Bank a degree of freedom, he was all too ready to request loans from it or to hamper its attempts to become a competitive force against the trading banks.

Electricity Trust of South Australia
In early September 1946, the Premier made a call on the bank to provide funds at lower than market interest rates for the Electricity Trust of South Australia (ETSA). When the Playford government nationalised ETSA, the Premier approached the 'socialist' Chifley government for a loan to compensate the shareholders. The government found, however, that it needed money to upgrade the Electricity Trust's facilities, and approached the Savings Bank for an instalment loan totalling £1,500,000 for ten years, recorded at £3/7/6 per cent per annum. At its next meeting on 20 September, 1946 the Trustees offered the Playford government £1.5 million over ten years and on 8 October 1947, the government made an immediate call on the bank for £500,000.[196]

Subsidising the government
On 2 November 1945 Premier Playford wrote to the Trustees requesting that they agree to an annual payment of £500,000 to the Housing Trust.[197] For 1945 the rate of interest was to be £1/10/– per cent per annum for a period of 42 years. Despite the potential loss of business to the Housing Trust, the Trustees agreed, without protest, to the Premier's request.[198] Between January 1946 and September 1952 the Savings Bank lent the Playford government a total of £8 million at 1½ per cent for a term of 42 years. Playford's deal to protect the bank came at a financial cost. The General Manager, reflecting in 1974 on the long history of the bank's loans to governments, calculated

that they were equivalent to a loss in revenue (as expressed in dollar terms) of $250,000 per annum between 1946 and 1974, – in total, a loss of $7 million in interest to the Savings Bank.[199]

Rundle retires as a Trustee after 41 years
On 22 January 1946 Joseph (Joe to almost everyone who met him) Rundle made a special appearance at the board meeting. Rundle had been a Trustee of the bank since 1905. He was head of Rundle Hotel Brokers and on many Adelaide company boards and President of the SA Bowling Association. Rundle was elected Chairman of the board on the 6 January 1935 until 31 December 1945. The minutes record that 'at the conclusion of ordinary business of the meeting the Chairman, N Taylor extended a welcome to Rundle, the former Chairman and with appropriate remarks handed to Mr Rundle as from his fellow trustees and the General Manager, a Mantle Wireless, as their token of their esteem and appreciation'.[200] Rundle was succeeded by Norman Taylor, who was the Chairman of a merchant import company.

The longevity of the Chairman
Taylor, who had received an OBE for service to welfare, notably crippled children, unfortunately died suddenly on 8 June 1947 and was replaced by Chairman of the Board, Len Hunkin. Hunkin was then Chair of the Trustees until he retired on 16 December 1971. He was replaced by G H P Jeffrey for one year and then Sir William Bishop became Chair of the Trustees until he was replaced by G Huntley from 1974 to 1976 who was replaced by the then government-appointed Bob Bakewell and finally by Lew Barrett in 1980 until the 1984 merger. The longevity of the board and its chairmen until 1974 provided the bank with continuity at the top but equally reinforced the stultification within the bank. The board, moreover, developed too close an association with the Liberal government, and tended toward paternalism and complacency from the top down. There developed an inward looking approach to banking which in the end created an institutional culture out of step with modern banking practices. Such an intransigent approach was evident in the bank's handling of the equal pay dispute and, we shall see, particularly in regard to its female officers.

Celebrating the bank's centenary
The bank carefully planned its centenary celebration for 11 March 1948. A book was commissioned on the bank's history and was prepared by Dr Charles Fenner under the directorship of A W W Cilento. Fenner was paid an honorarium of £50 for his book titled *Our Century*. A competition was held to find a poster to celebrate the 100 years of thrift and a reproduction of the prize-winning poster was hung in the main banking hall, which was 'gaily decorated for the occasion'.[201] On 10 March the Lord Mayor, Mr McLeay, held a civic reception for the Centenary celebration where the Chairman of the Trustees welcomed local and interstate guests and the president of the Bankers Association of New Zealand, Mr Connelly MLC, who had assembled for the occasion. In the evening, General Manager Neuenkirchen hosted 'a buffet dinner at his home at Kensington Park from where the delegates motored to view the lights of the city from Observation Point Belair'.[202]

50 *Things Fall Apart*

On 11 March the official ceremony was performed by the Governor, Lieutenant-General Sir Willoughby Norrie, who unveiled a bronze wall tablet celebrating the bank's service to the state. After the ceremony 200 guests, including the Governor and Lady Norrie, Chief Justice Sir Mellis Napier and Lady Napier, the Premier and Mrs Playford, the Ministers and their wives, the Federal Minister of the Army, Mr Chambers, the Leader of the opposition R Richards and Mrs Richards, Trustees and their wives and senior managers and their wives, were entertained in the staff recreation room.[203] That night a celebratory black-tie dinner was held at the South Australian Hotel where the Governor, the Premier, the leader of the opposition, Trustees, senior management and other dignitaries and their wives were in attendance. Premier Playford, in proposing the toast, said, undoubtedly with irony, that 'I know of no institution less political in its outlook and which has a greater opportunity of serving the people than the Savings Bank of South Australia'.[204] On 13 March 1948 a number of dinners were held for the staff and their partners. The Head Office function was held at John Martin's dining room where Chairman Hunkin gave special thanks to the public relations officer, Gordon George, for the celebration.[205] Other dinners were also organised around particular branch networks in the suburbs and country regions.

Equal pay
The Savings Bank's celebration of its 100th year was notable for the hierarchial divisions in the forms of celebrations. In the bank, junior staff were expected to know their place in the hierarchical order and this was especially the case with women staff members. The senior management and the Trustees of the Savings Bank were notably hostile to women receiving equal treatment and conducted a persistent campaign against equal pay and severance pay for women officers.

In September 1944 the bank had become concerned at the Australian Bank Officials' Association case before the Commonwealth Conciliation and Arbitration Commission regarding equal pay for women bank officers. The Trustees instructed Ligertwood KC to prepare a case opposing the equal pay claim. By the time the case appeared before Judge Foster on 5 June 1945 the bank discovered that Ligertwood was 'otherwise fully engaged on the Royal Commission investigating the activities of the Adelaide Supply Company Limited'.[206] The Trustees instructed Neil McEwin to oppose the equal pay claim.[207] Mr Richardson put the case for the Bank Officials' Association, Mr Derham for the Trading Banks, the State Bank of Victoria and the State Bank of South Australia, and McEwin for the Savings Bank of South Australia. Those opposing the equal pay claim challenged the jurisdiction of the Court and of the operations of the Economic Organisation Regulations upon the case at hand.

Judge Foster determined that he did have authority to hear the case. He said that banking was a 'male industry' and therefore, under the war-time regulations, the women were carrying out male work and were entitled to be considered for male rates of pay. Thus his adjudication on the matter was appropriate.[208] 36 of the bank's female clerks were subpoenaed to appear at the hearing to give evidence. From their evidence, McEwin informed Chairman Rundle that the Judge had discovered that there were clear anomalies in the banks' practices in which the women were employed under the Regulations, and that 'it was likely that the case would go against banks in general and against this bank in particular'.[209] Judge Foster recommended that the parties should seek a negotiated agreement.[210]

Both the Savings Bank and the State Bank belligerently refused to negotiate. They discovered, however, that the Commonwealth Bank was prepared to accept a pay scale of 85 per cent of the male rate.[211] The hearing went into abeyance while the High Court heard a challenge to the validity of equal pay and the Women's' Employment Regulations, using the Crown Crystal Glass Company as a test case. The High Court found that if a woman was substantially performing tasks of a male at some time since the outbreak of the war she could make application for equal pay.

In March 1946 Judge Foster recommenced the case and indicated that he would fix the rate of pay.[212] On 22 March 1946 he made an award, binding the bank to pay the temporary female clerks 90 per cent of the male rate.[213] In his decision Judge Foster admonished the Savings Bank for hiring the females as casual workers when clearly they were temporary workers and came under wartime regulations, and permission should have been obtained over their employment. Judge Foster rebuked the Savings Bank for paying so little attention to such an important matter as the National Security Regulations in regard to its employment of female staff.[214]

Secretary Linn was undeterred by the decision and rang both the local State Bank and the State Savings Bank of Victoria to see if a joint challenge could be mounted against the outcome, and he instructed the solicitors to explore all grounds for a challenge to the decision. He did mention, however, that the Savings Bank was reluctant to go it alone, given the criticism it received from the bench over its faulty employment practices, and said that he was 'not desirous of earning a further rebuke from the Court'.[215] In June, McEwin replied that there was no provision for an appeal and that in regard to the High Court 'he could see no grounds for a successful challenge of the decision'.[216]

Linn then prepared a report for the General Manager setting out the reasons why a challenge was not likely to succeed and how he had explored every avenue to mount an appeal against the judgement. He then noted that the decision only affected 36 women and that it 'will probably cost the bank less than £2,000 so far as retrospective pay is concerned and less than £1,000 as regards increases in salaries and that in any case the problem in a comparatively short period would solve itself by the majority of the girls leaving the service of their own voli-tion'.[217] Expressed bluntly, the Savings Bank went to the trouble of a three year legal battle to challenge the rights of 36 women for a miniscule amount of money. This was a matter of principle, not of money. Women had a moral responsibility to be housewives and not bankers and the bank was going to ensure that it reinforced this morality by preventing equal pay. The next challenge between the bank and its women officers over this moral position came in the same year, and it was over severance pay. Again it reveals a patriarchal culture that was already out of step with other banks.

Banking 'a man's world'
The assumption of the management was that banking always was and always would be a man's world. While this may also have been a general cultural norm it was held in a most extreme form by the Savings Bank. Moreover, to enforce its view, the bank was obliged to police its staff strictly. Given the unfavourable legal

experience of the equal pay case, the bank's management decided in 1946 that female staff would be employed basically as temporary staff. The expectation was that when a female officer married she would leave the bank and would not be entitled to the same entitlements as that of the men who received severance pay. When women remained on after marriage the management became alarmed and devised ways of dealing with the moral miscreants.

On 6 February 1946 Assistant General Manager Caire wrote to the General Manager over one case, that of Mrs Masters, saying she had joined the bank

> on 27 May 1929, and thus has been on the permanent staff for approx. 16 years 9 months. This means that in a little over 3 years she will have attained to 20 years' service, and in addition to then becoming entitled to a further six months' long service leave would qualify for a Retiring Allowance of approx. £465 based on her present salary of £280 p. a. It is usual with a typist or female employee that upon marriage she resigns, although I doubt if there is any understanding in writing ... (In the case of future female appointees there could well be a proper agreement covering this point).
>
> I judge, from discreet enquires I have made, that although her husband has been out of the Forces for 12 months, Mrs Masters, whose services were retained solely on account of the war, is in no hurry to tender her resignation. If she refuses to resign upon being requested to do so, the only alternative seems to be that she should retire (now if possible) under provision of Section 20.[218]

The General Manager then began to draft a policy for the Trustees whereby it would be a condition of employment that 'upon the marriage of a female officer she should forthwith tender her resignation from the Staff'. This decision became a General Order, 9 April 1946, to the effect that:

> No female officer on the permanent staff shall continue in the employment of the bank after her marriage except on the certificate of the General Manager that her employment is required in the interest of the bank.[219]

While wanting to ensure that there were places ready for the men when they returned from war service, the bank management realised it would have to retain a small number of their best female officers against what they perceived as the intense competition for experienced women office workers. So in early 1946 the management began to calculate how many experienced female officers it needed and offered them permanent positions so as to retain their services. On 5 April 1946, the Chairman of the Trustees Norman Taylor wrote to the General Manager informing him that the Trustees had stated that there were 16 permanent female staff and that the board had authorised the management to appoint up to 17 of the present temporary staff after examination and test of their efficiency and general ability.[220] A further 14 females would be appointed as temporaries whose duties were to be 'confined to typing, machine work and general correspondence'.[221]

Secretary Linn wrote to General Manager Caire that as of 1 April 1946 the bank employed 135 female clerks among whom were a number who desired to be transferred to the permanent staff. He concluded his letter by pointing out that as there was a general shortage of female typists and machine operators that an additional 14 female staff be employed, but that this would not have long term financial implications as the majority of these girls would be under 21 years of age and would not be affected for some time by the Women's Employment Award recently made in the Commonwealth Court of Conciliation and Arbitration.[222] Caire recommended that the board accept Linn's advice and employ more temporary women as well as the extra permanent staff, a view which was accepted by the Board of Trustees.

To determine which temporary female officers would be offered the position of permanency each head of department or branch manager was asked to send in a detailed report on any female staff member who might be offered one of the fixed positions. A number of examples will suffice to show the general paternalistic flavour of the responses to this directive by the managers. For example, Gordon George, Acting Public Relations Officer, wrote of Miss Margaret Robinson, who was 24 at the time, that she was an experienced typist, having previously worked at General Motors, and had 'obtained the Leaving Certificate of the University Examination. After passing the "leaving" she attended Miss Mann's Business College for twelve months. Miss Robins is conscientious and capable. She is refined and has a pleasant disposition. Her manners and general deportment are a credit to her home training and her college education (St. Peters Girls College.)'.[223]

Caire then collated all of these reports and made summaries of them for the Chair of the Trustees, Mr Taylor. Examples of these summaries are as follows. On Miss Ruth Wiling, Caire recorded that she was 17 years of age, had joined the bank in 1944, and was a very 'efficient and reliable stenographer. Possesses a very happy disposition and her only aim is to please'.[224] Of Miss Audrey Foreman, Caire wrote that she, 'was Dux of Adelaide Technical High School – Commercial. Is particularly alert and observant and takes a keen interest in her work. Conduct is good', she was 18 years of age and had joined the bank in 1941.[225] Similarly, Miss Nell Plunkett had joined the bank in 1945, was 17 years of age and was 'of a quiet disposition and has excellent manners. Particularly impressed with her progress. Was Dux of Adelaide Technical High School.'[226]

On 20 June 1946, General Manager Pedler wrote to the Treasurer seeking permission for the appointment of 15 female employees, who had been 'engaged during the war in a temporary capacity to take the place of junior clerks called up for war services', to the permanent staff.[227] Included in the 15 names were Miss Robinson, Miss Wiling, Miss Foreman and Miss Plunkett. On 6 August 1946 another 14 female officers were appointed to the permanent staff, following the assent of the Governor. Having secured the permanency of the female officers the bank wanted from the pool which had joined the Savings Bank during the war, management sought to close this door by passing a decree that forthwith any women employed by the bank had to work five years before applying for permanency. The management on 27 January 1947, then issued a general order, stating that:

> female officers appointed to the staff after 27 January 1947 shall not be declared to be on the fixed establishment until they had served for a period of at least five years.[228]

The effect of the 27 January 1947 order was to rescind the order of 9 April 1946 obliging women to resign upon marriage and thereby denying them a Retiring Allowance. What followed was a tussle between women staff, who had assumed that when they married they would be obliged to resign and receive some severance payments, and management. They then went to their professional association, the Australian Banker Officials' Association SA Branch (ABOSA), who supported them against the Trustees. On 1 November 1944 the ABOSA wrote to the General Manager of the Savings Bank on behalf of the permanent female officers, arguing that the 27 January 1947 edict discriminated against them and denied them the right to resign on marriage and therein the benefits of their retirement allowance, which they saw as a form of 'glory box' for their new life. Mr Barrett on their behalf wrote that

> Banking is not regarded to be a career industry for women. It is only in very rare instances therefore that a female is likely to remain in the service of the bank long enough to qualify for the Retiring Allowance.

Barrett added that passing of the new decree had

> hit members of the permanent female staff with all the force of an atomic bomb. They had regarded these General Orders as conditions of their employment and expected to receive any Retiring Allowance due to them when about to marry and their services were terminated for that reason ... many of them have refused attractive offers from business firms in which rates of pay were immeasurably higher. In addition in some firms they would have been permitted to purchase articles for their future homes at 'house prices' or at a discount, which would have meant considerable savings for them.[229]

The Trustees having received legal advice from the bank's solicitors, Messrs Baker, McEwin, Millhouse and Wright, that the order to oblige women to resign upon marriage was legal, they now sought clarification of that order in light of the January 1947 order of a five year probation period.[230] The solicitors replied that the January 1947 order clearly implied that female officers who remained on the staff after five years would be declared permanent. Secondly, as they were then on the fixed establishment they came under the provisions of the Act in regards to retiring allowance. A consequence of this logic was that if a female officer was obliged to resign upon marriage and was deemed on the permanent staff, she was entitled to the retiring allowance.[231] Compounding the problem was the fact that the bank had already paid the retiring allowance to two female officers, who had resigned in 1946 and thereby established a precedent. Moreover, the bank had paid a special allowance to those members of the staff and the returning officers who had been in the Services and those who remained behind, in the form of a 'victory bonus'.[232] So there was both the expectation and the precedent for rewarding those who had served the bank during the war.

The solution suggested by the solicitors was, firstly, to pay the retiring allowance to those female officers who served during the war; secondly, to put in place orders preventing female officers from being appointed to permanent staff, unless directed by the Trustees; thirdly, to reinstate the order obliging women to resign upon marriage. The effect of these three orders would be that no woman obliged to resign upon marriage would receive the retiring allowance after the new fixed date (1 December 1949).

The Savings Bank board accepted the advice of the solicitors and on 1 December 1949, instructed the General Manager to issue general orders to the effect that:

> Unless the Trustees otherwise direct no female member of the staff appointed subsequently to 1 December 1949 will be placed on the fixed establishment.
>
> No female officer on the staff shall continue in the employment of the Bank after her marriage, except on the certificate of the General Manager that her employment is required in the interest of the Bank.[233]

The General Manager then wrote back to the ABOSA saying that the previous conditions (except for the change in dropping the term 'permanent' from the directive) were now reinstated for the women who had turned to the Association for redress. The new rules, the letter noted, did not in theory exclude women from becoming permanent staff members but did make clear that they were expected to resign upon marriage.[234] By 1953 the only females in the bank who were on the permanent staff were a few of the typists and machine operators, the remaining females being temporary officers who were expected to resign when they married.[235] In 1955 the Savings Bank, in response to pressure from the ABOSA, on behalf of its female members, slightly modified this rule, allowing married women to remain in the bank up to two years after their marriage, on the proviso that they resigned first and were re-engaged as temporaries.[236]

Looking to modernise

In 1948 the Trustees received a report from the management in regard to mechanising the depositors' accounts as the first step in the mechanisation of the head office and then the branches. It was decided to make preparations for the mechanisation of the bank's deposits, beginning at head office. The Savings Bank saw itself as neatly positioned for a housing boom, with the Cudmore land and housing allotments scattered throughout the suburban area. It had established architect, drafting and legal services to support the home building program. It was now protected by the Playford legislation and looked to the Menzies government to bring stability to the Federal banking arena. The Trustees, however, during the 1950s and 1960s, became continually frustrated by the Playford government in their attempts to compete fairly for business. Moreover, the board and management became fixed in their ways and out of touch with both their staff and industry norms.

By 1949, the Savings Bank considered it was well placed to participate in the trends of home lending for mass produced houses as a part of the industrialisation of South Australia. Likewise the State Bank had gained valuable experience in the urban area to match its rural presence to participate in the expansion of lending during the boom years of the 1950s and 1960s. It remained, nevertheless, a bank for rural producers, particularly the co-operative enterprises, and a home builder for concessional loans. The State Bank would also feel that it was facilitating the modernisation of the state by making agriculture more mechanised. However, the dilemma for the State Bank was that it lacked a deposit base to escape government directives and constraints. It remained a niche rural bank.

3

Inward-looking modernism

Both public banks approached the post-war era with a sense of optimism that they were well placed to take advantage of the pent up demand for housing and the high level of savings in the community. The State Bank, in its 1925 Act, was given the foundations to use its rural branch structure to lend to the farmers and country residents for homes and modern farm equipment. The Savings Bank was centrally placed to use its credit foncier instalment loans to promote housing with the ability to lend up to 90% of value on a house to the level of £1,000. From 1946 the Savings Bank had bought land near the city for housing estates and was keen to use its high deposit base for lending to home buyers, as well as meeting the call from Premier Playford to provide funds to the government and the public utilities.

State Bank of South Australia
This part of the tale is recounted through the voices of the State Bank branch managers. From 1926, when branches were created, their respective managers would send annual reports to head office in July. These included appraisals of their regions, their annual deposit and loan accounts, their profit and loss statements, a report on their premises – including manager's house, and finally an overview of the performance of the staff. To gain appreciation of the State Bank the discussion will follow the managers' reports from the beginning of the branch network in 1926 through the depression, war and the boom years.

Renmark
In his first report from Renmark branch in 1927, manager, A D Chapman gives an indication of the difficulties the State Bank had in challenging the other trading banks in the country. He noted that the bank was at somewhat of a disadvantage as it did not have permanent premises. Moreover, in anticipation of the State Bank's opening its office the competition had shored up the better-off producers, leaving the State Bank with only the poorer fruit growers as its deposit and lending base. Chapman wrote in flowing but clear hand writing that the

> other Banks operating locally had ample warning of the likelihood of our opening and put into early effect their policy of defence. It is not suggested that had these circumstances been otherwise, the result to date would have been materially different, for 99 % of the likely clients were impoverished orchardists, hopelessly in the hands of the other Banks, and eager to grasp any opportunity to change their creditor masters. Essentially, this is a borrowing area.[1]

He added that Renmark is more like a 'terminus' rather than a 'centre', and outside of the fruit business the area had the feel that it was in a 'pioneering' stage.[2] There was, he said, 'so much need for capital but so few safe avenues to lend' but there was a sense of optimism in the district with the 'wine-bounty-British-preference position'.[3]

By 1928 the Renmark branch had only £6,000 in deposits. manager Chapman noted that Renmark was 'not the centre of this big district, as regards population. This is again demonstrated by the few Drought Relief applications put in through this Branch'.[4] He noted that the value of vineyards 'fluctuated remarkably' from the price of the bare land to £120-£150 per acre depending on the trade outlook.[5] He concluded with a comment that the branch was 'well settled in its fine new premises, and the bank secured quite the best site in the town when it built here'.[6]

In 1929 Chapman reported that the branch made its first annual profit of £781 with deposits rising by £1,543 and advances increased by £60,359. He observed that the figure could have been larger but for the directive from head office on adequate security, saying a 'large volume of Advance business was declined to conform with the approved policy of the Bank for this district'.[7] He then commented that 'on a conservative estimate £235,000 will accrue to the District from the 1928/29 crop of fruit'.[8]

In 1929, on receiving Chapman's report the head office became concerned over the growing debts in the region and consequently over the adequacy of security cover for many of the loans. Head office wrote to Chapman seeking more detail on these loans. Chapman took this personally, replying that he had but followed the lending policy of the bank and the criticism of his lending was unwarranted. Head office was incensed, saying it was their duty to have an overview of both bad and potentially bad debts. Chapman wrote that 'I should be interested to see a return from a Branch which was considered satisfactory. I can give you the type of report you want, if I know what is needed'.[9]

In his 1930 report Chapman wrote that for this region it was a 'year of struggle'.[10] Wheat was an 'utter-crop failure' and the fruit harvest while good was adversely affected by 'the over-supply of fruit on the market'[11]. The value of rural properties, on average, 'had fallen by 20% during the last three years'. However, he considered that all of the bad and doubtful debts were recoverable, with the possible exception of Moray Parks Fruit Company.[12]

In regard to the Moray Parks Fruit Company, Chapman reported that the operation of the packing company was marginal and it was 'touch and go' as to whether the bank's loan was covered by the proprietor, Milne Gibson, who also had a personal loan of £10,000 pounds with the State Bank.[13] Chapman calculated that £5,160 was at risk and this was covered by assets, mainly plant and equipment, including a fibrous bungalow, with an estimated worth of £5,330.[14] The Branch Inspector was reluctant to foreclose on Gibson at this stage and decided to extend the loan,[15] a decision which meant that the bank carried the company until it was placed in the hands of the receiver in 1968.

In 1931 the branch had made advances on fruit blocks to the sum of £37,818; on distillers and sheds, £78,495; fruit in sheds, £1,041; farms, £13,144; town and sundry, £21,078, totalling £151,576.[16] Chapman, commenting on the effect of the Depression, said that:

... values have fallen about 20% during the last three years. The market for Dried Fruits and Wine allows of a good 'peasant' living being made from Fruit blocks. It will not stand the old scale of living enjoyed by the older settlers in the past. The wheat growers appear to be in for a really good season, at last. It is a poor Banking district. There are ample borrowers, but few depositors, and the prospect ahead promises no change – unless the 'Empire as an economic unit scheme is fulfilled'.[17]

By 1932 Chapman wrote that the economy was picking up and that 'owing principally to Overseas Exchange, the Fruit industry is thriving and there is a good demand, at enhanced prices, for orchards'.[18] He did note, however, that the prosperity was built on the 'unstable factor of Exchange', saying that 'two accounts, that of Woodhams and McLeans, had run into debt in 1929 and were sold covering the debt.[19] The wheat position, he added, was still 'bad' and its future 'obscure'.[20] Some form of 'cooperative use of machinery on the farms would cut the heavy cost of working the farm but this was only in an indicative stage'.[21]

By 1933 Chapman again voiced his worries over the manner by which the co-operatives borrowed from the bank and then acted as if they were banks themselves, tying up the fruit industry by lending to the growers in return for supplies. He wanted the authority to place pressure on the co-operatives to stop them acting 'virtually' as banks 'making advances on future crops with the Bank's money'.[22] Chapman added that 'I think the time has arrived for a review of the policy of allowing the Shed to do all the Fruit advances. It was wise when advances against fruit on vines were being made, but a lot of it is legitimate Banking business now'.[23] Head office indicated that Chapman's observations had been noted but were not to be acted upon.

In 1934 Chapman took up the same issue in his report but with more vigour, berating the co-operative sheds for controlling the finances of, and exerting power over, the growers, saying that 'The Shed processed 4,466 tons, as against 3,816 last year and proved to be over-liberal in it's [sic] advancing against fruit last year, and is being correspondingly cautious this year'.[24] The Branch Inspector again refused to alter the lenient policy offered to the co-operatives.

Chapman, however, would not let the matter rest and in his 1935 report he noted that 'the RFG Co-op Ltd makes all the Fruit advances which would naturally come here. The Shed is virtually a rival bank, in this way – but you have ruled that it is to continue.'[25] Of the economic conditions, Chapman wrote, in somewhat telegraphic style, that 'the District is making a general slight headway – by virtue of the Overseas Exchange – return to par rates would be disastrous. Caution in advancing, is thus indicated, and good margins in security are necessary. Only skilled men and high yielding Fruit blocks, are safe to advance now'.[26]

In 1936 the new manager R B Taulaks noted that in his opinion this was an area of marginal farming, yet the farmers used borrowing to prop up their lifestyle. He commented that 'Fruit growers, with a few exceptions, appear to make a living only, and any accumulation of funds can only be accomplished by careful expenditure and extreme savings. Generally, I should say they are not prepared to live on what may be termed "the bread line."'[27] In 1937 Taulaks noted that in the fruit properties sold that year the values had risen. In regard to the referendum on marketing, he wrote that there was no 'depreciative effect on the home consumption price owing to the voluntary agreement'.[28]

In 1939, Taulaks took up the same bone of contention as his predecessor over the co-operatives. He noted that in seeking to keep control of advances, customers, when pushed by the Bank on their loans, 'merely arrange with a packing shed to pay the reduction asked for, and as the Renmark Fruit Growers Co-op. Ltd. has the majority of the growers as members, it follows that instead of getting the higher rate for our money, we receive through the Shed 4½%'.[29] Again the response from head office was to ignore the complaints and place no pressure on the co-operatives to stop acting as quasi-banks.

For the Renmark region the onset of the war boosted production as export orders to Britain rose, but the down side was the drain on male labour. Manager Taulaks in his 1940 report noted that:

> The war created a problem in regard to the disposal of surplus dried fruits exported. Negotiations with the British government for the 1940 exportable surplus resulted in the Government agreeing earlier in the year to purchase the remaining 50% of this export (sultanas, currants,) at a price based on the average price of the three past years. Then just before the end of June this was followed by a further agreement to purchase the remaining 50%. On the whole it has been a satisfactory disposal of the 1940 tonnage and one to be thankful for.
>
> War conditions appear to have affected the town business adversely (over 300 enlistments from the town and district and in some instances whole families have been removed).[30]

By 1942 Taulaks wrote that labour shortage had become 'a serious matter', as 'over 400 had enlisted and 800 people have left for the capital and other places where munition work or work in connection with armament production is being carried out'.[31] He added that, 'wives and families of soldiers in some cases have left and the balance can be said to belong to those seeking employment … The exodus has left its mark and quite a number of shops are vacant while the business firms remaining are suffering from the exodus'.[32] He complained that, while the branch had to carry a loss, the co-operatives in contrast were able to carry on with short term finance.

By 1945 Taulaks was able to report that while advances were down, with frost reducing the harvest by 30 per cent, signs were encouraging for a post-war upturn.[33] The prices for wine and spirits were made against advances by the government and the civilian consumption of dried fruit had risen 50 per cent.[34] The fruit had been harvested over the last two years by 'labour supplied by Land Army girls and RAAF personnel'.[35]

Taulaks noted that post-war planning had begun around Renmark with the provision of soldier settler land in the Chaffey area and at Murtho, across the River Murray, and an area on the western side of Renmark. There was concern, nevertheless, that demand did not warrant additional vine planting and that this was not justified on these plots unless they were of varieties not planted elsewhere. In regard to town business Taulaks wrote that 'some shops are still vacant but trading has been maintained. The Hotel is always full with guests, which brings additional income to the town'.[36] In regard to the bank's premises, he noted that 'these are in need of renovation' and said he was writing separately to the Branch Inspector on this matter.[37]

In 1947 advances had doubled from the 1945 level, being £87,426 mainly due to the overdraft account of Renmark Fruit Growers' Co-operative Limited being £36,132. There had been a miniboom in land sales but the cautious lending policy of the Bank limited the branch's ability to participate. Taulaks reported 'a number of sales of fruit blocks, with consequent financing of the purchaser, in all cases the prices have been high and it would have been impossible for us to advance figures against fruit blocks for security purposes'.[38] Total branch transactions were £5 million, being up £419,000 on the previous year, and despite 'adverse weather', profits at the distillery were up due to the Government-fixed price'.[39]

In 1948 Taulaks was replaced by Mr E S Newoly, who picked up on his predecessor's themes that, firstly, the branch's lending was restrained by too high security requirements, secondly, that head office needed to do something about the co-operatives acting as banks. He wrote that:

> I consider the advances against fruit blocks for a district of the size of Renmark is too low, however, we are playing very safe and have nothing to fear from a fall in values. I think more opportunity could have been taken to get fresh advance business offering with the return of War Servicemen especially in those cases in which we were interested as administrators of the Re-establishment & employment Act 2, 1945. This is a pity and no opportunity will be missed in future cases and even in the weaning of some from Institutions where they had no right to be in the first instance.[40]

He noted that there were only 251 town accounts in the branch, which he saw as 'disappointing for a town the size of Renmark'.[41] As for the bank's premises he wrote, somewhat shamefaced (and yet with more than a hint of hyperbole), that the opposition were goading him at the club because

> Their premises are attractive, spick and span and as such their Managers lose no opportunity to publicly, jocularly, and seemingly without malice, keep eternally requesting the information across the Renmark Club 'When are you going to paint the Bank'. I feel that I must respectfully report that the shabby appearance of our Banking premises is indeed a bad advertisement. It is quite the leading topic of the town and my opposition take mighty good care that it remains so.[42]

In 1950 there was an increase in advances of £75,952 and 105 new accounts were opened.[43] The increase in bank business, however, was made without any relieving staff, and seemingly without support from Adelaide, which prompted the manager to write in his report that the 'Staff have felt that too little appreciable and admittable knowledge is accepted by Head Office and furthermore comparable with other Banks we are ill equipped. It has been absolutely impossible to grant holidays. This together with long hours of overtime and letters from Head Office, one advising that if recreation leave is not taken it must be lost, is not conducive to a happy relationship and I regret having to report that morale is not as it should be. However we now have additional staff and look forward to a measure of relief'.[44]

In 1953 Manager Kernot provided an overview of advances, deposits and profitability from 1948 to 1953. Advances in 1948 were £73,994, in 1949, £114,714; in 1950, £190,660; in 1951, £208,088; in 1952, £302,993; in 1953, £161,885. Deposits in 1948 were £98,949; 1949 falling to £79,491; in 1950 falling again to £63,357; in 1951 rising to £86,531; in 1952 falling to £78,170 and in 1953 were £74,477. Profits in 1948 were £1,262; 1949, £1,727; in 1950, £2,482; 1951 they fell to £1,756; in 1952 profit jumped to £5,958 and in 1953, the profit level doubled to £10,032.[45] In explaining the fall in advances the manager noted that the Renmark Co-operative had decreased its profits by £14,000, and Moray by £8,000.[46] In analysing the low deposit level, Manager Kernot noted that 'the district is not wealthy individually and money available for deposits is very limited and the Savings Banks, both Commonwealth and State with their more attractive rates of interest command too heavy an appeal for us to compete'.[47]

It was a similar story for the Renmark branch through the 1960s with the branch having its trading adversely affected by its low deposit base and by the vagaries of the weather. The branch's position, moreover, was exacerbated when the trading banks were permitted to become savings banks. For instance, in 1965 the Renmark branch had overdrafts of £649,881 and made a profit of £18,180.[48] Manager Nankivell noted that:

> Most of our advances are quite safe, although there are three Bad and Doubtful ones which are uncertain. The two Co-operatives which are our main borrowers are well managed, and seasonal advances covered by stock account for a large proportion of their overdrafts ... The branch has difficulty in maintaining the number of accounts, due probably to the opposition from the trading banks plus the Savings Bank of South Australia which also operates cheque accounts.[49]

In 1965 the manager returned to the perennial theme of the power of the co-operatives and sheds arguing they remained a consistent brake on the growth and profitability of the branch. He said that 'the Packing Houses, such as RFGC Ltd control absolutely the financial structure of the growers, they virtually say whether or not a grower shall make his reductions to the Bank overdraft, by way of providing or declining finance'.[50]

The 1968 annual report for the Renmark branch showed a net profit of $38,855 with net overdrafts being $944,869 down from $1,180,689 in 1967.[51] The overdrafts in 1968 were related to three basic areas, fruit, cannery, distillery and packing with the net deficit from the Moray Park Fruit Pty Ltd standing at $269,392.[52] At the end of the 1960s the Renmark branch was still reliant on the co-operatives which were in turn dependent upon the international price of Renmark fruit and the fluctuations of the weather. In short, the history of the branch from 1927 to 1970 was one of steady progress, its future being tied to the co-operatives but ironically the branch was also in competition with them. The branch principally provided a service to the rural community rather than being a fully commercial proposition.

Kimba
In his first report from the new Kimba branch on the Eyre Peninsula on 30 June 1927, Manager L E Roake proudly wrote that 'it gives me great pleasure in advising

that since the Branch was opened on March 4th the business transacted had been great'.[53] With 101 accounts, the present season was a 'wonderful opening for the farmers and the crops around this district are looking equally as good, if not better than, those in Wudinna or Cowell District'.[54] Roake added, somewhat as an afterthought, that the branch had lost £385 for the year.[55] He was summarily removed from the Kimba branch.

In 1928, the new manager, Mr Matthews, reported that as he had inherited such a mess he was unable to immediately turn the branch around.[56] This was evident when Matthews, following the military-based management manual, sent a coded telegram of the branch's profit and loss position to head office as of the end of the financial year, which read: *Atlantic eight hundred and three pounds seven shillings and nine pence,*' Atlantic being the code word for loss.[57] In his report Matthews wrote of the increase in business by over 50 per cent but that the losses were due to the previous manager who had 'allowed the branch to drift'.[58]

When Matthews sent in the annual branch report and accompanying documentation in September 1928, the Branch Inspector was less than impressed with its presentation. Matthews received a stinging dispatch back from the General Manager, with Warren saying that he was embarrassed to present the branch's report to the board (then comprising R R Stuckey, Ed J Field, W L Summers and O Uppill):

> I am very disappointed in this return. In the first place it is nearly two months late, although requests have been made for it in the meantime. For this unprecedented delay I can see no possible excuse, and your failure to put forward some reasonable explanation is deserving of the severest of censure. As far as the actual return is concerned, it is of a very scrappy nature and its value almost negligible ... the fact that half of your report was typed and the remainder written has not improved its appearance for presentation to the board.[59]

Suitably chastened, Matthews made sure the 1929 report from Kimba was fully typed and in on time. Matthews wrote with some sense of satisfaction that because of careful management the branch return showed a profit of £37,[60] with increases in advances of £39,000 and 'no sales of land or stock for the year'.[61] This positive result, he noted, was achieved despite a severe drought. The report commented that 'the settlers are farming on a more sound basis than previously, realising the greater benefits that accrue from scientific methods than the haphazard methods which were practised at the foundation of the area'.[62] As for competition, there were two other banks in Kimba, the Bank of Adelaide with a staff of three and which was an agent for the Savings Bank of South Australia, and the Commercial Bank of Australia with two staff.[63]

In September 1929, General Manager Warren wrote a letter of praise and advice to Matthews saying that 'generally the return is a considerable improvement on the one submitted last year',[64] but he said particular attention should be paid to overdrafts and the branch should seek to use any upturn in the region to bring the farmers' debts down. He concluded his letter with the observation that a 'fair season in your district should enable you to place a number of your accounts in a better position'.[65]

While the region did have a good season in 1930 the international price for grain plummeted, causing a rise in farm debts. Matthews telegraphed another *Atlantic* dispatch recording the loss at £57/5/4.[66] In his report Matthews tabulated the acreage sown and the fall in the yields for the region in the following table:

1926/27, 72,417 acres sown. Yield 9.54 bushels
1927/28, 98,000 acres sown. Yield 2.92 bushels
1928/29, 136,060 acres sown. Yield 1.04 bushels
1929/30, 153,730 acres sown. Yield 1.28 bushels[67]

The implication of the fall in yield per acre, combined with the collapse in wheat prices, meant that the Farmers Relief Act supporting farmers in difficulty was so widespread in the Kimba region that it covered practically every property. Matthews wrote that the 'assistance granted under Drought Relief has increased considerably, and the time occupied in dealing with this has taken up a major portion of the day; in 1927 Drought Relief Accounts were 111, in 1928 they were 180, in 1929 these were 211 plus there were another 66 applicants pending'.[68] He concluded his tabulations by commenting that 'the Government has been called upon to assist 93% of the Acreage sown in the Kimba area'.[69] The report finished with the supplication that 'in placing this report before you I trust that the information contained therein will be satisfactory and enable you to follow the trends which have prevailed in this area during the past twelve months'.[70]

In his summary of bad and doubtful debts Matthews, as was the required practice, provided not just statistical information but an appraisal of the character of the borrower. Following standard procedures, Matthews used a series of stock phrases such as 'excellent character' or 'good and reliable' or 'honest man', 'satisfactory character', 'good worker', to send a coded message to head office about the borrower's characteristics. The head office used both the statistical information and the manager's judgements to make their own assessments of the borrower. There would sometimes be a mark in the margin (a tick or a question mark) or an underlining of the manager's comments to show the attitude of head office to the loan and to the Branch Inspector's approval of the judgement of respective managers.

For instance, Matthews reported in June 1930 that Ed Beriman, who had advances of £151 was a 'fair character'. 'This man', he wrote, 'is willing but is too old to work a Mallee scrub block. Security safe. Recommend account be cleared as soon as season improved; 300 acres sown'.[71] The head office noted the comments on the man's age, placing a cross rather than a tick by his name but still accepted the advice, placing the account in the 'satisfactory' category.[72] In contrast, when the branch manager wrote of Henry Crossman and his daughter Pamela, who were collectively operating on a property loan of £493, receiving Drought Relief, he said that they were 'Fair farmers but poor managers. Security safe valuation could be increased. This account will be cleared when opportunity presents itself. 400 acres sown'. Head office differed, placing this account in a 'doubtful' category and writing to Matthews insisting that the account be cleared 'as soon as possible'.[73] Similarly, E Haines with an advance of £1,238 was on Drought Relief and said to be a 'satisfactory character, an industrious farmer with 650 acres'.[74] Head office placed a cross by his account and sent back a note to Matthews instructing him to ensure that this 'account must be carefully controlled and every item of expenditure must be submitted to you'.[75]

In 1932, the new branch manager Mr Galloway, reported the Kimba region was deep in the grip of the Depression and the government moratorium on payments meant that the branch again recorded a loss. Galloway sent the annual telegram on 29 June 1932, to head office. It read, *Indian Bombard Becalm Abhor Pounds Banyan Shillings Abduct Pence* translated as a loss of £1,768/6/1.[76] In his report, Galloway recorded the reasons for the loss as government regulations on debt repayments saying that:

> Whilst the years operations have resulted in a loss of £1,768 it is pointed out that this figure is principally due to the necessity of having to reserve interest for the year totalling £2,331 and also not charging interest amounting to £453. Since the establishment of the Branch, £5,357 in interest has been reserved, and to date it has only been found advisable to transfer £194/11/6 of this amount to contingency account at Head Office. The necessity for reserving so large an amount is deplorable, but our activities are largely centred in comparatively newly established farming areas, which have not yet had time to prove themselves ...[77]

In 1933 Galloway again reported a loss, this time of £1,634, but concurred with one head office policy of holding a large reserve at Kimba because the area was 'newly settled and hence improved, coupled with the earlier drought and now generally depressed condition'.[78] He added that the Drought Relief charges on the land had meant that it placed 'price on the land in most instances well above its earning capacity' and subsequently 'no sales of land had been effected in the district during the year'.[79]

Galloway noted that rainfall in the region was unpredictable, being 3.29 inches in 1930, 6.80 in 1931, 8.38 in 1932 and 4.22 in 1933; however the average was 12 inches. Yields in this period rose from 4.32 to 7.64 and 8.61 with the price per bushel being 1/8d, 2/6d and 2/1d in 1933. He concluded his report by offering the sober evaluation that without reasonable rain 'I am afraid' conditions will 'not only [be] ruinous to a fair percentage of the settlers but will discourage others, and possibly create a lack of confidence'.[80] These premonitions were proven accurate when in 1934 rainfall was 3.29 inches but was slightly offset by a rise in the price of wheat to 2/3d per bushel.[81] Galloway's ability to present a clear economic overview was to stand him in good stead, for after World War II he went upward in the State Bank to be its Adelaide manager.

In 1935 the price of wheat recovered but the crop in Kimba was ravaged by grasshoppers. The combination of hard economic times, drought and pestilence, according to the manager had taken its toll. He added that many of the 'weaker farmers have given up the struggle or have been forced out by their inability to obtain any more assistance but this process of liquidation is proving expensive to the Branch and is demonstrating quite forcibly that heavy losses, probably inseparable from the pioneering of new country, are to be faced'.[82] The loss for 1935 was £3720/14/8. It was noted on the upside that the Commercial Bank had closed its office in Kimba, which had, in turn, benefited the State Bank. Moreover, the branch had acquired the assistance of their staff members, bringing the total to four, so as to deal with managing the Farm Relief account.[83]

In the tenth annual return from Kimba in 1936, Galloway noted that the price for wheat was rising but that in respect of reverted properties the district had about 'reached bed-rock'.[84] But two years later financial conditions had deteriorated further, the loss at the branch being £5,074 with an accumulated ten year loss of £19,958. He wrote that in 1938 conditions had improved for some farmers who did not now need debt relief, whereas for others hardship remained:

> Many more settlers had been declined Debt Adjustment and further assistance by the Farmers Assistance Board, and following the subsequent assignments, our already considerable number of reverted properties was augmented and the problem of management of this Branch seem to become more intricate than ever and the future appears just as dismal in respect of the weaker portion of Branch business, as has been the case for years past.[85]

In 1939 the new manager, J G Fewster, wrote, using inapt grandiloquence, that the Kimba district was suffering 'the effect of the Economic blizzard, which is set in slowly and is now being experienced at zero'.[86] He noted that he had not had the opportunity to inspect many securities, saying 'I have seen parts of the district under stress of drought conditions, bare and desolate looking, transformed in the course of a few weeks by the advent of rain to a glorious vista of green fields'.[87] One year later, Fewster had lost his infatuation with the region, reporting that he had moved about the district and that 'I am not very impressed with the potentialities, for general farming areas, of the hundreds of Buckleboo, Curtlinye, Canyarie, Wilcherry and Moseley except in isolated cases'.[88]

The year 1941 saw an accumulated loss at Kimba branch of £5,213/14/11.[89] What was notable about the correspondence for this year was the drain on the staff due to enlistments and the subsequent effect of the increased work load on those remaining at the branch.[90] On 6 June 1941 Manager Fewster wrote, blaming the delay in his annual report on bad and doubtful debts, that 'I regret to advise that owing to the magnitude of returns (71 names) and the complexities attending its preparation, I have been unable to complete same in time'.[91] On 9 June the Manager head office wrote back a stinging rebuke saying your 'handling of this matter is very unsatisfactory ... you must stand rebuked'.[92] Fewster did not take this slight lightly, replying on 13 August 1941 that:

> I appreciate that it is desirable to review these accounts [bad and doubtful debts accounts] on the limit expiry date when possible. But in view of the shortage of staff and the way it has been hacked about since August 1940, and the difficulties in arranging for share farming and subletting 44 or 45 reverted properties following a year of Drought with a dearth of farm labourers as a result of enlistments and migrations to other centres, to say nothing of other work I candidly resent being called upon to explain what you term 'the present unsatisfactory position'.[93]

General Manager Warren, in rapidly flowing style, pencilled his response over Fewster's text for his secretary to decipher. Warren noted that notwithstanding the War, the bank had to carry out due prudence in regard to bad debts, saying that 'It was quite sufficient to supply an explanation of the overdue limits without "resenting" what is after all necessary office procedure, justified by the long list at your Branch'.[94] Having made his point about under-staffing, Fewster let the matter drop.

With a rise in the rainfall in 1942 the pressure on the Kimba branch eased and this was evident in there being for the year only seven reverted properties that were sublet. Nevertheless, the annual report noted that despite the rain and the good prices for wheat and sheep there was the problem of a lack of 'local manpower' due to the War.[95] Fewster said that the good conditions saw overdrafts reduced in 90 per cent of cases. In 1943 he noted that the branch had lost one officer who was 'called up', reducing the staff to two.[96] In 1943 he reported that, due to enlistments, call-ups and migration to war industries, 'the womenfolk were lending useful assistance' on the land in grazing and wheat production.[97]

In 1945 Fewster reported that despite the lack of maintenance, due to the war effort, Kimba did have a high class of buildings, with 'good streets and footpaths and the inhabitants are served with a good water supply (laid on) and with an excellent Electric Light and Power service @ 1/5 per unit'.[98] He noted, however, that there was very little hope of incurring overdraft business beyond the £40,000 mark.[99]

In 1946 farming conditions in the Kimba region began to improve. The branch took the opportunity to deal with its doubtful debts. Overdrafts decreased by £1174 over the year, standing at £28,901.[100] Again in 1947, with good rainfalls, the area steadily recovered but the branch still recorded a loss of £117.[101] In 1948 the branch recorded a loss of £81.[102] On 30 June 1949 Manager Farquhar took pleasure in sending a telegram from Kimba to head office reading *Orient Cahoj Abahk Pounds Abboh Shillings Bafum Pence*, decoded as profit £64/12/4.[103] Overdrafts had decreased by £6,571 while accounts had risen by £2,732.[104]

The following year wheat prices were high, and with restrictions remaining on building materials and fencing wire, there was a rise in savings. Manager Farquhar noted that there was 'a very noticeable drift from horses to power farming and most of the tractor sales to date have been effected on a cash basis'.[105] The 1950 profit was recorded at £821.[106] This profit, Farquhar said, reflected the modernisation of farming in the Kimba region, with farmers 'borrowing to purchase farm implements [tractors], the building of new farm homesteads and for the better provision of water storage'. Farquhar concluded the report with the comment that this

> district in conjunction with the whole of Australia is enjoying a period of unparalleled monetary prosperity. During the past years, mostly bountiful seasons have been experienced, with prices of primary commodities reaching record levels, and farmers are consolidating their position which will help them to withstand a recession of prices which will ultimately follow.[107]

In 1951 the profit rose to £1,180 mainly due to interest on borrowing.[108] Head office replied that they were 'pleased' with the results but that the branch should 'not relax its efforts to increase the Fixed Deposits' and to 'keep a watching brief on the Account of Duncan & Co'.[109] The latter item referred to the prominent storekeepers in the town with two large stone shops, stone garage and storerooms, valued at £6,500.[110] In 1953 Farquhar moved to head the Cleve branch and was replaced by R A Fraser who had been at Mount Compass.

In 1954 Manager Fraser reported that the Kimba district was growing slowly with crops 'up and looking well and with 125,000 to 130,000 sheep' with 180,000 bags of wheat from the silo and the town itself was 'progressing with the High Street bituminised, RAOB Hall, Catholic Church, modern Lubritorium & Show Room'.[111] In 1955 Fraser felt confident enough to press head office on the issue of 'the poor state of the banking premises and the need for a new building; something other managers had been commenting on since the War, and whether the bank had reached a decision to sell the premises, as advised in the Branch Inspector's letter of 1954'.[112] The following year, pointing out that in 1956 the branch was falling behind the modernisation of the town, Fraser wrote that extensions and improvements were being made to the Kimba Soldiers Memorial Hall costing £15,000, and that there was a new service station and garage, three new 'modern shops' a green grocer and cafe.[113] Two new classrooms had been added to the school, and a cement brick fire station and a nine rink bowling green had been built. Fraser's pleading for a modern bank building fell on deaf ears in the head office and when he was transferred to Tumby Bay in 1959 the branch remained in a poor state of repair.[114]

In 1959, the new manager, G J Dyer, had better news to report, writing that the bank had successfully purchased a new site for the branch in the High Street which he said was 'ideally situated in the hub of the business section of the town. It is hoped that a building will soon be constructed of such a type that is becoming of a prosperous town'.[115] He pushed the claim for a total upgrade, including the manager's home, by noting that, in line with the growth in the town, the 'Bank of Adelaide has recently purchased a Housing Trust home for its Accountant. It is considered that the time is ripe for similar action to be taken by this Bank'.[116]

In 1961 Manager Dyer returned to the theme of a new manager's residence by noting that the 'condition of the bank premises and residence is deteriorating and the general appearance is very drab in comparison with the Bank of Adelaide which has been recently redecorated and fitted with modern furniture'.[117] Dyer concluded his report on a note of sadness and deference to his predecessor, writing that 'the late R A Fraser was held in high esteem by the customers of this Branch. He possessed the unusual ability to maintain popularity with all sections of the community during his term of office and his untimely death must be a great loss to this bank'.[118]

In discussing the season, Dyer noted that in 1961 the farmers were experiencing a good harvest of 1.4 million bushels of wheat but difficulties were being had in delivering the produce to market as the silos were full and a quota system was introduced. He said it 'was not unusual to see trucks lined up for a distance of half a mile from the silo'.[119] Three trains a day carried wheat to Port Lincoln. The town was booming with the construction of a new area school at a cost of £214,000 and the Kimba Community Hotel had made a record profit of £85,000 for the year.[120] In 1962 the branch's turnover was £5,901,853 which was an increase of over £2 million on the year before.[121] There was a record rise of 2,259 accounts, in part due to the Savings Bank transferring its agency from the Bank of Adelaide to the State Bank, but the branch still lost £6,090.[122] Dyer noted that the Public Works Committee was still considering the promised extension of the water pipeline from Iron Knob to Kimba but no decision by the government had been made.[123]

In 1964 Dyer proudly reported that the 'new bank Premises and Residence, erected by a local contractor, Mr J D Kayse' had been completed in December,[124] adding that 'our bank was fortunate and honoured to have the Official Opening performed by the Hon. The Premier, Sir Thomas Playford in February. The General Manager, Mr F A Galloway, Chairman of the Board of Directors, Mr G F Seaman and Board Members Messrs L T Ewens and A B Thompson were present and took part in proceedings'.[125]

The branch's turnover in 1964 rose by nearly £2,000,000, reflecting good rains and subsequently excellent farming and grazing returns.[126] Nevertheless the branch still recorded a loss of £4,441. The loss was to rise in 1965 with overdrawn accounts rising from £15,386 to £30,000.[127] Again it was the fickle rainfall which determined the profit levels of the farmers and graziers. The new manager, Mr Cairs, made the point that the area was undergoing modernisation and he was optimistic over the branch's future:

> Many customers of this branch have availed themselves of bank finance for advances to cover purchase of modern farming equipment, for development of their land, clearing of further areas of scrub land for increased production, the erection of modern homes and outbuildings; and renovation of fencing; the renovation of dams or the sinking of new dams. With modern equipment, and more scientific farming management, the old and the young farmers are proving this District's land capable of producing, together with the rest of Eyre Peninsula, one third of the State's grain crops. Rapidly increasing population and improved living conditions and standards, make long term prospects for the finance of primary production a sound proposition.[128]

The 1966 report converted the profit and loss figures into decimal currency, the branch recording a loss of $11,386 which was down by $1,708 from the year before.[129] Manager Cairs accompanied his report with a 'scientific' graph showing a direct correlation between the rise and fall in wheat production with the local rainfall, a point which had been made in reports dating back to 1928 but was now given a modern mathematical presentation.

In 1967 the Kimba branch's loss was $11,276.[130] In 1968 the loss was $8,633 due to a 50 per cent rise in interest received.[131] The Savings Bank Agency earned the branch $1,694, representing one third of the branch's commission.[132] In explaining the 1968 loss it was reported that the township was experiencing a tight situation with the 'hardest hit' sectors being motor vehicle and farm machinery sales. On the otherhand, 'the profit of the Community Hotel was averaging around $2,000 to $2,500 a month' and tenders were called for the 'erection of an 8 room motel block'.[133] The building of the motel extensions saw a decline in the bank's fixed deposits for 1969 of $35,000.[134] In 1969 overdrafts fell by $63,404 with total operations being over $20 million with the branch recording a loss of $1,236.[135] Accounts were also being lost to the Bank of Adelaide, which the manager said was competing vigorously for business. For instance, it was reported that C J and M K Symonds, a family of 'good connection,' had moved accounts because the Bank of Adelaide had provided a loan on 'unsupported Guarantee'.[136]

The trend of losing business from the Kimba State Bank branch to the Bank of Adelaide was a problem throughout the 1970s, due in no small part to the Bank of Adelaide insisting that any person taking out a business account with them must also transfer their personal accounts to the Bank of Adelaide. For the manager the highlight of 1973 was 'the connection of Kimba to the Polda Scheme giving the town a permanent supply of water. This will ultimately lead to a general beautification and upgrading of facilities. Moves have been made to establish a swimming pool and to install watering systems to ovals and the bowling green'.[137]

Overdrafts, however, remained high throughout the early 1970s, being $405,688 in 1970, rising to $435,407 in 1971, falling slightly to $420,345 in 1972, and again to $394,827 in 1973, and $324,170 in 1974. Total operations in 1974 reached $34 million, almost double that of 1971.[138] The manager, in a reflective mood, noted that the 'town of Kimba is going through a period of what I consider to be unsurpassed progress and the advent of a permanent supply of water, coupled with the past good season are the main contributing factors'.[139] Wheat delivered to the silos was over 5 million bushels and barley was 614,812 bushels, both record levels.[140] Nevertheless, the prosperity of the branch was tied to farming, and the weather. In sum, the State Bank was prepared to carry the Kimba branch, despite continual losses throughout the 1930s and 1950s, as a part of its service to the rural community. Even in the good years, many of the accounts were marginal or unprofitable.

Yacka

The establishment of the Yacka branch in 1927 was principally to service the wheat farmers of the Koolunga and Gulnara districts, in the area between the two large towns of Clare and Spalding. The 1928 report by the manager, Mr Rowed, set the tone for the whole history of the Yacka branch as a marginal concern. He said that since its 'inception on 12 March last [transactions] have resulted in a loss of £298/6/11, largely due to establishment expenses'.[141] Overdrafts were £4,280 and commitments £8,500. There were 51 accounts opened and 'many valuable connections secured' with about 15 accounts to be had'.[142] 'In 1929 the loss was £217/19/2, with no new deposits.[143] Mr Rowed reported that of the £26,098 in overdrafts, £24,406 were made against farming and grazing securities and no advances were made against fruit blocks or distilleries.[144] In 1930 the loss was £207/7/7 and Manager Rowed said that in regard to Yacka the State Bank's prospects were 'very limited,' although the Koolunga District, 9 miles from Yacka, had sent 'numerous requests to the Branch'.[145] With good seasonal rain, the manager said, somewhat over-optimistically, the 'possibilities are unlimited'.[146]

Given that the State was still in the depths of Depression it is not surprising that head office ran a black line under the word 'unlimited'.[147] The 1931 report showed that head office's scepticism was justified, as the Yacka branch recorded a loss of £234 due to the 'continued unfavourable conditions'.[148] Manager Rowed's report in 1933 was poetically sober, saying that, owing to the abnormal conditions, 'a state where perplexity prevails', losses had accrued, but with 'the prospect of better prices for wheat and wool, it is confidently expected that the farming community of this District will surmount their difficulties'.[149] The turnaround in prices over the next four years saw the branch record a profit of £186 in 1937.[150] In 1937 advances against farming and grazing securities was £58,184, and against the town and miscellaneous securities £5,881.[151]

In defending the branch's loss of £107 in 1941 the manager, Mr Giffen, drew a stark linkage between the grid of weather, yields and price. Giffen said that the dry season saw a decrease in the wheat yield from 58,413 bags in 1940 to 11,750 bags in 1941 with the price at 3s and 5, 1/4 d per bushel which he calculated would 'not be sufficient to meet production costs'.[152] By 1945 the manager commented that prospects were improving but that the district was dominated by a number of family farms and this resulted in tightly held family holdings. He said, 'it does not seem likely that new-comers needing assistance will come into the district as the process of "handing down" from father to son is fairly certain in practically all cases'.[153] Advances had steadied at £47,734 and the branch made an actual profit of only £30, again showing how much of the branch's services were not on a strictly commercial basis.[154]

By 1954 the manager wrote in a reflective but confident mood that this

> is a rich and fertile locality and the settlers are in a very sound position, even though the average holding is small, most being around the six to eight hundred acres. The Depression years are still very vivid in their memories (and mine) and the lessons of that period have been well learned, and there are few, if any, who have not built up reserves to help tide them over the lean years which undoubtedly lie ahead.[155]

Throughout the 1960s it was steady progress in the Yacka branch without any major upturn in deposits or advances. In 1961 the branch suffered a loss of £4,011, being £304 less than that for the previous year.[156] Despite the loss the manager was optimistic, with the extension of electricity he anticipated that prospects would improve:

> ... this Branch is on a very sound basis and should continue indefinitely. All the older customers and most of the younger still remember the years of the Depression, and show very careful deliberation in making any decisions affecting finance. However, with the advent of the first E.T.S.A. single wire power loop, a number have branched out and purchased Electric stoves, Hot Water Systems and larger Refrigerators to give some, up to now, unaccustomed luxury.[157]

Despite this hope for a turnaround, the branch in 1967 made a loss of $11,787, which the manager called 'a most favourable result in comparison with that of the two previous years in which losses of $13,738 and $13,240 were recorded.'[158] In explaining these losses the manager noted that the Yacka district had experienced its driest six months since 1862, and as a result farmers were 'grazing sheep on the roadside'[159]. Town business was quiet, although several people had shown interest in property for 'retirement purposes,' but the promised bridge over the River Broughton had not eventuated.[160] In 1969 economic conditions had only marginally improved, with the loss being $6,459 as against $8,903 in 1968 but with the number of accounts declining.[161] By 1974 the branch's profitability had not progressed, recording a loss of $25,753, 'an increase of $4,253 on the previous year'.[162] Again, these figures dramatically show that the Yacka branch provided a service to the rural community but not at a profit to the State Bank.

Millicent

In contrast to the Yacka and Kimba branches, the Millicent State Bank branch was able to carve out a profitable niche market in the prosperous South East of South Australia. The Millicent branch opened in 1950 and steadily grew, in a region which Manager J C Taylor called 'over banked' (with competition coming from the ANZ, ES&A, Bank of Adelaide, the Bank of New South Wales, the National and the Savings Bank).[163] By 1960 the branch was beginning to show a small profit. For example, in 1961 the bank made a modest profit of £57 as compared to a loss of £112 in 1960.[164] The rise in business with advances, increasing from £31,531 in 1960 to £42,498 in 1961, prompted the manager to write to head office requesting 'an additional female' staff member, but this was declined.[165] He wrote again the following year strengthening his claim by arguing that such an appointment would allow for the 'training of the males in particular in higher duties'.[166] His request was again refused.

Initially the attitude towards the growing south east fishing industry was one of suspicion, as this profession, according to the manager in 1962, attracted many 'undesirable types' to Robe and Kingston.[167] The managers took some convincing that commercial fishing was a business sound enough for large loans. In 1962 the manager's report observed that professional fishing was a

> precarious one, and as a result attracts a certain type – the majority of which could be termed as non-progressive and unreliable. However, the industry is an important one, and the bank is at present administering 23 loans granted under the Loans to Producers Act with uncalled balances totalling £38,146. The SAFCOL factories at Robe and Beachport process the catch for export, and there appears to be an assured market at profitable prices for all concerned.[168]

By 1963 the branch was beginning to recognise that the fishing industry was worth lending to and that many migrants were 'hard working' and had long term plans to be successful commercial fishermen.[169] The 1963 annual report noted that there was a growing trend for bigger boats whereby the profits were ploughed back into purchasing 'larger new vessels' which were 'fully equipped with modern devices'.[170] The report pointed out that what was preventing the expansion of the fishing industry was government restrictions over the size of the catch. Moreover, the manager noted that there was intense competition for business in the region, prompting 'unethical modern banking practices being adopted'.[171]

When the government did liberalise the Fishing Act in 1964 this only resulted in a drop in earnings for the fishermen and a further concentration of the industry, as those with the capital began, as the manager expressed it, 'turning to even larger vessels', so as to dominate the industry.[172] By 1964 the annual report commented that crayfish were in danger of being fished out and that the new government restrictions were timely and would consolidate the position of the owners of larger boats but place at risk the 'same poor types' who were attracted to fishing to make a living.[173]

By 1964 the annual report noted that the timber mills were 'operating continuously, with all available males and a reasonable number of females working shift work with the result that employees earn substantial wages'.[174] This led the manager to suggest that 'this bank should follow the modern trend in Banking to the extent of at least advertising, there are still a big percentage of "old

Australians" ignorant of the functions of this institution, let alone the vast "new Australian" community, and this cannot be expected to improve in the face of the terrific volume of Advertising, specially trained Staff and facilities, Door Knocking campaigns, and other modern "gimmicks", adopted by the Other banks'.[175]

In 1965 the growth in the export industry for crayfish pushed up the price of fish and led to additional boats which were, the manager reported, 'better equipped cutters to enable greater distance to be covered'.[176] By 1965 it was recognised by the State Bank that 'larger boats are now viewed as a necessity to enable fishing of grounds far from the base', and for the managers this meant they had to be prepared to lend on the upgrading of fishing vessels.[177] The manager wrote that 'hard working' owners were now positioned to ride out the bad seasons and gain from the growing price of crayfish and shark, both for export and the domestic market.[178]

By 1966 the advances from the branch had risen to over $4 million, a rise from $2.6 million in 1965.[179] The rise in deposits reflected both the good seasons in primary production and fishing. Moreover, the Apcels mill account rose due to the expansion of the timber mill. The manager returned to the theme of the 'rat race' of modern banking, noting that the lowering of interest rates by the bank's rivals had adversely affected deposits.[180]

By 1967 the Millicent manager was writing that the South East 'over banked'.[181] Nevertheless the advances of the State Bank that year had risen to $5.6 million, a rise of $1.5 million over 1966.[182] The Apcel mill was becoming the bank's major account having increased its overdraft facilities by $450,000 during the year.[183] By 1969 the annual report noted that over 800 people were employed at the mills and that Cellulose Australia Limited was under the cloud of a takeover threat by Australian Paper Mills (APM).[184] There was a concern expressed by the primary producers, however, that the forestry industry was causing irreversible environmental damage, notably to the water supply because of the extension of the drainage system, which would have profound effects on farming. The manager reported that 'the water table has fallen drastically to the detriment of the larger areas of established pasture land'.[185]

Despite these environmental concerns, dominance of the mills in the district remained unchallenged. By 1971 the Annual State Bank report noted that the Apcel Mill had embarked on a $12 million expansion program and had an overdraft facility with the branch of $7.3 million with the mill producing 25,000 tons of paper per annum.[186] The report noted that APM had taken over Cellulose and was engaged in reducing its employment numbers by 'streamlining its production system'.[187] In 1974 the branch recorded a profit of $151,355 which was a decrease on the previous year's profit of £221,285.[188] The profit reflected the prosperity of the region and of large accounts, including $3 million in the Apcel Pty Ltd account and over $1 million to Cellulose Australia Limited.[189] The range of business transacted at the Millicent branch extended from timber processing to primary produciton, fishing and real estate.

In short, the Millicent branch had grown in strength since its beginnings in 1950. The progress of the branch, nevertheless, was hampered by the competition from the other banks which had broken from their pre-war conservative mould of banking and were lending freely and even chasing business, rather than letting it come to them. Moreover, the trading banks were capturing their customers through the promotion of 'one stop' banking where a customer could have a wide range of accounts 'under the one roof'. Equally the trading banks were using their credit arms (eg. Esanda with the Wales) to provide 'top up', 'cocktail' loans to their customers. Despite the strength of the competition the State Bank had carved out a niche market in Millicent, especially in the fishing and timber industries.

Southern branch – King William Street South
The Southern (Adelaide) branch opened in 1957. By 1961 the branch in King William Street, near the Central Market was firmly established in the region with a profit of £13,311, with advances being £236,303.[190] The 1961 annual report noted that the branch's advances were 'dominated by the South Australian Fisheries Account Number three' which was basically the the Port Lincoln tuna factory where the balance had risen from £106,000 to £179,010 in the previous twelve months.[191] Business in the south of the city, however, was slow, in part due to the credit 'squeeze' orchestrated by the Menzies government, and in part by the lateness of the State Bank in establishing a city branch system. Manager Riding noted that in anticipation of competition the opposition ensured it held tightly onto the 'good business'. As a result the branch was only receiving 'a stream of weak propositions'.[192] The main customers of the branch were listed as SAFCOL, Red Comb Egg Cooperative Society Ltd, Vuepak, Freeman Wauchope, Balhannah Cooperative, Keller Earthmovers – all of which, the report noted, 'had excellent years'.[193]

Manager Riding reported that the 1961 government-induced downturn had produced a 'flat' real estate market in the Adelaide city precinct and commented that there was a 'total abandonment of the speculative building industry, [which was] probably an excellent thing for the genuine home seeker'.[194] In regard to his staff, Riding reported that 'my banking experience exceeded the combined experience of the remainder of the staff by *three* times. With this very young staff we have handled £14,626,602 in current accounts for the past year, as against £12,476,193 for the previous year'.[195]

The 1962 report, again written by Riding, noted that an excess of receipts over expenditure had reached a record of £16,329, against £13,311 for the previous year.[196] In offering a précis of the branch's 'most prominent customers', Riding noted that, 'SAFCOL had a record Tuna season and satisfactory crayfish exports; Balhannah Co-op suffered a drop in the apple crop but the rest of the business was well maintained. Central Distributors [publishers of Greetings Cards] had an excellent year in tune with the "instant" craze [of sending cards] replacing the need for correspondence'.[197] Likewise, Century Products, an engineering firm had a substantial rise in business this year.[198] In contrast, Custom Builders, a speculative building firm had a 'very depressed year'.[199] Freeman Wauchope saw a drop in timber sales, and likewise, Keller Earthmovers recorded a slight drop in business. Red Comb Egg Co-operative while 'obtaining a greater share of the State egg packing trade', had a 'difficult year due to falling prices'. Windsor Poultry had a reduced turnover and therefore a fall in profit, and Motor Traders saw a fall in sales.[200] Similarly, hotel business recorded a slight fall-off in customers and the Central Market showed lower figures for the large stall holders. There was active competition for business between the Commonwealth, ANZ and Wales in the southern sector of the city. Ridings said that the bank had 'something to learn in business promotion' from its opponents and he recommended, 'with due respect', that a conference be held on dealing with advances.[201]

In 1963 the Southern branch recorded a profit of £17,776, but this fell to £12,167 in 1964.[202] The fall in profit reflected the narrow base of the branch's business as it was directly attributed to 'the Tuna situation', depletion of stocks causing a drop in profit for SAFCOL.[203] The manager reported that the proposed plans for improvements to Victoria Square road diversion and the planning of a fountain had upset the local traders and he considered that it would only lead to a further flow of business away from King William Street to Gouger and Grote streets.[204] In closing, he mentioned that during the year 20 country staff had used the holiday flat which was attached to the branch.[205]

The tenth annual report of 1965 saw a profit of £21,282, again showing that the 'annual profit' of the branch was tied to 'the fortunes of the Canning, and crayfish exports'.[206] Reflecting on the ten years of the branch's history, Riding noted it was 'free from one penny of loss from bad debts', with current account transactions having risen from £17 million in 1963 to £22 million in 1964, to £27 million in 1965.[207] In regard to prospects for growth, Riding noted that the 'rebuilding of the Central Market, and the new Police Building, I feel will do something to move the centre of gravity a little more to the South, and gradually improve our position'.[208]

The profit for 1966 was $36,046, the second best result achieved by the branch.[209] Riding commented that 'Once again, the dominating influence of SAFCOL advances has been felt. Their purchase of the MV 'Espirito Santo' without proper budgeting brought about an acute shortage of working funds, followed by pressure on our part to improve liquidity. As a result, a greater tonnage of tuna was exported to the USA and this has lead to a shortage of Tuna stock for the home market'.[210] The $100,000 that SAFCOL had to spend to make the 'Espirito Santo' seaworthy, he said, came as a 'shock' to the Southern branch and the company had approached the Commonwealth Development Bank for a concessional loan.[211] The branch manager gained the clearing account from the Stock Exchange of Adelaide.[212] As for the southern precinct, he reported that it was moving into the modern era, saying the 'new CAGA House which joins us, is a welcome addition to the neighbourhood. This building alone cost $340,000 and its air conditioning more than the whole of our premises. Its cost of cleaning alone is six times that of our premises'.[213] He added that the City Council intention of 'closing off of Victoria Square has not been received favourably in this section of the City'.[214]

Throughout the 1970s the Southern branch's prosperity turned on the co-operatives, notably SAFCOL, Red Comb, and Balhannah, with the branch having around 400 accounts and the total deposits rising from $118 million in 1968 to $180 million in 1972.[215] In the 1975 annual report of the Southern branch, profit was $268,950, a massive rise on the previous year's profit of only $50,000.[216] Again it was SAFCOL which increased its securities from $1.3 to $4.4 million, boosting the branch profit level. Equally, the transfer from the Adelaide office of the Public Service accounts added to the glowing picture.[217] The manager reported that none of the accounts lost were of any value and this included the West Adelaide Football Club which, when refused a $75,000 overdraft for the purchase of players, shifted its accounts.[218] Given the publicity associated with this shift, the manager deemed it necessary to comment that 'indications and observations I have made since that time convince me even more that the bank's decision was correct'.[219]

The 1979 annual report noted that deposits rose by $616,577 to $2,405,558 with the major depositors being the Public Service Association accounts, Freeman

Wauchope, Balhannah Co-operatives, United Farmers, Century Products, Red Comb Co-op and SAFCOL.[220] A new account, the Australian Breeders Co-operative, was mentioned in the report as a group of thoroughbred breeders who had formed a co-operative society for the purpose of marketing yearlings and thoroughbred horses of all ages. The report noted that 'the Directors sound like a who's who of racing with such names as C S Hayes, D C Brown, A E Trim (Chairman) H E Neck, etc. Breeders have been unhappy with selling arrangements for some time and the Breeders Society is to build a selling complex on leased SAJC land at Morphettville Racecourse. Since 30th of June 1978 overdraft accommodation totalling $1,150,000 has been approved for the Breeders Society'.[221]

In the 1980 annual report, Manager Dittman commented that the 'Australian Breeders Co-op. in its initial year of operations was quite successful. Against a budgeted figure of $2.6m for the first Annual Yearling sale in February last the actual turnover was $3.9m. Subsequently all age and bloodstock sales have exceeded all expectations and the Breeders Society looks to the future with confidence'.[222] Nevertheless, manager Dittman noted that with 'all new ventures' … 'experience is the best teacher', and the 'Directors have gained a lot of "know how" from the first year of operation'.[223] The 'downside' for 1980 was the collection of sundry debtors, some of whom it was noted had 'dragged on into the 120 days outstanding category'.[224]

The 27th annual report of the Southern branch in 1982 reported that business had substantially increased and the branch recorded a profit of $1,097,751 a rise of 59 per cent on the previous year.[225] As was the pattern, the main demand for loans came from the co-operatives and long-standing accounts and it was customers 'utilising their facility to a greater extent' rather than new loans which were boosting the branch's profits.[226] The largest accounts were SAFCOL, Cavandale Homes, Freeman Wauchope, the Public Service Association, and Red Comb Co-operative. Concession loans were also granted to the RSL Croydon & Kilkenny, State Opera of SA and the Department of Corrective Services Social Club. Manager Fray put the progress of the Southern branch down to 'a steady rate of growth' and the potential was there for this 'steady growth to be maintained'.[227]

In sum, the positive results for the Southern branch in the period 1957 to 1982 reflected its lending to successful co-operatives, which had rural connections. That is, although the State Bank had become a fully-fledged trading bank in 1926, the bulk of its business was from rural loans. In the case of the Southern and the Millicent branches their success was in niche markets, notably timber mills, the fishing industry, and the co-operatives. In the cases of Renmark, Kimba and Yacka, their fortunes were tied to farming and they were never in a position to compete effectively against the trading banks. In cold, hard profit terms, neither the Yacka nor Kimba branches should have been opened. In terms of serving the rural community both of these branches filled important economic and social roles in their respective towns. In short, the State Bank had advanced from the 1940s through an incremental process. Each branch learnt from the previous year and made slow changes to its lending practices. The board continually kept a watchful eye over the branch managers, ensuring that procedures were adhered to and aspirations kept in check. Concomitantly, individual managers could expect to move up the hierarchical ladder by adhering to past practice and by following the culture of seniority, each man counting off those above him, who might retire or die, for a chance at the next rung. The approach was steady growth, which was restrained by a lack of capital and government support and by the power of the trading banks where the wider range of its services gave them the edge over the State Bank.

Savings Bank 1945 to 1970

The Savings Bank of South Australia entered the post-war period with a pool of funds which could be lent on housing. The Depression experience showed the bank that instalment loans were a safe form of lending and that the pathway forward was to learn from the mistakes of the State Bank's 1,000 Homes plan. The aim was to lend to middle class and the upper working class families and to develop modern homes built using contemporary materials. In 1946 the bank promoted its architectural services, reporting that 'hundreds of enquiries have been received since the decision was made'.[228] The Savings Bank Trustees said that the bank had appointed as architect G Beaumont-Smith who had prepared 'a book of 27 attractive designs from which people who intend to build homes with financial assistance from the bank would be able to choose'.[229]

The bank's architectural strategy was, however, upset by the shortage of building materials. As a result the erection of homes was reduced to such a level that the architects had little work to do. In 1948 the board decided that, due to the bottlenecks in the building industry, it was reluctantly closing the Architectural Department. Nevertheless this was only a minor setback in the bank's housing plans and its intention to modernise its lending.

Modernisation through mechanisation

On 7 January 1950 the General Manager received a report from the Systems Officer, A W W Cilento, that 12 national accounting machines at £971 each had arrived in preparation for the mechanisation of the ordinary deposit accounts in Adelaide and selected branches.[230] The board delegated to the Systems Officer the task of preparing a report for the board setting out the date for the operation and the logistics of the change. There were regular updates presented to the Board of Trustees throughout the early part of 1950, with the program for mechanisation being tabled at the 10 August 1950 board meeting.[231] The report recommended that the transformation of the 165,000 accounts occur over the last weekend of September 1950.[232] The board agreed to the date for mechanisation but was reluctant to close the bank on the Saturday. The Systems Officer's report recommended that the whole weekend be set aside for the change and that if the Adelaide office was to remain open then additional staff should be rostered on for the task. Cilento's report commented that:

> The success of the proposed operation will depend largely on the willingness of the bank's staff to work voluntary overtime on Saturday afternoon and evening and on Sunday. In this connection, and recognising the need for the utmost co-operation from all concerned, it is further suggested that consideration be given to offering one day's leave, to be taken later at the bank's convenience, in addition to the penalty rates of payment prescribed by the appropriate award or agreement, to all staff members who work overtime on both days. Such a gesture by the bank, in my opinion, would help to produce an atmosphere conducive to enthusiasm and sustained effort by all affected.[233]

The preparation was conducted along military lines, which was befitting an organisation which had 219 officers who had just returned from war service. Cilento spoke of mechanisation as requiring 'skilful organisation, a clear detailed and well-defined plan of action, unified control, and the briefing of selected officers for specific tasks'.[234] The officers were to be briefed in committees and by written instructions so that they would 'become familiar in advance with the features of the general plan and, in particular, with the details of their own part in it'.[235] The plan was military in its structure and detail, it established teams with set tasks for such matters as the transference of records, the rostering on and off of canteen staff for meals, and the designation of drivers to use the bank's fleet of cars to collect staff early on Sunday morning. The bank received assistance from the National Cash Register company in supplying support staff for the mechanisation. The manager of National Cash Register Company flew over from Sydney to witness the operations and 120 staff were rostered on in teams, working long shifts throughout the weekend to complete the task.[236]

In appraising the operations, Cilento reported that all the accounts were transferred in a 'highly satisfactory operation' and both the staff and the customers had been impressed with the speed of the new mechanised system which had evoked 'keen public interest'.[237] Concluding his remarks with praise for the men serving under him, Cilento said:

> This report would be incomplete without reference to the excellent response by those officers rostered for duty to all demands made upon them during the transitional period. They worked willingly under conditions of strain for long hours and by their sustained efforts enabled all essential work to be completed within the available time. Many were showing signs of exhaustion by Sunday evening but, with an earnestness characteristic of most officers of this bank, remained at their posts until directed to cease duty.[238]

The Savings Bank was committed to the task of modernising not just its procedures but also its business direction. The major block to the Savings Bank's expansionary plans, however, came from government. Chifley's nationalisation campaign propelled the Savings Bank under the protective wing of Premier Playford. Playford regarded the Savings Bank as one component of his industrialisation program and made annual calls on it to fund the Housing Trust and public utilities. As we have seen, when the Savings Bank Act was passed the Premier regarded it as a form of 'gentleman's agreement' whereby the government would offer protection in return for annual borrowing for general revenue and specific purposes, notably for the Housing Trust and ETSA. Moreover, Playford regarded the Savings Bank as a subsidiary financial player in South Australia.

Empire
The internal culture of the Savings Bank was complex. On the one hand, there was the desire to be modern and competitive with the other banks, on the other hand, there was a hankering for old symbols, must notably that of the 'mother country'. For instance, in mid 1953 the Savings Bank began its preparations for celebrating the visit of the Queen in 1954. The King William Street frontage was elaborately decorated with flags and floral tributes. The bank's annual report, in bold print, recorded that:

> The outstanding event of the year was the visit to the Commonwealth of Australia (and to this State) of Her Most Gracious Majesty Queen Elizabeth II and his Royal Highness the Duke of Edinburgh. This was the first visit paid to Australia by a reigning monarch and the presence of Her Majesty in Australia has done much to further cement our ties with the Homeland.[239]

This sentiment echoed that of the bank's 1948 pamphlet, *Highlights From History*, distributed to all schools as part of the bank's centenary celebration in 1948. In this pamphlet the first royal visit in 1867, that of Prince Alfred the Duke of Edinburgh, was juxtaposed against the first steam train trip in 1856. Such over-blown monarchical sentimentality laid the Savings Bank open to parody. This happened in 1955 when the bank was lampooned in a spectacular way when in a 'prosh stunt', students from the University of Adelaide enacted Sir Anthony (Charles Stokes) and Lady (Ann Levy) Eden attending a 'Summit' at the bank's King William Street Offices.[240] This mock visit captured such public attention that it brought King William Street to a lunch-time standstill.

The board was undeterred by this publicity and soon after this incident invited the Governor to unveil a bronze wall plaque to celebrate the bank's reaching the target of £100 million in deposits. The annual report recorded that on 8 December 1955 'the Governor Air Vice-Marshall Sir Robert George unveiled the tablet in the presence of Lady George and a large representative gathering of citizens'.[241]

Thrift giving way to hire purchase: restraint to excess

While the Savings Bank board was enmeshed in a monarchical culture which celebrated the past and stability, society and the financial markets were changing around them at a rapid pace. By 1954 the Savings Bank management began to believe that intensified competition and new financial products were undermining the bank's philosophy of thrift and the morality of the population. In addition, the board saw these financial changes as threatening the place of the Savings Bank in the financial markets in South Australia. This thinking was evident in a report to the branch managers given by the Acting Public Relations Officer, P L Ferrier in February 1954. Ferrier began his address by saying that the 'primary motives for a man to work are really animal, to have food for his family and self, to provide shelter, and to be adequately clothed. Following on from there, our present mode of living induces him to live in a community, and to follow an occupation which provides not only his basic wants but also gives him ego satisfaction, job satisfaction, security and many more secondary requirements.'[242] Warming to his task Ferrier then spoke of the 'opposition', which he said was no longer just the Commonwealth Bank but hire-purchase companies which were breaking records. 'One well known store in Adelaide', he said, 'has made great progress on its time payment system and now stands third for sales of all large stores in Adelaide. "Spend before you save" seems to be a dangerous motto being adopted by more and more South Australians and too often court cases are reported of people disposing of goods to which they have no title'.[243]

Trading banks become savings banks: the excess of lending

In 1956 the Menzies government granted the trading banks the right to take out savings bank licences. By granting them savings bank licences Prime Minister Menzies was simultaneously placing them on equal footing with the

Commonwealth Bank and directly challenging the public savings banks. The trading banks, moreover, had direct and indirect links with hire-purchase and major financial corporations and thus could play off the regulated and unregulated markets. The adverse consequences of this decision were immediately evident to the Savings Bank, with intense competition occurring for its deposits and over home loans. In 1946 the Savings Bank proudly proclaimed that 86 per cent of South Australians held at least one account with the Savings Bank. By 1970 the Savings Bank deposits were $416,407,306, holding 50 per cent of savings bank deposits in South Australia, but steadily fell to be 46 per cent by 1984.[244]

In short, the changes to the Federal Act allowed a challenge to the very heart of the Savings Bank of South Australia's existence, its deposit base. Even though the Savings Bank offered higher interest rates on its deposits and lower rates on home loans, the broader offerings by the trading banks/savings banks undercut this historic advantage. The trading banks were using their corporate market strength to take deposits from the savings banks. To retain market share the savings banks had to reverse the process by using their deposit base and branch structure to become trading banks. Such thinking, however, went against the whole tradition of the Savings Bank of South Australia and the board did not contemplate such a radical response. Rather the Trustees expressed their indignation at the betrayal by the trading banks. When the Trustees did decide to fight back they found many forces marshalled against them, including those political interests both in and outside parliament that supported the private banks.

The press in Adelaide in the 1950s, moreover, was unsympathetic to the plight of the Savings Bank. This negative response was not surprising given the cross directorships between the Advertiser Ltd and the Bank of Adelaide which existed at the time, and this connection was evident in the media group's strong advocacy of trading banks becoming savings banks. The media highlighted the dominant position of the Savings Bank with £107 million deposits, and the Commonwealth Savings Bank with £31 million in deposits in South Australia, and bemoaned that these amounts gave the public banks an impenetrable market share which would deter private competition.[245] By January 1956, the media was abuzz with the rumours that both the Bank of New South Wales and the ANZ Bank would soon open savings banks in South Australia with the Bank of Adelaide indicating that it was also exploring such a move.

It took until 1961 before the trading banks began their assault on the savings bank deposits in South Australia. When the move did come it was in a most damaging form for the Savings Bank as it was from the Bank of New South Wales which had for nearly one hundred years developed a strong business relationship with the Savings Bank. The relationship ended on 29 August 1961 when the General Manager of the Bank of New South Wales, H Marshall, sent a somewhat belated letter to the General Manager, Caire, advising him that it was the intention of the Bank of New South Wales to open a savings bank in South Australia as of 1 September 1961.[246] Given this was in effect three days' notice his concluding comments that 'We take this opportunity of expressing our deep appreciation of the association which has continued between our institutions',[247] read as somewhat disingenuous (Letter received 29 August 1961). On 31 August Caire wrote a curt reply saying the bank regretted the move, and indicated he would be in Sydney late in November and would make his last courtesy visit to the Bank of New South Wales.

At the board level the immediate response to the move by the Bank of New South Wales was anger, and the management was requested to calculate the cost of closing all of the bank's accounts with the Bank of New South Wales. At that time the Savings Bank had £2,528,750 deposited in the Bank of New South Wales and the management reported that a precipitous move to immediately withdraw this amount would lose the Savings Bank £15,382 in interest.[248] The board decided that this was too high a price to pay to show its disapproval and decided on the more prudent strategy of gradually phasing down its holdings. The bank immediately withdrew the £60,000 it had as a short term deposit with the Bank of New South Wales, and transferred this and its travellers cheque business to the Bank of Adelaide.[249] The board decided it had little alternative but to extend its own branch and agency network to compete against the Bank of New South Wales.[250]

In January 1962 the Savings Bank management became equally concerned when it heard a rumour that the Bank of Adelaide was secretly setting up its own savings bank branches and was already poaching customers in anticipation of the change.[251] The board decided to set up an investigation of the matter. On 9 May 1962, the Savings Bank received a formal notice from the Bank of Adelaide informing it of its intentions of moving into the savings bank arena. The General Manager of the Bank of Adelaide, Mr West, wrote to Cilento notifying him that due to competitive pressure it was 'essential' to enter the savings bank field and compete with the Savings Bank. He concluded his letter with the gentlemanly comment that 'I would assure you that it is our earnest wish to maintain and continue the cordial relationship which has for so long existed between our respective Institutions'.[252]

The entrance by the Bank of Adelaide into the savings bank field was as serious a threat to the Savings Bank's business as that of the Bank of New South Wales. A month earlier the board had received notifications of the entry into the savings bank arena of the National Bank and the Commercial Bank.[253] These changes were received with concern but their entrance into the savings arena did not warrant the same strategic shift in direction as that of the Bank of New South Wales and the Bank of Adelaide. In response to the move by the Bank of Adelaide, the Savings Bank decided that it had to establish branches of its own to offset the loss of the 34 agencies and 36 branches that had operated through the Bank of Adelaide. In 1956 the Savings Bank had 87 branches with six under construction. The need to compete against the trading banks saw an extensive building program and by 1966 there were 121 branches and 738 agencies throughout South Australia.

A cocktail under one roof

The Savings Bank branch network was a visible and practical means of competing against the trading/savings banks, but the trading banks had the power to outperform the savings banks through the extent of their services. That is, the trading banks offered their customers trading, savings and hire-purchase facilities all through the one institutional structure. The trading banks successfully promoted this facility by advertising that it was now possible to do all your 'banking under one roof'. These banks evaded the Reserve Bank's restrictions on home loans by mixing loans from the savings bank with those of their financial subsidiaries and this became colloquially known as a 'cocktail loan'. Naturally, these advantages were readily exploited by the trading banks and cut substantially into the Savings

Bank business. The Savings Bank quickly realised that old loyalties were little protection against such powerful competition. It began to place pressure on the government to allow it to compete fairly against the trading banks, a move that went against the ideology of the LCL government which gave primacy to private enterprise and the network of interests associated with it, which came to be known as the Adelaide establishment.

Building modernism
The Savings Bank board, however, considered it was still a modern institution. In keeping with this view, in 1955 it built a new city branch in Hindley Street. The building was promoted as ultra-modern, combining practicality with progress. It was to have a frontage of 212 feet to Bank Street and 20 feet 10 inches to Hindley Street with entrances in both streets. In its press release the Savings Bank said that the building was to be built from the 'most modern ideas in multi-storeyed building construction' and was to be 'fully air-conditioned, equipped with high-speed gearless lifts and bank staff amenities'.[254] The building was to have 'garbage disposal units, postal chutes and refrigerated drinking fountains on each of its eight floors and the ground floor columns would be finished in granite, with the exterior being an aluminium facade which was to be glazed with special heat resistant glass'.[255]

The bank's promotion of modernisation was typical of this period. For instance, a book written in 1958 to celebrate the hundred years of the *Advertiser* spoke of South Australia's progress in the usual terms of population size (875,000), annual value of production (£275 million), exports (£123 million), the diversity of the economy (manufacturing, mining, agriculture and commerce) and so on. It then went on to comment that this economic progress was visually complemented by the modern architecture springing up around the city, including its 'modern airport', its 'modern Adelaide Boy's High' and the *Advertiser's* modern multi-storey buildings in the 'functional mode'.[256] Modernisation was equally reflected in the establishment of the South Australian Symphony Orchestra and the flourishing theatre which were 'signs of maturity' for South Australia.[257]

School banking
In the face of competition the Savings Bank decided to stress its core values of thrift and delayed gratification by placing stress on its school banking services. In 1945 there were 70,537 school bank accounts with a credit balance of £255,232. Through its promotion and the rise in the population, by 1956 there were 809 school bank agencies and the total number of accounts was 123,379 with a balance of £1,000,312.[258] The board in response to reaching the million mark expressed its gratitude to all those who had given 'voluntary aid in the task of developing the habit of savings in young minds', from the Minister of Education down to school principals and teachers who acted as agents for the bank.[259] In recognition of this support and to celebrate the million milestone the board provided 'a commemorative gift of a framed reproduction of an original portrait of Captain Matthew Flinders to every school in the State'.[260] The board also decided to augment school banking with the introduction of awards for students, as well as teacher training scholarships for overseas study, prizes for speech nights and school sports awards.

Putting the bank in its place

In response to the move by the trading banks into the savings sphere, the Savings Bank of South Australia decided to approach the Playford government to allow it to offer cheque accounts. In 1958 the board wrote to the Premier seeking to have its Act changed so as to provide its customers with cheque account facilities. As a consequence, the Premier instructed Under-Treasurer Seaman to investigate such a provision. After examining the situation in Victoria, Seaman wrote a report opposing such provision, calculating that the cost of operating cheque accounts would be two and a half times that of ordinary deposit accounts and thereby would reduce the level of profit and potential revenue to the government.[261] Seaman wrote that the 'most heavily losing accounts are clearly those with local commercial people – the grocer, the chemist and the like. These people do not carry substantial balances but put through large numbers of transactions involving heavy staff work and little or no revenue'.[262]

Having been informed of Seaman's opposition the Savings Bank Trustees obtained a copy of the report and had management set out a detailed reply. The response contested the assertions made by the Treasury, in particular those on the calculations on costs. The Trustees insisted that it was essential that the Savings Bank have a cheque account facility or the decline in deposits would be greater than that predicted by Seaman on the costs of cheque accounts,[263] an argument which eventually found a receptive ear from the Premier.

As soon as Playford indicated publicly he was prepared to allow the Savings Bank cheque account facilities, the trading banks demanded reciprocal rights to offer non-profit organisations cheques free of stamp duty. When challenged in early October 1961 by his opposition number in the parliament, Playford did not reveal his hand, only saying he had equal sympathy with both claims. Shadow Treasurer Don Dunstan asked whether the trading banks would be allowed to have the same exemptions as the Savings Bank, in regard to non-profit accounts. Premier Playford replied that the matter was under investigation but that once it was known that the Savings Bank had requested 'the right to operate cheque accounts' this would immediately bring a 'request from the trading banks to allow them freedom from stamp duty in support of non-profit accounts. Honourable members will see that an extension of that facility would embarrass the finances of the Treasury'.[264]

On 23 October 1961, Playford wrote to Chairman Hunkin saying that he wanted to be assured that the bank would retain its policy of offering the best value for depositors. He said that while private cheque accounts 'would almost certainly be well received by your customers, and that it would be some counter to possible loss of business to private savings banks, I am, nevertheless, concerned that you should maintain your ability to pay interest on deposits at a rate significantly higher than other banks for that is by far your greatest competitive appeal'.[265] On 31 October Premier Playford wrote to the bank notifying them that cabinet 'had before it a request from the Associate banks that the exemption from stamp duty for cheques drawn by a variety of non-profit organisations be made the same for all banks upon which such cheques may be drawn. You will appreciate that this request undoubtedly is to some extent the result of publicity given to the proposal that authority be granted for your bank to provide extended facilities for cheque-operated accounts'.[266]

The bank replied that it should retain the exemption because it was a public institution and not one where profits flowed to shareholders outside the state. Chairman Hunkin wrote that the Savings Bank had operated cheque accounts for friendly societies and all other societies, unions and local authorities since 1912, as had the Commonwealth Bank, and this situation had never previously been attacked by the private banks and it had only emerged because of the entry of the Savings Bank into the cheque account field. The bank added that the Savings Bank 'is a State instrumentality holding its assets for all and on behalf of the Crown. It is essentially a mutual and co-operative institution. There are no shareholders as such nor any distribution of profits and its funds are largely invested in the State'.[267]

Having suffered Premier Playford's procrastination on the cheque account issue the bank wrote again to the Treasurer arguing even more strongly that the cheque account facility was essential to the bank and to the government if for no other reason than to counter the claim by the trading banks of 'doing all your banking business in one Office'.[268] On 16 November 1961 Playford replied that the bank's letter was being considered and asked the bank to send further comments on the operation of private cheque accounts.[269] The bank did so, arguing for full cheque account provisions including the capacity for personal overdrafts on cheque accounts.[270] Under-Treasurer Seaman was still a stumbling block as he wrote to the bank saying he remained opposed to the provision of cheque accounts by the Savings Bank, preferring that this provision remain with the Bank of Adelaide and the State Bank.[271] The Trustees urged that the Premier introduce the legislation in the November sittings of parliament, as the Savings Bank was losing valuable business to the trading banks. But on 7 December 1961 Premier Playford wrote to the board informing them that the amendment to the Act had been 'held over for reconsideration by Cabinet early in the next Parliamentary session'.[272] The Trustees were alarmed at the implication of this news, as it indicated that there was strong opposition within the cabinet to their cheque account proposal. The board decided to have the newly appointed knight of the realm, Sir William Bishop, intercede with cabinet members presenting the bank's case.

When Sir William Bishop attended the April 1962 board meeting he said that over Christmas he had private discussions with cabinet members on the Savings Bank's behalf, indicating its desire for full cheque account facilities. He reported that while there was some cabinet support for a limited cheque account facility there was, however, strong opposition in the cabinet room to any overdraft facilities. Nevertheless, he said, a more restrictive cheque account proposal, which did not threaten the trading banks, would get through cabinet and the parliament.[273] Bishop said that the wisest option for the board was to put aside the issue of overdraft facilities on personal cheques for the moment but to obtain what was possible with a limited cheque account facility.[274]

When Playford then agreed to support the Savings Bank offer of a selective cheque account arrangement, the bank provided him with notes to argue the case in the parliament. The Savings Bank again urged the Premier to proceed immediately as it was losing customers on a daily basis. But Playford decided to delay the bill until the next session of the parliament. When nothing seemed to be happening in the first session of parliament in 1962, the Chairman of the Trustees wrote to the Treasurer urging him to 'expedite' the amendments as the National Bank and the

Commercial Bank were entering the savings bank field, as was the Bank of Adelaide.[275] Nonetheless, it took until the 18 September 1962 before the bill was presented to the parliament. When it was tabled it contained mixed blessings for the Savings Bank: the bill provided the bank with its limited cheque account facilities but extended the exemption from stamp duty on cheques drawn for non-profit societies to the private banks.[276]

National clearing house for bank cheques

When the Savings Bank acquired the right to offer cheques it was soon pressured by the Australian Bankers Association (ABA) to subscribe to a national clearing house for cheques. What followed was a protracted period of negotiation over the terms by which the Savings Bank would enter into the national scheme and how it would protect its historic role of offering cheques free for non-profit organisations and local government.[277] In the end the Savings Bank agreed to a compromise position whereby it would gain the national clearing house support from the ABA but only at a concessional rate. The Savings Bank's bill rate was approximately half that of the trading banks and it was permitted to continue its practice of concessional loans, as long as it did not promote this service.[278]

Again matters were made more complicated by the involvement of the State government, which inadvertently had publicly promised the local government that there would be no charges on their cheque accounts. Sir Lyell McEwin boasted in the parliament of the Playford government's role in providing the concessions sought by local government.[279] The Savings Bank Trustees were embarrassed and had to write to the ABA, explaining how the government had acted independently of their secret agreement. The ABA was prepared to overlook this matter as long as it was just an aberration. The trading banks, nevertheless, placed pressure on the Reserve Bank to prevent the Savings Bank from poaching local government and non-profit society accounts from them. Reserve Bank Governor H C Coombs raised the issue with the Savings Bank management when he visited the bank in January 1963. The managers reassured the Governor that the bank would not unfairly take clients from the trading banks.[280]

The Queen's representative

The nature of savings banking business in the 1960s was changing rapidly. The Savings Bank nevertheless clung to the past, to Queen and Empire. In its literature, the bank continually highlighted the visits by respective Governors to the bank. For instance, the minutes record that on 3 May 1962, Sir Eric Bastyan KBE, CB, Governor of South Australia inspected the bank. The board minutes record that: 'His Excellency had joined the members of the board and the General Manager and Assistant Manager at luncheon in the private dining room. The Trustees were delighted to have the Governor stay on for coffee in the board room and sign the visitor's book, before wishing him and his ADC, Captain Lewis farewell'.[281] The annual report was to call the visit the outstanding event of the bank's year.[282]

Modern marketing

While clinging to Empire the Savings Bank management was, nonetheless, prepared to adopt the market techniques of America. For example, the advertising campaign of the bank for 1961 was a combination of tried and true promotion, highlighting the bank's place in South Australian banking history, and the sponsoring of the popular children's television program the Mickey Mouse Show. The Savings Bank's slogans for the year were 'Add Zest to your Life: Salt Some Away' and 'First in the State since 1848'.[283] The advertisements targeted 'The Empire Games' and 'The Book of the Year' (ie. a Savings Bank pass book). In that year advertisements in the cinemas, which had been so popular during the war years, were to be 'discontinued' in favour of television and radio advertisements.[284]

Concomitantly, in July 1961 the Public Relations department decided that there should be a unifying campaign which linked the bank's South Australian origins with its new focus on television. The decision was to phase out sponsorship of the Mickey Mouse Show and the Mickey Mouse money boxes and to phase in sponsorship of the local product, Humphrey B Bear. On 17 May 1962 the bank's sponsorship of the Mickey Mouse Show expired and was not renewed. Instead 'spot ads' on television and radio were adopted.[285]

Again, borrowing from America, a feasibility study was conducted in 1961 on whether the bank should build a drive-in branch, in this case, on Anzac Highway at Plympton. Following the examination of the potential of such a novel approach to banking the management advised the board that at that moment it could not recommend such a move for South Australia.[286] Alongside these marketing campaigns were the traditional sponsorship of sporting and community groups, notably, the Adelaide Festival, the Pembroke Girls Choir and the Eisteddfod, a tradition of philanthropy and community involvement which could be traced back to when the bank provided prizes for academic merit at school speech nights and final year education certificates from 1927. Since that date the Savings Bank played a significant role in the lives of many South Australians, principally in the arts and sporting sponsorships.

Dialogue between the State Bank and the Savings Bank
By mid 1962, the State Bank had become alarmed at the intense trading bank competition. The Savings Bank's commitment to the South Australian community did not, however, stem the outflow of deposits or loans to the trading banks. In response to overtures from the State Bank, the Savings Bank Board considered a form of co-operative arrangement. For its part, the State Bank was also feeling the loss of accounts and its lack of ability to capture clients from the other banks.[287] The Savings Bank Trustees indicated that it might be time for more collective action to compete against the private banks, and formal discussions were commenced. By the end of 1962 an agreement was reached between the two banks in which each would operate as agents for the other. While the State Bank was interested in a more formal merger, the Savings Bank board was reluctant to go beyond a trial period of agency co-operation.[288]

In the meantime, the Savings Bank was having to respond to the regular requests from the Playford government for funds to facilitate its industrialisation program. For example, in 1962 the Premier made his annual demand for advances to the Housing Trust and the Electricity Trust.[289] In July the Savings Bank agreed to lend £1,675,000 to the Housing Trust and ETSA, with £500,000 allocated to ETSA immediately, and £250,000 to the Housing Trust.[290] Then the bank board agreed to a public loan to the

South Australian Gas Company for £498,550 at 4⅞ per cent.[291] On 19 July 1962 the Premier wrote to extend loans under the Homes Act from 30 to 40 years. After considering this request the board agreed to making long-term loans for government revenue.[292] On 7 August the Premier wrote to extend the ETSA loan to £1,775,000. The Trustees replied that its funds were fully committed but that later in the year funds might become available to meet the Premier's request.[293]

Savings Bank arrears: 'there but for the Grace of God'
Despite the boom in the 1960s, bank arrears remained a problem and were still closely monitored by the Savings Bank Board. Arrears statistics were presented to the board every six months and these reveal that bad luck, bad management or economic downturns (or often a combination of all three) could rapidly place borrowers into difficulty, a position often exacerbated by the lack of adequate public welfare provisions at either the federal or state levels. For example, following the 1961 government-induced downturn, the bank kept a close watch on accounts in arrears. From these reports it can be seen that arrears were often the result of a combination of factors. For instance, Mr D of New Queenstown had a loan of £1,325 on a property valued at £3,400 with arrears of £108. The assessor's remarks were that the 'mortgagor has not worked for approximately 5 years – result of head injury in accident at GMH', he was receiving £5 per week invalid pension, and Mrs D £3 a week in pension, with the mortgagor paying £24 per quarter mortgage.[294] In an even worse position was Mr C of Northfield who had taken out a loan in 1959 for £2,250 and had accrued arrears of £147. He had been 'incapacitated and confined to a wheelchair as a result of electrical shock while employed at ETSA and was receiving £12/12 per week'. The report noted that the mortgagor 'was unable to manage financially and a group of friends is now administering his affairs and paying £27/1 a month to the bank'.[295]

Mr M of Seaton Park had arrears of £96 due to being retrenched by GMH in March 1961, at the age of 66 years. He had three school-age children, and his only income was the old age pension of £5/2/6 per week supplemented by the wage of his 14 year old daughter who had just started work, and they were jointly paying the bank £14 per month which in effect reduced arrears by £5 per quarter.[296] Mr R of Clearview owed £121, he was a bricklayer whose arrears were caused by sickness.[297] Mr P of Enfield, with arrears of £148, was an unemployed labourer due to a leg injury and was dependent on social security of £4/2/6; in this case the second mortgage was held by the Financial Corporation of Australia, which was reluctant to act until the mortgagor obtained work.[298]

Brothers A & K Ch of Hampstead Gardens were store proprietors whose arrears of £126 were caused by the 'fall off of business', they were paying off the mortgage at $5 per week to extinguish the arrears.[299] As an aside, having weathered this storm, the brothers went on to be highly successful local businessmen. Mrs H of Sturt had arrears of £87 caused by her husband being out of work and being taken seriously ill. She was now working at a hospital and paying £6 per fortnight.[300] The bank and the Noarlunga Council were also in dispute over arrears connected to the Ocean Line Drive-in.[301] Mr H was a piano tuner who was out of work due to becoming deaf but was now employed as a fitter and turner and was paying his arrears.[302] Mr B of Elizabeth East had arrears of £49 caused by family sickness. He had 'one child in the Children's Hospital and wife suffering from anaemia', but he promised to clear arrears as soon as was possible.[303]

The bank was critical of hire purchase arrangements which the management and Trustees regarded as an affront to the ethic of thrift. However, the bank showed tolerance towards those in arrears, especially to borrowers revealing a commitment to clearing their debts. Often accounts in arrears had the Housing Trust as second mortgagee and the bank worked closely with the Trust to monitor each loan. The trend was reminiscent of the 1930s where the bank sought to keep families in their homes. There were, however, cases where the Trust repossessed the home. There was also a degree of moral superiority and paternalism which shaped the decisions over clients with hire purchase problems.

For example, Mr J of Greenacres an unemployed slaughterman owed £40 and was an irregular payer and in foreclosing on the loan it was noted that the arrears were 'believed to be due to HP [hire-purchase] debts'.[304] Mr H of Para Hills with a loan of $7,900 owing $274, was a welder, who was paid $43 per week, with three children (15, 12 and ten). His arrears were caused by 'excessive hire-purchase commitments ($60.50 per month) and a period of 2 months unemployment'. Unless he paid $10 per week Notice of Sale was to be issued.[305]

Mr B of Morphett Vale had worked as a book binder and had a loan of $6,750 owing $316 arrears and 'due to excessive hire-purchase commitments [he] has failed to honour his undertakings and Notice of Sale should be made'.[306] Mr H of Para Hills, who was a car assembler for GMH, 'suffered periods of unemployment and had a car on hire-purchase had promised to pay $16 per week but has fallen behind in payments. It was recommended that a Notice of Sale be prescribed, unless this amount was regularly paid'.[307] Mr B of Salisbury East had arrears of $177 and was a storeman on $44 per week; arrears were deemed to be caused by unemployment and hire-purchase payments of $40 per month.[308]

The Arrears Committee was also less sympathetic to those in difficulty from a 'broken home' than from families where the male breadwinner had lost his job. For instance, Mrs W of Elizabeth Downs had an original loan of $6,000 with arrears of $200. Her husband had left her and she obtained work at GMH but had to resign because ill health. Her only income was $22 per week maintenance plus for each child $18 endowment. She had three children; her 11-year-old son had recently had an ear operation, which entailed high chemist costs, and the hospital bill was only partially covered by medical benefits. Mrs W had approached the bank saying she was unable to pay any mortgage and was seeking a Housing Trust rental home. A notice of sale was issued.[309] Similarly, Mr S, a motor mechanic of Brahma Lodge, had a loan of $6,480 and arrears of $260, 'arrears caused by wife deserting the husband and precipitating his suffering a nervous breakdown'. The house was vacant and he was believed to be working in Whyalla. A notice of sale was to be issued.'[310]

Waiting in line for a loan

At the other end of the Savings Bank's housing loan business was the long queue for a home loan. For example, in February 1963 the bank informed the Reserve Bank that it was lending at a rate of £550,000 per month with a long waiting list for loans totalling £1,800,000, and applications were being settled between 13 and 15 months.[311] The Reserve Bank pointed out that as the other savings banks did not keep waiting lists, unless it was for specific lodged applications, it was difficult to assess the accuracy of the pent up housing demand. The Reserve Bank did inform the Savings Bank that the three major lenders for housing in South Australia were public banks, the State Bank, the Savings Bank and the Commonwealth Bank.[312]

1965 talks on amalgamation versus co-operation
In early 1965 the State Bank again approached the Savings Bank of South Australia inquiring as to whether their co-operation might be more formal. The State Bank was keen to see if co-operation could be more comprehensive and Mr Taylor, the Chief Inspector of the State Bank, 'interviewed' the Savings Bank manager, pointing out that the competition from the Bank of Adelaide was particularly affecting country accounts and that perhaps even amalgamation might be called for in some country branches. Following a series of discussions between the two public banks it was decided that an agreement was not appropriate at this stage but in specific circumstances a more formal co-operative arrangement could be made between particular branches.

The 1965 election: socialism versus capitalism; 'Hands off the Savings Bank'
In 1962 the Democratic Labor Party (DLP) had raised the issue of merging the Savings Bank and the State Bank but this remained dormant until the 1965 election where the role of public banking became the prominent political issue of the campaign. The Liberal Party decided to highlight in its campaign the claim that the ALP was going to merge the State Bank and the Savings Bank as part of a socialist plot. On 3 March 1965 the Liberal Party took out full page advertisements in the *Advertiser* with the heading 'Hands off the People's Savings; Keep the Savings Bank free from Political Interference'.[313] Asserting that opposition leader Frank Walsh had called for the amalgamation of the Savings Bank and the State Bank so as to get at their deposits, the advertisement carried lines in bold 'Don't let this happen. Don't let ANY politician use your bank for political purposes.'[314] The LCL government, the paper noted, would move an amendment to the State Constitution to make it 'beyond the power of any government at any time to interfere with Savings Bank deposits, except by referendum from the people'.[315]

Two days later, the Labor Party inserted its own full page advertisement with the banner heading: 'Hands off the State Banks'. The ALP argued that it was Premier Playford who had extracted £4,000,000 as long term unsecured loans from the Savings Bank for his government,[316] and that the 'Trustees were paid by the Government only 1½ p. c. interest, while they had to pay 2¼ p. c. to the depositors. It's your money he's taken'.[317] The Labor Party said that if elected it would legislate to allow:

> our public banks to compete with the private banks. The Savings Bank has lost hundreds of accounts, because Playford has denied the State banking systems the right to run both trading and savings accounts in the one office, as the Commonwealth and private banks do. Playford has put millions of our money – the accounts of the Electricity Trust and other state undertakings – in the hands of private banks who compete with the State and Savings Bank.[318]

Frank Walsh said that the merger of the two public banks would allow these banks to provide hire purchase loans for its customers, and added that he also wanted both banks to have the right to offer the same overdraft facilities as that of the trading banks or the Savings Bank of Victoria.[319]

On the same day as the ALP placed its advertisement in the paper, the *Advertiser* came out with all guns blazing carrying a front page leader, blazoning the claim 'No Case for Bank Amalgamation'. The paper carried an editorial arguing that 'both the Australian Labor Party and the Democratic Labor Party have made amalgamation of the State Bank and Savings Bank of SA a platform plank in their election campaigns'.[320] The Premier's rejoinder of legislating against any interference was 'prompt and reassuring':[321] 'An intriguing feature of the proposal, smacking as it does of socialism, is that it aims at eliminating one of two thriving, efficient and it would seem indispensable concerns. Labor would appear to be courting serious difficulties to contemplate even minor changes to a mammoth banking edifice in which 83 out of every 100 South Australians have accounts and, it follows, a sentimental, as well as a financial stake'.[322]

After the victory of the Labor Party in the 1965 election the Savings Bank and State Bank entered discussion as to what to do if the new government carried out its promise to merge the two banks. The Savings Bank Board, while in public it opposed an amalgamation with the State Bank, wrote in confidence to the State Bank saying that if there was a merger the Savings Bank would pursue overdraft facilities. The letter concluded with the observation that if there was a forced merger then this would at least assist in its 'defence against private banks'.[323]

The victory of Walsh did not, however, see any moves to amalgamate the two banks. In the first two years of the Labor government there were no moves to merge the banks. When Don Dunstan replaced Walsh as Premier in 1967 the Liberal opposition began to probe him as to his intentions in regard to the banks. Robin Millhouse asked whether the government was going to honour the ALP election promise of merging the Savings Bank and State Bank. Premier Dunstan said the issue was still being investigated but that the initial findings were that the Savings Bank was at a disadvantage because it could not offer overdraft facilities.[324] When the opposition raised the matter again, Dunstan spoke only of widening the functions of the State's public banking system so as to eliminate duplication and increase mutual co-operation, adding that no 'legislative action would be taken this session' in regard to the two banks.[325]

The legislative inertia remained when the Liberals won the 1969 election and Steele Hall was elected Premier. Rather than confront the discrimination against the Savings Bank the new Liberal government spoke of increasing the competition by allowing the building societies to take on more trading bank investment facilities. The Savings Bank wrote to point out that this only intensified their disadvantage and that it was essential that the bank be given overdraft facilities.[326] Hunkin then went to visit Treasurer Pearson and was told that the Treasurer was sympathetic to a change in the Act and that the bank should provide him with the necessary information on the reasons for overdraft facilities for their customers.[327]

Personal loan provisions
Following Pearson's encouragement the Trustees set up a sub-committee to develop amendments to make the bank more competitive with the private banks. In early October 1968 the bank management informed the Trustees that 'from a competitive point of view the most urgent additional powers required are those

Inward-looking modernism 91

relating to advances by way of overdraft, personal loans, and the power to invest in trustee securities'.[328] He judged that there were dangers for the bank if the bill entered the parliament in its current form, in that 'the question of the appropriation of net profit may be raised. Even if no action were initiated by the Government, it is possible that an amendment might be moved by a member when the bill was introduced into the House'.[329]

In November 1968 the bank suggested an amendment to its Act whereby it could lend freely up to one twentieth of its entire funds, urging that this amendment be considered in the new year by the government.[330] The Trustees established a sub-committee comprising C A D Walker, L V Hunwick and J H Wilton to develop the proposed amendments. When they approached Under-Treasurer G F Seaman on 4 November 1968 for a change in the Act he advised them that it was not possible to consider the amendments in the current session. He said, however, that if the bank wanted the amendments, especially that of loans to depositors, then the board should present the amendments to the government as soon as was practical in the new year for a possible tabling in the February session of parliament.[331]

On 12 December 1968 Hunkin as Chairman of the Trustees wrote to Treasurer Pearson (he insisted the letter should be hand delivered) presenting the case for the amendments to the Act. The letter said that in the view of the board, since the entry of the trading banks into the savings bank field in this state, that there

> had been a steady diminution of the bank's former share of the ordinary savings market. In particular, the aggressiveness with which some competitors have exploited the advantages which they enjoy in relation to the making of loans and advances, by requiring intending borrowers to transfer all their savings bank business to them, has, in many cases, resulted in the loss of accounts customers of this bank.[332]

Know your place
On 17 December 1968 Treasurer Pearson replied in a perfunctory manner that the government was as yet not committed to changing the Act.[333] The board was extremely disappointed but continued to press the issue. Nearly 12 months later it obtained a positive response from the government when, in August 1969, they were informed that the Treasurer had advised the cabinet that he intended to move amendments to the Savings Bank Act in the new year. The Treasurer, however, set the limit for personal loans at only $1,000.[334] This alarmed the Trustees as they realised that this meant that the bank would still remain uncompetitive. In a pointed way the Trustees indicated that the limit implied a political intention on the part of the government to ensure the Savings Bank remained tied in competition with private competitors.

The Trustees wrote to the Treasurer openly showing their collective displeasure, saying that:

> It is most disappointing the Cabinet should see fit to even contemplate the second condition [a limit of $1,000 on personal loans]. It must be assumed that Cabinet, in arriving at this decision, would be motivated solely by a desire to further the interests of the bank and its depositors ... The size of the individual loan should be determined by the purpose for which the loan is made, the capacity of the borrower to meet his commitments and the extent to which

he has contributed in the past and may contribute in the future to the bank's deposit funds and hence its investment capacity.[335]

The Trustees indicated that if the cabinet was to set a limit it should be $3,000 as $1,000 would be 'inadequate for the purchase of vacant land by young people contemplating marriage, the purchase of a range of durable goods by young couples with "teen-age families", the purchase of farming machinery and development of farming properties, "carry-on" finance for clubs and societies, bridging finances for housing probates'.[336]

Treasurer Pearson replied that the:

> Cabinet and Parliament could not possibly accept such wide amendments. Cabinet has agreed to proceed upon the lines set out in the letter of 14 August 1969. Whilst I should be prepared to submit to Cabinet for consideration a rather higher limit than $1,000, I should need some quite substantial argument and cases to justify a higher figure. A limit of $3,000 seems far beyond what can be justified for personal loans. Parliament would not authorise your entering the normal field of the Trading Banks in financing commerce, industry, and current production.[337]

Having been instructed by the Treasurer that the government would not allow the bank to be competitive with the trading/savings banks, the Trustees suggested a compromise position in that the loan limit be set at $1,500, which they said would be preferable to the one suggested by the Treasurer.[338] The cabinet accepted the compromise. On 20 November 1969 the Treasurer introduced into the House the amendments to the Act with the loan limit being set at $1,500 and this passed without amendments.[339]

1968 - the Savings Bank's 120th year

The Savings Bank celebrated its 120th year in a modest manner. The bank developed plans to computerise the head office accounts and establish on-line banking at selected branches. The annual report noted that the bank had 133 fully equipped branches, a rise of 50 since the advent of trading/savings bank competition. There were 1,109 officers in the bank, 785 males and 324 females. The bank had 902,0000 operating accounts and aggregated funds of $409 million. School banking was operating in 807 public and private schools and there were 1,322 special purpose savings deposits in factories and offices. As of 30 June there were 27,522 mortgage loans with balance outstanding at $151,290,861. Since 1848 the bank had lent $272,000,000 of which over half, $165,000,000, had been lent since 1958. Between 1941 and 1965 the bank had lent $75 million to government and semi-government authorities, including $19 million to the Housing Trust and $34 million to ETSA. New loans were made to local authorities amounting to $6 million.[340]

The bank promoted its 120th year in the form of pictorial representations of the historical progress of South Australia, taken from reproductions of etchings held in the Art Gallery of South Australia and by promoting its home lending to families, through the depiction of a 'modern family'. In the advertisement, a grey-suited husband is seen watching over his young son presenting his first pass book to the teller at the modernised Port Adelaide branch, watched over by the wife/mother attired in air hostess motif, with blond older daughter holding a teddy.[341] The next slide in the montage has the family at a barbecue lunch outside their modern home in the Adelaide Hills, the husband in weekend attire, barbecuing the chops and sausages on his tripod portable BBQ, the son asking the father a question (maybe when will the food be ready), the wife looking on, cup of tea in hand, over a prepared table, the daughter directing all her attention to patting the dog; while two young boys in the background (friendly neighbours) are giving a wave as they pass by.[342] The depiction matched the Savings Bank's philosophy that this was a male world where the place of women was as an adornment, whose role was to nurture and to passively watch on.

Married female officers: one year continuation of employment
In December 1968 the Trustees noted that due to particular banking needs female officers were continuing employment after marriage on a special case basis. The board also noted that there had been a reduction in male applicants to the bank and public service and that it might be advisable that female officers be permitted, at least, to make an application for continuation of service in the bank after marriage.[343] The board also noted that some female officers wished to ascertain up to 12 months before marriage whether they might continue in employment of the bank as married women.[344] The board, in response to these requests from the Australian Bank Officials' Association (ABOA), agreed that female officers would be allowed 'to apply to continue in the service of the bank after marriage' but it still remained the prerogative of the board as to whether the bank would concur with such an application, and also that 'authority be given for a period of up to one year in advance to continuance of employment of selected female officers [after their marriage]'.[345]

Managers' attitude survey 1968
In 1968 the management had decided to hire external consultants to survey the managers' attitude to head office. The results alarmed the senior management as they discovered to their dismay that two thirds of the managers felt that the relationship between them and management was 'unsatisfactory'.[346] The managers complained that head office was 'inflexible' and did not allow for autonomy at the branch level nor delegate responsibility to branch managers. The managers felt that even when decisions which would benefit the bank's profitability were suggested they were refused because they were not strictly in keeping with instructions from head office. The managers complained that there was little chance for delegating responsibility as over 50 per cent of the bank's officers were juniors (under 21 years). The management considered that one way of dealing with this problem was to recruit fewer females as this would reduce the 'total turn over of the staff' and build up continuity within the branches'.[347]

Cricket talk
In keeping with the male culture of the senior management, talk about cricket was the common tea room conversation opener for the senior managers and often featured in job interviews as an unconscious test of the suitability of a candidate to fit into the bank's culture. In this regard, the Savings Bank management consistently sponsored cricket in South Australia. The bank, however, still regarded the game as an amateur occupation. This was most evident when one of the staff, the

champion cricketer and footballer Eric Freeman made his regular request for leave to play cricket for the State and Australian teams. Upon each request the board would tally his leave entitlements and then when these were quickly eroded, expect him to play for his country on leave without pay. For instance, when Freeman was selected as a member of the Australian team to tour England in 1968, he was granted special leave without pay from 7 May 1968 to 9 September 1968. Similarly, in 1972 when Freeman applied to the board for leave to represent South Australia against Western Australia in the Sheffield Shield it was noted that he had 'already exhausted his annual leave and that the bank would grant him special leave without pay so that he could represent his State'.[348]

In January 1972 Freeman again wrote to say that it seemed unfair that as he was employed as a promotions officer by the bank and used prominently in the bank's promotional material and campaigns, that he was being penalised when playing for his country and for the State cricket teams. He said he found it financially onerous that he was expected to use all of his annual leave and then to take leave without pay at a personal cost to himself when selected to play for his country.[349] When he met with board intransigence, Freeman decided to resign from the Savings Bank. Upon hearing of Freeman's predicament, Sir Donald Bradman contacted the General Manager to intercede on Freeman's behalf. Sir Donald's request met with an instant change of heart. The General Manager contacted Freeman informing him that he could use his annual leave until it was exhausted and after that time 'special leave would be provided making up the difference between his 'sporting pay' and his 'bank salary'.[350] In proposing the motion to the board the General Manager noted that Freeman had been granted 315 days leave without pay since his employment in the bank.[351]

The bank regularly sponsored the State cricket team providing a general funding for the team and offered $10 per catch taken in each Sheffield Shield Game. As a reward for the South Australian cricket team winning the Sheffield Shield in 1975/1976 season the bank presented $250 as a special bonus to the team and promised that should the team repeat the performance in 1976/77 the bonus would rise to $500. The cheque was presented at a special dinner in the board dining room with invitations being sent to cricket captain Ian Chappel and Sir Donald Bradman.[352]

Empire meets the 'mods'
The annual report of 1970 began with the Trustees recording their pleasure that on 4 December 1969 his Excellency Major-General Sir James Harrison made an official visit to the bank and after the mandatory inspection, including an examination of the new electronic data processing system, was entertained at luncheon by the Trustees and senior management. Len Hunkin was still Chairman of the board. Chris Hurford had resigned from the board to contest the seat of Adelaide and was replaced by Lew Barratt, a leading Adelaide accountant. The report was notable for its use of economic modelling and the contrast between the old men of the board and the depiction of female customers in bright 'mod' clothes, beehive hair-dos, (white) leather boots, to match the report's orange and purple geometrical designs based on the lines of modern colourfield paintings. The bank's board and senior management practices were based on the past, yet the bank was trying to give the appearance of being economically up to date and 'fashionably hip' in its products and services.

By the beginning of the 1960s both the Savings Bank and the State Bank were constrained by their respective legislation and lack of support by the Liberal or Labor parties to compete effectively against the trading banks. The thinking within the two banks was that the past served the present and that they were only niche financial players and even if they wanted to be full trading/savings banks there was little support in the parliament for such a move. Moreover, there were strong forces in the private sector which were against full public competition against the private banks, especially the Bank of Adelaide. As we shall see in the next chapter Premier Dunstan began to change the political environment which disturbed the respective boards, especially when the new premier began to promote the idea of a merger of the two banks.

4

Don Dunstan's plan for modernisation

As the decades of the 1950s and 1960s unfolded the two banks commenced operation with high hopes of becoming modern banking institutions. The objective was to modernise the banks to be a part of the industrialisation of South Australia. The banks were, however, unable to benefit fully from the changing economy because of political restrictions and their staid cultures. The banks' complacency was assaulted from the outside by the Premier. The early 1970s became a period of resistance by the banks to Dunstan's attempts to modernise them from the outside. Ironically, when Dunstan resigned from office due to ill-health, the two banks decided that his plan had merit and approached the new government requesting a merger. That is, in the late 1970s with the fall of the Bank of Adelaide came a period where the public banks sought to prod a procrastinating Premier Tonkin into letting them merge so as to modernise. It was in the early 1980s that the newly elected Premier John Bannon responded positively to the banks' request for amalgamation.

Outside political forces for change: Dunstan's modernisation by stealth
When Don Dunstan became Premier, in his own right, on 30 March 1970, the South Australian economy was languishing, with Playford's major industrialisation program having stalled by the early 1960s. Dunstan's plan for revitalising the economy was to extend economic development into diverse fields, notably the arts and education. He considered that the public sector had the capacity to take a lead in developing South Australia. In modernising the economy Dunstan sought to coordinate the State's finances. First he established the State Government Insurance Commission (SGIC) in 1972, with much resistance from the insurance industry and the Opposition. Then the Premier turned his attention to the two public banks. Dunstan was of the view that as the Savings Bank was 'nationalised' by Playford it should respond directly to him and be more integrated into his plan to modernise the economy, a view directly opposed by the Savings Bank Trustees who fought to retain control over their business and profits. The Savings Bank Trustees, having developed, over long years of Liberal governments, a modus operandi with Premier Playford, were highly suspicious of the Labor government. The Savings Bank nevertheless was dependent upon the new government to overcome the disadvantageous position in which the Liberal government had placed it.

After the 1970 election victory of Dunstan, the Savings Bank wrote to the new Premier requesting an increase in the personal loan limit from $1,500 to $3,000. In supporting the application, the board pointed out how the previous government had not approved the bank's upper limit and as a consequence, the bank was 'losing first-class business and in some instances good customers'.[1]

Dunstan said he was sympathetic to their request and would present the rule change to his cabinet. Given that the Savings Bank wanted something from him, Dunstan decided that it was a good time to request something from them, so he pushed his idea of a merger between the Savings Bank and the State Bank. As an initial tactic Dunstan sought to develop a rapport with the Trustees by indicating to the Savings Bank that he would support their application for an increase in the borrowing limit and would ensure that the changes to the Act would have an expeditious passage through the parliament.[2]

Getting voices on the boards
While the Savings Bank was preparing its amendment to the Act, Dunstan simultaneously introduced two bills into the House of Assembly to alter administrative arrangements within the Savings Bank. He had informed the Trustees that these were but administrative adjustments to the Act. The amendments seemed innocuous enough but their effect was to allow the government to assert more control over the Savings Bank Board. The first change allowed a director to be on both the Savings Bank and the State Bank boards. The second amendment was to change the method of appointing the chair of the Savings Bank Board from that of a Trustee decision to that of a government appointment. In addition, the term of office of board members was reduced from four to two years. The effect of these alterations was to allow the government to appoint the Chair of the board and for a person to be on both the boards of the State Bank and the Savings Bank.[3] Having the numbers in the lower house Dunstan's amendment passed without any opposition.

The Savings Bank Trustees were taken aback when they read the bill to discover that what they thought were mere adjustments in annual leave arrangements, in practice fundamentally altered the manner of the appointment of the Trustees and their terms of office.[4] This only confirmed their suspicions of Dunstan and their worst fears that the government was seeking to gain control over the Savings Bank. The Trustees were, however, in a quandary as what to do as they were still waiting for the Premier to upgrade the overdraft amounts for cheque accounts. The board decided that Chairman Hunkin should formally write to the Premier protesting over the changes and the lack of consultation on the alterations in their term of office.[5] The board decided to meet Dunstan's stealth with their own behind the scenes manoeuvres.

The opposition were alerted to the amendments and debate in the Legislative Council became acrimonious, where it was alleged that there was a plot by the government to control the Savings Bank. C R Story said the amendments were aimed at amalgamation, saying the government wanted 'a combination of the State Bank and the South Australian Savings Bank which was a brain-child of the Hon Hugh Hudson'.[6] Story argued that the government's intention was to control the deposit funds of the Savings Bank and he saw something 'sinister' in the amendment to the Savings Bank Act which allowed 'the government, not the trustees themselves, to appoint the chair of the Savings Bank Trustees'.[7] Similarly, Murray Hill argued that if the amendment was carried 'the same person would be able to hold office on both banks' and this was linked to the 'political history of the proposed marriage between the two organisations' with 'the sole aim of the Labor government of controlling depositor funds'[8].

In contrast, the elder statesman of the Liberal opposition, Sir Arthur Rymill, supported the bill saying that 'I think I should declare my interest, as I am a director of a trading bank which in a way compares with the State Bank, and a director of a savings bank which is, I suppose, competing with the State Savings Bank. I see nothing wrong with the bill or the amendments to it … I see no reason why a member of the board of one bank should not be a member of the board of the other. They are both government institutions and are not competing with each other in any major way'.[9] Rymill went on to argue that he also supported the government's right, as the shareholder, to appoint the Chair of the board, saying this would 'modernise the charter of the bank'.[10]

Given that Premier Dunstan had yet to pass the legislation on cheque account limit, the Trustees decided that the best course of action was not to be seen as publicly attacking the government. The board members, however, had recorded in the minutes their concern that 'the amendments had been introduced by the government without the knowledge of either the Trustees or management. No opportunity had been given to comment on the proposals or add to them. One of the proposals had, in fact, been framed to take from the board the long-established privilege of electing its own Chairman. The members decided to write to the Premier expressing their disquiet at not being consulted over the amendments'.[11]

When the Under-Treasurer wrote to the board, in regard to the (new) limited terms of office, informing them that the appointment of Mr Jeffery as Chairman and Mr Huntley as a Trustee would be only until 1 January 1972 and not until 1975, the board decided to fight back. The Trustees immediately sought legal advice as to the terms of the present Trustees and the implications of the new Act. The bank's solicitors replied that in their opinion, the current chair, G H P Jeffery, was entitled to be covered by the old legislation and hold office for five years, until 31 December 1975, and not the new two year provision. The Trustees then wrote to the Premier pointing out this legal opinion and asking him to uphold the previous terms of appointment[12]. Having received this legal advice, Dunstan decided to delay his plans of appointing his own man as Chair of the board, until the current board's term of appointment expired. He wrote in early February informing the Trustees that Jeffrey's appointment would be, in accordance with previous undertakings, to the term of his retirement.[13]

1972: up-dating the Act

In February 1972 Dunstan informed the Trustees that he would change the cheque account limit as requested. On 14 March 1972 the amendments to the loan limits, from $1,500 to $3,000, were presented to the parliament and were gazetted on 14 April 1972.[14] Dunstan nevertheless ensured that he retained a lever over the bank as he refused to grant an extension of the repayment period beyond three years. Consequently, the Trustees wrote to the Premier seeking to extend the repayment schedule to five years, and said the Act needed a major overhaul as it looked like a 'patchwork quilt'.[15] The Trustees suggested to Dunstan that the Act be brought up to date by removing outdated clauses, particularly those requiring the approval of the Governor for staff changes and the appointment of agents. In addition, the

Savings Bank wanted to adopt a number of the lending practices used by the trading banks, and presented this to Premier Dunstan as beneficial to both the bank and the Treasury, saying it would have the effect of 'strengthening the bank's position and [of] providing the Government with Revenue'.[16]

Dunstan told the Savings Bank Trustees he was sympathetic to updating the Act but suggested that perhaps as the Savings Bank was entering into traditional trading bank business that it was now time to consider a merger with the State Bank. Chairman Jeffery wrote to the Premier opposing such a suggestion, stressing, however, that unless the bank could become more competitive in its own right then this would have a negative result for both the Savings Bank and the Treasury.[17] Jeffery argued that the bank had social obligations in its charter which restrained its level of profit and therefore it needed to have higher earning accounts to offset these obligations. He said the bank still offered 'uneconomic public service, where the margin between costs and earnings is small' and the 'high interest rates on deposits' were even more of a drain on profits and, in fact, 'except for the income from reserves, in some years there would have been no surplus'.[18] As such the Savings Bank was merely seeking to expand the range of its services into the trading bank arena just to maintain its position in the market place and Jeffery said the board saw no benefits in a merger with the State Bank.

Dunstan replied that if the Savings Bank wanted to expand into the field of the trading banks it should unite with the other state-owned bank, the State Bank. Such an amalgamation, he said, would give the new bank the ability to 'extend to some of the largest trading, commercial and profit making businesses in the country'.[19] He added that:

> Whilst I have considerable sympathy with the desire of the bank to protect and extend its savings bank business against competitors by giving wider and more comprehensive services, such a generalised extension into trading bank business presents problems. However it does seem to me that there are possibilities, by some closer arrangement with the State Bank than presently exist, of achieving your present objective and perhaps of achieving even more favourable results expanding the bank's lending practices into the trading bank field.[20]

Premier Dunstan, at that time, was receiving deputation from the ABOA over what they saw as the archaic management system in the Savings Bank, where the authority of the senior management could not be challenged. The ABOA wanted rights of appeal in regard to promotions and classifications. Dunstan said that he has some sympathy with these demands but wanted to extend them to include industrial democracy, which in practice would place an Association member on the board of the Savings Bank.[21] After a year of negotiation the changes to the Act, however, were minimal, principally restricted to rights of appeal and not full industrial democracy.

In accordance with the amended Savings Bank Act the General Manager notified the board that the bank had established both a Classification, and an Appeals Committee. Assistant Auditor-General K J Boland was appointed to the committees. In supporting the external appointment, the General Manager said Boland filled the same role in the State Bank; therefore, given the closer relationship with that bank, it might be an advantage to have the same person on these Committees, and that his appointment was 'acceptable to the Australian Bank Officials' Association'.[22]

Married female officers: surplus to requirements
In regard to staffing matters the Savings Bank was reluctant to make any reforms, and perceived all suggestions from the outside as a threat to the bank's independence and history. The most glaring evidence of how far the Savings Bank's management was stuck in the past was in its attitude to its female officers, in particular, to its belief that a married woman's place was in the home and not in banking. Such a view brought the bank into conflict with its female staff and the ABOA. As the following account shows it was only the passing of anti-discrimination legislation which changed the bank's practices.

On 11 February 1971 the Savings Bank Board agreed to the recruitment of three juniors per month up to a total of 29. Recruitment proceeded until June when it became evident to management that the rate of wastage had slowed down. Whereas it had been anticipated that 60 officers would resign in the first six months of the year, only 42 had done so. As a result management considered that it was over-staffed, attributing this situation to two factors: firstly, the general lack of government employment, and secondly, the 'continued employment of married females and the application of new salary scales'.[23] Management noted that there 'are 55 married female officers in the service and it is considered this is an opportune time to review the results of our [1968] policy of continuing female officers in employment after marriage'.[24] It recommended that:

> Of the married female officers now serving 10 have been married for 2 years or more. It is considered that some movement should be engendered into this group, in the interests of future recruitment, salary savings and the maintenance of morale.[25]

The minutes record that the retention of married females 'can be expensive salary-wise' and there is a 'constant need for a flow of junior female officers through those routine jobs which do not rate the skills of the more experienced officers'.[26] The board decided to halt junior intake for 1971 and to 'terminate the employment of married females who had been married for 2 years or more' and to make this a general policy directive as of 30 September 1971. The married women were to receive one month's notice of the termination of their employment.[27]

The women promptly went to the ABOA which sent a letter of protest to the General Manager and a copy to Premier Dunstan.[28] The ABOA's view was 'that married female officers employed at the present time could be expected to have believed that, when the bank permitted them to continue in employment after their marriage, their employment was to be on the same basis as that of male officers, i.e. until such time as they themselves wished to terminate their services, or retirement'.[29] On behalf of the Premier/Treasurer, Under-Treasurer Seaman wrote to the bank expressing concern over the termination letters and expressed his opposition to the bank's policy in regard to married women's employment.

The Trustees were unmoved by these protests, saying that the employment of married women was their prerogative and was offered as a privilege to the women and not a right. The board wrote that 'prior to December 1968 female officers were not permitted to continue in the service of the bank but that after that date certain females, on a selective basis, have been permitted to continue'. All female officers, they stressed, 'knew the conditions of employment and the right of the board to terminate the employment of married women' when they joined the bank. They added that in any case there was the need to keep open places for 'school leavers'.[30] The ABOA did not accept this explanation and replied that the decision towards the married women showed a general attitude to the bank's staff whereby any 'employee can at any time be fired'.[31]

The ABOA then sought to shame the bank into changing its policy, threatening to go public on the matter unless the bank changed its mind. The ABOA wrote that, 'We had hoped that a more enlightened and humanitarian view of the "master-servant" relationship would have eventuated from further consideration of the situation in which some of the bank's married female officers find themselves'.[32] The Association concluded their letter with a threat that it would take the matter to Commonwealth Conciliation and Arbitration Commission but hoped that a public confrontation could be averted.[33]

Having been threatened with public exposure for their discriminatory practices the Trustees decided to fight back, and instructed the management to carry out an investigation into the employment conditions of female officers in other banks. They were somewhat surprised to find that their practices were out of kilter with the rest of the banking industry and discovered that even in their sister savings banks there was no discrimination between male and female officers in regard to employment after marriage.[34] The bank discovered that in the State Bank there was 'no alteration' in female officers' conditions of service as a result of marriage.[35] Likewise in the Commonwealth Bank female officers did not resign on marriage and the only alteration was 'the notification of name change'[36].

Notwithstanding this evidence, the Trustees remained intransigent on this matter and wrote to the ABOA reaffirming their prerogative to terminate the employment of the married women.[37] Nevertheless, in the face of the evidence and the threat of being forced to defend their anomalous position before the Commission, the board beat a tactical retreat and inserted the caveat that this did 'not apply to those officers whose continuation after marriage was approved prior to 7 June 1971'.[38] The ten targeted women were therefore allowed to remain in the bank but the board still retained the right to fire any woman officer upon her marriage. In short, nothing had changed for the board from 1945 to 1972 in regard to its attitude to women officers in the Savings Bank and, for that matter, their place in society.[39]

Equal pay
The equal pay case in 1969 which was based on the principle of equal pay for equal work, had no impact on the Savings Bank. However, in 1971 the Trustees soon became concerned when female pay in the banking industry came before the Commonwealth Conciliation and Arbitration Commission. On 6 August 1971, Commissioner Portus handed down a decision which increased the female salary rates as prescribed in the Private Banks' Award. The ABOA wrote to the Savings Bank requesting a flow-on of this decision. The Savings Bank initially opposed the rise but after discovering that the Bank of Adelaide was going to pay the new award the Savings Bank decided it had no choice but to implement the new rate. In making

the decision the Trustees were informed that the new pay scale was applicable to women aged over 18 years and that this only affected 61 female officers, involving an increase of $30 per annum, raising the salary from around $1,495 to $1,525 per female officer a year. Despite the paltry nature of the rise there was a pencilled directive alongside the board minutes instructing the management to minimise the recruitment of women eligible for equal pay and that the bank was 'not to recruit females over 17 years in 1972'.[40]

Even when in 1972 the Arbitration and Conciliation Commission revisited the equal pay decision of 1969, and decided to apply the principle of equal pay for work of equal value, the Savings Bank held back, waiting until they were legally obliged to pass on any pay rises to female officers.[41] Under pressure from the ABOA, the board agreed that women should have equal opportunity for promotion.[42] In accordance with this change in view it was decided that all positions were to be open to all officers, whereas it was previously the practice to invite applications for such positions from male officers only.[43] Nevertheless, the Trustees still held the view that women should resign from the bank when they married, a practice which remained until Premier Dunstan's anti-discrimination legislation in 1975. In keeping with the Savings Bank's moral attitude towards women as the basis of 'family thrift', it was decided to celebrate the bank's 125 years with a donation to mothers.

1973: Savings Bank's 125th birthday

The Trustees decided to celebrate the bank's 125th birthday on 11 March 1973 with a publicity campaign of a $10 donation cheque given to mothers who had babies born on that day.[44] The bank used its sporting heroes, Eric Freeman, Malcolm Blight and Russell Ebert to present the cheques to the mothers. The bank spent $3,000 on press publicity to highlight the growth in deposits over the last 25 years from $121 million to $500 million, the rise in staff from 546 in 1948 to 1,258 in 1973 and the number of savings accounts from 582,817 to 956,434. The growth in services to be noted included cheque accounts, personal and demand loans and the introduction of computerised banking. The bank spent $27,500 on staff dinners at twelve different centres with the total number of guests invited being 2,600.[45]

Empire and the celebration

In celebrating the bank's 125th year the Trustees were confronted with a problem of protocol. In short, it was usual practice that a new Governor was invited to inspect the bank and have a private luncheon with the Trustees. The Governor's office indicated to the bank that the new Governor, Sir Mark Oliphant, would be able to make his inaugural visit to the bank on 24 May 1973. The dilemma for the bank was that this date fell well after the celebration date and the Trustees were concerned that if the Governor was invited as just one of a number of eminent persons on 11 March then this might be seen as a slight on the Queen's representative. After much rumination the board noted that, 'as customary in the past, the first visit to the bank by a new Governor should be a special occasion in itself. It is suggested that it would be preferable not to associate such a visit with the bank's 125th Year celebrations and risk the presence of other distinguished guests lessening the importance of a Vice Regal visit'.[46] So it was decided to hold a special celebration visit on the day, specifically for Governor Oliphant, which was then to be followed by a luncheon with other distinguished guests, including the Premier Don Dunstan and His Excellency the Governor and the leader of the opposition, Bruce Eastick, and former premiers Tom Playford and Steele Hall. Also invited were Lord Mayor W Hayes and the Chairman of Advertiser Ltd, J Bonython.[47]

School banking: the thin edge of the wedge

In November 1972 the management of the Savings Bank became alarmed when it discovered that the Westminster School had given exclusive rights for its school banking requirements to the Commercial Bank. The bank wrote to Westminster School noting that it had provided long-standing banking services not only to the school but also to the Methodist Church and associated institutions (eg. Prince Alfred College, Methodist Ladies College, Lincoln University College) and Methodist students for many years.[48] Westminster was, however, unmoved. The Savings Bank then sought the assistance of Premier Dunstan to place pressure on the School Council to change its mind.[49] Dunstan wrote to the school supporting the Savings Bank, pointing out it had previously provided services to the school as had the State Bank and the government. The school replied that their choice was taken because of the service provided by the Commercial Bank, notably a loan for the School Chaplain's residence, and was an initiative from the School Council and not one of the Commercial Bank.[50] The bank then wrote to all the parents at the school who had accounts with the Savings Bank asking them to make private arrangements for their school banking needs and set out how the bank had served the cause of Methodism in the State.[51] The School Council stood firm against all of this pressure and reaffirmed its exclusive contract with the Commercial Bank.

The issue here was not so much the decision by the Westminster School but the extreme lengths the Savings Bank went to in order to protect its previous dominance in school banking. The Trustees and management were also showing a general concern at the decline in school banking and what that meant for the philosophy of thrift. The Savings Bank management was still committed to the concept of instilling savings from an early age but recognised that school banking was costly to operate. Concomitantly, the sense of banking loyalty was also beginning to wane as customers shopped around for the best interest rates on both their deposits and loans, and school banking was now less popular among school children, especially high school children, than in the heydays of the 1950s.[52]

State Bank re-evaluates its corporate role

While the Savings Bank began the 1970s deeply concerned over Dunstan's plan for modernisation and the growing threats to its patriarchal and paternal administrative model, the State Bank was keen to become more commercially competitive. This desire was hampered by its small deposit base, which restricted the ambit of its lending to concessional housing loans and to serving the rural industry including the many co-operatives' accounts. The deposit level had been consistently around the $40 million mark since 1968 and was dependent upon fluctuations in the rural economy. For instance, in the financial year 1973-74 the bank's deposits jumped from $46 million to $67 million and this rise was due solely to record harvests and high prices for rural produce. In 1970 deposits stood at $40 million with loans (mainly via overdrafts and long term commitments) at $31 million and advances on homes at $83 million. By 1974 commercial loans were $51 million and home advances at $142 million.[53]

By 1974 the State Bank was aggressively pursuing corporate business. These loans were still mainly connected to its rural banking roots but began to be more market oriented, especially those for rural properties and the co-operatives. Examples of the State Bank's commercial loans can be seen in the following major accounts held at the Adelaide office. At this branch in 1974 total credit commitments were $22 million. The largest loan was to Southern Farmers with a line of credit amounting to $4.5 million, followed by Thomas Hardy & Sons $3 million, Amscol $1.5 million, and Co-operative Insurance $1.5 million.[54]

50 per cent profit goes to State revenue
In 1974 Dunstan sought to end the 'gentleman's agreement' that had been made between Premier Playford and the Savings Bank Trustees in 1946. The Dunstan government moved amendments to both the State Bank and the Savings Bank acts obliging them to pay 50 per cent of their annual profit to the State treasury. When he presented the bills to the parliament Premier Dunstan justified his action by noting that 'neither the State Bank nor the Savings Bank were required to pay income tax. If these institutions were required to pay such tax at this time, they would be required to pay 47½ per cent of their profits by way of taxation. It does not seem unreasonable that such a contribution should be required as it were in lieu of the income tax otherwise payable'.[55]

Bruce Eastick for the opposition criticised the intent and the wording of the bills, and as it applied to the previous financial year the 'opposition was opposed to both the revenue raising component and its 'retrospective provision'[56]. Dunstan replied that he was but following precedent as it was the Hall government which applied the principle of putting part of the State Savings Bank profits into the Treasury. 'He said that the State Savings Bank of Victoria has been required by a Liberal government to pay half of its net profits to State revenue and the Rural Bank of New South Wales has also been required by a Liberal Government to do so. The Commonwealth Savings Bank and the Commonwealth Trading Bank have also been affected by Liberal governments in the same way ... The principle of retrospectivity in relation to previous net profit was established by the previous Liberal Government.'[57]

The bills passed both houses of parliament and the two public banks were forthwith obliged to pay 50 per cent of their profits into state revenue.

An external review of the two banks
Dunstan decided that he might prompt the banks to agree to a merger by exposing to them their financial backwardness. To that effect, and against the objection of the banks, he employed two interstate financial experts to conduct a review of both banks. On 7 April 1975 the Premier obtained cabinet approval for the appointment of Sir Walter Scott and Sir John Marks to conduct an inquiry into, and report on, the Savings Bank and the State Bank. The never published terms of reference were:

> To examine the character and operations of the Savings Bank of South Australia and the State Bank of South Australia and, having regard to modern banking practice both in Australia and overseas and to the broad public and social objectives implied by the statutory character of the banks, report on (a) New or expanded areas of operation and service considered necessary if a full

range of banking services is to be provided with economy and efficiency (whether or not such activities are provided for in the bank's present charters). (b) Means by which, either separately or jointly, the banks may further enhance the services provided to the State and its people, including personal banking services, and the management of funds for the general benefit of the community.[58]

The report pointed out that to ensure confidentiality the investigation would be limited to interviewing the directors, Trustees and the banks' chief executives. The interim report set out a series of 'principles for the optimum development of the banks'. The report stated that the Savings Bank 'offers its depositors a higher rate of interest than other savings banks in South Australia and lends funds at rates lower than others and the bank is the major lender of housing loans in the State, at interest rates lower than any other institution except the State Bank. It provides a number of special, and less profitable, services including the encashment of personal and social service cheques, and facilities for customers to pay their electricity accounts, water rates, and insurance premiums to the State Government Insurance Commission'.

In terms of the functions of the State Bank, the report noted that it had administered a number of Acts: Advances for Homes (1926–70), Loans to Producers (1927–62), Loans to Settlers (1930–72), Loans for Fencing and Water Piping (1938–52), The Vermin Act (1931–67), Student Hostels (1961–), and conducted general banking business. The report contended that the latter meant, in practice, the provision of banking facilities to customers who had difficulty with other trading banks. Its main function was supporting rural industry, co-operative organisations and the housing sector. While it had the power to provide discount of commercial bills and grant personal loans it had not exploited these facilities.

It was estimated that the State Bank and the Savings Bank were both growing more slowly than their counterparts. The report found that between 1969 and 1974 the Savings Bank deposits rose 49 per cent whereas other savings banks grew 123 per cent. The State Bank's deposits rose 74 per cent whereas other trading bank deposits rose by 102 per cent and the State Bank had only 7 per cent of the State's total deposits. The State Bank had 373 staff and 35 branches whereas the Savings Bank had 1,418 staff and 142 branches (plus 700 agencies).

The Savings Bank's range of services was restricted by its legislation and by its traditional approach of offering higher rates on its deposits and to special accounts and advances. The Savings Bank was offering 0.5 per cent higher interest rates on its deposits than all other banks and held some 50 per cent of the savings deposits in the State. It offered deposits stock (to compete with term deposits) special purpose accounts (such as Christmas Savings and School Savings), and advances were made to the State government, statutory and local government bodies, non-profit making organisations such as hospitals, local councils, clubs, churches and charities. The Savings Bank was involved in mortgage loans for rural and development projects and home mortgage loans, and was the major lender for housing finance in South Australia. The Savings Bank had offered personal loan facilities but was hampered by government regulations over the amounts and duration. At the time the limit was set at $5,000 over five years. The Savings Bank had a cheque account facility for both profit and non-profit making organisations and personal customers. With profit making bodies the accounts had to be in credit and channelled through the State Bank.

The State Bank offered a wider range of services but these were driven by community financial needs rather than commercial considerations. The State Bank offered cheque account, overdraft facilities, mortgage loans, insurance underwriting, foreign exchange transactions, sub-underwriting, interest bearing deposits and certificates of deposit. The total overdraft facilities comprised only a limited number of accounts in a selected sector (eg. rural co-operatives). According to the report, the State Bank was overly reliant on funds from the state government. In 1974 the Treasurer advanced to the bank $21.4 million and in addition there were advances on the Home Building Accounts of $148 million with deposits being $67.7 million. The State Bank did not make any calls on the national or international money market for capital and this was in the opinion of the authors 'not consistent with modern banking practice'.

A similar finding was made on the Savings Bank's lack of modernisation. The Savings Bank, the report said, was overly reliant on deposits to fund its activities. While holding some 50 per cent of the savings bank deposits in the state this figure was not stable and had fallen significantly since the introduction of savings-trading banks in South Australia. Marks and Scott's report concluded its overview of the Savings Bank by predicting that it was unlikely to improve its market share and therefore the only way it could grow was by a rise in savings deposits, which, this report considered, was unlikely.[60]

In addition, the authors of the report noted that the Savings Bank's strategy of attracting deposits through higher interest rates was proving costly, as customers in general were moving from low to high interest bearing accounts. The bank could meet this challenge by lowering its profit margins, but since 1975 it was obliged to pay the government 50 per cent of its surplus over expenses and this would have other implications on whether it could offer unprofitable services such as school banking. The other option was to lower management expenses which were seen as too high. In 1974 they stood at half the interest paid on depositors' accounts, or $13.6 million, which was considered by the authors as revealing systemic inefficiency.

Marks and Scott's report concluded that the two banks were basically not equipped to offer modern banking services. The authors based their findings on the principal criteria of net profit as the basic test for modern banking, and as the two banks placed service provision over making high profits they were by definition not modern. The report also noted that in overall attitude and operations the two banks lagged behind their competitors. For instance, the report found that the two banks' advertising and images were by no means in keeping with international practice and standards. Their management structures were notable for the duplication of scarce managerial skills.

Given the structural problems, the conclusion of the report was that the Savings Bank needed a trading bank arm and the State Bank needed the breadth of the Saving Bank's deposits to create a basis for higher profits and modernisation. The authors recommended, with a hint of self interest, that the two banks should begin a phased merger and that they were ready to be consultants in that very process. The benefit of such an integration was, they said, that a unified bank would increase access to external funds for the bank and more funds for its customers. Allowing for a management system which better used the skills of the managers would lead to the 'rationalisation' (read *reduction*) of staff and branches as was occurring overseas. Such a rationalisation would increase the profit level of the newly merged bank. The new bank, the report pointed out, would need to find means of becoming more independent from the government and far less reliant on government funds. Marks and Scott's report observed that the Savings Bank managers were less than impressed with their State Bank counterparts perceiving them as merely overseeing a 'sluggish' and narrowly focused bank.[61]

Once they received their copies of the report the two banks were respectively outraged. The Savings Bank Trustees wrote a draft reply on behalf of both boards expressing their 'strong disagreement' with the 'key recommendation' put forward in Marks and Scott's report. The letter made it plain that they regarded the report as being politically driven and having a pre-conceived conclusion in mind, that of a merger which prejudged the evidence which was collected. The letter said 'it is difficult to escape the conclusion that the document merely reflects the quandary of trying to rationalise a predetermined direction'. The Savings Bank, for its part, said it opposed the idea of the Savings Bank using the State Bank for trading bank services as they considered this as being merely a form by which the Savings Bank was to 'subsidise the State Bank'. The Savings Bank stressed that integration could lead to higher risks, and it rejected the notion that the Savings Bank was uncompetitive.

The letter concluded with an implied political threat to Dunstan if he should try and merge the banks, saying:

> It must also be recorded that enabling legislation would have to be put through the parliament and in the current circumstances particularly its passing may prove difficult to achieve and in any event the obvious publicity which would arise could have very damaging portents. The confidence and loyalty of its [the Savings Bank] depositors rests solidly on a policy of no political interference over a term of 130 years. Should this be put in jeopardy and, if so, to what end?'
>
> By way of summing up ... the Savings Bank, which is servicing around 50% of the business available, has held its place in the face of aggressive and well-armed competition. It is acknowledged that neither bank has profit as its primary motive, but as a banking fundamental operating surpluses must be generated to strengthen reserves ... banking is among the most highly labour intensive industries and its problems have been compounded over recent years with dismaying speed. It is our firm opinion that while we cannot support the proposed integration, in the light of the evidence submitted in its favour, we would wholly agree with any measure designed to bring the two banks into a closer and mutually beneficial relationship.[62]

The Savings Bank said it was opposed to 'rationalisation' of services or an expansion of its corporate banking as these had the potential to adversely affect its customers. It argued that 'attending to one corporate customer at the counter may take as long as attending to ten or a dozen savings bank depositors', a claim which reveals how serving depositors predominated the thinking of the board. It added that the bank was indeed modern, as witnessed by the 'installation of the new on-line computerised banking systems which will be amongst the most modern in the world'.[63] In light of the hostile response from the two banks to the report, and especially the Savings Bank's implied political threat, Premier Dunstan decided not to go ahead with a merger and paid the consultants out, with a fee of $14,500 for their services.[64] He had to wait until 1976 before the Chairman's and his deputy's term of office expired on the Savings Bank Board. Once that happened he could influence more strongly the thinking in the bank. He let the matters raised in Marks and Scott's report rest until the next year.

Sex Discrimination Act
On 19 August 1975 Premier Dunstan sought leave from the House to introduce a bill for an Act to 'render unlawful certain kind of practices of discrimination and promote equality of opportunity between men and women generally'.[65] Clause 16 of the Act dealt specifically with discrimination on marital status, making it illegal to discriminate on the grounds of sex or marital status and preventing discrimination on imputed characteristics of one person against another person.[66] The bill received bipartisan support and became law on 14 October 1975.

At the Savings Bank board meeting of 30 October 1975 the Trustees for the last time gave approval for the continuation of the services of 11 female officers after their marriage and then received a report from the General Manager on the Sex Discrimination Act.[67] The General Manager then moved amendments to the bank's employment practices so as to equalise the conditions of service for both men and women. Equalisation was to occur in the areas of superannuation, permanency of employment, retirement age and marital status (except that a female had to notify the bank of any change of name after marriage).[68] It was also noted that the bank was implementing the equal pay provisions of the Arbitration and Conciliation Commission for male and female officers.

Integrating the boards
As soon as it was legally possible Dunstan moved to appoint new Trustees on both public banks and to have joint Trustees on both banks. Earlier on, in 1973 Dunstan had appointed to the State Bank Board E R Howells, a Sydney money market expert to assist in modernising its fund management. Immediately this became a political point of contention between the government and the opposition. Robin Millhouse asked Premier Dunstan why a Sydney resident was appointed to the State Bank Board. Dunstan replied that

> the Government decided that it was advisable to have on the boards of the Savings Bank and of the State Bank in South Australia a banking expert of considerable stature, someone who had considerable experience in the use by the banks of the money markets and of international financing. Neither bank board had someone with this experience on it ... We believe it was necessary to add this expertise to our boards and, consequently, Mr Howells has been appointed to the State Bank board'.[69]

In 1974 Dunstan appointed Howells to the Savings Bank board. He then appointed the chair of the State Bank, Mr Seaman, (the former Under-Treasurer) to the Savings Bank Board. The next move in the plan came when Jeffery's term of office expired on 30 December 1975, and Dunstan immediately appointed the head of his own department, Robert Bakewell, to chair the Savings Bank Board. Bakewell was also on the State Bank board. Finally, an ex-Labor member of parliament, Ernie Crimes, was appointed to both boards, in what the Premier described as a temporary measure while his worker participation legislation was being debated. When the latter legislation was passed Dunstan said Crimes would resign and his place would be filled by a bank officer elected or appointed onto each board. In the end his industrial democracy plans did not eventuate but by then the government had a strong representation on both bank boards.

At the first meeting of the board in 1976 it was recorded that G H P Jeffery was retiring from the board, having been a member since October 1963 and Chairman since 1 January 1972. Sir William Bishop also retired after serving on the board since 7 February 1946. The board passed a motion of appreciation for the 'long and distinguished service' of both men and expressed its 'appreciation of the valuable contribution they had made to the bank'.[70] Bakewell was appointed by the government as Chair of the Trustees with Ernie Crimes replacing Sir William Bishop on the board.

At the commencement of 1976 Premier Dunstan had at last gained a strong voice on the Savings Bank Board and could influence both public banks through his cross-board membership on the State Bank and the Savings Bank boards. There were three joint members on the boards (Bakewell, Howells, Crimes), and each board contained the chair of the other bank on it (Howells, Bakewell). It was not so much that the three were strictly Dunstan men, rather it was the perception that they were that caused suspicion and animosity.

For the Savings Bank management, suspicion was confirmed when immediately upon being appointed to the board, Bakewell broached the issue of more co-operation between the Savings Bank and the State Bank. In response the senior management wrote to Premier Dunstan protesting about Bakewell's action and his efforts to unilaterally explore co-operation between the two banks.[71]

Then on 12 February 1976 Bakewell wrote to the General Manager, A G Shepherd, saying that 'whilst you were interstate, I took the liberty of having a few words with Mr Drew on personnel matters, and following this discussion, I think it would be very useful if he could let me have his comments on ... training courses for the staff, the calibre of Branch members between the ages of 40 and 50 years and the potential of officers aged between 24 and 40 years and the grading of officers'.[72] The Chief Manager's response was one of indignation, notifying the Chairman that he would inform the whole board of the request saying that 'any statement of information obtained from the management by any individual Trustee was also to be furnished to every other member of the board'.[73]

Nevertheless, the General Manager sent Bakewell's request to his assistant who forwarded it to the personnel manager. On 12 March Shepherd replied to Bakewell and the Board of Trustees that very little training was available for the staff and that training was 'carried out as opportunity presents itself'. Moreover, he said the bank did not have a specific program to select its more capable officers but rather had them involved throughout the bank and, at that moment, they were engaged in the 'inauguration of the new [computer] system and in the introduction of Bankcard', and to shift them to specific training programs was deemed by the General Manager as 'highly dangerous to the bank's success in this area'.[74] The report noted that 'officers of high calibre and potential' were 'spread very thinly when the magnitude and wide range of the business is understood.'[75] In terms of technical expertise General Manager Shepherd indicated that innovation came from above, saying that there is 'a rule that the Deputy General Manager will act as Chairman of all internal committees and the Chief Manager, Banking shall be a member of every committee dealing with proposals regarding banking operations. I would wish these practices to continue'.[76]

The General Manager's reply showed not just an over-sensitivity to the request into the training of the staff (or the lack thereof) but a resentment that the Chairman was making such an inquiry. The implied assumption was that the Chairman was acting at the behest of the Premier. The reply again exposed the raw nerve touched by the previous findings of Marks and Scott's report on the bank's lack of modern practice in regard to staff training and development.

No-confidence motion against Premier Dunstan
The Savings Bank's distrust of both Bakewell and Dunstan saw the board turn to the Liberal Party for protection. On 10 February 1976 opposition Leader Tonkin moved that the House 'no longer have confidence in the Premier and Government of this State'.[77] In supporting his motion, Tonkin began by citing 'the matters that have come to light following the appointment of Mr R D Bakewell (Director of the Premier's Department) as Chairman of the Board of Trustees of the Savings Bank of South Australia, and of Mr E H Crimes, the former Labor member for Spence, as a trustee are so serious that no lesser motion will suffice'.[78] Tonkin then outlined his criticism of these appointments as 'jobs for the boys' and as a concerted effort to control the Savings Bank Board.[79]

Tonkin reiterated the case made in private by the Savings Bank to the Premier over the government appointments to the board and the bank's opposition to Marks and Scott's report. Tonkin noted that cabinet approval for the external inquiry was made without 'any prior reference to the existing trustees' and that the Trustees, when they had received the findings, pointed out 'the several contradictions in the report' and there was 'disagreement as to who was responsible for meeting the fee payable'.[80] Tonkin noted that despite factual weaknesses in the report the government was moving stealthily on its recommendations to integrate the Savings Bank, State Bank and Industries Assistance Corporation activities, 'with funds being able to transfer freely between each section of the one organisation'.[81]

In his reply, Dunstan implied that he knew where Tonkin had got his confidential information from, and he contended that unlike Playford, he had never directed the Savings Bank to invest in any way, and that:

> Whoever wrote that brief and gave it to the Leader, did not tell him some of the essential background and that is unfortunate for the Leader ... At no time have I given a single direction to the board of Trustees of the Savings Bank on where their investment should go ... before the terms of reference were agreed on, the Chairman of each bank discussed them with me. The inquiry then proceeded. We received a first-phase report, which I found unsatisfactory. It did not cover the terms of reference and, after consulting with the bank Chairman I asked for further work to be done to complete the assignment that had been made. Further material was sent to me, and that was discussed with

the Chairmen of the two banks, who both pointed to several errors in the report, and some unsatisfactory features of it, in their view. I accepted their advice and told Sir James Marks and Sir Walter Scott that we did not intend to proceed further.[82]

Deputy Premier Des Corcoran tried to turn the political attack back on the opposition by noting that Sir Arthur Rymill was both head of the Bank of Adelaide and a prominent member of the Liberal Party, and maybe this had something to do with the Liberal's opposition to the integration of the public banks. He added that, as 'Sir Arthur Rymill is Chairman of the board of the Bank of Adelaide he is afraid that this move may have some effect on that bank's operations and so is every other private bank. What the Leader and Deputy Leader of the Opposition have said this afternoon is akin to the suggestion that as depositors they should "take your money out of the Savings Bank and the State Bank of South Australia and put it into a private bank"'.[83]

The Opposition's no-confidence motion was lost on party lines but the resistance to the integration saw Premier Dunstan retreat from his plans to merge the two banks. It was clear to the Labor Party from this incident that there was strong opposition from members of the Board of Trustees and management of the Savings Bank to working with the State Bank and that they had been quite willing to leak material to the Liberal Party. As well, there was considerable opposition from the business community and from the media to the merger. The *Advertiser*, which had interlocking directorship with the Bank of Adelaide (notably Sir Arthur Rymill was its Deputy Chair and was Chair of the Bank of Adelaide board), said that placing Robert Bakewell on the Savings Bank Board was just an attempt by the government 'to take control of the $750 million funds of the Savings Bank'.[84]

Given the resistance to the integration of the public banks, it is not surprising that Premier Dunstan, in the Chifley Memorial Lecture in late July 1976, described Adelaide as a city under the sway of a 'financial Royal Family'.[85] He said that 'the three bulwarks of conservatism in South Australia, the Bank of Adelaide, the *Advertiser* and the SA Brewing Company, are bound together by common directors and family ties. The three companies have harmony of interest at board level. The 15 men who sit on the boards of those three companies in single or multiple capacities hold 98 directorships between them in almost every top South Australian company'.[86]

Co-operation

Despite the growing hostility to a merger the two public banks did agree to continue to co-operate on mutually advantageous projects. By the end of 1976 the boards of the State Bank and the Savings Bank agreed to establish a joint committee to discuss co-operation between the banks.[87] The joint committee comprised the chairman of each bank and one other board member of each bank plus the respective general managers. The committee's first meeting was on 29 April 1976 and it explored mutually advantageous arrangements. In October 1976 the two banks agreed to co-operation between their branches in Robe and Kingston, including the use of a State Bank officer within the Savings Bank.[88] As well, the banks developed a credit card facility known as Bankcard, which they jointly provided as of October

1975. Further, the State Bank was given access to the computer network of the Savings Bank.

Outside financial forces for change
Having defended their independence from Dunstan's merger plans, both the Savings Bank and the State Bank were then confronted by fundamental alterations in world financial markets. In August 1971 the international financial market was fundamentally changed with the collapse of the Bretton Woods Monetary Agreement and the subsequent destablisation of the Australian currency. For the public banks in South Australia this seemed quite remote, yet within a decade both banks were placed under pressure to abandon their conservatism and embrace the open market. Nevertheless, in many respects the 1970s was a period of business as usual for the banks. For instance in 1976, the Savings Bank continued its support of public enterprise, with a loan of $3 million to ETSA.[89] Loans to statutory authorities and public bodies included $900,000 to the SA Meat Corporation, $2.5 million to the Pipeline Authority, $500,000 to the Adelaide Festival Centre and $5.5 million to the Housing Trust.[90]

Similarly, 1977 began as usual with plans for the Savings Bank Trustees' annual tasks. These included presenting the bank's awards for community services, preparing the arts, sports and community sponsorships, evaluating the candidates for the overseas scholarships for teachers, and preparing the school student prizes.[91] It was reported to the board that the Royal Show sponsorship was to cost $7,300 for the year, which was in keeping with the usual expenditure.[92] The Trustees also set aside $1,500 to promote Her Majesty Queen Elizabeth's Silver Jubilee appeal for the purchase of a grand organ for the Festival Theatre. The board again sponsored the State cricket team with its cash for catches being set at $20 each for the 1977/78 first-class cricket season.[93] Following the successful sponsorship of the 1975 inaugural Festival of Arts youth program, called Come Out, the bank sponsored the event again in 1977.[94]

In March 1977 the Trustees again lamented the Savings Bank's inability to provide overdraft facilities. A report to the Trustees noted that when the Savings Bank in 1973 was prevented from offering 'overdraft facilities to its customers' it had as an alternative provided business credit cheque accounts but these had proved 'to be ineffective', with the bank continually losing 'all kinds of accounts to other banks'.[95] The General Manager indicated that the Savings Bank was at a disadvantage in comparison to its Victorian counterpart which could offer overdraft facilities while the Savings Bank had to rely on operating through the State Bank for overdrafts. He believed that this was unsatisfactory because customers preferred to do all their banking with one institution.

In 1978, the Savings Bank management discovered that the Rural Bank of New South Wales was having significant success using women to market loans, under the slogan the 'feminine touch in banking'.[96] The experiment had proven highly successful in terms of an increase in business and in improving the image of the bank. The Trustees decided to investigate the matter with the possibility of copying the exercise. On 16 March the bank proudly announced it had launched a Women's Information Service for loans targeted at women customers. The campaign cost $121,150 to promote banking services for women.[97] The bank was, at the same time, equally keen to promote its continued support for the 'Miss Sportsgirl Quest' and the women's mid-week squash competition.[98]

State Bank

In the face of a more uncertain global financial future the State Bank decided to compete more intensely for local commercial business. In 1975 the State Bank moved into the field of credit cards, visa and Bankcard and bought a 5 per cent share in Beneficial Finance Corporation to provide specialist services to its customers. In 1975 the State Bank's total income was $20 million, rising to $30 million in 1977,[99] despite South Australia suffering the worst drought in its recorded history. The bank also had a 51 per cent rise in its net profit, which was $3,322,814.[100] In 1977 the State Bank Board retained a hands-on approach to lending and this can be gauged from the following Minutes of the 21 December 1976. In attendance were G F Seaman (Chairman), J R Dunford (Deputy Chairman), E R Howells, R D E Bakewell and A F Kneebone. Minutes of the previous meeting were confirmed. Then a list of applications for the Commonwealth-State Housing agreements were dutifully agreed to. The General Manager provided an account of funds at call in Elder's Finance to the total of $65 million. A balance sheet was then presented of fortnightly trading showing deposits at hand being $118 million; overdraft advances at $70 million; home building fund at $219 million; investments $12.7 million plus debenture stocks to Beneficial Finance, ETSA, SA Gas, securities totalling $58 million. The fortnightly statement of major accounts, Apcel, SA Fishermen's Co-op (SAFCOL) and Foster Clark were then received and individually discussed.[101]

What then followed was an extensive report of the finances of the Barossa Co-operative Winery and its request for 'seasonal accommodation' as the Reserve Bank had raised concerns over its lending which stood at $5.4 million.[102] It was recommended that the matter be deferred until more detail was obtained on the nature of the loan guarantees. The Orlit Account was then examined. The bank was keen to expand into the building industry and saw this account as increasing its business reach in this field. Orlit had assets and liabilities of just over $19 million and its profits had risen from $421,487 in 1973 to $1.5 million in 1976. The company was described as operating housing construction in all states, bar Tasmania. Due to the rise in interest rates as a consequence of the devaluation of the Australian dollar, the company wanted to restructure and sought a stand-by facility of $2 million. This was agreed to as long as Orlit provided a $5 million letter of credit.[103]

Next item for consideration was the Myponga Co-operative which sought a loan of $33,500 to upgrade its plant, and following an outline of its financial position, this was approved. Then followed an examination of the Loxton Co-operative Winery & Distillery which requested a loan of $119,000 to build a new cement building to accommodate staff and cellar wine sales. Again this was approved.[104] The report supporting the loan indicated that the Loxton Co-operative had concluded a successful year raising its profit from $733,000 to $1.9 million and was now under the 'dynamic' new manager, Mr Linn, who had 'considerable drive in the selling field'.[105] It was noted in passing that $400,000 of the rise in profit had been at the expense of growers.[106]

Dunstan a friend of the Savings Bank

While the State Bank was seeking to expand its commercial business from a low capital base, the Savings Bank was continually restrained from moving into the corporate arena. In 1977, the Savings Bank Board approached the Premier to extend its services to those of its customers who changed their accounts from a personal to company basis. Dunstan had been initially suspicious of this change when it was made some years before, considering that it was only going to benefit the most wealthy rural families. The Savings Bank had worked assiduously to convince the Premier that their intentions were based on the principle of equity. The bank pointed out that the trading banks were poaching their clients when they changed their status from personal to company accounts and this related to small rather than big rural businesses. As such, their request was a defensive move based on fairness rather than an offensive campaign to move fully into corporate lending.

When presenting the bill to the parliament Premier Dunstan said that he 'did not put the amendment forward when they were originally proposed by the bank board at the time when Mr Jeffery was Chairman of the board ... After a thorough examination, I put them forward now as they specifically supported the small family'.[107] The opposition, however, saw the move as threatening the private trading banks and inexplicably as a back-door move at amalgamation. The leader of the opposition, David Tonkin, said the amendment would 'remove the limitations on trustees and enable the bank to lend money to commercial bodies, by definition, as well as to individuals ... I have been in touch with several trading banks in this State and have obtained their strong opinion that the passage of this legislation will put the Savings Bank of South Australia on a similar footing to that of the average trading bank. This Bill is a clear and blatant first step towards the amalgamation of the two banks'.[108]

The wording of the bill said that the bank was to offer 'extended services' and this terminology was opposed by the opposition. Heini Becker asked 'was it the intention of the government to enable the Savings Bank of South Australia openly to enter normal trading bank operations? That is what we want an assurance from the government about'.[109]

Dunstan replied that:

> It is not the intention of the Savings Bank to enter normal trading bank business at all. The reason for this proposal have been specifically given and they are confined to that area ... In a changeover of operation from an individual basis to a company basis in order to extend facilities to those people is not simply protecting the existing business of the bank: it may involve some extension of business. However, the aim of the section is certainly not to allow the Savings Bank to enter into general trading bank business in any significant way.[110]

Given that the idea had come from the Savings Bank, Dunstan was surprised at the vehemency of the opposition's response to the bill. The opposition in the Upper House opposed the bill arguing it was turning the Savings Bank into a trading bank without Reserve Bank supervision. In defence of the bill, the government again claimed that Sir Arthur Rymill (who was no longer a member of parliament) was behind the opposition's motion to oppose the bill. This accusation was denied by Murray Hill who said with indignation that 'Sir Arthur Rymill has not been in touch with me for about 12 months'.[111] The opposition moved and passed an amendment to the bill which struck out the words 'to extend', and this saw 10/10 division with the Speaker casting his vote for the amendment. The government then moved that the bill be the subject of a conference between the two houses.

Dunstan said he opposed the amendment, saying 'I cannot imagine anything more absurd than this amendment ... The effect of this is to prevent the bank from acting in other than a purely protective way about existing business. The effect is, and is intended to be, to prevent the bank from acting as an effective competition in relation to its business as compared to other banks'.[112] The consultation between the two houses saw an amendment agreed to which gave the bank the ability to expand its lending accounts but only to small business. The Opposition amendment said that 'to extend the services of the bank to that body, where in the opinion of the trustees, that body is a small business only, the proprietors of which are persons who could normally be expected to establish accounts with the bank'.[113] After debate over the wording, the motion was passed by both houses of parliament on 8 December 1977.

The Savings Bank was now in an intriguing position as it had until then been suspicious of the Labor government over its intention to merge the two public banks. It had looked to the Liberal Party to defend its interests but now found that the opposition was not prepared to allow the Savings Bank the legislative room to compete against the private banks. By 1978 it was quite evident that the Savings Bank was seeking to place itself in the field of corporate lending and personal loans and that Premier Dunstan was prepared to back such a move. There is a historical irony in the situation that just as the bank and the Premier were coming to like minds Dunstan's term as leader was to be prematurely cut short because of ill health, brought on by the death of his second wife. Dunstan's personal tragedy was noted by the Trustees when in the minutes of the meeting of 16 October 1978 it was recorded that the board had sent a letter of condolence from all the Trustees 'to Premier Dunstan at the passing of his wife Ms Adele Koh'.[114] On 8 February 1979 Premier Dunstan collapsed in the parliament and from his hospital bed he announced his resignation as Premier and as a member of parliament. He was replaced by Des Corcoran as Premier. Three months later, banking in South Australia was to be fundamentally transformed by the collapse of the largest private trading bank, the Bank of Adelaide.

The Bank of Adelaide falls
On 9 May 1979, the stock market was awash with rumours that the Financial Corporation of Australia (FCA), an arm of the Bank of Adelaide, was in trouble. On that day there was an abnormal run on the Bank of Adelaide. On 10 May 1979 the Adelaide Stock Exchange officially queried the bank about its position. The Bank of Adelaide had, since February 1979, been seeking to find a way of dealing with the losses which FCA had accrued on inter-state property speculation. The FCA had shareholder funds of $53 million and the Bank of Adelaide had shareholder funds of $67.7 million, but the FCA had borrowed $337 million for its investments and needed somewhere between $30 million and $60 million just to avoid breaching its trust deeds. The FCA, headed by an entrepreneurial banker, Ray Turner, had been investing in property in Sydney and Perth. The downturn in these markets left the FCA exposed, an exposure which the Bank of Adelaide was unable to cover.[115]

On 21 May 1979 a formal agreement was reached between the Bank of Adelaide and the ANZ group in which the ANZ would acquire the shares of the Bank of

Adelaide with an exchange of 15 ANZ shares for 44 Bank of Adelaide shares. The deal struck with the ANZ, at its simplest level, was valuing the Bank of Adelaide shares at $1.25 each, which (on the face of it) was below the market price of the shares, estimated to be $1.70. This prompted a shareholder outcry and extensive media debate. The intention was that this agreement would be then put to a meeting of shareholders as soon as possible. The next day Sir Arthur Rymill, after 27 years as Chairman of Directors of the Bank of Adelaide, resigned.

A group of shareholders pushed for and obtained an inquiry into the ANZ deal and the reason for the losses. After this delay, there was an extraordinary General meeting of the Bank of Adelaide shareholders held in the Adelaide Town Hall on the 15 October 1979.[116]

In the meantime there was a change of government. Premier Des Corcoran called a snap election on 15 September 1979, which the Labor Party lost with a swing of 11 per cent to the Liberal Party and David Tonkin was elected as Premier. He was reluctant to rescue the Bank of Adelaide or to express a view over the competing claims on the value of the Bank of Adelaide share price.

In the build up to the public meeting, the Bank of Adelaide held discussions with the Reserve Bank on how to manage the meeting.[117] It was decided to present only the ANZ option and to exclude any discussion of an overseas buyer. It was left to Sir Arthur Rymill to present the case for the ANZ offer, which he did by pointing out that the directors 'were morally and legally bound' by the Reserve Bank to accept the ANZ offer. Rymill indicated to the meeting that the two major shareholders, John Martin & Co and the AMP (who between them owned 20 per cent of the shares) fully supported the ANZ takeover. After a long meeting, notable for its shareholder anger at how the bank had got itself in such a dilemma and for the distress shown by some shareholders over the historical loss, there was an 88 per cent acceptance of the takeover offer.[118]

There was a final chapter in the saga to unfold. A group of shareholders, the most prominent of which was a Mount Gambier businessman, Alan Scott, made a legal challenge to the decision. This led to a hearing before the Master of the Supreme Court, J Boehm, in early November 1979. The basis of the challenge to the ANZ takeover was that a better price could have been obtained if the bank had been more diligent in its pursuit of other options. Elliott Johnston QC, representing the dissident shareholder group, questioned Sir Arthur Rymill as to why other alternatives to that of the ANZ were not pursued with more vigour. Sir Rymill's response was that the Reserve Bank directive had tied the hands of the directors and that the ANZ offer was the best that was available in Australia.[119] Elliott Johnson accused Rymill of withholding information from the shareholders over Norman Young's role in organising a rescue of the Bank of Adelaide.[120] The dissident shareholder action was withdrawn only days before the ANZ offer lapsed. On Thursday, 6 December, 1979 the Bank of Adelaide was removed from the stock exchange, ending its 114 years of banking history in South Australia.

The demise of the Bank of Adelaide left a trading bank vacuum in South Australia. Nevertheless, the Tonkin government was unwilling to allow the Savings Bank or the State Bank to fill this gap. Rather, Tonkin in direct contradiction to the stand he took against Dunstan, sought to exert more control over the Savings Bank.

The State Bank

The State Bank was keen to fill the vacuum left by the demise of the Bank of Adelaide and sought to expand its commercial activities. However, the State Bank's lending was still dominated by its rural roots and the extent of its ambitions was kept in check by its small deposit base. The foray into corporate lending gave the managers an opportunity at risk management. Nonetheless, the board of management kept a watchful eye on the managers' corporate lending.

A snapshot of the growth and diversity of the State Bank's activities, after the fall of the Bank of Adelaide, can be seen from the following record of the State Bank board meeting of 15 January 1980. In attendance were G F Seaman, J R Dunsford, Professor K J Hancock and W F Nankivell. The meeting went through the usual overview of assets, the monthly account, insurance claims, staff matters, maturing investment and then discussed special cases. The General Manager, Brian Robertson, reported on a request for an over-draft facility to A H Lightburn indicating that the company was formed in 1919 and was trading profitably until 1976 when it ran into difficulties, making losses of $379,000. In 1977 Lightburn had dispensed with its unprofitable products and concentrated on concrete mixers, hydraulic jacks and washing machines and spin dryers.[121] As a result of the restructuring the company believed it would run at an annual profit of $500,000 and for the first five months of 1979 had a profit of $144,123. It was seeking to transfer its account from the Commonwealth Trading Bank to the State Bank if a working draft of $1 million was provided. Estimated assets were $3.8 million with $1.3 million unsecured assets. The board indicated that given its concerns over the level of security that the bank would be reluctant to approve an immediate discount line of $500,000 and so deferred the matter until more evidence on the borrowers security could be furnished to it.[122]

At the same meeting a loan to facilitate the Red Comb Co-operative Society's takeover of Scholz Chemicals was sought. Red Comb requested a $400,000 loan to purchase Scholz who was a chemical manufacturer at Gawler for horticultural, agricultural and veterinary products.[123] This would make Red Comb's total requirements from the bank to be $1.5 million.[124] The bank estimated its assets at $2.9 million and its subsidiary, Farmer Brown, at $2.9 million. Scholz Chemicals assets were recorded as $3.9 million. The loan was approved.[125]

A good deal of the board's monthly business, nevertheless, was taken up with the co-operatives, who made up the State Bank's largest borrowers and whose position was politically sensitive. For instance, in February 1980, the board lent $934,000 to the thriving Dairy Vale Metro Co-operative, which had a profit of $1.5 million.[126] In contrast, on 1 March 1980 the board was confronted by a financial crisis at the Southern Vale Co-operative. What made this issue of some concern to the board was that the bank had received adverse publicity over what was depicted as undue financial pressure placed by the bank on the co-operative. The consensus of the board was that the Co-operative was in such a poor financial position it was up to the government to guarantee the Southern Vale Co-operative or allow the bank to follow sound banking practice and place it in the hands of liquidators. At its next meeting the board was informed that the government had come to the rescue of the Co-operative and undertaken to fund the bank $400,000 as a sufficient amount 'to pay the growers an average of 63.4% of legislated prices for grapes delivered to the Co-operative during the 1980 vintage'.[127] The board agreed to the government's rescue plan.

Berri Fruit Juices Co-operative Ltd, which had loans of $2.3 million, requested a loan of $120,000 for acquiring property for storage space to complement blow-moulding of bottles, pasteurising, cordial and peel manufacturing plants.[128] This was readily approved. SAFCOL, which had loans of $2.7 million sought an extension of $400,000 on its overdraft to extend its Wright Street premises and $55,000 to install racking and the purchase of a fork lift truck for its cold rooms.[129] This was approved. Berri Co-operative Packing Union Limited, with loans of $350,850 applied for a loan of $347,000 for the purpose of a new packing house, offices and laboratory. This request was approved.[130] The Barossa Co-operative with loans of $3.1 million, sought an increase in loan priority up to $6.5 million with the support of the Reserve Bank. Again this was approved.[131]

Co-operatives and politics
At the beginning of July 1980 the Riverland Co-operative had become liable for $359,949 interest on overdrafts. Normally this amount would have been added to the overdraft but the government wanted to change this system and institute a 'scheme of arrangement' with the unsecured creditors.[132] The Deputy Under-Treasurer had approached the Chairman of the Board and was advised that 'the [Tonkin] government would be embarrassed in those negotiations for a scheme of arrangement if the bank included that amount in its current overdraft limit'.[133] As a result of this request the bank was asked to place in a special account $3.34 million which would be secured by the government.

The board was made conversant with the troubled financial history of the Riverland Co-operative and was furnished with board minutes from October 1979, showing that it had then requested reliable cash flow figures from the Co-operative. At that time, the bank had advised that if the Co-operative's problems continued it would need a government guarantee to meet its shortfalls. The Management Report to the board indicated that the bank's administration had little confidence in the Co-operative's assertion that it could turn the business around, saying that:

> It would seem that the people responsible for the decision to keep the cannery open and enter into the 'Project Riverland' deal are under the misguided belief that ... next year the society will turn the corner and that things will be better then. The chances of this happening are remote as a business with sales of $25 M can not hope to service a debt structure of $16 M (not to mention suspended L. P. A. loan of $2.58 M). How can it hope to achieve this when machinery is worn out and when marketing of its products is outside its control and in many lines, the profit is virtually negligible?[134]

As the State Bank saw it, the Riverland Co-operative had entered into a foolhardy agreement with growers, offering a guaranteed price of $210 a tonne for peaches based on 58 cartons of fruit per block, but was only receiving 30 to 50 cartons per tonne of fruit. Moreover, wastage was so high that around $25 per tonne of produce was ending up in the rubbish dump.[135] Fruit over 10,500 tonnes had been purchased and collected before the Co-operative saw the error in its pricing and by then the loss was in excess of $1.1 million.[136] As a result, the bank was understandably reluctant to lend any more capital to cover the $7.789 million needed to meet costs and the board decided that the Co-operative was not to be bailed out unless the government provided a full guarantee.[137]

At the 17 December 1980 board meeting it was reported that the government had supported the Riverland Fruit Producers Co-operative and had requested a further $423,000 to meet urgent creditors for which the government would take full responsibility.[138] The government indemnified the State Bank for $3.76 million against loss but for the bank this left money at risk in the 'Jon' account amounting to $1.26 million and the loss of interest on the loans and outstanding 1978 season payments of $167,000.[139] The total amount needed to be guaranteed was $5.2 million. The board heard from the receiver that the amount owing to the bank 'may be fully recoverable'.[140] The dilemma for the bank was that the receiver's estimation of the Co-operative's assets (land building, plant, etc.) were insufficient to guarantee the loan. As a consequence, the board decided to write to the Treasurer to receive a full formal 'acknowledgment of the government obligation and undertakings'.[141]

Resisting political pressure
In July 1980 Premier Tonkin wrote to the State Bank board seeking an under-write loan for the building of a Hilton hotel in Victoria Square.[142] The management considered it as too high a commercial risk for the bank to undertake a loan. Having refused the deal on commercial grounds the board was again pressured by the Premier/Treasurer to change its mind and to join a financial consortium to build the International Hilton Hotel. The proposal came before the 1979 August meeting of the board where it was presented with figures on the proposed building, indicating that its estimated cost was $39 million.[143] The construction cost provided by Fricker Brothers was broken down as follows: construction costs $26 million, design cost $3.5 million, fittings fixtures $4.2 million, financial borrowing costs $5 million.[144] On these estimations the board was reluctant to become involved.

In considering the proposal, the board noted that the security offered was, firstly, a government guarantee, secondly, a second debenture over the assets guarantee by the shareholders and developer, and lastly, a personal guarantee from the directors. The board was informed that the management placed 'little reliance on the value of the security, apart from the government guarantee'.[145] It noted that upon completion the building would be sold to the Superannuation Investment Trust for $39 million and it would be after this sale that the bank would be paid out. The motion put to the board by the Chair was that, despite the project being 'commercially unrealistic', the board resolved to 'give the matter further consideration if so requested by the Hon. Treasurer'.[146] The point at issue was not so much the political pressure but the resistance to it by the board of management.

Following the collapse of the Bank of Adelaide, the Savings Bank explored with Premier Tonkin the prospect of expanding its level of investments into the corporate sector. Tonkin told them his government was utterly opposed to allowing the bank to move into the traditional trading bank field. Instead Premier Tonkin said he wanted the power to appoint not only the Chair of the board but the Deputy Chair. As well the government wanted to have an oversight of staff levels and to appoint senior staff in the bank,[147] an attitude in stark contrast to the 'hands-off' approach Tonkin had taken when leader of the Opposition. Lew Barrett, then Chair of the board, said the board was surprised at Tonkin's change in political position, in regard to interfering in the affairs of the Savings Bank, but was prepared to discuss the amendments with the government.[148]

The bank's solicitors suggested that the bank give ground on the Deputy Chair position and compromise on its investment strategy so as to gain some ground on the bank's lending. The amendment recommended by the solicitor was to indicate that the bank should have the power to make corporate investments but these were 'for the investment of depositor's funds at adequate short term'.[149] The bank unsuccessfully argued that all it wanted to do was copy the investment practices of the public banks in Victoria. The Tonkin government was, however, only ready to allow for minor changes to the Act.

A fundamental re-think: merge to survive

The failure to gain government approval to expand its investment program saw the Savings Bank management evaluate its position and seriously consider a full merger with the State Bank. An internal report commissioned by the General Manager revealed that in 'all aspects of its business' the bank was 'losing market share'. In terms of savings bank deposits in South Australia the total percentage held by the Savings Bank stood at 50.8 per cent in 1972 but was down to 36.6 per cent in 1981. The prime reason for this fall was the increase in deposits in Building Societies and Credit Unions. In terms of all banks the Savings Bank total deposits were 32.7 per cent in 1972 falling to 28.3 per cent in 1981. Taking into consideration deposit stocks, the total deposits were 53.8 per cent in 1972 down to 49.1 per cent in 1981.[150] It was clear that to attract and keep deposits the Savings Bank would have to offer and market higher interest rate accounts.

In short, the comparative advantage which the Savings Bank established in 1945 by offering higher interest rates on deposits was being eroded by the building societies and credit unions, and by the trading/savings banks offering specific high interest savings accounts. With declining deposits the Savings Bank was having less funds to lend on housing or to statutory authorities, a problem compounded by the change to the Act in 1980 where 50 per cent of loans had to be in housing mortgages. The bank's response had been to reduce its General Reserve Fund, which fell from 5.32 per cent in 1972 to 3.82 per cent in 1981. The dilemma for the bank in this strategy was that in using its Reserve funds to provide a substantial contribution to profit the decline in the reserve ratio would eventually affect both the surplus to the government and the amount of funds available for loans.

It was in the light of these trends that the management began to explore the idea of dividing the bank along a savings/trading bank line, akin to the Commonwealth Bank. Ken Matthews prepared a paper to this effect. The expectations were that such a division would see the trading bank arm making initial loses and draining resources/capital (around 3:1) from the savings bank and would 'require a substantial change to current lending policy'. An advantage would be that 'mortgages would appear as a satisfactory percentage of deposits and could justify a reduction in mortgage lending'.[151] The bank, however, would have to switch into 'higher earning assets' in 'maintaining [its] profitability'.[152]

Financial deregulation

Following his investigation, Ken Matthew, as Acting General Manager, wrote to Premier Tonkin seeking further changes to its Act which would give the bank a more commercial focus, principally through bills of exchange. The letter defended this move by arguing that since Treasurer Howard, on behalf of the federal government, had recently deregulated the savings bank market the Savings Bank had now lost its comparative advantage.[153] Financial deregulation meant that the Savings Bank had to compete more with the trading (savings) banks just to retain its market share. 'I do not perceive of the bank as another trading bank; however the trustees must be responsive to changing market circumstances'.[154]

In August 1981 Premier Tonkin wrote to the Savings Bank expressing concern over the current amalgamation of trading banks and indicated his desire for the Savings Bank and the State Bank to undertake discussions to 'ascertain what steps might be taken to provide as efficient and effective services to the community through both banking institutions'.[155] The Premier and Minister for Trade and Industry, Dean Brown, also wrote to the bank informing them that the State Bank was investigating the potential of a merchant banking subsidiary.[156]

Under pressure from the banks, Premier Tonkin was coming around to the bank's point of view that the Federal deregulation of the savings banks had altered banking but it was not prepared to take the step of an amalgamation. Instead, only minor amendments to the Savings Bank Act were permitted. In January 1982 the Act was amended, raising the maximum amount that could be lent on an unsecured basis from $5,000 to $15,000.[157] In thanking the Premier for his prompt action on the Savings Bank's request, General Manager P J Simmons wrote that the increase in the overdraft amount 'will allow the bank to compete with the other financial intermediaries in a more equitable basis and assist in the retention of existing business and the gathering of new business'.[158]

The amendments to the Act also allowed the Savings Bank to accept bills of exchange and to take out shares in local companies, with the approval of the Treasurer. The clauses that were of most concern for opposition leader John Bannon were firstly, that the changes to employment provisions increased the number of prescribed officers and decreased the power of the Appeals Committee to hear disputes over promotions. Premier Tonkin said the changes were needed to give the Trustees more options in 'flexible manpower planning'.[159]

The second issue of concern to the opposition was the removal of investment provisions for lending only in South Australia. Of particular worry for opposition leader Bannon was the openness of the new investment clauses which meant that the bank would be able to lend on residential mortgages outside of South Australia. Bannon moved an amendment, supported by the government, that the bank 'not lend on residential properties outside of South Australia'.[160]

In speaking to his amendments, John Bannon praised the 'thrift' role of the bank, and spoke highly of the institution. He noted that the Savings Bank of South Australia had assets of $1,300,000,000 and current housing loans were $446,700,000, with deposits of $1,200,000,000 and that the government was to collect $4,300,000 that year after collecting $2,700,000 the previous year. Moreover, he said the 'bank has another important function as far as the community is concerned, which dates back to its very origins in the middle of last century and that is, as a repository for the savings of the ordinary people of this State. Indeed, the Savings Bank of South Australia has been a traditionally appropriate repository for a vast bulk of the population's savings from the very first year when, as children, they started saving through the school bank, through the rest of their lives'.[161]

Bannon's emphasis on the Savings Bank as a traditional savings bank was ironic timing as the Savings Bank Board had finally decided that it wanted to be a joint savings bank/trading bank, and wrote to Premier Tonkin seeking approval to merge with the State Bank. The Savings Bank considered that if it was to change, that change should be fundamental. As such, the objective of the new bank was to be a 'full service' and 'commercial' bank.[162] Premier Tonkin, however, procrastinated on the merger, only moving tentatively in the direction of amalgamation before he called the State elections on 6th November 1982.

By 1982 the two banks were looking to merge in a climate of political and financial change which eventually saw the financial market deregulated. The two banks desired to modernise and protect their market share but they were now in an era of higher risk than when this idea was first muted in 1965 and promoted by Dunstan in 1976. In 1982 Bannon had floated the idea of a public bank to fill the gap left by the Bank of Adelaide and was keen to foster the merger, but was wary of being seen as too close to the bank for fear of a repetition of 1976. No-one seemed to understand or take cognisance of the reasons for the fall of the Bank of Adelaide and what it implied for a bank spreading out from its regional base. Similarly, no one seemed to see parallels with the appointment of the entrepreneurial banker Tim Marcus Clark with the experience of the Bank of Adelaide subsidiary, the Finance Corporation of Australia and its 'over-optimistic' manager, Ray Turner. The next half of the book tells how the culture of the banks was transformed and how this destroyed the combined bank.

Part II

Telling Times

5

Open for business: the new destroys the old

The reader will perceive a different structuring of the narrative in this section of the book. In part, this change is due to the shift in the empirical foundation, from bank records to two public enquiries, Samuel Jacobs' Royal Commission into the State Bank of South Australia and Auditor-General Kenneth MacPherson's investigation into the State Bank of South Australia (SBSA). This chapter is also structured around a dialogue between Premier Bannon's political reasoning behind the formation of the SBSA and Commissioner Jacobs' legal reasoning on the failings in the bank's composition.

Loss of faith in the public sector: embracing the modern private market
The vacuum created by the demise of the Bank of Adelaide was the impetus for the merger of the Savings Bank and the State Bank. The Tonkin government procrastinated on merging the banks and it was left to newly elected Premier Bannon to enact the legislation which saw the banks amalgamate. The merger occurred in a period of declining support for public sector endeavours and a stagnating local economy. The process of merger talks occurred in the lead up to the 1982 election where the Labor Party under John Bannon sought to capitalise on the faltering economy and the seemingly floundering Tonkin government.

In 1982, when the two banks made their request to Premier Tonkin to merge, the South Australian economy lagged behind the rest of Australia. The Tonkin government espoused the ideology that the problems with the State's economy were due to 'big government' which, according to economic orthodoxy, 'crowded out' private investment. As such, Tonkin set about reducing the public sector to give room to the private sector.

In keeping with this ideology the Tonkin government decided that statutory authorities would have to justify their existence before a government-dominated Upper House Committee. In November 1981 Tonkin introduced a bill to have statutory authorities referred, by their respective ministers, to a Legislative Council select committee.[1] It would be up to the minister to recommend which of the statutory authorities would be referred to this Legislative Council select committee.

Opposition leader John Bannon argued that the intention behind the bill was not modernising the public sector. Rather, the bill had little to do with public sector efficiency and accountability and more to do with both ministerial patronage and power over statutory authorities.[2] The real stumbling block to the bill were government members in the Legislative Council, particularly, Ren De Garis, who wanted to expand parliamentary rather than government power over statutory authorities.[3] In face of the divisions in its own ranks the Tonkin government retreated, but in doing so came to hold the position that statutory enterprises should be independent of both the government and the parliament.

In this new ideology the public sector was seen as the problem, not the solution, to the state's economic development. The decline in public sector expenditure, however, combined with the failure of the private sector to come rushing into the supposed space, saw the South Australian economy languish. The onset of a national recession and widespread drought in 1982 exacerbated the crisis in the State's economy and set the stage for a close election. It was a combination of both the government losing, and the opposition winning that produced the 1982 election outcome. John Bannon became the new Premier.

Bannon and making the state serve the private sector
In 1982 the Labor opposition had devised a strategy whereby public funds would be pooled for private-led investment initiatives. At its simplest level, the opposition's economic strategy was to use good housekeeping to accumulate finances to be lent to the private sector on commercial grounds. In his political rounds with the business community, Bannon said that he had discovered that, with the demise of the Bank of Adelaide, there was no substantial trading bank head office in South Australia and business leaders had to fly interstate for funds or were ignored by the banks and financial institutions. He stated that:

> I was concerned about bodies like the AMP. There was no real investment in South Australia at all, at that stage, and they had their local board. I remember meeting them, and they said, well our problem is that we're here as a brief to the AMP and our problem is that there was no interest in South Australia. Everywhere you went, you were getting this kind of reaction, we had just been written out of the financial calculations. The conclusion was, okay there had to be self help we had resources here, we had investment funds and let's mobilise them.[4]

1982 election
Unbeknown to Bannon the Savings Bank and the State Bank had jointly approached Tonkin requesting a merger. Ever cognisant of the 1976 experience of Dunstan, in May 1982 Bannon tentatively tested the waters on his idea of pooling public sector finances for private sector investment. He spoke of 'mobilising the State's financial sector' and of 'creating a SA Enterprise fund to stimulate economic activity'.[5] Bannon's May Economic Statement went on to say that a Labor government would 'ensure a closer co-ordination (and integration) of the services of the State Bank and the Savings Bank of South Australia'.[6] Bannon gave the idea an electoral embellishment in his November election campaign speech, when he said that the closer co-ordination between the public banks would be 'an engine for economic growth',[7] a rhetorical phrase that was to come back to haunt him in the Royal Commission into the State Bank of South Australia (1992). In defence of his rhetoric Bannon said that the phrase 'engine of economic growth' was:

simply that financial resources could be mobilised to invest in the restructuring of South Australian industry. It was apparent that we were in rust bucket conditions and that the financial institutions in the East were not interested in, nor knowledgeable enough to do anything with industry. We had been written out of the financial calculations, and the conclusion was that there had to be self help, we had resources here, we had investment funds and let's mobilise them. That's what I meant by an engine of economic growth.[8]

The ALP's 1982 election strategy of appealing to the business sector went some way to disarming small business which had vigorously campaigned against the Corcoran government in 1979 (under the slogan, 'Stop the job rot').[9] The strategy placed the Liberal Party at a disadvantage in that the ALP was offering an alternative to the Tonkin government's indecisiveness over economic policy and its public sector job reduction strategy.

Moreover, in keeping with the Americanisation of Australian politics, the ALP set about constructing their campaign around John Bannon as the leader. His marathon running was now used to imply dedication to solving South Australia's problems in the long run. Bannon was presented as a sound economic manager and as a tough calculating political strategist (especially for his tactic of isolating the Left in the ALP, notably Peter Duncan). This image was quite distinct from that of his student political days where he was noted for his debating skills and for his passion for a cause. This transformation in image is captured by a conservative contemporary of his, the novelist Nicholas Hasluck, who drew the contrast between Bannon the student debater and the political leader, when he recalled that in student politics, Bannon was a 'fiendish' opponent, who was a 'fiery orator with an unparted 'pushback' hair style and a purposeful glint in his eye, a far cry from the dulcet-voiced Premier of today'.[10]

A neutral public sector: 'doing more with less'

When Bannon was elected Premier he told his first Cabinet meeting that the ministers should resist the temptation to purge their departments. Instead he told the new ministers to take the high moral ground and treat the public service as neutral, relying on their expertise to promote growth. Nevertheless, Bannon argued that the public sector had to 'do more with less',[11] an outcome which would be achieved by more efficient use of resources. What this phrase was meant to signify was that the Bannon government did not intend to reintroduce Dunstan's state-led policies on the economy. Rather, the phrase was aimed principally at the business community, indicating that the new government was looking to the private sector to stimulate an economic recovery in South Australia.

Merging to modernise

Upon winning the election Bannon received a joint congratulatory letter from the boards of the Savings Bank and the State Bank which, to his surprise, also included a request for a merger. Premier Bannon replied that he favoured such a move and agreed that the two banks should exercise responsibility for their merger.[12] To facilitate the amalgamation a small working group was established, known as the Merger Advisory Group (MAG). The MAG was dominated by representatives from the old banks. It comprised three persons from each of the banks, from the Savings

Bank, Lew Barrett (Chair of the Board of Trustees) with A G McEwin (Deputy Chair) and P J Simmons (Chief General Manager); from the State Bank, Professor Keith Hancock (Chair of the Board), Justice O'Loughlin (Board member) and P E Byrnes (General Manager) and three members from the state public service, namely, Mr Guerin, the head of the Department of Premier and Cabinet, R D Barnes, from Treasury, and Ian Kowalick, from the Department of State Development.

Merger: a 'bold new approach'
In its final annual report of 1983 the Savings Bank of South Australia gave prominence to the announcement of the merger saying that:

> On the 18th of May, [1983] the Premier of South Australia, the Honourable John Bannon, announced that his government firmly supported the proposal by the Savings Bank and the State Bank to initiate early action to amalgamate the two banks. He also announced the formation of a special working group to facilitate consideration of questions which will necessarily come before the Government.[13]

The 1983 State Bank annual report spoke of the merger saying that 'the proposed amalgamation will result in the bank being the biggest in South Australia, with approximately 34 per cent of all bank deposits, and employing 2,500 people'.[14] The report said that the bank looked forward in the words of the Premier, 'to bring about a bold new approach to banking which will benefit all sections of the South Australian economy'.[15] The Savings Bank carried over to the new bank assets of $1,545 billion, and the old State Bank brought with it assets of nearly $918,043,000, so that at the time of the launch it was reported that the new bank would have total assets of $2.6 billion.[16] In April 1984 the Savings Bank of South Australia had acquired Beneficial Finance Corporation at a price of $50.5 million, of which the old State Bank held an 8.6 per cent share.[17]

How to be a modern bank – be fully commercial
The MAG considered that the best way that the new bank could become modern was to be like the major banks in Australia. Kowalick recalled that the thinking on the MAG was that the new bank would, 'as far as practicable, operate in circumstances comparable to national operating banks'.[18] As such, it was decided by the MAG to exclude the term 'savings' from the new bank's title; it was therefore decided to call the bank the State Bank of South Australia. The intention of the MAG was that the new bank should be founded on a legislative base 'that would enable it to become an active, innovative participant in the South Australian economy and financial markets' and function 'as closely as possible to a fully commercial enterprise, competing in the market place'.[19] In keeping with this objective, the MAG sought to ensure its charter expressed a dominant commercial focus and limited government involvement in the running of the bank. This condition was made more acute by the Savings Bank Trustees' long memory of the efforts of Playford, Dunstan and Tonkin to influence the lending and administration of the Savings Bank. The MAG set tight restrictions on the manner by which government could give advice to the new bank.

There was general agreement between the MAG and the government that the bank should be an independent entity. In the eyes of the MAG, the government's role was to be like a passive shareholder, to appoint the board and then leave the bank to achieve its commercial objective. Bannon was sympathetic with the notion that the bank should be commercial and relatively autonomous from the government but had some reservations over how independent the bank should be and indicated that the new Act should at least allow for formal consultation between the board and the Treasurer. The debate in the parliament reinforced the perception that the bank was to be independent of the government of the day.

Commercialising the new bank
Shortly after the bank's last annual report was tabled in the parliament, the debate began on the draft bill. On 28 October 1983 the MAG had sent the draft bill to the government and the next month the bill was presented to the parliament to create an Act for the State Bank of South Australia. In the parliamentary debate Premier Bannon echoed the ideology of the MAG when he said that the new bank 'should operate in conditions as comparable as practicable with those in which private sector counterparts operate'.[20] Similarly, opposition leader John Olsen agreed with the private focus, adding that the bank should be so highly commercial that it could spread its lending outside of South Australia. He added that the new bank should create 'a wide range of lending and other financial services, and it would have a greater capacity to offer full international banking services and [should] have no commercial advantage over its private sector counterparts'.[21]

In supporting the commercialisation of the bank, Olsen raised his concerns over whether the government would intervene too heavily in its commercial operations of the bank, and in particular over the appointment of the board, the policy direction of the bank, and finally, over the siphoning-off of profits to pay for government programs.[22]

The Premier's response was to note that the relationship between the government and the bank was a 'co-operative and consultative one', and to comment that the bank 'would be consulted over policy but basically the bank would be autonomous from the government in making policy decisions'[23]. The government, he said, could put proposals to the bank and its board which the bank was 'required to give serious consideration … but the action that it takes is ultimately the prerogative of the bank'.[24] In response to a question on the bank's prudential responsibilities in terms of the Federal Banking Act, the Premier noted that the new bank was not bound by the Act to be under Reserve Bank guidelines but that it was the intention of the government to ensure that the bank did voluntarily comply with these guidelines.[25]

The debate in the Legislative Council mirrored that in the House of Assembly, with the opposition contending that the bank should operate as a private bank with no advantages from, nor overt interference by, the government. The government's reply was to stress that the Act protected the bank and ensured its autonomy from the government. The relationship, as set out in the Act, was clearly one of the bank being 'at arms length' from the government. An interesting twist to how autonomous the bank should be occurred in the debate in the Upper House. Leigh Davis asked Attorney General-Chris Sumner whether the government would instruct the SBSA to act in the interest of local companies and provide them with funds so they could defend themselves against take-over bids from corporate raiders outside South Australia.[26] Sumner replied that

> One cannot have it both ways. Either one wants a bank which is substantially independent of the Government and which the Government can influence only indirectly by appointments to the board and by the Treasurer's making suggestions to the bank under the clause that we have already mentioned, clause 15 (4), which requires the bank to consider any proposals that the Treasurer makes; on the other hand, some people might expect a policy that involves acting as a white knight in take-overs or in other ways influencing the bank's investment decision.[27]

The debate between Davis and Sumner touched upon a contradiction within the Act. The contradiction was between a state bank serving the interest of the State, and a state bank acting like any other private bank, investing interstate and overseas and carrying out commercial activities, which may be profitable to it but not necessarily in the interest of the state. The dilemma was that if the SBSA was to conduct a high percentage of its business outside the State then this would raise concerns over the local expertise to supervise this activity, given that the Reserve Bank was only acting in a voluntary capacity in regard to a state institution.

As both the State Bank and the Savings Bank had so little business outside South Australia the likelihood of such a transformation seemed hard to imagine. Unfortunately, as we shall see, that is exactly what happened. Likewise, the Act carried in it a contradiction between it being fully commercially driven by the profit motive, yet serving South Australia by doing what it did in the past, providing concessional home loans and rural finance. That is, in Clause 15 (2), the board was instructed to 'administer the bank's affairs in accordance with accepted principles of financial management and with a view to achieving a profit'. Nevertheless, in a gesture to the past the Act instructed the board to administer the affairs of the bank with a view of promoting 'the balanced development of the State's economy' and 'the maximum advantage to the people of the State, and shall pay due regard to the importance both to the State's economy and to the people of the State of the availability of housing loans' (Clause 15 (1)).

The SBSA and the board soon came to interpret these clauses to mean that if it pursued corporate business, it was following accepted banking principles, and as long as it conducted the same local business, such as providing home loans, it was fulfilling its charter of benefiting the state's economy. How far the bank board thinking on this change differed from the past can be seen in 1989 when the annual report deemed housing as not being fully commercial but an activity carried on by the bank to meet the 'social obligations of its charter'.[28] In other words, by 1989 housing, which was the old banks' core business, became regarded by the new bank as but a social activity. The 1989 SBSA annual report noted that the bank's 'commercial' lending to business enabled it to continue its 'social role' of lending for housing.[29] The report said that:

> Activities by the bank and its subsidiaries, such as corporate lending, merchant banking and funds management, provide the strength to make

home lending decisions which, in a period of high interest rates, are often more social than commercial in nature.[30]

Undoubtedly, in a period of high inflation home lending is less profitable than corporate lending, but over time this can level out. Moreover, home lending is far safer than corporate lending. The point was, as Ian Kowalick noted, that by 1989 there was an uncritical view in the bank against housing loans. Kowalick, who was on the MAG and then in 1988 joined the SBSA, found that the new commercial culture in the bank falsely regarded home lending as unprofitable. He commented that:

> I don't think the emphasis on housing development necessarily meant that it was in an uncommercial way and whilst at times it is popular for banks to suggest that housing does not make money, I don't believe that that is the case.[31]

Balanced development meant being commercial

Similarly, while the Act allowed the bank to lend outside South Australia, the thinking in the government was that this would be done with a careful eye to safe and profitable loans. The bank was beginning from such a low base and with so little experience of anything but home loans in South Australia that it was not imagined that loans overseas and interstate would begin to be the force driving the bank. In any case Premier Bannon assumed that the management and the board would control this lending. Premier Bannon commented that:

> One would expect that the board of the day, in entering into obligations or lending, would have regard to the impact of its policies on the State's economy and not expose itself too greatly to interstate or other loan arrangements. But, really it had to be a matter for judgement of the board. That is why one has a board of the bank and why one has skilled staff administer policies.[32]

When the bank fell under the weight of its unprofitable loans outside of South Australia, John Bannon mused that:

> Now you say a lot of those (non-performing) operations were offshore and interstate and so on and how could they directly impact on South Australia as such, and I hadn't fully addressed that question, because that was bound up in the general profitability issue. But whenever something was proposed like, we'll open up an office in Brisbane, my immediate response in those areas was, is it going to be profitable?[33]

Consultation

The MAG approach to consultation was that the SBSA would retain as much independence as was possible from the government. In Bannon's view the new bank was going to have to consult with the Treasurer and the Treasury on its operations, and therefore there would need to be formal provisions in the Act for this consultation. This view was written into the bill and was spelled out in Clause 15 (3) which stated that, the 'board and the Treasurer shall, at the request of either, consult together either personally or through appropriate representatives, in relation to any aspect of the policies or administration of the bank'. Additionally, the board was obligated to 'consider any proposals made by the Treasurer in relation to the administration of the bank's affairs and shall, if so requested, report to the Treasurer on any such proposals' (Clause 15 (4)).

Consultation or 'riding instructions'

Premier Bannon told the parliament that this consultation simply meant appointments to the board would follow the practice of the past. Bannon's model of consultation was based on previous procedure and was more formal but somewhat less interventionist in the SBSA's affairs than the Playford or Dunstan, or even the Tonkin, governments. Consultation became the most heated issue in the parliamentary debate on the State Bank of South Australia bill. The leader of the opposition, John Olsen, said that the opposition was concerned that the government would not just appoint the board members but would give them specific instructions. Olsen said that the consultation clauses could be read as being 'tantamount to riding instructions to anyone appointed to the board'.[34] Bannon replied that this was neither the intention of the government nor permissible in the bill. Rather, all that the clause allowed for was that the government could put proposals to the board, to which it was 'required to give serious consideration … but the action that it takes is ultimately the prerogative of the bank'.[35]

The tension in the bill over consulting in practice became resolved by regular perfunctory meetings (four to six weekly consultations) between the Premier, Treasury officials, the Managing Director of the bank and the head of the board. These meetings became symbolic in that there was the semblance of consultation but little substance. At these meetings it was Tim Marcus Clark who led the Premier through the bank's accounts and business and implied that the bank was able to serve the past and forge ahead within its commercial direction. Bannon said that at these meetings the bank management

> took great pride in discussing its commitment to housing, explaining how new and innovative housing finance was, and how people could walk off the street and get home loans and things like that. It was in the regular meetings I had with the bank, housing was always highly featured, and was used as a kind of indicator of the general health of the bank.[36]

Similarly, Bannon considered that he was dealing with just another statutory authority which was running its own affairs. He took limited direct involvement in the bank, relying on the board, commenting with some bitterness that:

> The thing I've had to labour under most is the fact that the bank to me was, in some senses, quite peripheral to the issues I was dealing with and handling, with full on attention, and on a day to day, hands on, basis. The bank was being managed by the board, it just sort of swung into my vision and swung out again, from time to time, and that was inevitable.[37]

In keeping with much of modern management practices the monthly meetings between Clark and Bannon were mainly briefing sessions by the bank to the Premier.[38] In the latter Royal Commission, Commissioner Jacobs however, argued that Bannon did inject some sense of meaning into the consultation in regard to the politically sensitive matter of interest rates. Expressed in commercial legal terms, this intervention was used as evidence by Commissioner Jacobs to refute Bannon's claim of having a 'hands off' approach to the bank. In this case, the rarity became the legal refutation used by Jacobs, to find Bannon guilty of interfering in the bank for political ends and not keeping the bank 'at arm's length'.

The first instance of the non 'hands off' approach was in September 1985 when Premier Bannon summoned Clark to a meeting to request the bank 'not to raise rates until after Christmas, unless forced to do so by inexorable pressures of the market',[39] a request the bank concurred with, leading Commissioner Jacobs to say that:

> it is an irresistible conclusion that the Treasurer temporarily forsook his 'hands off' role and his perceptions of a commercially independent bank. Contrary to his expressed desire on other occasions that the bank's decision-making should recognise the advantage to the State of profit-orientated decisions, he was willing and anxious on this occasion to sacrifice that advantage in the short term for the political advantage of his Government ... The ALP election material proclaimed that John Bannon acted to hold down housing interest rates.[40]

The second instance of Bannon discussing interest rate policy with the bank was in the context of the federal election in 1987, where he proposed that the bank not pursue an interest rate rise immediately before the election as this would be interpreted politically. Commissioner Jacobs said that this request involved political benefits to the ALP.[41] According to Jacobs, the third and most significant request by Premier Bannon to restrain interest rates was in September 1989. The government went to the people on 25 November 1989. The request for a restraint on housing interest rates led to a discussion at the 28 September board meeting, where it was agreed to defer the rise 'pending satisfactory arrangements with the Treasury'.[42] On 2 October Bannon agreed in principle to the bank being subsidised for the delay in interest rates and the bank received $2 million in compensation. Following the election the board increased its interest rates as of 1 January 1990.

Commissioner Jacobs' concluded that

> The evidence does not warrant an affirmative finding that Mr Bannon himself made a proposal at that meeting in terms of a categorical request for political favours. But he knew that the proposal to hold interest rates involved the bank acting to its financial detriment in a way which would avoid political odium and might well attract support to his Government; and he could not have failed to realise that the bank board was alive to that implication.[43]

When Jacobs stood down as Commissioner due to ill health he was replaced by John Mansfield, who wrote the final report. In this, Commissioner Mansfield noted that in legal terms there was 'no wilful neglect' on the part of the Treasurer and Under-Treasurer in the arrangement over interest rates. Mansfield added that he accepted that Treasurer Bannon had 'acted in the honest and reasonable belief that he was entitled to act the way that he did and that he acted always for what he believed, rightly or wrongly, to be in accordance with, rather than in opposition to, the fulfilment of his obligations.'[44]

Bannon noted that on interest rates:

> The irony was that these things which somehow make it seem sinister were all publicly stated positions. I mean to the extent I as a politician put pressure on the bank it would obviously, publicly and privately, in this area of the cost of housing to the ordinary person, be political. But in the end of the day it wasn't that portfolio that brought the bank under; on the contrary, if all their business had been as good as their housing business then they'd be all right.[45.]

The point Bannon was making is that he would have been criticised by the media and his party for not acting politically. Moreover, it was the corporate lending, not housing loans, which brought the bank down. His political actions in legal terms, however, became read as a different truth, as a judicial refutation of his claims that the bank operated independently from the government. The refutation found the contradiction so central to legal discourse which Commissioner Jacobs, as an eminent jurist, was looking for. It gave him the proof of Bannon's interference in the bank. In this judgement Bannon was found doubly guilty, for on the one hand politically interfering in the bank's deliberations on interest rates and, on the other hand, not interfering in the bank to prevent its imprudent lending. In commercial legal terms, Jacobs was astutely pointing out the contradiction in Bannon's position. In the final analysis, Bannon was the minister who was obliged to protect the taxpayers, because it was the government who was guaranteeing the bank. As such, if Bannon intervened on one matter, interest rates, he should have intervened to protect the taxpayers.

Profits: the past is obliterated by the present

In drawing up the initial draft bill, the MAG sought to give the sole rights over profit appropriation to the board. The government, naturally, opposed this recommendation and set out an arrangement whereby the bank had to consult with the government over the level of the flow of profit to the Treasury. The government argued that the SBSA had to operate like other public banks and pay the government, firstly, an amount equivalent to federal taxation and secondly, pay an amount that reflected a return on capital. This was translated into the Act in terms of the new bank paying to Treasury 'a sum equal to the income tax for which the bank would have been liable under the law of the Commonwealth', (Clause 22 (1a)) and secondly, 'having regard to the profitability of the bank and the adequacy of its capital and reserves, determines to be an appropriate return on the capital of the bank'. (Clause 22 (1b)). The return to the government was therefore equivalent to tax payments and to the level of profit generated by the bank.

On this arrangement Bannon commented that the government's thinking was that there was a *quid pro quo* at work in regard to profits. In return for negotiation between the bank and the government over the payment of a dividend, the bank could, in general, be allowed to retain its independence from the government in other matters:

> At the end of the day, bearing in mind the considerable autonomy which the bank had generally, it was not reasonable that the board of the bank should be able to dictate the return to the government. Our view was that the pres-

ence of a guarantee and the fact that the government was the owner of the bank meant that through the government the community should have the final say in the amount of the return ... the requirement to disclose any difference of opinion on this matter, as a matter of practical politics, was a restraint on the Treasurer. In my experience, in situations like that, the onus would be on the Treasurer to justify rejecting the recommendation of the board. So, while the Treasurer was given the final say, there was a significant restraint imposed upon his ability to reject the view of the board.[46]

Bannon made the same point in the parliament, saying that as the bank was a public enterprise the government had the right to consult with the bank over the annual profit.[47]

Opposition leader John Olsen sought to fix the amount of profit paid to the Treasury, via a formula, which stated that the sum would be a prescribed amount in terms of a return on capital 'equal to the prescribed rate for that financial year' or 'one half of the net operating surplus for that financial year – whichever is the less'.[48] Olsen stressed that the bank should not have a 'return greater than the Australian savings bond rate or 50 per cent of the net operating surplus'.[49]

Bannon replied that this 'was not acceptable', saying that the 'bank and the government have mutual interests, and it is in the interest of the government and the State that the bank operates effectively and profitably'.[50] He pointed out that the clause relating to the profit transfers would restrain the actions of a Treasurer and that in any case the bank had an effective comeback if it ever considered that too high a demand for profit was placed upon it. He said that in practice, the 'Treasurer is in receipt of a recommendation, no doubt based on the account of that year and, no doubt, accompanied by the board's assessment of the bank's profitability, and the balances for ensuing years and so on. They are all part of the decision-making of the board, and the board makes a recommendation to which the Treasurer must pay regard. He must pay due regard: it is a requirement by law and, if he does not, that also means that he is in breach of the Act'.[51]

The government successfully opposed Olsen's amendment in the House of Assembly. The issue was taken up in the Legislative Council by Leigh Davis, who noted that the old State Bank 'was obliged to provide half its operating surplus to the Treasurer',[52] and that, in 'the case of the Savings Bank of South Australia, as it is now constituted, there is a fairly complex formula. It appears that in 1982, 47 per cent of the operating surplus was paid, and about 48 per cent was paid in 1983. We have an existing practice where both the Savings Bank and the State Bank, for all intentions and purposes, pay about half their operating surpluses into Treasury annually'.[53] As such, Davis argued the government should therefore accept the amendment of the Opposition. In reply Attorney-General Sumner echoed the points made by Premier Bannon, saying:

If the Treasurer wants to take more than is recommended by the bank, that is placed on public record for the Parliament and the whole South Australian public to see. The government is the elected body of the community. It is very amenable to public opinion. And to what the community wants. If the community felt that the government was placing banks in jeopardy, I am sure it would let the government know about it.[54]

Once established 'at arm's length' from the government it was very difficult for the Treasurer to intervene, as this would send out signals to the press and business sector that either the government was interfering in the SBSA for party political purposes, or that the bank was not operating commercially. Both messages would have adverse ramifications for the bank, and, as the Treasurer was the Premier, for the Bannon government. This imperative was strengthened by Bannon's desire not to have a no-confidence motion moved against him, as had happened to Dunstan. Similarly, the opposition was shadow boxing over the issue of profits as it also wanted to ensure the profits of the SBSA flowed to the government, when it won office. There was a strong incentive, therefore, for the Premier and the SBSA to keep the bank's commercial practices removed from the political arena.

Don't blame me – blame Bannon

The flow of profit from the bank to the government became a point of contest at the Royal Commission. The ex-Chair of the SBSA Board, David Simmons, supported by the other ex-directors, claimed it was the government's 'push for profit' which drove the bank's uncontrolled growth.[55] Simmons also asserted that the manner by which the bank had to obtain capital through the SAFA arrangement disadvantaged the bank and was a structural pressure driving the growth of the bank. Both claims were disputed by the State Treasury which calculated that the bank had a 'no better than adequate profit performance over the period' and that 'when taken as a whole the bank's funding and profit transfers to the Treasury did not disadvantage the bank.'[56]

Treasury's submission in regard to the cost of capital was backed by an independent analysis from BT Corporate Finance on the funding of the bank. BT Finance found that:

> Over the period 1987–1991, the assumed minimum cost of equity for SBSA has been less than the estimated total cost of equity for major Australian listed banks. Our analysis also indicated that the assumed minimum cost of equity for SBSA has also been lower than the cost of various subordinated quasi-equity issues of the sample banks. The implication is that the assumed minimum costs of equity for SBSA over the period may have been relatively low given the risks of an equity investment in the bank'.[57]

The Auditor-General, Kenneth MacPherson, concurred with the Treasury's calculations, pointing out factual errors in Simmons' submission over the tax take and profit flows from the bank to the Treasury, and he regarded the Treasury's evidence as an effective counter to Simmons' claim of a 'push for profit' and the too costly provision of capital through SAFA.[58] In contrast, Commissioner Jacobs in his first report asserted that there was a 'profit enhancement culture' within the bank and that the capital needs of the bank were met by SAFA on terms that 'were more advantageous to SAFA than to the bank'.[59]

The final report by Commissioner Mansfield somewhat differed from that of Jacobs and concurred with the Auditor-General in finding that:

> The processes associated with funding the bank did not lead the bank to engage in operations that have resulted in either material losses or in the bank

holding non-performing assets. He [the Auditor General] has specifically rejected submissions to the contrary made on behalf of the non-executive directors ... Put simply, it could not be proved that whatever care or lack of care, or other conduct, led to the bank procuring its capital funding as and when it did was a cause of the bank's financial difficulties. Without that causative element, no action for damages on behalf of the bank against persons involved in that process could succeed.[60]

Simulated returns: profit versus profitability

Expressed in more technical terms, the critical figure in the bank's financial troubles was not capital nor profit but profitability. That is, what was crucial was not the profit level but profit in relationship to assets. The growth in the bank's profits was disproportionate to the return on its assets. In short, as the SBSA's assets grew the return on these assets actually fell and proportionately the risk was intensifying. While all eyes were on the appearance of profit per year, the figure not fully appreciated by the government, and Treasury and directors was the decline in the level of profit on each asset acquired. Growth became growth for growth's sake because the assets acquired accrued only marginal benefits, or at times turned into liabilities. This is evident by counter-posing the profit figures with the assets figures. In 1984 the $4.8 million profit was on assets of $2 billion. In 1985 the bank had a pre-tax profit of $37 million on assets of $4.1 billion. In 1986 the operating profit was $41 million on assets of $6.4 billion. In 1987 the profit was $52 million on $7.8 billion. In 1988 the profit was $69 million on assets of $11 billion. In 1989 the profit was $97 million on assets of $15 billion. In 1990 the bank made a book loss of $397,000 and on assets of $21 billion.[61]

Expressed in the simplest terms, by 1986 the SBSA had reached a plateau in profitability. Thereafter profits or assets declined, and yet it was not until 1991 that the perception of a profitable bank was to be shattered. It is only in hindsight that the issue of profitability became evident to Premier Bannon and only as a consequence of the Auditor-General, Ken MacPherson's, report. It is not surprising then that Bannon, who had but followed the bank's fortunes at a distance, was taken by surprise at the bank's supposed sudden turnaround in fortunes. When asked as to why he had not raised the issue of profitability he replied that:

> It was never put to me in those terms. Assets were increasing, profit was going up. That was the context. So from someone like myself, not trained in the reading of banking details, the figures, in terms of rates and returns and so on, depended very much on other analysis. There were things that stood out, the bank would say isn't it terrific these assets were going up, it goes to show we are carrying out our brief. Our profits were up fine, maybe some reduction in it at the time but you can understand that because of the economic circumstances in which we were operating, End of story.[62]

The board

Unlike Dunstan's approach, the method adopted by Premier Bannon in regard to appointees to the State Bank Board was to ensure that the board was not only seen to be – but was actually independent of his government. Appointments via the provisions in the Act basically followed past practice by premiers of appointing local business figures to the board. Ironically, the politics of the appointments to the board were not for the government to control the board rather the reverse. Bannon placed people on the board who were perceived to be more sympathetic to the opposition than to the government. A case of 'what is termed, in public policy literature, satisficing'. He commented that all seemed satisfied[63]. He said that:

> I was conscious of the vulnerability of financial institutions based on the 1976 experience of the Bank of Adelaide. I felt it was vital that there should be a feeling of assurance about the board in a political sense, and for that reason, sought to provide continuity between the two previous bank boards, including some of those persons who had then been appointed by the previous Liberal government. So if the Liberals wanted to complain, they would be complaining about people they actually said were the bank directors. That's where I say [John] Olsen and [Dean] Brown and others can't escape responsibility for that situation.[64]

Bannon's strategy of safe appointments to the bank board meant that the SBSA had a board dominated by local business men when the bank was becoming a national and international commercial player. A quick thumbnail sketch of the State bank board will show you that it was a bank based on past practice. Lew Barrett, the Chairman, was a chartered accountant and was the former Chair of the Savings Bank. He was also Chair of the Royal Adelaide Hospital, Honorary Treasurer of the Adelaide Children's Hospital, President of the Council of the South Australian Institute of Technology, a committee member of the Australian Kidney Foundation and a director of Beneficial Finance, Poseidon Limited, M S McLeod Ltd., Bounty Investments and Wakefield Investments. He was a member of the Adelaide Club, and considered in its broadest terms could be regarded as part of the old 'establishment' so reviled by Dunstan. While reflecting the past values of the Savings Bank in remaining autonomous from government, he was a strong supporter of Tim Marcus Clark's project of rapidly commercialising the bank.

Professor Hancock was an economist by training and Vice-Chancellor of Flinders University and had been a member of the (Vic) Martin Committee set up by Treasurer Keating to place his imprimatur on financial deregulation. He then came to prominence when he headed a review into the Australian Industrial Relations system, before becoming a judge in the Industrial Court. While a member of the Adelaide Yacht Club, his elevation in life was not due to hereditary wealth or business connections but academic reputation and financial competence.

Rob Searcy, like Lew Barrett, was a chartered accountant and the head of a leading accounting firm, Milne, Stevens, Searcy, Hill & Company. He was a director of Television Broadcasters Ltd, and a director of the Adelaide-based merchant bank CCF Australia Ltd. He was a Trustee of the old Savings Bank and was on the executive of the Neurological Research Foundation and a national director of the Australian Brain Foundation, and was also a member of the Adelaide Club. He had attended St Peters College and studied economics and accountancy at the University of Adelaide and was a member of the Royal Adelaide Golf Club, and featured in the 'blue book', published in 1980, on prominent people in South Australia.[65] Again, he was someone from the traditional mould, and he could perhaps be regarded as a member of the old Adelaide establishment.

In keeping with both the history of the Savings Bank and the State Bank there were ex-politicians on the board. Bill Nankerville was a former director of the old State Bank, rural producer and ex-Liberal member of parliament and he was a member of the Adelaide Club. Don Simmons and Molly Byrne, former Labor ministers were community appointments to the board reflecting the old fashioned way of making appointments. From the public sector there was Keith Smith, director of the Department of State Development, who held senior management posts with Henry Jones IXL and was previously the Managing Director of Kaiser Stuhl Wines and a director of Penfolds Wines. Like Hancock, he had only a fleeting role to play on the board.

Tim Marcus Clark was the son of a prominent Sydney retailer, went to Scots College in Sydney and completed an MBA at Harvard in Boston. Clark was Director of Miller Andersons in Adelaide from 1960–66, and when it went into difficulty he worked in retailing and banking. He was the Commercial Bank's representative on the committee which facilitated the merger with the much larger Bank of New South Wales to form Westpac. He was also a director of a number of companies, notably, Marac Holdings and Henry Jones IXL (where John Elliott cut his entrepreneurial teeth) and with the New Zealand entrepreneur, Allan Hawkins, of Equiticorp. He was a member of both the Melbourne and Adelaide Clubs.

The Chair of the board after Barrett was David Simmons. Simmons was a former Trustee of the Savings Bank and a corporate lawyer. He was the senior partner in the Adelaide law firm Thomson Simmons and Company and became the director of Beneficial Finance Corporation, along with 130 other companies, of which around a third were connected with the SBSA group. He also held shares in 57 South Australian companies, including a whole range of Adelaide small and medium sized firms involved in such diverse activities as property development, broadcasting, wine, carpets and furnishing and trustee firms, including the Raptis group, MS McLeod, Wolf Blass Wines and Solomons Ltd. The latter company was formed by Myer Solomon who had challenged the Bank of Adelaide board over the takeovor bid by the ANZ Bank.

There is a symbolism here in that Simmons was representing a prominent Adelaide company which was prepared to stand up against the (dominant Anglo-Saxon) 'old' establishment legal networks. There was a certain political construction here of a lawyer representing businesses who were distinct from the major law firms in Adelaide which had given legal advice to the establishment enterprises in South Australia over one hundred years.

Simmons was the secretary of Ramada International Pty Ltd, which was headed by the property developer Bill Sparr. The jewel in the crown of the Sparr group was the $70 million Ramada Grand Hotel complex at Glenelg, which was funded by the State Bank and Beneficial Finance – and went into receivership. Also, Thomson Simmons and Company put together the legal intricacies of the REMM–Myer Complex deal. Moreover, the law firm entered into a joint venture with Beneficial Finance to build a new $12 million office building in Pirie Street. Finally, according to calculations made by the *Advertiser*, Thomson Simmons and Company received more than $1.2 million in legal fees from the State Bank group in 1990–91, representing 40 per cent of the legal fees paid by the Bank Group for that year.[66]

The involvement of Simmon's law firm with the Bank Group, according to Clark, became a point of contention between him and Simmons. When he appeared before the Parliamentary (Stephen Martin) Inquiry into banking, in September 1991, under privilege, Clark claimed that his relationship with Simmons deteriorated from mid 1990 because he questioned Simmons over companies he was involved in. Clark alleged that:

> ... the deterioration in my relationship with the Chairman also appears to have coincided with my concerns expressed about the financial position of entities associated with the Chairman. David Simmons was Chairman of both the bank and Beneficial Finance Corporation, his law firm was a major legal adviser both to the group and many of the group's customers and he was closely associated with entities which had major exposures to the group, some of which at this stage were having financial difficulties. His law firm was a major legal adviser to both the bank group and many of the group's customers.[67]

When he appeared before the Parliamentary Inquiry, Simmons denied Clark's claims. His counsel Abbott QC, pointedly argued that his client regarded Clark's allegations 'as nothing but a slur on the character of my client. Worse still, we suggest that those allegations would not publicly be made other than on an occasion such as this where Mr Marcus Clark is protected by the privileges that witnesses before this inquiry enjoy.'[68]

A spokesperson for Thomson Simmons and Company said in the firm's defence of Clark's accusations that their involvement with the Bank Group was but a reflection of the size of the firm and that there was a degree of competitive rivalry about the claims. Mr Farrugia on behalf of the firm said that they 'were criticised for innovation and for a whole range of things we did in building our practice. We have acted properly and built our practice on hard work'. He added that 'it was common practice for banks and their subsidiary companies to have a lawyer on its many boards'.[69]

Tony Summers was appointed to the board in 1987, when Professor Hancock was elevated to the Industrial Court. Summers was the head of a small agri-business in the Adelaide Hills, which was acquired by Adsteam. In this capacity he had met Premier Bannon and so impressed him that Bannon had no hesitation in appointing him to the SBSA Board. The buy-out of his company gave Summers the capital base and reputation to be appointed head of the one of Adelaide's oldest pastoral businesses, Bennett and Fisher. He was also chairman of many of Bennett's subsidiaries, notably, R M Williams and Ditters, and a director of Dalgety Farm Ltd. Although never a student at the school (rather he attended Urrbrae Agricultural High School) he was connected with St Peters College through fund raising activities. He was also involved in the restoration of St Peter's Cathedral and had been at times Chair of both the Adelaide Festival Trust (a fundraising body), and the Adelaide Festival Arts Board (a decision making body), Chair of the highly political National Farmers Federation fighting fund, and a member of the Adelaide Club.[70] He was symbolically associating his newly acquired wealth and position with that of the 'old' establishment and an anti-union perspective.

Mr Summers was thrust into adverse public light in 1990. In that year Bennett and Fisher was sued by the sugar giant CSR over what was claimed as an act of deceit by Summers, in that he sold the Anchor Group to the company for $23.7

million but subsequently CSR valued Anchor at only $1.6 million. Later that year Summers was pressured by the Australian Securities Commission over the payments made to him of $2 million in management fees over the previous seven years. In July 1990, it was revealed that a property his wife purchased for $190,000 in 1983, was sold some six years later to Bennett and Fisher for $4.5 million. At the time the property was valued at $500,000 by the Valuer-General's Office.[71] The Australian Securities Commission and the Adelaide Stock Exchange pointed out to Bennett and Fisher that, as the purchase represented more than ten per cent of the assets of the company, it had to be ratified by an extraordinary shareholders' meeting, which was held on 23 November 1990.

At the meeting the purchase was opposed by one of the company's largest shareholders, the AMP society, and by many small shareholders. After a long and raucous meeting the purchase was eventually ratified, but only after Denis Gerschwitz (the head of SGIC), at the time a director of Bennett and Fisher, exercised a proxy vote on behalf of the SGIC. The media reported that the ratification was against the wishes of the small shareholders. Soon after the Managing Director, Summers, left the company, and went to England to pursue religious studies. In 1993 Bennett and Fisher, under pressure from a consortium of banks, was placed in the hands of receivers. In 1995, a reconstituted Bennett and Fisher made an out of court settlement with Summers.

Over time the basic structural composition of the board remained the same, although there were marginal changes to its membership. In 1985 Robert Bakewell was added to the board. There was a certain irony in this appointment as Bakewell was previously at the centre of Dunstan's aborted attempt at integrating the old banks. He subsequently became Chair of the Savings Bank from 1976 to 1980 and then went on to be the State's Ombudsman. Upon retiring as Ombudsman he was a consultant to the auditors, Touche Ross, who had conducted consultancies for the SBSA, before he was appointed to the board. He retained an interest in business consultancies, including a politically controversial one associated with the activities of the Adelaide Casino, where he was paid $200,000 a year to provide advice to the Malaysian-based consortium Genting, who ran the casino. Under pressure from the Liberal Opposition a review of the consultation process was undertaken by the Arnold government in 1992. The review alleged (though this was never legally proven) that Bakewell gave Genting 'intimate details' about the Adelaide casino which may have been used by Genting in respect of its casinos in Perth and Kuala Lumpur. Following the report's findings, the Labor government abolished Bakewell's position.[72]

Rod Hartley, when he became the Director of the Department of State Development, replaced Keith Smith on the board. Hartley left State Development to head the prominent local corporation, MS Mcleod Ltd, a company with which Lew Barrett and David Simmons had connections. Under Hartley, Mcleod Ltd. went through a controversial program of diversification with the focus shifting from a broad-based wholesale firm to a more specialised concern with a focus on the duty free business. The company suffered a financial crisis which saw the painful divestiture of subsidiary companies, the most prominent being that headed by the internationally renowned, locally respected (and naturally aggrieved) wine-maker Peter Lehmann who then successfully floated his own wine company. Hartley then left MS Mcleod Ltd to become an independent consultant.

In short, the board had members who were predominantly local business identities, some of whom embraced the entrepreneurial spirit of the 1980s; others were from the old banks with traditional business practices. In practice, the board was regularly snowed under by the quantity of paperwork, prepared for them by the management, and by the technical nature of contemporary banking. Nevertheless, their support or acquiescence in accepting the growth dynamic of the bank in the 1980s regularly saw them agreeing to large loans without sufficient evaluation of all the risks involved in the proposals. The non-executive board became overly reliant on the managers, in general, and on the Managing Director in particular, to provide the critical appraisal of the lending proposals before coming to them. The board's deliberations became one of trust; this is typical of boards in general. In the late 1980s, however, it was this trust of an over-stretched management which contributed to the bank's downfall.

While the bank grew and appeared to be successful there was a good deal of prestige and monetary rewards attached to being on the board. As well, as the bank was a significant large player in the local economy dominated by small business, there was a natural flow-on of goodwill to the bank. Tim Marcus Clark also presented the directors with opportunities to head subsidiary companies of the SBSA group, so that while the directors were only paid according to restricted salary levels – a restriction governed by Bannon's belief that serving on such boards was a public duty – they could gain extra income by being on these subsidiaries.

For instance, in 1990, the Chair of the board, David Simmons, boosted his public 'chairman's cheque' of $19,600 with a top up of $64,498 by serving on sub-committees and subsidiary boards, bringing his total return from the bank to $82,098.[73] Similarly in 1990, Rob Searcy was paid in $50,000 total by the bank; Bob Bakewell, $39,718; Rod Hartley, $27,525; Tony Summers, $29,051; Bill Nankivell, $23,295; with Molly Byrne the only board member receiving the base rate of $10,025.[74] In 1989, the previous Chair of the board, Lew Barrett, had received remuneration of $74,665.[75]

The conservative practice soon gave way to the imperatives of the 1980s. As the SBSA grew so fast and so embraced the dominant culture of the era, the SBSA board fundamentally changed both the old thrift philosophy and the over-cautious practice of lending. In their place was too often a trust in management and its ambitious lending plans. The philosophical distance travelled from the old board to the new board can be gauged by recalling that the first trustees of the Savings Bank in 1848 were not paid for their services, took their turn as tellers and were precluded from either depositing money or borrowing from the bank.

From the outside the board seemed to be retaining the appearance of a public sector board, serving the State and adhering to the virtues of civic duty. But, in the Auditor-General's opinion the board was not independent enough from the managers, rather it did not step back and analyse the submission of the lenders and thereby failed to act as a check and a balance on the bankers.[76]

In the end, the Auditor-General notes, the board did not use its collective 'common sense' to question the submissions presented to it.[77] As soon as the bank began to live out its desire to be a major bank the old board practices of cautiously and painstakingly assessing all major loans was swamped by the imperative for quick decisions over complex corporate deals. The only person on the board with significant experience in commercial banking was the Managing Director who was also the driving energy behind the bank's desire to be a major financial player.[78] The board unwittingly shared this desire and until it was too late did not fully realise the dangers that the bank was entering into or to challenge the Managing Director when doubts began to emerge about his leadership.

There was something more than shared desires and a sense of achievement in the failings of the bank to live up to the past philosophy of thrift, it was both banking knowledge on the board and the style of Clark. As David Simmons contends, Clark was a formidable opponent on the board to anyone challenging the competence of the lending strategy or management skills of the bank. The flavour of his confrontational style is captured by the Chair of the board, Mr Simmons:

> Mr Clark was the only banker on the board. He was extremely intelligent and articulate and, at least initially, his mastery of the business of the bank over-awed the board. Mr Marcus Clark also had a very forceful personality and, by dint of good background briefing and clever debating skills, was usually able to gain the ascendancy in any board discussion. Any board member who took it upon themselves to query anything said or done by Mr Marcus Clark would usually find him or herself in a debate which they were certain to lose. On those infrequent occasions when Mr Marcus Clark may not have been anticipating such a debate, he would invariably deflect that criticism or concern by suggesting that the matter was already the subject of review by management and/or would form the subject matter of a separate paper on another date. The skill with which Mr Marcus Clark dealt with expressions of concern by directors was matched by an impressive command of the subject matter which went with being a hard working Chief Executive.[79]

Both Hartley and Simmons expressed the view that Clark dominated the board and it was difficult to deal with Clark on both a professional and a personal level. There was a sense that at a personal level the bank and Clark merged. Clark, it was said, had a 'love of the bank'. It was, as Michael Abbott QC implied in the Royal Commission, an unhealthy love, a possessive love in that he saw the bank as 'his bank'.[80] Simmons also suggested that this love was somewhat excessive, saying that Clark 'spent an enormous amount of time on bank business. Indeed, the bank appeared to be his life. For a significant proportion of the time as Chief Executive Officer, his wife and family remained in Melbourne and, with no extraneous commitments in Adelaide, he was able to spend many hours on bank business over and above his normal working week'.[81]

There are parallels here with the manner in which United States President Ronald Reagan presented his presidency as based on his love for America and, on the basis, criticism of his ideas and policies became diverted by the accusation that those making them were un-American.[82] Similarly, criticisms of Clark were muted by the representation of his commitment to the bank. The directors were principally concerned with Clark's domination of the board and not the direction of the bank. As Bannon noted, the criticisms of Clark that filtered to him were over his domineering personality, his 'positive drive and not that he was leading them in the wrong direction'.[83]

In the period up to 1989 the board concurred with the direction in which the Managing Director was taking the bank, they also benefited from the prestige that went with the media's plotting the progress of the bank to be Australia's fifth largest grouping. After 1989, however, the non-executive directors were becoming concerned that the Managing Director had an unrealistically optimistic vision of market trends. As a result, the relationship between board members – especially Hartley, Searcy and Simmons – and the Managing Director began to deteriorate. The board then sought to exercise some control over him.

The failure of the non-executive directors to deal with the Managing Director led to the claim that they were a 'weak' board and that Bannon should have done something to strengthen the board. On paper, however, the board was representative of the Adelaide business sector and did not appear to be particularly deficient or an atypical board in the 1980s. This is the point that Bannon makes in his defence, commenting that, 'I believe that the composition of the board of the State Bank was not out of line with the composition of the boards of the major banks. While the composition of any two boards is not the same, the sort of person on the State Bank can be found on the boards of the major banks'.[84]

The lack of Treasury expertise on the board

The noticeable absence from the board was that of the Under-Treasurer. When appointing the board Premier Bannon was aware that such an appointment would raise opposition from members of the old boards. This view was confirmed by Rob Searcy, who told the Jacobs Royal Commission that: 'There was a general feeling on the board of some disquiet that if a Treasury representative was seen to be on the board of the bank then the customers of the bank would see that government had been in involvement with the bank and would react adversely'.[85]

Rather than have a Treasury person on the board Premier Bannon wanted Treasury to evaluate the bank from the outside, by judging the direction of the bank's commercial decisions and overall performance. He went further than this, however, by arguing that such a form of accountability would be compromised by placing a Treasury person on the board. His rationale was as follows.

> I felt that the Treasury role should be to provide me with advice on the bank and to the extent that the Under-Treasurer or senior Treasury official would be compromised by the decision, and that it was not appropriate to have someone there [from Treasury].[86]

The board simulated control

Bannon contended that given the political constraints this board 'stacked up' against any other bank board in Australia[87]. Royal Commissioner Jacobs had a different opinion, arguing that the board lacked the strength and ability, and at times the desire, to stand up to management. He noted that the 'board as a whole lacked hard-headed business and banking experience'.[88] Jacobs was highly critical of Clark as Managing Director for the level and quality of information flowing to the board. Commissioner Jacobs, in keeping with his judicial evaluations, looked for individual rather than systemic causes for the board's failings. He accepted the board's claims that they did not exercise more authority over Clark because of their belief that he had a 'close rapport' with, and the 'confidence' of, the Premier.[89] Again this finding reinforced the conclusions of Commissioner Jacobs that the Premier as the person legally responsible for the guarantee had to accept responsibility for the situation within the bank.

Tim Marcus Clark and the desire to be number one

Tim Marcus Clark was the driving force behind the SBSA's transformation. He was responsible for shaping the commercial culture within the bank and was the dominant influence in the bank's recruitment program, and in the promotion and remuneration packages of the senior managers. Clark was appointed in the context of making the new bank more commercially orientated than the old State Bank or the Savings Bank. The MAG engaged a head hunting firm to find such a person to make the new bank more commercial. They came up with three names, one of whom was Clark, at the time a middle-manager in Westpac.[90] He was interviewed by representatives on the old board, Professor Hancock and M F O'Loughin from the State Bank, and Lew Barrett from the Savings Bank. While not having had experience at running a large organisation, Clark indicated that it was very much his desire to do so. Hancock, who had been chair of the old State Bank board, said that Clark, 'dearly wanted to get his hand on the tiller, and there was no prospect of his ever doing so in Westpac'. He added that Clark was willing to 'come to a small bank when he could be playing in the big league'.[91]

When Tim Marcus Clark was head-hunted to merge the old banks and be Managing Director of the new SBSA, he seemed on paper to be well credentialed. As mentioned previously he had been a director of Miller Anderson in Adelaide and in the 1970s was a director of a series of companies, Marac Holdings, Henry Jones IXL, Australian Capital Fund, General Credits and Commercial Bank Insurance. Clark had one of the much vaunted credentials of the 1980s: a Master of Business Administration from Harvard (Boston).[92] When challenged, he had a penchant to use his MBA as affirmation of his superior approach to business organisation. In a world where meetings become a staple diet, Clark was skilled at chairing them, meticulous in his preparation, and astute at getting at the heart of the matter. His sober attire reflected the image of the conservative banker, the butt of jokes in films and television drama.

But there was another side to Clark. There were many parallels between Tim Marcus Clark and two other 1980s entrepreneurs, Alan Bond and John Elliott, especially in their profound optimism over the potentialities of the market and the private sector. However, whereas Bond and Elliott were larger than life, Clark was a more private person. This tendency to maintain his privacy stemmed from a knife attack on him in 1980, when he was a lending officer in the Commercial Bank.[93] The media speculated somewhat wildly over the motive for the attack, advancing claims that the notorious drug runner Roger Wilson had known Clark and that they had had a falling out. These accusations were never proven. The mystery deepened when Wilson mysteriously disappeared just after the knife attack on Clark. Given the unsubstantiated media speculation and sensationalism over the supposed connection between Wilson and himself, it is understandable that Clark was highly sensitive about his privacy.

At Westpac he had worked with Alan Hawkins, who departed at the same time as Clark to set up an entrepreneurial business in New Zealand. Hawkins said of Clark that 'he's the most positive person I've known', adding that 'under Westpac we came up against the management by committee, a style which always inhibits action'.[94] Upon leaving Westpac, Hawkins set up the company Equiticorp as his vehicle for takeover bids, investment and currency deals in New Zealand. Hawkins rapidly rose to prominence in New Zealand, but following the share market crash his actions became more desperate, and in the end he had to face fraud charges in New Zealand, a case where Clark was given limited immunity to give evidence against Hawkins. Hawkins was found guilty and served time in a New Zealand prison.

For his own part, Tim Marcus Clark said that he was appointed because of his commercial 'experience and because I was aggressive and optimistic'.[95] The first chair of the SBSA Board, Lew Barrett, a strong supporter of Clark at the time, said of Marcus Clark that he was 'a very aggressive, entrepreneurial chap, keen to see the bank do well, keen to see the State Bank with Tim Marcus Clark become Australia's number one bank'.[96] David Simmons noted that Clark was 'not so strong on banking, but as a retailer he was fantastic [he was] more of a salesman than a banker, a brilliant salesman, one of Australia's best.'[97]

The desire to be recognised

In sum, Mr Clark seemed an ideal candidate for the period of financial deregulation. He was an aggressive competitor with 'the will to win' and was committed to the bank being number one, with him at its head. He was an excellent salesman in an era where all aspects of life were now becoming commodities. The terminology of the market became the language of all spheres, and Clark the salesman appeared to be the man for the era, the man to lead the new bank into the ever burgeoning commercial world. He had not, however, any experience as a Chief Executive of a large banking organisation but made it clear that he desired to do so. As Barrett observed, he had the burning desire to make the new State Bank the number one bank in Australia. He saw the means of translating this desire into reality by capturing corporate clients and Clark sought to instil into his management team his own optimism and determination to make the deal. He wanted managers who could grasp the opportunities presented by the market and expand the bank's assets. This desire could only be fulfilled by displacing the big four Australian banks: Westpac, the National Australia Bank, the ANZ and the Commonwealth Bank.

The commercial discourse and Tim Marcus Clark

When challenged Tim Marcus Clark was adroit at shifting styles to match his audience. Behind closed doors of the board meetings he could be charming, but if challenged he could be assertive. When challenged by Bannon, however, he became open and apologetic, owning the problems and implying he had already thought of the solutions. Such a technique allayed Bannon's concerns and he could then forget about them. On this Bannon made the observation that:

> If you are in the normal course of business and dealing with people, particularly in my position, you are often in a situation of confrontation and argument. As such, if I say to somebody this performance isn't good enough, their natural reaction is to explain to you that it is better than you apparently realise, or the reasons why that performance is not up to par. Now that was never Mr Clark's style. His response to that sort of questioning invariably would be to acknowledge the deficiency and not take a defensive position. To, indeed, assist the analysis of the problem, and then to explain systems in detail, what he thought were the appropriate steps, to deal with it. Now if you are confronted with somebody responding in that way it is a little hard not to

believe that they have it in hand and to have confidence in the way they are tackling it.[98]

During his time as Managing Director, Clark was seen by the business sector as a dynamic leader – the press spoke of him as a 'dynamo', and accepted uncritically his line that the 'State Bank is the catalyst in what happens in this State'.[99] As well, Clark had the support of the opposition. For example, when Clark renewed his contract in 1988, the then leader of the opposition, John Olsen praised him enthusiastically, saying that:

> As a result of Mr Clark's smooth and efficient amalgamation of the State and Savings banks, the State Bank now takes its place in the market place as an enterprising competitor on equal terms with the private banks. Mr Clark has also exhibited a determination to maintain the bank's independence from government which has added to its credibility in the market place.[100]

As a result of the general support for Clark, Bannon accepted uncritically that Clark was running the bank in a commercially competent manner. It was only in late 1990 that Bannon began to doubt Clark's capacities. Up until then Bannon took Clark's appearance as if it was backed by real substance. For example, at the same meeting when Clark declared his involvement with the troubled Equiticorp company and spoke on the collapse of the National Safety Council (Victoria) he informed Bannon that, incidentally, he had just been appointed as Chair of a joint automobile venture between Toyota and Holdens. Such a juxtaposition, Bannon contended, did not at the time seem deliberately contrived, but it did have the effect of retaining Bannon's uncritical support for Clark. He said: 'Now I'm not saying he did that deliberately, it did coincide, but you can understand my view of him was coloured by the view of him that others were getting as well in those contexts'.[101]

Bannon added that he did not socialise with Clark and only had close working contact with Clark when the latter was appointed Chairman of the Grand Prix Board. In Bannon's opinion Clark

> did a brilliant job there. His style of chairmanship, to me, his ability to delegate, his ability to solve problems was very apparent and so the chief executive of the bank was also wearing the hat of the Grand Prix chairman, who I actually knew better in that context and understood better what he was doing because it was in my purview, and that obviously coloured my response to his capacity.[102]

To challenge Clark meant dissecting the representation that dominated the 1980s, that selling was the basis for success. The dilemma for the SBSA board members was that when the bank broke from its past and became a national and then a global corporate bank, the board members were swept up in the rise in assets without adequately questioning whether the ever-present desire for growth could be sustained given the regional past of the old banks or whether it was being conducted at too high a risk. The board, the government and the parliament all put faith in the market and globalisation. Equally, all these actors did not realise that such an approach could lead to the destruction of the past at so rapid a rate. In six quick years nearly 150 years of banking was destroyed.

The destructive side of modernisation exacted its toll on the new State Bank of South Australia which embraced the 1980s acquisitive culture of greed without the wherewithal to assess the risks it was taking. The next chapter provides a statistical overview of what went wrong and why, an overview which gives empirical weight to the argument that the bank grew too fast in a deregulated environment where the risks had been enhanced.

6

From a thrift to an entrepreneurial bank: what went wrong?

On Monday 2 July 1984 the doors of the new State Bank of South Australia (SBSA) were opened for business. Cutting the ribbon to signify the merger of the two old banks, the Savings Bank of South Australia and the State Bank of South Australia, was Premier John Bannon. He was flanked by the Chair of the board, Lew Barrett, Deputy Chair Professor Keith Hancock (the previous chair of the State Bank), and the Managing Director of the bank, Tim Marcus Clark. The ceremony was a simple one, in keeping with the history of the merged banks. In the next six years this history, based on prudence and thrift was displaced by credit and acquisitiveness, with the bank being transformed from a local retail bank to a global commercial entity.

Opening up for business: touching the parochial heart-strings
A television campaign that preceded the launch of the SBSA belied the shift the bank was taking. The advertisement identified the new bank with the history of the old banks and was accompanied by panoramic shots of the South Australian landscape. The thinking behind the campaign according to Clark, was to appeal to the emotions of South Australians. He told a collective meeting of managers that the campaign aimed to present a 'birds-eye view of South Australia' via the use of sweeping camera shots taken from a helicopter so as 'to reach the hearts of the television viewers.'[1] The shots of the landscape were accompanied by 'words from Australia's best known poem [Dorothea McKellar's 'My Country'], with a special verse written for South Australia... The words are spoken by a young girl – anyone's daughter – as though she has just learnt the poem. But the sunburnt country is about the whole of Australia. So the advertising people wrote some special words to appeal to the state pride that beats in the heart of every South Australian'.[2] The intention of the commercial was to create in the mind of the viewers an 'indivisible association' between the new State Bank and South Australia.[3] The advertising campaign sought to tie the new State Bank to the historical development of South Australia.

When the two banks merged in 1984 the bulk of their combined business was lending for home ownership. At the time, house loans constituted 62.5 per cent of the SBSA's loan portfolio and these were principally funded from retail deposits which constituted 85 per cent of the bank's deposits. What lending there was outside South Australia was due in the main to the acquisition of Beneficial Finance Corporation (BFC) by the Savings Bank in April 1984. While BFC did have assets outside the state (around $400 million) they were principally in real estate, the retail market and loans to small business concerns. In 1984 the SBSA had only a minor banking office in London, which it took over from the Savings Bank, and this was its sole overseas operation. In 1985 the overseas business of the SBSA totalled a mere $36 million.

In the first Annual Report of the SBSA, Tim Marcus Clark spoke of continuing the proud history of banking in South Australia established by the former banks. The 1984 Report emphasised that the SBSA was 'the only bank that has its *heart* in South Australia'.[4] Clark's report spoke of building on the strengths of the old bank in lending for housing and to farmers, adding that the bank was to 'develop into a new force in servicing the commercial and corporate sector'.[5] The Managing Director noted, however, that the bank was 'aggressively seeking a larger slice of the small business, corporate, commercial and international sectors'.[6]

The past as pastiche
To an outsider, the impression given by Clark's report was that the past was guiding the future. In practice, the new corporate ending was not only swamping the retail banking side of the SBSA but was also propelling the bank into markets it had no past experience of nor expertise in. It was this new direction and the speed of its uptake which destroyed the SBSA and yet it was one that at the time was depicted as progress, as the final recognition that the bank was modern and now in tune with market trends. Corporate lending it was agreed by both the bank and the parliament would be the agency for modernising an out of date institution. The SBSA management so aggressively pursued corporate business, however, that by 1986, the bank was beginning to grow out of control, and was doing so at a pace that was producing a declining level of profitability. Rather than slow the lending, the new corporate management decided paradoxically to intensify its corporate lending. By 1991 corporate loans had risen to 64.2 per cent of the bank's loans and accounted for 83.9 per cent of the loans that were non-performing.[7] By then housing loans in South Australia (while growing in real terms) contributed only 14.7 per cent of the bank's loans.[8] The bank was by then borrowing 82 per cent of its funds from the wholesale money market, using the government guarantee to obtain the capital so as to lend to corporate clients.[9] In seven years the SBSA had moved from a bank funding its loans from deposits to one, almost totally dependent on the international money market.

Giving lie to the advertisement that the SBSA had its 'heart' in South Australia was the fact that two thirds of the bank's business was now conducted outside of South Australia. The image of serving South Australia, cultivated for over one hundred years, was now mythical. The corporate business conducted interstate and overseas dominated lending but was justified on the grounds that it gave the bank its profits to service the 'unprofitable' housing and rural loans. But in the end it was the corporate loans which proved to be unprofitable and the housing loans which were the profitable core of the rescued bank's business.

Discarding prudence
Between 1984 and 1991 the State Bank of South Australia shed its values of thrift and prudence, mythologised as virtues of the nineteenth-century woman (who was once the Savings Bank's emblem), and adopted the entrepreneurial spirit of the 1980s where men made the deals. The transformation of the SBSA's lending was

evident both in its quantity (rising from $3 billion to $21 billion) and in its direction from housing and rural loans to corporate lending. To match this lending the SBSA changed its capital structure, moving from self reliance to dependence on the international money markets, a transformation from the constructive to the destructive side of capitalism.

The internal culture of the bank matched this new direction. The system of seniority was replaced by the hiring of staff regarded as possessing the technical ability to conduct the corporate loans. Equally, those from the old banks who were prepared to embrace the new culture were retained in positions of power. Managers who were critical of the cultural shift in the bank were often relegated to the sideline or sometimes pushed out of the bank altogether. The new entrepreneurial managers had little trouble borrowing money to lend to corporate clients, as the SBSA had a government guarantee, and there were many clients who were pursuing money to invest in assets which were growing faster than the rate of inflation. The dilemma was how to lend while minimising the risk to the bank. As early as 1986 the management was given clear signals that its lending was not returning an adequate level of profit to match its growth strategy. Faced with the decline in return on assets, the management decided paradoxically to accelerate the lending. By 1990 the speculative risks that the SBSA had been taking destroyed 'the bank that thrift built', and along with it the old State Bank of South Australia and its commitment to rural people and concessional housing loans in the state.

The new bank wanted to be a player in the 'big boy's game' of global finance and speculation. Ironically, the history of the old banks facilitated this shift. In particular, the Savings Bank never fully came to terms with the place of women in banking and society, and its inwardly looking old-fashioned ideas was a fertile basis for the new corporate bankers to claim these were anachronistic in the 1980s. When the SBSA leapt into the 1980s it had little historical experience to guide it and what history it had was swamped by the pace and size of the bank's growth. Here the inward looking past of the banks, fostered by respective governments in the 1950s and 1960s, provided the basis for a destructive rush into commercial lending in an era of financial deregulation.

The intensity of the present: doing the deal

> the bank's corporate lending displayed the characteristics of being driven by the need *to do the deal*. The application of sound policies and procedures was sacrificed to the desire to write new business.[10]

Doing the deal was the dominant private banking philosophy of the day, it was brought to the bank by Clark, and soon replaced the faith in thrift, a displacement fully supported by the old boards who dominated the MAG and then adopted by the new board. The drive 'to do the deal', with its rush to beat the opposition to the corporate clients, became the all pervasive drive of the senior managers, and their lending was supported by the board. In this frantic clamber for corporate clients, thrift gave way to credit financing and savings – the core concern of the old banks – became a residual component of the SBSA. In this the SBSA was merely following the major banks in Australia who recognised with deregulation that capital could be acquired overseas and deposits were a costly means of funding loans and providing services.

Doing the deal to beat the competition

> There are numerous examples of senior officers, for a variety of reasons not the least of which was to perceived need or desire ' to do the deal', inadequately and in some cases recklessly assessing proposals and failing to act in a responsible and prudent manner. The attitude that there was a need to complete the transaction quickly because if they did not, someone else would, seemed to pervade and characterise senior management's actions. The spectre of the competitor always waiting in the wings was constantly put forward as the reason for rushing so many transactions, many of which involved millions of dollars.[11]

A new breed of bankers was recruited, and those who came over from the two merged banks were inducted into or openly embraced, the new culture. The aim was to beat the competition to the corporate clients. The clamber for this business became intensified by financial deregulation which not only allowed the entrance of 15 foreign banks but also fundamentally altered the rules of the game of banking. The SBSA competed in this game without a history of the old rules and therefore tended to copy whatever the opposition was doing. It was a strategy based on a misguided hope that the other bank knew what they were doing. In this faith in the market, the new managers could find material sustenance in their own remunerations. The motivating force behind the managers' actions became to closely related to self-interest. Couched in the new language of the day, it was claimed individual self-interest equalled collective good. That is, the new corporate bankers were encouraged to pursue self-interest as this would (*ipso facto*) trickle down to others, in this case the taxpayers, in the private banks it was the shareholders. The new moral mission of the bank was no longer to instil prudence in the 'working people' but to encourage clients to access credit. For some of the managers in the bank this was a breath of fresh air, blowing away the paternalistic, patriarchal and patronising attitudes of the past.

Being a player in the big league

The corporate managers (recruited or re-invented) saw themselves as superior to the 'old retail bankers' they had replaced and to the rest of the public servants in South Australia. The desire was to be like a private banker. Moreover, in the process of seeking to realise this desire, the bank's culture became transformed from that of a public bank to that of a private bank. The bank measured its growth against that of the other banks, initially against the other state banks, and when the SBSA began to pass their 'sister' banks, its desire became focused on displacing the big four banks (the Commonwealth, the ANZ the National and Westpac) – or the 'big boys' as they were less than affectionately known within the bank.[12] By 1989 the bank was promoting itself as the seventh largest banking group in Australia.[13] It was lauded in the financial press as the dynamic new force in banking. By 1990 the SBSA was proudly boasting that it was now the fifth largest banking group.

Growth for growth's sake

> The one thing that all parties giving evidence to my investigation agreed upon was that the bank failed because 'it grew too fast'.[14]

The acquisitive culture that took hold in society and then in the bank was neither restrained by government control, nor in the SBSA's case by the shareholders. Rather, for the managers there was a pool of money to dip into to lend to business clients. From the outset the bank called on this money and grew at a rate faster than that of any other bank in Australia. In 1985 it grew by 27.5 per cent, in 1986 by 52 per cent, and in 1987 it grew by 25 per cent. Amazingly after the share market crash of 1987, when other banks began to become conservative lenders, the SBSA grew by 39.5 per cent in 1988.[15] The bank was now unable to stop itself, increasing its lending as the boom turned to bust. In 1989 the bank grew by 36.6 per cent, and notably its lending was geared to the high risk sector of the market, commercial property, where it lent over $1 billion in 1989 alone. In 1990, when the recession was looming and the bank recognised that it had a liability crisis, it could not stop its lending spree but grew by an incredible 40.7 per cent.[16]

Table 1 Comparison of bank group growth measures

year	Increase in total assets			Increase in operating profit after tax		
	Banks consolidated %	State Banks %	SBSA Group %	Banks consolidated %	State Banks %	SBSA group %
1985	21.9	26.0	27.5	18.2	17.1	N/A
1986	26.4	34.0	52.8	8.5	22.9	8.4
1987	15.8	21.5	25.0	8.9	(10.0)	0.3
1988	19.8	25.4	39.5	46.1	39.7	44.7
1989	21.4	25.2	36.6	2.7	(121.5)	36.8
1990	11.7	19.3	40.7	(36.5)	(5.6)	(73.5)

From Table 1 it is evident that the SBSA was growing faster than both comparable state banks and the banking industry as a whole.[17] Moreover, as the growth figures for 1988, 1989 and 1990 reveal the SBSA grew fastest after the share market crash and property industry's boom to bust cycle. At the onset of the recession in 1990 the bank was growing at four times that of the industry. A growth of 40.7 per cent in 1990 when banks as a whole reduced lending by 36.5 per cent is a clear indication of both how out of control the SBSA was and how 'reckless' its lending had become.[18]

Meaningless planning

> Make a loan, book the profit and make another loan. It was the excesses of the 1980s at its worst, conducted by a State Bank guaranteed by the people of South Australia.[19]

The growth in the bank's assets was unplanned. The SBSA management did have both a strategic plan and a profit plan, but these were more symbolic than meaningful indicators of where the bank was going. As the following table shows it was only in one year, 1987, that the plan and the outcomes matched. In every other year growth far outstripped the plan. In fact actual growth between 1986 and 1990 was $14 billion of which only $8 billion was planned.[20] In short, 38.7 per cent of the bank's growth was above the plan – the plans were irrelevant to the direction of the bank.[21] Table 2 below indicates the disjunction between planned and actual growth trends.

Table 2 Projected asset growth – bank

Year Ended 30 June	Strategic Plan Projection $M	%	Profit Plan Forecast $M	%	Actual $M	%
1985					739.4	27.5
1986	931.0	25.8	1,168.3	34.7	1,902.1	55.5
1987	1,717,1	24.6	1,311.7	24.4	1,514.2	28.4
1988	1,367.4	20.8	1,302.2	19.5	2,829.0	41.3
1989	1,156.7	13.1	1,398.3	14.5	3,156.1	33.1
1990	2,603.0	20.6	3,409.0	26.9	4,611.6	36.3

Everybody's doing it

During the 1980s, banks as a consolidated group showed continual growth, increasing their assets by over 10 per cent between 1985 and 1990 and in some years by over 20 per cent.[22] Even in the high risk years the banking sector still grew, by 21.4 per cent in 1989 and by 13.1 per cent in 1990. As a specific banking group, the state banks grew faster than the other banks but their level of profitability was lower. Initially the level of doubtful debts was lower in the state banks but after 1989 it was much higher than the other banks. Looking at the broader comparison between 1985 and 1990, the four major Australian banks (the Commonwealth Bank, the National, Westpac and the ANZ) averaged an after-tax return on net assets of 14.0 per cent whereas the SBSA returned 9.6 per cent.[23] The bank's return was in line with that of the State Bank of Victoria before its merchant bank subsidiary, Tricontinental, fell, implying that both banks had grown at too high a risk and at a cost to their profit margins. In turn, this suggests they were lending to more risky clients, turned down by the other banks, an implication clearly evident in the following tables on credit quality measures.[24]

Table 3a Comparison of bank group credit quality measures:

	Doubtful Debts Expense / Average Receivables			General Provision for Doubtful Debts / Receivables		
Year	Banks Consolidated	State Banks	SBSA Group	Banks Consolidated	State Banks	SBSA Group
	%	%	%	%	%	%
1985	0.40	0.30	0.50	0.90	0.20	0.50
1986	0.53	0.33	0.27	0.79	0.59	0.45
1987	0.72	0.33	0.28	1.02	0.63	0.41
1988	0.74	N/A	0.40	1.03	N/A	0.46
1989	1.27	1.93	0.80	0.94	0.93	0.49
1990	1.44	1.46	1.59	0.77	0.95	0.47

Table 3b Comparison of bank group profitability measures:

	Operating Profit after Tax / Average Net Assets:			Net Interest Income / Average Total Assets		
Year	Banks Consolidated	State Banks	SBSA Group	Banks Consolidated	State Banks	SBSA Group
	%	%	%	%	%	%
1985	15.9	9.5	6.5	3.40	3.30	3.80
1986	13.3	10.4	10.1	3.12	2.79	3.16
1987	11.4	7.1	6.3	2.94	2.34	2.61
1988	12.6	N/A	N/A	3.31	N/A	2.58
1989	10.8	(2.0)	10.3	3.12	2.43	2.05
1990	6.4	2.6	2.7	3.02	2.18	1.72

Thus in comparative terms, the SBSA was as the above tables indicate expanding at a rate faster than any of its competitors but at a cost to its profitability. By 1990 the SBSA group had grown to be larger than the State Bank of New South Wales and was 29 per cent of the size of the Commonwealth Bank.[25] In the period between 1986 and 1990, the SBSA increased its total assets by 216 per cent, compared with the average of the big four of 84 per cent, and the average for the State Banks of New South Wales and Victoria, and for the R & I in Western Australia of 107 per cent.[26]

Table 4 Growth in Bank Assets

Bank	1984 $'m	1990 $'m
State Bank of South Australia	2,683	17,300
State Bank of New South Wales	5,787	18,382
State Bank of Victoria	7,512	N/A
Rural and Industries Bank of WA	2,311	8,271
Commonwealth Bank	14,730	53,391

Symbol of success: appearance of profit, not profitability

The outward appearance of success was rising profits but this disguised an underlying weakness, the decline in profitability. To those outside the bank, notably the government, the rising levels of its profit and the fact that profit predictions were coming in on target gave them the sign that the bank was successful. In 1986, the bank predicted a profit of $35.1 million and it was $33.6 million; in 1987 it anticipated a profit of $41.9 million it was $40.8 million; in 1988 the budgeted profit was $47.7 million it came in at $55.5 million; in 1989 the budgeted profit was $65.8 million and it was $78.5 million; and in 1990 the budgeted profit was planned at $88.1 million but fell to $35.9 million and this was an artificial figure.[27]

Taxes as a symbol of success for the government

The second symbol of success was the rise in the flow of revenue to the government. In 1985 the SBSA paid $5,832,000 (on assets of $3.4 billion), in tax revenue, rising to $9,839,000 in 1986 (on assets of $5.4 billion); $31,250,000 was paid in 1987 (on assets of $6.8 billion); $46,000,000 in 1988 (on assets of $9.5 billion); $88,101,000 transferred to the State Treasury in 1989 (on assets of $12.6 billion), and $24,000,000 in 1990 (on assets of $17.2 billion) – and a fictitious payment of $21,026,000 was recorded in 1991 when the bank was rescued by the government to the amount of $950 million (on assets of $20.1 billion).[28]

The profit flow gave the Bannon government the sign it was looking for in regards to the entrepreneurial bank; it seems as if neither the Treasurer nor the Treasury looked for other signs of how the bank was going. If they had they would have seen that from 1986 onward this level of (profit) transfers was coming from a higher and higher level of assets. In banking terms, the implication was that the SBSA was growing at a cost to its profitability and therefore was likely to be making cuts in its margins and taking on higher risks in its loans. In other words, each rise in the level of profit was coming at a disproportionate rate of rise in the SBSA's assets, implying the poor quality of the assets acquired by the bank and the high risks it was taking. The following table gives an indication of the disproportionality between the bank's growth and its profit.[29]

Table 5 State Bank of South Australia Group: Key financial information as at 30 June

	1991 ($'000)	1990 ($'000)	1989 ($'000)	1988 ($'000)	1987 ($'000)	1986 ($'000)	1985 ($'000)
Net Interest Income	257,483	311,542	267,271	244,100	185,701	164,795	139,970
Operating Revenue	508,005	530,921	463,790	329,505	252,826	211,443	180,472
Doubtful Debts Expense	1,733,272	218,374	71,256	26,336	11,454	8,174	8,835
Operating Profit	5,011	(397)	97,022	69,518	52,081	41,000	37,016
After Tax	21,065	24,093	90,811	66,443	45,864	26,164	24,133
Dividends paid to SAGFA	21,026	24,093	88,101	46,000	31,250	9,839	5,852
Total Assets	21,620,272	21,142,063	15,028,946	11,003,257	7,893,767	6,451,221	4,130,398
Total Liabilities	20,242,266	19,760,770	13,672,661	9,992.848	7,301,625	6,040,568	3,760,218
Net Assets	1,378,006	1,381,293	1,356,285	1,010,409	592,142	410,653	370,180

From a thrift to an entrepreneurial bank 157

For the government the critical figure was the dividends paid to the Treasury. In terms of its stability, however, the SBSA's profits should have been weighed up against its total assets. By comparing the two columns (operating profit and total assets) it is possible to see the dramatic decline in the SBSA's profitability from 1986 onward. As the Auditor-General notes:

> The figures outline the dramatic growth (573 percent) in the Group's asset base over the period 1984–1990. From 1985–1989 operating profit before tax rose quickly (162 per cent), but was less than the growth in assets over this period (264 per cent). In 1990 the Group actually made a loss before tax, but its assets grew by 41 per cent.[30]

From 1985 to 1990 the bank's total assets (as distinct from the group assets) grew by 404 per cent but the bank's profitability did not grow along with its assets base. Rather there was a declining rate of profit on the rising assets. For example, in the period 1985 to 1989 the bank's assets grew by 270 per cent but its operating profit before tax rose by 179 per cent, that is, a rate nearly 100 per cent below that of the increase in assets.[31] In 1990 the bank group grew by 41 per cent but actually made a loss.[32] Here was the ultimate fictitious world where the bank's assets rose by over $6 billion in 1990 but the bank recorded a loss and was carrying an estimated $3 billion in doubtful debts, all in a year when the board was told by the management that the bank was consolidating its lending.

The bank was acquiring assets at low margins, implying it was taking on corporate clients for little benefit and at higher risk to the shareholders. Additionally, the bank was front-end loading its loans, so that the loan was more profitable in its early years and less profitable in the later years. So when the bank began to take on high risk loans there was the compounding problem of a decline in the returns on the previous loans. To be blunt, there was growth but often for little or no purpose on the bank's profit level.

Illusory banking
By 1990 the SBSA was making record loans, breaking all previous asset growth figures, but losing an unprecedented amount of public money. There was immense lending activity most of it outside of the state but at too high a risk for a bank guaranteed by the taxpayers.

In its last two years the bank group's assets nearly doubled in size. In the same period its doubtful debts were rising faster than its profits. In 1988 the average of its doubtful debts was 0.27 per cent on per average asset, rising to 0.80 per cent in 1989 and 1.77 per cent in 1990.[33] While the bank in general was following the market trends in taking on higher risks its lending was out of kilter with the other banks in 1989 and 1990.[34]

In 1990 the Managing Director was optimistically projecting growth for the next five years. The board finally began to recognise that this was unrealistic and the directors pressed the Premier to hold an external inquiry into the bank. Eventually, he agreed and this obliged Clark to allow an external evaluation of the bank. The review by J P Morgan showed that the bank had so many doubtful debts that the government had to bail out the SBSA with a $970 million loan (rising to $3 billion in the next two years). The initial rescue package was around three times the accumulation of six years of profit of the SBSA, and the final indemnity was ten times that of the bank's profits over this period.

Here was a public bank which grew from $3 billion to $21 billion dollars in assets, making an accumulated book profit of around $269 million between 1984 and 1990 before it had to be rescued to the amount of $3 billion dollars in 1991. After six years of debt reduction, the Group Asset Management Division (the 'bad bank'), which inherited these bad debts was able to sell off assets of $1.2 billion. Ironically, the 'good bank' after 1991 has returned a profit of $80 million a year, principally on housing loans. The bank had come full circle to its 1984 position, only to be privatised, with the public carrying the losses.

From a retail to a wholesale bank

As Table 6 below shows the capital funding of the SBSA was fundamentally transformed in two years, from 1984 to 1986. From 1986 onward the SBSA was dependent upon outside sources for its funds and had to find high levels of profit to meet its interest bills on the money borrowed. The table shows how in three years after the merger the funding of the SBSA had been profoundly changed and by 1990 the funding was totally transformed.[35]

Table 6 Division between retail and wholesale funds – State Bank

Year	Retail %	Wholesale %
1984	85	15
1985	N/A	N/A
1986	45	55
1987	38	62
1988	32	68
1989	25	75
1990	18	82

The old banks had used their deposit base to fund loans, but by 1986 the capital structure of the bank was transformed with over half of its capital coming from outside its own resources. In short, the old State Bank and the Savings Bank operated in the retail market for their funds and lent in the retail market for housing, rural loans and government instrumentalities. In 1984 the newly formed State Bank only turned to the wholesale market for 15 per cent of its funds, and by 1990 wholesale funds constituted 82 percent of the funds for its lending. The bank became dominated by its borrowing on the wholesale market and its lending to the corporate clients with two thirds of its assets outside of South Australia. Moreover, as the Auditor-General noted, the capital borrowed by the SBSA through the government agency, SAFA, was at an advantageous rate to the bank. In sum, it was obtaining cheap money for its lending and its borrowing was fully backed by its government guarantee.[36]

Dangerous diversity

When the SBSA was formed, corporate loans constituted only $464 million out of the initial asset base of $2.6 billion. By 1990 corporate lending constituted 38 per cent of its lending assets, and 60 per cent of its problem loans were in this sector.[37] In 1984 housing loans amounted to 62.5 per cent of the SBSA's interest earning assets but by 1990 they constituted only 14.7 per cent of the bank's lending. In contrast, in 1990 housing loans accounted for a mere 2 per cent of the bank's non-performing loans. In 1990 foreign loans made up 34.8 per cent of the loan portfolio and were responsible for 24.7 per cent of non-performing loans.[38] As the accompanying table shows, by 1990, 65 per cent of the bank's lending was being conducted in the corporate sector and this contributed 82 per cent of outstanding loans.[39]

Table 7 Loan portfolio

Loan Portfolio	Proportion of Loan Portfolio %	Proportion of Non-Performing Loan %
Australia:		
Housing	14.7	2.0
Retail Personal and Business	13.0	13.0
Corporate	37.6	60.4
New Zealand:		
Housing (United Banking)	7.6	1.2
Corporate	9.9	11.6
Other International:		
Housing	0.5	–
Corporate	16.8	11.9
	100.00	100.00

When the SBSA ran into difficulty it was not from its (old) retail sector but from its (new) corporate loans. In its report on the bank, J P Morgan estimated that as of 31 December 1990 the SBSA's exposure to retail lending was 2.5 per cent of which only 2.0 per cent was in the non-accrual category (i.e. loans not returning any money to the bank).[40] The bank had lent 1.9 per cent to public administration of which 0.2 per cent was not accruing money.[41] In contrast, the bank's highest exposure was to finance, which was an exposure of 25.8 per cent and this sector had non-accruals of 12.8 per cent.[42] It had an exposure to property of 22.4 per cent of which 51.9 per cent was in the non-accruals.[43] In sum, the SBSA had ventured into areas of lending which were of much higher risk than that of home loans (the basis of the old banks) with almost no experience of such lending but at a rate in excess of that of the major corporate banks.[44]

The optimism of commercial property

The bank executives, especially those in BFC, had according to the Auditor-General a 'reckless optimism' in the safety of commercial property.[45] The nature of the bank's lending in this high risk sector can be seen in the fact that during 1989 lending for commercial property comprised 72 per cent of total commercial approvals, an increase of exposure of $1,008.6 million (doubling the exposure) in one year.[46] The exposure by the bank to commercial property exceeded 20 per cent of risk assets, which went against Reserve Bank prudential guidelines.[47] In the case of Beneficial Finance its exposure to property accounted for an extraordinary 60.09 per cent of its risk exposures.[48]

Table 8 Exposure of the risk portfolio per industry

Industry	Bank per cent	Beneficial per cent	Group per cent
Property and business services	15.38	47.03	23.58
Construction	7.07	13.06	7.51
Finance, Investment, etc.	44.52	16.04	38.59

In brief, the bank group was over-exposed to commercial property, one of the riskiest sectors of lending in the late 1980s, and this was a significant cause of its bad debts. In making these loans the bank and, especially, BFC was convinced that property was always safe. Between 1985 and 1990 the corporate banking exposure to commercial property was to increase by more than 1,675 per cent, rising from $101.9 million to $1,809 million in these years.[49] In 1989 at the time when the commercial property market was over-heating, the bank lent an amount in excess of $1 billion dollars, from $801 million to $1,809.7 billion, of which commercial property comprised 72 per cent of total commercial approvals.[50] In 1988 and 1989, while the Reserve Bank cautioned against lending on commercial property, the SBSA increased its loans to this sector by 125.9 per cent and to developers and contractors by 154.8 per cent.[51] To the taxpayers' regret the SBSA treated the Reserve Bank's caution too lightly.[52] By December 1989 the bank's total exposure to commercial property exceeded 20 per cent of its risk assets (of which over 50 per cent was in the CBD districts of Sydney, Melbourne, Brisbane and Adelaide).[53]

Table 9 Exposure to developers and contractors

As at June	Exposure $M	Proportion of Corporate Loans %	Proportion of Total Risk Assets %
1985	74.1	7.94	4.38
1986	190.6	6.57	4.33
1987	346.5	12.24	7.30
1988	611.2	14.25	8.56
1989	1,577.5	27.39	13.01

As Table 9 shows the SBSA exposure to developers and contractors grew at a remarkable rate given that the bank group had no experience of this market.[54] The SBSA had moved into a culture of which it had no experience and one that was highly volatile yet it ignored the external warning signs that it was conducting high risk business.[55] When it began to attract clients in the period following the share market crash of 1987 it did so without recognising the short and long term risks it was taking. Yet no one intervened to prevent this risky lending, instead the executives making the loans depicted them as beating the other banks to the entrepreneurs, the heroes of the 1980s.[56] The share market crash had wiped out half the value of the Australian share index, yet, rather than reducing its lending, the bank expanded its assets in what was then becoming an over-heated market.

Last spin of the dice

Many of the entrepreneurial clients the SBSA attracted to its corporate books after the share market crash were often seeking quick profits to ward off other banks and sought a last gamble on property to make a high return. But when the property boom turned to bust the SBSA was left with bankrupt clients and high interest obligations on the money it had borrowed to lend to them. The SBSA having been quick to make the deal, was now confronted by clients without the funds to meet their interest payments and commercial property worth far less than anticipated. When the property market turned down the bank found itself with a devalued asset and a non-performing loan. It could not sell the buildings as there were no buyers and if the SBSA had sold at disposal prices this would have had a snowballing effect on the rest of its property portfolio. The bank even found it difficult to rent out these properties. The SBSA then had little choice but to hang on to the buildings, carrying the interest payments until they could be disposed of in an orderly fashion. It was then left to the 'bad bank' group, the Asset Management Division, to carefully dispose of these assets.

Abandoning South Australia

The old banks were specifically established to serve the South Australian market. The SBSA was meant to carry this tradition forward and become more commercial in the process. Within six years of its formation the bulk of the SBSA's business was being conducted outside of South Australia. As the following chart shows 65 per cent of the bank's exposure was interstate and overseas and this constituted 61.8 per cent of its doubtful (or non-accrual) exposures.[57] Just as the SBSA had moved into markets of which it had little experience, the managers also spread into regions in which they had limited knowledge. Here the SBSA's endeavours were far worse than that of the Bank of Adelaide, both in the extent of its losses on commercial property, notably on the eastern seaboard.[58] As the table (100) below reveals, as of October 1990 nearly one in two of its loans interstate were non-accruals.

Table 10

Geographic Area	Total Exposure Per cent	Non-Accrual Exposures per cent
South Australia	34.8	38.2
Interstate	31.1	46.8
Overseas	34.1	15.0

Overseas speculation

The extent of how far the SBSA was in unfamiliar markets can be seen in its expansion overseas. In 1984 the SBSA had an asset base of only $22 million but in 1985 the board agreed to a strategy of overseas expansion. The SBSA expanded overseas in three major waves. The first wave was from June 1985 to June 1986 when the assets overseas rose from $36.1 million to $395 million.[59] The second wave was from June 1986 to December 1991 when assets grew from $395 million to $1,037.2 million.[60] The last wave was from December 1988 to September 1990 when assets rose at an extraordinary rate from $1,207.9 million to $7,999.7 million.[61] As the following table (11) shows, the bank's expansion overseas occurred in a period after the share market crash of 1987 and especially in 1990, when the property bubble burst and Australia slipped into recession, ahead of the rest of the world.

Table 11 Growth in income earning assets – overseas operations

Period Ending	$A'M
June 1985	36.1
March 1986	346.4
June 1986	395.6
September 1986	782.6
December 1986	613.6
March 1987	690.0
June 1987	719.1
September 1987	852.5
December 1987	1,037.2
March 1988	968.9
June 1988	971.7
September 1988	1,088.7
December 1988	1,207.9
March 1989	2,173.8
June 1989	2,537.1
December 1989	4,426.3
June 1990	6,880.4
September 1990	7,999.7

Alongside the growth in what is termed 'incoming assets', was the rise in the bank's off-balance sheet 'contingent liabilities'.[62] These included foreign exchange transactions, interest rate swaps, cross currency interest rate swaps, contingent swaps, interest rate futures, guarantees, letters of credit and bill endorsements. The growth in the off-balance sheet contingencies was from $2,976 million in June 1986 to $36,693.7 million in November 1990, falling to $27,220.2 million in February 1991.[63]

Table 12 Growth in off-balance sheet business – Total contingent liabilities

Period Ending	$A'M
June 1986	2,976.0
June 1987	9,920.0
June 1988	10,291.0
December 1988	22,430.0
September 1990	34,546.9
November 1990	36,693.7
December 1990	31,956.7
February 1991	27,220.2

The fact that the SBSA was in this world of 'high finance' is alarming in itself, but as the above Table 12 shows the sheer extent of its involvement says a lot about the reality that had gripped the bank management.[64] The bank from South Australia was now in the heady world of international high finance, competing against banks that had been involved in this rarefied atmosphere for decades (if not in some cases for centuries).

Creating an illusion
The bank's expansion overseas was based on illusion rather than profit. In 1989–90 the return on average overseas earning assets was 0.01 per cent; in money terms the bank had invested nearly $8 billion overseas to make a loss of $6,396,000 for that financial year.[65] It came as no surprise then that it was this area of lending which Royal Commissioner Jacobs termed 'crazy'.[66] The bank management justified its expansion overseas on the grounds that there was more profitable business to be had elsewhere than in South Australia and that the profits earned would flow back to the State Bank. The board was all too ready to share in this illusion, despite the facts that the overseas operations were growing at an uncontrolled rate recording either marginal returns or substantial losses.[67] For Commissioner Jacobs this economic logic was not supported by the profit returns on the overseas investment.

Those little town blues
The claim of serving local client needs overseas was the rationalisation given to the board and Premier Bannon as to why the bank should establish a branch in New York. In November 1987 the bank board decided to open a New York office, and for tax minimisation purposes and to get around Reserve Bank regulations, this expansion included a Cayman Island sub-branch. The New York office engaged in risk-taking activities, including leverage transactions (loans with a high debt to equity ratio, 3:1, or higher) and mezzanine finance (subordinate lending which can be of a high risk nature with spreads of 8 per cent) in a market of which it had no experience and in a country where there was quite a different banking culture.[68]

In June 1990, the SBSA had assets of $1,750 million in New York and the return on its assets between 1988 and February 1991 was an accumulated profit of $4.9 million.[69] The overall return on assets in New York in 1991 was only 0.22 per cent, with 40 per cent of the branch's outstanding loans being from high leveraged transactions.[70] The bank's lending in New York was uncontrolled by head office, and lending increased by 81 per cent between July 1990 and February 1991 when the board was advised by the New York branch that it was consolidating its portfolio and not making new loans.[71] The bank's ill-considered expansion into New York is captured in the following exchange between Commissioner Jacobs and Premier Bannon.

> *Commissioner Jacobs*: If you had thought to yourself 'This is crazy', would you have said so?
> *Premier Bannon*: If I had thought it was crazy, yes, which would suggest that the bank had gone crazy, I suggest.
> *Commissioner Jacobs:* That thought didn't cross your mind.
> *Premier Bannon*: Not at all.[72]

The image thing
Commissioner Jacobs regarded the bank's expansion into New York as a failure on the part of the Treasurer/Premier Bannon to challenge the grandiose plans of the

bank. He considered that the bank's expansion for its adventures overseas were 'unconvincing if not silly'.[73] In defending the board, Lew Barrett said that the reason for going overseas was that the SBSA wanted to be no longer seen as a small regional bank but one that was international and this was the 'real reason' for the board's desire to expand overseas.[74] As Commissioner Jacobs observed the most obvious feature about the bank venturing overseas was that it wanted to be a 'major player in the big league'.[75] It wanted to create the image that it was a successful international bank even if this meant in the short term losing money.

Auditor-General MacPherson was also of the view that the New York venture was of a high risk character and was scathing of the management for engaging in such lending. In his criticism, he in particular criticised Trevor Mallett, the manager of overseas operations, for misleading the board (by omissions) as to the high risk character of the New York branch's lending. These omissions, he concluded, prevented the board from discharging its duties prudentially.[76] Mallett in his submission to the Auditor-General's inquiry defended management prerogative to determine the risk of a loan whereever it might occur, saying that:

> 'debt is debt' whether it be in Australia or New York. Just for the record, if the board delegated me a discretion, it was a total discretion. So far as I'm concerned the activities of management within discretions were Management's responsibility, not the board.[77]

Nevertheless, as the Auditor-General regarded this answer as too superficial and unconvincing and he said it was not shared by other executive officers.[78] To be blunt, there is a marked difference between taking on debt in a market of which you have historical knowledge and an understanding of its culture and one in which the competition is fierce and the culture foreign. MacPherson was equally critical of Mallett for withholding information from the board as to the high risk character of the bank's New York operations. The bank's entry into New York was a dislocation from the bank's past – and certainly of marginal worth.[79]

In regard to Mallett, the Auditor-General said he erred in not drawing to the attention of the board the high risk 'nature of the corporate finance activities of the New York Office' adding that 'Mr Mallett's withholding of the information sits uneasily with his description of the difficulties of exercising effective control over the off-shore branches'.[80] Likewise, MacPherson considered that Clark , his deputy Kenneth Matthews, along with Mallet and Chris Guille failed to adequately keep the board informed of the Reserve Bank concerns over the level of the SBSA's exposure.[81]

Never say no
The bank's philosophy for overseas lending was neatly summed up by Mallett, who in discussing the bank's lending in New Zealand, said that 'our style is not to say no (you can't have a loan) but to say how we'd do it'.[82] In short, the SBSA was always looking to find ways of saying 'yes' to a loan. As the following table on the profit and loss results for overseas, on-balance sheet investments reveal losses in New Zealand were over $2 million with an expenditure by the SBSA of over $1.5 billion. The Auditor-General was highly critical of the role of both Mallett and Clark in the bank's exposure in New Zealand. MacPherson singled out the failure of Mallett and Clark to inform the board, in 1988, that the SBSA's loans were at risk

because the New Zealand economy was 'headed for a major disaster' as constituting 'a dereliction of their duties to the bank and the bank board'.[83]

Table 13 Profit/Loss results from overseas branches

Year Ended 30 June	London GBP'M	New York $US'M	Auckland $NZ'M
1986	0.459	–	–
1987	0.266	–	–
1988	0.321	–	–
1989	1.196	0.2	(0.3)
1990	0.233	1.7	(11.5)
February 1991	(12.773)	3.1	(1.845)

As the above Table 13 indicates, the SBSA's loans overseas were of little or no benefit to the bank's profitability, only intensifying the risk the bank was taking in its financial transactions.[84] By February 1991, the SBSA had at risk $325.5 million in exposures from overseas investment with a total of $5.2 billion invested outside of Australia for marginal returns.

Beneficial Finance Corporation

> Although Beneficial Finance's total assets represented only about 13 per cent of the total assets of the State Bank Group, its loan losses represented about 43 per cent of the Group's total loan losses, and its total losses were about 42 per cent of total Group losses.[85]

Just as had occurred with the Bank of Adelaide and its financial subsidiary FCA so too with the SBSA; it was its subsidiary, BFC which was lending at far higher risk than the parent bank. In this regard the Auditor-General considered that BFC's lending was so out of control that it could be deemed 'reckless'.[86] He noted that by March 1990 60 per cent of BFC's $3 billion lending program was of an entrepreneurial kind outside of what was supposed to be its core business (that of lending for real estate and equipment purchases).[87] He noted that its corporate division was run by 'irresponsible managers who speculated wildly in commercial property, driven by little more than the thought for the next sale'.[88] By 1990 Beneficial Finance's lending had caused it to accumulate a disproportionately high level of bad debts.[89] While BFC represented around 13 per cent of the bank's assets its poor lending resulted in BFC being responsible for 42 percent of the bank group losses.[90] The Auditor-General considered that the Corporate Services Division of BFC was basically its engine room,

> paid no attention to the basic principles of credit risk management, blithely assumed the continual availability of unlimited funding regardless of the term of its exposures or their cash flows, and assumed that commercial property development was eternally and unerringly profitable. The division was run by irresponsible managers who speculated widely in commercial property, driven by little more than thought for the next sale.[91]

In relative terms, the Auditor-General regarded Beneficial Finance as being one of the country's leaders in profligacy and imprudence with its growth uncontrolled and its risk taking of rash proportions. He wrote that:

> The 1980s has become known as the period of corporate excesses. Beneficial Finance's corporate behaviour must rank as an example of the worst kind of excesses that were prevalent during that period.[92]

MacPherson is of the view that the BFC managers received inflated salaries. For instance, the Auditor-General commented that by June 1990 Baker's total remuneration package stood at nearly $525,000 which was more than double the packages for the heads of the Commonwealth Bank and the State Banks of New South Wales and Victoria.[93] In addition, the salary packages for another six senior executives in BFC stood at $200,000 or more.[94]

The nature of BFC lending had been transformed from one of small real estate loans, equipment leasing and consumer finance (the old core) to corporate loans and commercial property (non-core). By March 1990, sixty per cent of BFC's business was non-core.[95] BFC, according to the Auditor-General, speculated too freely on commercial property, 'with an unquestioning faith in the inevitable profitability of commercial property development projects'.[96] Likewise in their operating joint ventures the managers had a tendency to lend too freely. As the Auditor-General argues, 'the very nature of the relationship between Beneficial Finance and its joint venture partners encouraged profligate lending, and the growth of businesses beyond the capacity of the partners to manage. Inevitably, significant losses resulted and, equally inevitably, it was Beneficial Finance, as the financing partner, that paid the costs'.[97] That is, BFCs chief executive officers Reichart and Baker's strategy 'was to seek out small entrepreneurs and offer them a joint venture with unlimited finance to grow, uncontrolled by normal funding constraints, involving taking an unacceptable risk that is tantamount to gambling'.[98]

In short, BFC was in the high risk end of the market, lending money to clients who were conducting businesses of whose operations BFC did not seem to have adequate knowledge. Moreover, in general terms the directors failed, in MacPherson's view, to come 'to grips with the reality of the operation of Beneficial Finance'.[99] Baker, who in 1990 was touted as the replacement for Tim Marcus Clark, in Auditor-General MacPherson's view, 'must bear the heaviest share of the blame'. He 'displayed a serious lack of understanding of his duties as Managing Director' simply promoting growth without due regard to prudential policies or procedures'.[100] Of Baker's assistant at the top, Erich Reichart, the Auditor-General was quite scathing, saying:

> Mr Reichart must take a heavy share of the responsibility for the financial position of Beneficial Finance in February 1991. Mr Reichart single-mindedly pursued assets growth, with a one-dimensional faith in high-profile property developments that bordered on recklessness. I am simply at a loss to understand how the second most senior executive in Beneficial Finance could then, and judged by his submission to my Investigation, still now, pay such complete disregard to the realities of the cyclical nature of the commercial property market, and to the need for a financial institution to be able to fund

its activities. Mr Reichart seemed to have only one thought – that commercial property investment was good. The risks associated with the fact the investment was long-term, with long-term negative cash flows, seemed never to enter his head.[101]

In Reichart's defense his strategy was fully in keeping with the banking culture of the 1980s; where the objective was to loan to entrepreneurs who were investing in assets which were rising faster in value than the rate of inflation. In general, BFC's tactic was to lend on commercial property, which had been an area of escalating asset value. However, when the market became over-heated in 1989 the asset value fell as dramatically as it had risen. It took some years for the value of commercial property to rise, unfortunately for the SBSA and the BFC the upward correction in the market came far too late.

In September 1990, when the bank investigated BFC lending, it discovered that 71.8 per cent of BFC's loans under the $20 million mark were at risk, amounting to $2.38 billion. Concomitantly, of the 24 clients with loans in excess of $25 million there were 12 loans which were non-performing, the total exposure being $870 million.[102] Between 1986 and 1989 BFC grew at three times the rate of its competitors, growing by 326 per cent compared to the average of 103.9 per cent.[103] The growth of BFC was facilitated by a plethora of off-balance sheet companies and trusts which made it difficult to analyse or bring under the control of the bank itself. This was compounded by the tendency of the BFC board of directors to have 'paper meetings' as alternatives to convening board meetings thereby undermining the power of the board to control the managers.[104]

When it began BFC was lending within the historical charter of the State Bank. In July 1984 BFC lent on average $25,000, almost all in real estate property.[105] The 1986 annual report described corporate lending as representing 6 per cent, corporate finance in 1987 rose to $411 million but by June 1988 it had risen to $766 million, a rise of 86 per cent, while corporate lending in 1988 represented 39 per cent of all loans.[106] By 1988 BFC had moved into the realm of financing property projects and into joint ventures outside of its past experience or historic expertise at an unprecedented rate.[107]

BFC grew by 48 per cent ($245 million) in 1985, 39 per cent ($295 million) in 1986, 9 per cent ($95 million) in 1987, 46 per cent ($526 million) in 1988, 36 per cent ($595 million) in 1989 and 18 per cent ($412 million) in 1990.[108] BFC's growth for its last three years was basically unplanned – the actual growth of $1,534,000,000 exceeding the planned growth of $726 million by $807 million, or 111 per cent.[109] Actual asset growth between 1988 and 1990 was double that budgeted. According to the Auditor-General strategic planning and budgets were 'largely irrelevant'.[110] BFC's unplanned growth in financial areas where it had 'little previous experience' at a rate in excess of any of its competitors lead MacPherson to raise the 'suspicion that BFC's credit assessment standards were imprudently low'.[111]

In short, both BFC and the Bank Group grew too fast in diverse areas which it had no historical collective memory of and in an unplanned manner.[112] The SBSA group was transformed from a South Australian retail lender into a corporate entrepreneurial banker only too ready to lend to entrepreneurs all over Australia, and in London, New York and New Zealand. The bank was altered from a bank essentially servicing South Australia to one that had two-thirds of its assets outside the state. Moreover, even its lending to corporations in the State seemed to produce fleeting results with the three big monuments to the bank's lending, the Remm–Myer complex, the Australis office block in Grenfell Street and the State Bank building, all being sold at a loss. The SBSA was remodelled from that of a successful regional retail bank to a global corporate bank which collapsed under the weight of its debts.

As early as 1986 the bank was confronted with a mismatch between growing assets and disproportionate returns on those assets. Expressed simply, the SBSA was growing but at a cost to its overall level of profitability. In 1986 the bank then made the fateful and fatal decision to chase assets to match its borrowing from the international money markets. In the end the share market crash, property slump in 1989 and the recession of 1990 exposed the weaknesses in this strategy. The SBSA was over-exposed, notably in commercial property with little chance of recouping its money quickly and with the international creditors now demanding repayment.

The bank's initial successful growth hid the declining profitability, as did the uncritical media image of the bank as the most successful (state) bank in Australia, headed by the (dynamic) Tim Marcus Clark. The image of the SBSA as a winner, as a successful entrepreneurial bank, lasted until entrepreneurial banking came under question and then the weak link in the financial chain, the state banks, were cleansed from the market. In 1990 the SBSA, as the Bank of Adelaide had before it, became the victim of its desire to be a national player and to the excesses of its subsidiary. The internal desire to be a player, however, was made from a position of weakness. The State Bank had neither the staff, the experience nor the culture to be a global corporate bank. As the next chapter will show these weaknesses were disguised by the transformation of the SBSA's culture from that of a public to a private bank. In the process of transformation few were given the power or the incentive to look prudentially after the shop. There was, in effect, inadequate checks and balances on the bank's lending.

7

Who's looking after the shop?

As we saw in Part I of this book, the administrative history of the Savings Bank of South Australia and the old State Bank of South Australia could be characterised as authoritarian, paternalistic, and patriarchal. From the respective boards downward the administration was one of caution, prudence and a 'hands on' approach to lending. Each decision was checked and double checked, with the boards overseeing all the major decisions of the managers. Expressed simply, the administrative history of the merged banks was one in which there was more concern with minimising risk via administrative controls than in taking risks by being out in the market place.

When the two banks merged in 1984 this culture was quickly replaced by one of acquiring corporate business and expecting the administration to catch up with the lending. Whereas the old banks had too many checks and balances, the new State Bank of South Australia seemed to have too few. As Auditor-General MacPherson expressed it, the 'essential feature of the prudent management' [is] 'assets and liabilities management [and] the most startling feature of the State Bank operations, is that before late 1990, it did not exist. Until 1990, there simply was no overall management of the Bank's assets and liabilities'.[1]

This chapter draws out the implications of the SBSA's pursuit of corporate growth without any effective assets and liabilities management system. The old banks with their inward looking cultures became highly susceptible to the new private sector approach brought to the SBSA by Tim Marcus Clark. The SBSA senior management became divided between the new breed of bankers, loyal to and dependent on the Chief Executive Officer, and the old bankers, most of whom had no experience of wholesale banking but were concerned as to the lack of prudential controls. They were easily caricatured as yesterday's men not in tune with the culture of the 1980s.

The culture outside of the SBSA in the 1980s was one of speculative capitalism, where the deregulated financial market created an environment of asset acquisition. The media lauded the entrepreneurs who were using debt financing to take over companies. The SBSA pursued these entrepreneurs as an expression of making the bank more commercial. Unlike its major competitors, the SBSA however had little history of such corporate clients and limited systems to manage the loans and to evaluate prudentially the risks the bank was taking.

What was surprising about the SBSA was not that it was tempted by the speculative culture outside, rather it was that it never realised it was so deeply in trouble until it was too late. That is, by 1986 there was tension within the SBSA management that the bank could not absorb its growth nor manage prudentially its liabilities, yet the desire for growth remained. Moreover, the bank 'took off' from 1988 onward when the risks in the market were greatest. A major reason for this foolhardiness was that there was no overall coherent system of managing risk within the bank.

This chapter is first concerned with revealing the lack of control over lending within the bank. Secondly, it will offer reasons as to why there was never an effective system to oversee and regulate lending within the SBSA. Moreover, the chapter will explain how the SBSA disregarded the warning from outside the bank as to the risks it was taking.

Doing it alone

> Mr Clark's imperative was to diversify and grow, and there was nothing to stand in his way. The economic environment of the day was ideal. Deregulation opened up new markets and new opportunities. As a State bank, the Bank was not subject to the formal supervision that did exist. He was the only director with any banking experience, enabling him to dominate the board. There was no share price to worry about – just profits. There was an unlimited supply of money to fund the Bank's expansion – the Government guarantee meant that it could borrow whatever funds it needed, as and when it required them, without any real need to plan.[2]

The transformation of the SBSA from a retail to a wholesale corporate bank was articulated in the debates on the State Bank Act. The Act indicated that the bank should be both a corporate bank and a home/rural lender. The implication was that the board should steer the bank in this dual direction. The debate on the Act indicated that the board and the managers should look after the bank. The government should be 'at arm's length' from the SBSA. The new entrepreneurial Chief Executive Officer took the Act as a mandate to turn the SBSA into an international corporate bank and to be run without political interference. Clark's skill was in corporate trading and had limited experience of the second major aspect of corporate banking, asset management. The pace of the SBSA's growth and the sheer size of its corporate loans saw the traditional home and rural lending completely swamped by the wholesale lending.

The past offered little assistance in the bank's new direction as the previous prudential structures of the merged banks was geared to retail lending which was relatively simple in operation. Moreover, the lack of structure for gauging loans was compounded by the absence of collective memory of lending to corporations. Additionally, in a deregulated financial environment there was a high demand for experienced corporate bankers, notably in Sydney but also in Melbourne. Additionally, the Managing Director in the opinion of the Auditor-General unfortunately created an 'autocratic environment' which ensured that senior managers were dependent upon him.[3]

Prudential management from outside the bank was equally a problem. Under the Act, the State Bank was autonomous, yet responsible to the Treasurer, to respective private auditors and, in a voluntary manner, to the Reserve Bank. All of these external checks relied heavily on what the bank told them was happening inside the bank, and all in the end were unable to stop the bank's demise. That is, the State

Treasury had no experience of supervising a corporate bank and had few staff who knew this financial area and was hamstrung in its operations by the Premier blocking it from 'second guessing' the bank. The Reserve Bank did have the expertise and the ability to place the SBSA's lending and profitability in historical indices and comparisons with other banks and on market trends. Nevertheless, its supervision was only voluntary and was obliged by its Act to supervise those institutions which legally and formally came under its ambit.

As such the SBSA was forging new grounds with little internal means of control and the outside supervision was more symbolic than of substance. The old banks relied on their boards to oversee their business activities, keeping their distance both from the Treasury and the Treasurer. In the new SBSA the board's autonomy was retained and was assisted by the private auditor. Additionally, the Reserve Bank made visits to the bank to appraise its progress and raise issues with the senior managers. The effect of this was to place predominant weight for prudential supervision of the bank's business onto the management and board. The major reason for this, according to the Auditor-General, was the lack of leadership from the top over prudential management within the bank.

This lack of control over lending was criticised by MacPherson when he commented that:

> The organisation structure of the bank meant that there were no internal checks or controls on the growth. The bank was organised into highly autonomous business units, with the objective of making those divisions accountable for their profitability. There was no overall authority which exercised control. The Executive Committee was mired in detail, and ineffective, Mr Clark's focus was not on prudent control, but on growth and profitability.[4]

In short, the SBSA was very much on its own in assessing its credit transactions and this made the flaws in its credit management more acute. For the bank as a whole these flaws were critical, however, because for the managers keen on lending the advantage of so much autonomy was in rising annual remuneration packages. The lending managers vigorously guarded their prerogatives to lend and there was too little attention and respect for systems of control over prudential lending.

The role of Chief Executive Officer

> The bank's inaugural Chief Executive Officer, Mr Clark, was the bank's growth hormone ... The story of the bank is one of a professionally aggressive and entrepreneurial Chief Executive without sufficient appreciation of the need for prudent banking controls and management.[5]

The Auditor-General considers that Tim Marcus Clark was the driving force behind the SBSA's asset growth. He was responsible for shaping the growth culture within the bank and was the dominant influence in the bank's recruitment program and in the promotion and remuneration packages of the senior managers. Clark was appointed in the context of making the new bank more commercially orientated than the old State Bank or the Savings Bank and saw his role as driving the cultural revolution within the SBSA as fulfilling his employment brief.

Changing the culture

In changing the direction of lending Clark set about inculcatng into the SBSA a new entrepreneurial culture.[6] This new culture regarded corporate banking as superior to that of the retail banking which had dominated the business of the two merged banks.[7] In keeping with this logic the corporate bankers considered that they had to be paid at more commercial rates than their predecessors. The new corporate bankers were rewarded far in excess of the 'old' bankers and therefore had to justify their salaries by attracting more and more business. Once they had achieved that objective, they then had to justify the subsequent hike in their salary by drumming up more business. Their superiority was constructed on the treadmill of continually doing the deal. The SBSA's culture and system of material rewards became structured around growth. It was at one level growth for growth's sake but at another it was growth for higher remuneration.

Those who upheld the past and the bank's social responsibilities were construed by Clark as living in an 'outdated culture'.[8] He spoke of applying a 'new broom' to this culture.[9] To achieve this end he began a recruitment campaign so as to bring a 'fresh approach' to management, unconstrained by 'old-style thinking'.[10] In this process the bankers from the merged banks who questioned the style and skill of the new 'technocrats' were marginalized and some made redundant in this process.[11] As the Auditor-General observed, the weaknesses in the bank's competence were in no small part due to its recruitment polices. He noted that:

> One director expressed the view that, at senior levels, the bank was increasingly staffed by 'technocrats' ie people with technical, rather than banking, skills. Mr Masters, has asserted that one of the reasons for the Bank's difficulties was attributed to the fact that it 'kept bringing in personnel from areas outside banking and replacing traditional bankers with 'whizz kids'[12]

Three years after the merger the bank had effectively been transformed and this occurred in no small part tue to the recruitment of new personnel.

The new managers

> The all-encompassing, isolated and subjective nature of Mr Clark's dealing with senior management, however, had the potential to create – and did, I am satisfied, create – an autocratic environment. The dependency thus generated between senior executives and the Managing Director was unhealthy, and hence inappropriate. The inappropriateness of the concentration of power lay in the risk that this ensuing dependency would sway the judgement of senior management or stifle the criticism or dissent which individual or groups might otherwise have felt free to express.[13]

When the SBSA began its recruitment drive for senior managers the labour market for experienced corporate bankers was extremely tight. Federal Treasurer

Paul Keating had just deregulated the financial market, and fifteen foreign banks had opened their doors for business in Australia. Additionally, Sydney had become the country's financial hub. As a consequence, the SBSA found it difficult to recruit corporate bankers to Adelaide. This, however, did not dampen the bank's ardour to be a corporate player. It recruited non-bankers and those with academic banking qualifications but with little or no banking experience. It was under the apprehension of losing staff that Clark said the bank had to pay the new recruits relatively high commencement salaries (at the 75th percentile mark as set out in bank surveys) to lure them to the SBSA and then continue to pay them high salaries so as to prevent them from being head-hunted by the opposition.[14] As Auditor-General MacPherson observed, the SBSA 'was successful in retaining its recruits as no senior executive was poached by another bank but that might just say something about the quality of the SBSA's senior staff'.[15] Expressed more negatively, it could be that no other bank might have wanted the SBSA managers.

The recruitment policy of the SBSA reinforced the sense of difference within the bank. Among many bankers from the merged banks the feeling was that their knowledge and skills were being devalued and that the SBSA was replacing them with inexperienced 'technocrats'.[16] These had to prove their superiority. Their personal sense of identity became linked to being a player and beating the 'big boys' in the corporate banking game.

The new management were competing at a significant disadvantage as the bank had rudimentary corporate banking structures. As a result, without an effective administrative system in the SBSA its operations became a world of rituals. There would be the annual strategic planning meetings setting the direction of the bank and presenting planned targets for growth and direction. Six months later there would be the profit plan to augment the strategic plan. The actual pace of trading soon outstripped the strategic and profit plans and the bank's direction began to be set more by where the deals were being made than by any foresight. The SBSA in the end just grew for the sake of growing and it could do so because it took too little interest in prudential management but had 'an obsession with growth, and with profit-reporting, as ends in themselves'.[17]

The 'can do' culture
The administrative weakness was intensified by the cultural revolution brought to the bank by Tim Marcus Clark. Clark was an ardent advocate of the 'cultural' approach to management, a philosophy which is influential in a range of American business schools and popularised by Thomas Peters and Robert Waterman in their book, *In Search of Excellence,* and in the popular metaphoric business guide, Sun Tzu's *The Art of War*. This approach was seen as radical in the 1970s because of its preference for action, as Peters and Waterman express it, the emphasis was on 'do it, fix it, try it'.[18] By 1980 this approach became a part of the lexicon of business jargon. It espoused the virtues of 'just doing it' and then building the support structures around the sales. That is, an organisation's administration needed a continual cultural revolution to keep the sales momentum up. When challenged as to the efficacy of this approach, Clark tended to use his Harvard MBA as a credential backing for his style.[19]

174 *Things Fall Apart*

An example of Clark's style of management can be seen in his appointment of Stephen Paddison as Chief Manager Personnel in 1985. Paddison had only just joined the SBSA and his training was in information technology. In appointing Paddison to manage the bank's personnel and recruitment program, Clark said that he wanted:

> to change the personnel culture in the bank and I thought you can't do that with the existing personnel people and I wanted a total change, and I asked Steve Paddison to go and run personnel, and he said: I know nothing about personnel, and I said: I want you to use common sense and nothing else. I said: I don't want you to know the way banks are run or the way banks look after people. I said start from scratch and then you've got to go and work it all out and, you know, find people and talk to people and come up with the best way to run personnel, and I thought he did an outstanding job in restructuring our personnel division.[20]

Clark's placement of inexperience staff in positions beyond their training had the effect of making them reliant on his authority and tended to intensify his power over them.[21] This power was reinforced by his hands-on approach to their remuneration packages.

Clark considered that his recruitment policies had created an 'outstanding team' of senior executives.[22] Nevertheless, the SBSA was to acknowledge, after the government bail out, that the 'recruitment process tended to rely overly on networking and head hunting – sometimes of mediocre candidates'.[23] The Auditor-General noted that even where managers showed expertise and tried to be in control they were 'required to operate under sustained pressure in order to meet ambitious growth targets, whilst embarking on a self-education campaign'.[24]

MacPherson was critical of Clark's recruitment policies and procedures. Equally, he regarded the board's decision to give the Managing Director extensive powers to appoint the senior echelons without effective review by the board as a fundamental mistake. Such a move shifted the balance of power to the Managing Director and away from the board. Given the bank was embarking on new corporate lending, the Auditor-General considered that the board should have exercised more direct control over Clark.[25] Instead, the Managing Director was given a free hand to manage the SBSA even though he had little experience of 'mainstream' bank administration, in comparison to his experience as an entrepreneurial banker.[26]

Once recruited the senior executives were inculcated into a remuneration system which was highly subjective and overly dependent upon the opinion of the Managing Director. For instance, Clark's annual performance appraisals of the managers were based, he said, upon a concern for the 'total' person because he said State Banks 'look after people'.[27] In keeping with this adage, Clark said he examined the managers for 'their responsibility to the bank, their responsibilities in their home situation, and their responsibilities to the community'.[28] However, the Auditor-General found that there were no set objectives or norms in these appraisals and, if they occurred at all, they were 'informal, obscure, arbitrary and subjective'.[29] The lack of objectivity by Clark in dealing with staff led

MacPherson to comment that Clark's assessment of the senior staff 'created an environment where there was a risk of senior executives compromising the independence of their judgement.'[30] Moreover, the concentration of power held by Clark made for an 'unhealthy' and 'far-reaching dependency' by managers 'on the Managing Director'.[31] Expressed more bluntly, the environment within the SBSA senior management implied that the bank 'looked after their people' as long as they in turn accepted unquestioningly Clark's philosophy. For instance, Clark said bonus payments were made on profit and not growth, but the Auditor-General disputes this claim, regarding the bonuses as a means by which the Managing Director asserted his power over the managers and tested whether they had been full inculcated into the culture of the SBSA.[32] It was, in short, a commitment to Clark's growth strategy which lay at the base of rewards in the SBSA.[33]

Power and reward

> Mr Clark set the remuneration as a result of his subjective assessment ... The concentration of power arising from the informality, secretiveness, and subjectivity of the performance assessment process created an unusually strong and far reaching dependency on the part of the senior executive echelon on the Managing Director and on the satisfaction of his expectations.[34]

By establishing an appointment, remuneration, and a bonus system that was highly dependent on him the Managing Director created a form of control. All senior executives had to deal with the arbitrary and subjective exercise of power by the CEO and interiorise his outlook. Tim Marcus Clark's evaluations were shaped by his optimism in market forces and his surveillance was founded on testing whether the managers were both in the market place doing the deals and loyal to him. For many of the senior managers this was a test which was easily absorbed as it was consistent with their ideological convictions and was reinforced by a generous remuneration package.

The extent to which the SBSA had entered the 1980s corporate world can be seen in the salaries granted to the managers. Remuneration packages in the SBSA matched those of the major interstate private banks but were far in excess of salaries in the public sector in Adelaide or in public banking in Australia. Two examples will suffice to show this point. Stephen Paddison became Chief Manager Personnel in 1985 rising to General Manager Retail in 1987, and then became Chief Manager Australian Banking in 1989. When he was promoted in 1987 Paddison's remuneration package was $105,000, rising to $401,822 in 1990. The Auditor-General, commented inquisitively that:

> Indeed Mr. Paddison's career progress within the bank is astounding, for its speed, and the scope of responsibilities entrusted to him. The wisdom of the use made of Mr Paddison's skills, and of the responsibilities assigned to him has, however, been criticised in other quarters, largely on the grounds that Mr Paddison's virtually complete lack of prior banking experience imposed serious limitations on the effectiveness of his work, as did the rapid changing focus on his activity.[35]

The second example is that of Trevor Mallett who was one of the few experienced bankers recruited to the SBSA management. Mallett joined the bank in 1985 and became Senior Manager Corporate Banking. In 1986 he went to head the International Banking Division of the bank, acquiring the additional division of Treasury in 1988, losing Treasury in 1989, and was Chief Manager Corporate and International Banking in 1991. Mallett's remuneration package rose from around $75,000 in 1987 to $303,000 in 1990.[36] It was Mallett's opinion that there was nothing 'special' about the SBSA because it was government owned, rather for him it was like a private bank:

> would I have treated (control and supervision of the overseas branches) any differently because it was the State Bank of South Australia? My answer is no. I mean, consistently, it's only in recent times that I'm fully coming to grips with the fact that this is a government bank. I really came into this organisation with no experience of anything other than private banking and for many years it was as though we were a private bank.[37]

It is important to remember that while Paddison was seen as Clark's prodigy within the bank, Mallett was Clark's assistant in its overseas ventures, notably in New Zealand. In assessing the reasons for losses made by the bank overseas the Auditor-General criticised both Clark and Mallet, saying that the investments 'were not adequately or properly supervised, directed and controlled'.[38] MacPherson was also highly critical of the quality of Mallett's reports to the board which, the Auditor-General says, 'were not, under all the circumstances, timely, reliable and adequate'.[39] The Royal Commission recommended that investigations be undertaken to determine whether civil proceedings could be brought by the bank against Mallett for 'gross negligence' on two overseas acquisitions.[40]

In short, as MacPherson expresses it, remuneration and promotion were tied to being a member of Clark's team and to his growth philosophy. Resistance to Clark's philosophy was permissible so long as it did not threaten the bank's newly established philosophy. Resistance outside of these parameters was met by the collective opprobrium of the other managers and the exercise of the power of Clark.

For instance, when Graham Ottaway opposed the bank's growth strategy at the 1988 Strategic Planning Conference, calling for consolidation he was demoted. On this the Auditor-General indicated that after his confrontation at the Conference with Clark, Ottaway was 'relieved of his duties as General Manager, Corporate and International – a key business-generating unit of the bank which he had headed since 1986 – and put in charge of a support function designated Group Services'.[41] He returned to a position in retail banking the following year, but he is reported to have again raised concerns that the SBSA 'lacked leadership' saying the bank 'was going backward'. Soon after these comments he was dismissed.[42]

Asset and liability management
In his investigation of the prudential management of the SBSA, the Auditor-General said he was amazed that it barely functioned at all. In regard to asset and liability management, Macpherson said that:

> The most significant – and startling – feature of this aspect of the State Bank's operations, is that before late 1990, it did not exist. Until 1990, there simply

was no overall management of the bank's assets and liabilities. This part of the bank's activities was completely without co-ordination. The emphasis was on growth and profits.[43]

In regard to asset and liability management, Clark set the systems in place but they contained fundamental problems. In his statement to the Royal Commission Clark noted that in meeting the commercial charter of the bank three important committees were formed: the Executive Committee, the Lending Credit Committee (LCC) and the Asset Liability Management Committee (ALMAC). Clark added that 'all these committees were run on a formal basis, with a Chairman, and a secretary who organised the papers and the meetings, and kept minutes. These minutes were then distributed to the Directors of the State Bank along with their other board papers'.[44]

In his appearance before the Martin Inquiry Tim Marcus Clark said that 'the way I managed the bank was as follows: because I had to build a new team and was on a three-year contract, I followed a team approach involving the senior people of both the merging banks. I delegated authority and autonomy throughout the Group. A number of committees were set up. I was Chairman of the Executive Committee and an ex-officio member of other committees.'[45] Inside this formal structure there was an uncritical acceptance by this team of the bank's growth culture, and the pursuit of self-interest by the senior managers was the driving force behind the team.

The Executive Committee
In regard to the highest strategic committee within the SBSA, the Executive Committee, Clark claimed it was run on professional lines. According to Clark:

> The Executive Committee was charged with the responsibility of advising the board on the strategic direction of the bank. The Committee was in effect set up to bring together the collective knowledge and experience of the bank's senior managers so as to plan the bank's future. In general we met every two weeks. Meetings were formal, and the committee operated by considering papers which were submitted through the Board Secretary – the business of the committee was to implement the policies agreed by the board; to consider and make recommendations as to what sort of future policies and strategies might be appropriate, and to review the operations and the performance of the State Bank Group.'[46]

In contrast to Clark, Auditor-General MacPherson considered that the Executive Committee never fulfilled its allocated function, rather was merely an expression of Clark's will:

> The Executive Committee functioned as the senior management organ of the bank. It was however never formally constituted by the board, and the board did not delegate any powers to the Committee ... The role, functions and powers of the Committee were never defined ... Constitutionally, the Executive Committee was merely the alter ego of the Chief Executive Officer. Whilst it was perceived as the decision-making centre of the bank, it in fact occupied too much of its time on trivial matters. and was handicapped by an excessively large membership.[47]

The Lending Credit Committee (LCC)

Likewise, the Lending Credit Committee, which Clark said was established to critically analyse the lending proposals coming up from the line managers, failed to do so. Instead it seems to have reinforced the growth mentality of the bank.

Auditor-General MacPherson observed:

> a majority of the Lending Credit Committee were line managers, that is, in charge of the Lending divisions of the bank. It is, in my opinion, wholly inappropriate for a credit committee to be dominated by individuals whose junior staff are responsible for bringing lending submissions before the Committee whose members had, by virtue of adoption by the bank of its strategic plan and annual profit plans, a firm personal objective of meeting asset growth in the division for which the particular member is responsible, in particular periods. What was lacking from the bank's credit approval structure, at Lending Credit Committee level and below, was a procedure under which lending decisions would be rigorously and objectively analysed by a person not having a commitment to asset growth for its own sake.[48]

The Auditor-General stressed that the bank's structures for assessing loans were vulnerable to individual self-interest overriding the interest of the taxpayers. In regard to the Lending Credit Committee he notes that:

> all officers of the bank who participated in lending decisions at the Lending Credit Committee level and below were motivated either wholly or partly by corporate desire for growth in assets. It is abundantly clear that this was a major failing within the lending structure of the bank prior to 1990. In forming this conclusion, I have also had regard to the fact that many members of the Lending Credit Committee, in the period under review, were participants in a bonus scheme, or were otherwise entitled to bonuses, which reflected growth, in a particular year, in loans written by the division of which the officer was a senior manager.[49]

Moreover, the lack of consistency and continuity in the membership of the Lending Credit Committee further weakened the sense of responsibility over lending. On these failings in the LCC, MacPherson commented that: 'membership fluctuated in two senses; first, the number of attendees at meetings ranged from three (in breach of its charter) to seven; secondly, members did not attend – and were not required to attend – every meeting. Strictly, it was a misnomer to describe the Lending Credit Committee as a committee. A consequence of which was that the accountability of individuals was weakened'.[50]

MacPherson's opinion was supported by the team from JP Morgan (the merchant bank called in to review the SBSA in late 1990) who noted that the LCC

> is constituted of a 'revolving door' of individuals who do not consistently review all credits. This can give rise to abuses (e.g., stacked committees), individuals participating who have little interest in the procedures, and some participants who may not have well developed credit expertise. All the

members of the GCC [the LCC changed its name to the Group Lending Committee] have other day-to-day responsibilities and may not have time to review a large quantity of credit submissions in any depth. We believe this system stifles accountability. So many people are part of the approval chain that responsibility can be attributed to any part of the organisation.[51]

That is, there were no clear cut lines of accountability at the top to monitor lending. The self-enclosed and self-confirming management culture was founded on lending and on defending the right to lend. Additionally any semblance of prudential control was swamped by the sheer magnitude of the lending. The lines of control lacked objectivity and were encased in the enterprise culture of growth. The internal culture within the bank was a mirror of the prevailing culture outside its walls, which the SBSA sought to imitate.

Asset and Liability management
On 28 June 1984 Clark wrote a memorandum to the board indicating that he was acting on the board's directive over sound assets and liabilities controls by establishing an Asset and Liability Management Committee (ALMAC).[52] His methods reflect his revolutionary management style rather than a traditional response to issues. Clark appointed Graham Ottaway as Chief Manager Finance, which placed him in charge of the SBSA treasury section. You now had in charge a manager with no background in treasury matters and a department which had rudimentary accounting techniques. That is, the Savings Bank had only two treasury personnel whose principal activity was dealing with the Reserve Bank account. Ottaway raised with the Managing Director the limitations in the structure he inherited from the Savings Bank and his lack of qualifications and experience in this area but Clark, in his 'can do' style, 'assured Mr Ottaway that he had confidence in him'.[53]

From the outset the new bank had no experienced staff in treasury who could manage the rapid growth in the bank's assets and liabilities. Ottaway said that at the beginning the treasury 'simply set up a phone system' which was 'very simple, very straightforward – essentially riskless business at that stage'.[54] Ottaway commented that the first ALMAC seemed to him at the time professionally run. In hindsight, when questioned by Macpherson, he said that:

> I don't know what an expert would expect of an asset liability management committee so I don't really know. We thought that we were doing an effective job at the time but then as time went on and one learned about the sophistication of organisations that had computer models to help them out and economic reports and as new models were developed, swaps and all sorts of synthetic assets, none of which I personally had knowledge of, one could see that an asset and liability management committee comprised of people with that sort of expertise are going to do something quite different from the sort.[55]

The Auditor-General observed that Ottaway's submission provided a 'telling insight' into the origins and development of the bank, saying that:

> At the time of the merger, nobody in the bank knew what was going to be required and that by the time the requirements were understood, the bank had grown so quickly, and the business had become so large and changed in its nature so much, that the timely introduction of appropriate systems and procedures had become an almost impossible task.[56]

To assist him in his duties in late 1984, Ottaway hired the merchant banker Jim Hazel. Hazel said that when he took the job the bank's accounting was very rudimentary and that it had no way of planning its future and there was no system for forecasting its cash flow. Ottaway noted that:

> I made the point regularly, it was somewhat laughable that, an institution like a bank that was assessing credit had no cash flow forecasting ability of its own and that it merely relied on its ability to pick up the 'phone and raise money. It became one of those things, like many things in the bank, that became 'wish list' items'.[57]

Without a system to know the cost of its funds and loans the bank priced according to what they perceived as that of the market.[58] Hazel commented that Clark 'drove sales and assumed that if you had sales, you would earn profits ... there was a lot of 'gonna' about establishing an effective pricing and cash flow forecasting system'.[59] The effect of not knowing the cost of the funds and the pricing of wholesale lending led to undisciplined credit transactions where managers were not fully aware of whether the loans they were making were profitable.

In July 1987 when Hazel was appointed to head the SBSA's subsidiary, Ayers Finnis, he was replaced by Mallett. Mallett was then head of International banking and he took on the treasury role as an extra responsibility. Hazel had advised against appointing Mallett, saying that 'it looked stupid for someone who had a full-time job running International banking to suddenly be given another job which someone had been at full-time before and merge the two together'.[60] The Managing Director could not be dissuaded from his course of action.

Women in a man's world
At the same time as Mallett absorbed the treasury role into his International banking responsibility, Julie Meeking was appointed to the position of Senior Manager, Money Markets. She had an academic background and had practical experience at treasury, having previously been employed as head of Treasury and Foreign Exchange in the merchant bank Michell NBD Ltd, and had worked as Manager, Treasury, with Adelaide Steam Ship Co Limited (Adsteam). She noted at the time of her appointment that treasury 'really lacked a lot of experience'.[61]

Meeking was committed to upgrading the bank's asset and liability management. She sought to introduce transfer pricing within the bank so that each lending division knew the actual cost of making their loans. She also attempted to develop a system of marking the bank's treasury portfolio to market, so that the bank knew on a day to day basis the profit on assets to be realised.[62] Without transfer pricing and 'marking to market' profits on assets could be selectively made while losses on corresponding liabilities were being disguised. Meeking sought to ensure that the treasury had a balanced balance sheet, and finally, to develop a cash flow forecasting system.

She felt hampered in her efforts to make the treasury effective by the fragmented character of the institution and the resistance from the lending divisions to make their loans accountable to credit control systems. For example, the introduction of transfer pricing was resisted by the line managers as it affected their profits and consequently their bonuses. In the submission to the Auditor-General she provided an instance in 1989 where Paddison stated at a meeting in New York that 'Retail banking made a return of 33% on capital'.[63] Meeking replied to her cost, 'that figure was fictitious, and that there were some $7 million monthly recurring costs that were not being attributed and probably could largely be attributed back to Retail banking'.[64]

Paddison disputed these claims and said that it was inappropriate to single out retail banking from the other division as they were all subject to a similar accounting system. The Auditor-General replied that: 'On its face that submission is correct, but it must be remembered that Paddison was, at all times, a member of the bank's Executive Committee, and if the bank's accounting policies were inadequate he can not completely disclaim responsibility'.[65]

Meeking's efforts to introduce and consolidate an asset and liability system in the bank were hampered by the lack of support she obtained from senior management. In passing it is interesting to note that the women managers in the bank in charge of 'good financial housekeeping' were confronted by senior male managers unsympathetic to their efforts, who regarded such systems as inferior to doing the deal. Another example of this attitude was in 1990, when the Chief Manager Group Audit, Chin Wing Sun, sought to develop an effective internal auditing system. She was hampered by Mr Matthews who failed to support her. Like Meeking, Chin had an altercation with Paddison when she attempted to assess his department, which was then Corporate Banking. Paddison wrote to her saying it was 'inappropriate for the audit department to concern itself with how these responsibilities [credit and pricing] are divided and exercised'.[66] He added that 'I would wish to sound a word of caution that I will strongly resist the intrusion of Group Audit into areas which I believe are the proper province of management'.[67]

In the Auditor-General's opinion Paddison's opposition to an asset quality audit of his department reflected 'adversely on the discharge, by Mr Paddison, of his responsibility for the prudential management of his portfolio of the bank's assets'.[68] In regard to Paddison's 'warning off' Chin, the Auditor-General was of the view that his action did 'not reflect what would be expected of a senior executive on an important matter of accountability'.[69]

Funds

In early 1989 Steve Taggart was recruited from the bank's London office to become Chief Manager, Australian Treasury. Taggart said that he found that the skills of those working in treasury 'were just below par' and that 'we were trying to run an aggressive treasury and match the bigger players, I guess, without the tools to be able to do it'.[70] In the Auditor-General's opinion 'with the exception of Ms Meeking (whose area of responsibility was restricted), Mr Taggart was the first in charge of the bank's treasury operations who was appropriately qualified for the task.'[71] Apart from these two individuals MacPherson found that the treasury throughout almost the entire period of the SBSA's existence lacked sufficient expertise within its prudential tasks. In brief, the treasury staff were required to carry out tasks which were beyond their experience (and often expertise) in an atmosphere of growth but with the lenders having an ample supply of funds, guaranteed by the government. Taggart told the Auditor-General that the ALMAC did not know its function, did not have the data to do its task, and instead concentrated on peripheral issues. He said that it also did not understand cash flows; it was as if the SBSA 'was managing this big bucket of funds where money was going in and out but in terms of properly measuring the cost of capital and how it was allocated and all those type of things which also fit into asset and liability side, there was not any sort of policies in that area, so it just was not happening well enough'.[72]

Go and 'write assets'

Taggart indicated that control was secondary to writing new business, 'the behaviour that was rewarded was profit for the business units that the people were running' and that those 'people [were] being quite handsomely rewarded for generating profitability'.[73] In 1990 Taggart tried to elicit support in slowing the lending to match the limitations of the bank's treasury. He was quickly put straight by Clark about the bank's culture when the 'Managing Director at that time said that basically while he was running the bank we would continue to write assets and so we had to go and rethink our whole method of presenting the problem to people'.[74]

The Auditor-General concurred with this view on prudential control being seen as a hindrance to growth, saying that 'the operational divisions of the bank were either unwilling, or incapable, of modifying their behaviour to conform with the requirements of asset and liability management'.[75] He then reiterated his damaging findings that 'until 1990 there was simply no overall management of the bank's assets and liabilities. The evidence establishes that this part of the bank's activities was completely without coordination. The emphasis was on growth and profits'.[76] MacPherson is equally critical of the board members for not having due regard to ensuring themselves that asset and liability management was operating effectively. MacPherson criticised the directors for not taking 'steps to obtain a better understanding of the intricacies of asset and liability management'.[77] He was nevertheless more critical of Clark for not giving 'asset and liability management the emphasis it deserved', saying that Clark was 'the only person in possession of all the relevant organisational and operational facts and in a position of authority such as to enable him to coordinate the bank's activities; but there is no evidence that he did so'.[78]

In MacPherson's view the bank's prudential systems were comprehensively inadequate:

> The poor quality of lending decisions made by officers and institutions within the bank in the period under review was partly a consequence of the non-existence of policies, partly a consequence of the inadequacy of policies which did exist, partly a consequence of non-compliance with policies, and partly a consequence of a culture within the bank which created a pre-disposition to lending money without adequate assessment of the creditworthiness of the borrower. Furthermore, the bank's policies were not only often inadequate, they were often flouted by Management, in some instances, by the board itself.[79]

As the bank evolved the drive for growth had became the norm. It also became a systemic necessity as a means of compensating for previous faulty lending practices. That is, from its outset the bank had adopted the practice of charging disproportionate fees at the time of the loan which resulted in inflated profits in the early years of the loan but left the bank facing the potential for lower profits in subsequent years. It has been calculated that without the front end fees 'the reported profit of the bank would have been reduced by almost a third to one half'.[80] Moreover, as the Auditor-General inferred, there was a personal reason for the managers to adopt the practice of front end fees: 'though there is no evidence (and there is unlikely ever to be), to the effect that the practice of taking the disproportionate front end fees was activated by any ulterior motive there is warrant for an inference – which I draw without hesitation – that the practice was engaged in with the intention of inflating the reported profits of both divisions within the bank and the bank itself'.[81]

Expressed pointedly, the inference in the Auditor-General's evaluation was that the managers were driven by self interest to front end the loan fees. As a result, when the bank's profits began to decline there remained a strong imperative to increase the level of lending to shore up the bank's profits against the structural fall in profits. The managers were impelled to lend more just to maintain the status quo in terms of profits and bonuses. At the very time when the financial market was becoming riskier, as firms were beginning to feel the delayed effects of the share-market crash and their rush into property, the SBSA's imperative was still to lend. The bank was eager to write more loans to offset its falling profit so that in 1989 and 1990 there was this unholy alliance between the bank, lenders and clients of the SBSA to make loans in a desperate effort to retain the status quo.

Asset and liability management
In sum, the SBSA was an institution suffering from an imbalance between its lending and regulatory systems. The bank's focus was on lending and in making quick decisions on loans. Between 1984 and 1991 it had no trouble in meeting and surpassing its lending targets. During this whole period the SBSA was never able to consolidate a system for dealing with its assets and liabilities until it was too late to save the bank.

The disparate character of the systems within the bank made it difficult to obtain reliable information on the loans. Equally, the committees overseeing the loans seemed to be dealing with trivia and not the substantive issues of prudential control. In practice, from its origin until near its demise, the SBSA had no way of knowing the extent of the risks it was taking nor whether in the long run its lending would prove profitable, a situation compounded by the faulty method of front end loading its loans. As the Auditor-General noted, 'the overwhelming weight of the evidence is that, until about the beginning of 1990, no proper attention was given to the need to manage the assets and liabilities of the bank and, equally important, the Group in an overall sense'.[82] To reiterate, MacPherson contends that the responsibility for this fundamental weakness lay with the management and the board, and that 'the Managing Director and board failed in their duty' to oversee asset and liability management before 1990.[83]

The board

> ... the Board of Directors was the governing body of the bank charged with responsibility to administer the bank's affairs and to control the Chief Executive in his performance of his management function. A reasonably prudent board – whatever its skill – would have done much more than the board did. It was not beyond the capabilities of the non-executive directors to take commonsense measures, and to stand no nonsense.[84]

At the time of the merger, the old boards were active in the setting of the goals of their respective banks and in the decision making process. As we saw, if anything the old boards were overly involved in checking and double checking the management and the lending decisions which tended to delay loans and stymie the initiatives of the managers. In contrast the new board was too reliant on management. It often acquiesced to the lending proposal and became overly reliant on the expertise and advice of the managers.

In this sense, the SBSA Board was typical of many boards in the 1980s who were too dependent on management. The board was, however, responding to the direction of the Act in making the SBSA more commericial. As the SBSA grew and became a large player in the local economy dominated by small business there was a natural flow on effect to the businesses associated with the directors. There were also the opportunities offered to directors to head subsidiary companies of the SBSA group, so that while the directors were only paid according to set levels, they could top this up with remunerations from being on subsidiary companies of the bank.

In regards to lending, the board was charged, by the Act, with the tasks of running the SBSA in accordance with acceptable banking principles and with the objective of making a profit. The first board of directors was appointed on 28 June 1984 and at that meeting it delegated lending to particular authorities in the State Bank's management and established a series of prudential guidelines. With regard to lending the board initially set its parameters based on the practice of the old banks, with the board retaining a hands on approach to large loans. The guidelines required the board to approve loans being 'greater than $2.5 million and of any exposure to single entity or industry in excess of 20 percent of the bank's "risk assets" and the LCC was delegated to transact loans outside of these limitations'.[85]

When the management began to pursue corporate clients not only did the sheer quantity of lending increase, so also did the size of the loans. The $2.5 million limit soon became unrealistically low for approval by the board and led to a situation where the board was continually involved in lending decisions and where the extraordinary became commonplace. That is, the ceiling now was too low for those making decisions in the $100 million range, especially when management insisted that the decisions had to be made as quickly as possible in order to beat the competition. Additionally, sharing in the common goal of making all of these lending decisions led the board to became somewhat complacent over large loans. Equally, the speed, complexity and rising volume of the lending applications increased the board's reliance upon the expertise of the management and on the leadership of Tim Marcus Clark.

Within a very short period of its operations the SBSA Board began to be fundamentally altered by the sheer amount of loan requests. In response to frequency and the magnitude of the loans needing approval, the board began to distance itself from lending decisions. Firstly, the board set up a sub-board with the responsibility for facilitating approval of loans. Then in the late 1980s the board raised the ceiling on loans so high as to effectively to remove the board altogether from the lending approval process. In doing so, the board, as the Auditor-General expressed it, was making a choice 'to exercise little control over lending'.[86] The board's response to the pressure to continually make quick decisions on loans, and their lack of collective expertise, was starkly different from the historic role boards had played in management. The result was that the board lost its ability to always act as an objective constraint on the lending and instead became another chain in the approval process. In the end, MacPherson contends, to 'the extent to which lending proposals came before the board, they did so for 'noting' or 'confirmation' only'.[87]

The board in effect became dislocated from its past and engulfed by the intensity of the 1980s. In this change a contradiction emerged, where the board was officially the final arbitrator of large loans but, as a collective body, neither had the time nor the technical expertise, apart from Tim Marcus Clark, to make the critical evaluations over a loan. The board nevertheless was still involved in decisions on large loans and at the same time abrogated power over the decisions to the managers. By doing so the board in MacPherson's view contributed to the SBSA's fall. The board had acquiesced to the fundamental transformation of the bank without realising the implications of that transformation on the lines of accountability over lending. In a strident criticism the board, according to the Auditor-General, failed to even take 'common-sense' measures to control the bank's lending.[88]

He notes that as early as October 1985 the board was complaining of the 'technical nature' of some board papers and the perfunctory, and at times misleading, character of other submissions. Once the character of the bank's lending and borrowing had changed the non-executive directors found it difficult to challenge the knowledge and expertise of the bankers. The lack of experience in banking became an impediment to the discharge of their duties. This weakness was accentuated by the manner by which information was presented to the board and the pressure-cooker atmosphere where speed of response was deemed essential. The Auditor-General noted the board was continually asked to make rapid responses to loan requests and approve them despite the fact that as 'often as not, lending submissions which reached the board did not facilitate useful analysis'.[89]

'In short', MacPherson noted, 'I am driven to the conclusion that the Managing Director and the board failed in their duty. Although, of course they cannot be expected to have carried out the assets and liability management themselves, they should have ensured that this important function was being attended to, and that appropriate systems and procedures were in place well before the steps that were taken during 1990'.[90] The decision making of the board soon began to resemble that of the managers, with quick decisions being made on loans, with 'round robin' telephone calls becoming too common a practice rather than as a device to be used only in an emergency.[91] Board members were individually agreeing on complex loans over the phone and then ratifying them at the next board meeting. As the

Auditor-General noted 'I am satisfied that, in relation to the lending business of the bank, the board lacked the experience, information and, on occasion when it utilised the round robin procedure, the appropriate forum, in which to make properly considered decisions'.[92]

In the end, as soon as the bank began to grow the old board structure of assessing all major loans was swamped by the imperative for quick decisions over complex deals. The board did its best to carry out its duties but was unable collectively to control management. A position made most difficult by the board being inadequately informed by the managers and at times manipulated by them.

The Reserve Bank of Australia
The internal controls within the bank struggled to control growth. This struggle was equally evident in regard to the checks on the bank from the outside. When the Act was introduced into the parliament Premier Bannon said that he expected the SBSA would operate within the Reserve Bank of Australia (RBA) guidelines. In terms of the RBA, Bannon commented that 'I was aware that while the Reserve Bank of Australia did not have control over the State Bank as a matter of law, it complied with Reserve Bank requirements, but I believe that regular meetings took place between the Reserve Bank and the State Bank. I knew that the RBA had requirements as to capital adequacy and as to the general conduct of banking business, I was advised from time to time that the State Bank was indeed complying with Reserve Bank requirements'.[93]

When the new SBSA was challenged on its lending by the RBA, a guild type of mentality developed among the SBSA managers whereby the Reserve Bank was regarded as an old 'gentlemen's club' not in tune with the SBSA's new commercial focus. RBA's warnings over the SBSA lending was systematically discounted by the SBSA's management and subsequently went unreported or were underestimated by the board. The SBSA held the position that as it was a state bank it was different from the other banks and that its Act only obliged it voluntarily to obey Reserve bank rules. When pushed by the RBA to comply with the regulations the bank would find excuses for why they could not immediately do so. It was only the Reserve Bank's power to hinder the SBSA's expansion overseas which enabled it to gain SBSA compliance.

Tea and scones with the Reserve Bank

> ... I think you need to understand that the formal discussions with the Reserve Bank are at what is somewhat jokingly referred to as 'tea and scones' level – a very general level.[94]

Clark saw the arrangement with the Reserve Bank as only a 'gentleman's agreement' without any legally binding status.[95] Clark was imbued with a certain private banking attitude which was hostile to the RBA's formal and painstaking approach. Putting it more bluntly, as the Auditor-General did, Clark treated the RBA with 'disdain',[96] a disdain which he seemed to have fostered among the SBSA's senior management

Unlike other banks in Australia where the Managing Director dealt directly with the RBA, from the outset Clark delegated this responsibility to his deputy, Kenneth

Matthews. Matthews had a long history as a manager in the Savings Bank, nevertheless, in the new SBSA structure his role was more symbolic than effective. Matthews was, however, only a nominal deputy to Clark. That is, despite being second-in-charge, Matthews, as the Auditor-General noted, 'had no people of substance reporting to him', instead 'they reported to Clark'.[97] Moreover, Matthew was not, in the opinion of MacPherson, 'sufficiently aware of operational matters to adequately perform his task', rather he was 'dominated by Clark'.[98]

The RBA, however, mistakenly, saw Matthews as a 'substantive number two' and not as merely a 'conduit of information'.[99] The RBA assumed that as Matthews was the person dealing with them, he had the power to ensure there was compliance with the RBA's guidelines. In practice, Matthews was dependent on Clark to make the SBSA comply. According to the Auditor-General, Clark made it clear to the senior managers that they had to decide where their loyalties lay, either with the RBA or with him and his bank. The Auditor-General noted that 'in almost every respect, that question was answered in favour of their Chief Executive Officer'.[100]

The choice Clark presented to the managers was graphically displayed at the September 1986 consultation meeting between the SBSA and the RBA. The RBA officials at that meeting raised their concerns over a number of issues - firstly, the SBSA's failure to meet the RBA's prudential guidelines, and secondly, the State Bank's reluctance to allow the external auditors to send, independently, their reports to the Reserve Bank; lastly, the SBSA's rapid growth when the bank's profitability was 'static' and when there was only a 'marginal return on the bank's assets'.[101] Clark, in responding to these concerns, proceeded to 'own' the problems and indicate that he was going to do something about them. He admitted that the SBSA was growing 'too fast' and that 'growth exceeding 30 per cent could lead to indigestion', adding that he was aware of weaknesses in the SBSA's management saying that 'below the top 20 members of the management team there were some real challenges'.[102] Clark commented that the bank was going to achieve an 'efficient information system' and that the SBSA had a 'lot of catching up to do on its management information system'.[103]

The following year, when the RBA pursued the matters it had raised in 1986, Clark took umbrage. That is, unlike Bannon, who assumed that Clark actually did own problems and not just offer signs that he did, the RBA officials in 1987 began to push Clark on the issues raised before, especially over when the SBSA would send its external auditor's reports to the RBA. At that point, according to the RBA minute of the meeting, Clark 'abruptly left the meeting'.[104] This departure soon became 'common knowledge' within the bank and appears to have set the tone for the senior managers attitude to the RBA's supervision.[105]

For its part, the Reserve Bank was so concerned by Clark's abrupt departure from the consultation meeting that the Governor of the Reserve Bank wrote an official, short diary note to the effect that 'I hope Mr T Clark will cool down. If not it may be invidious but necessary to indicate to other authorities how our relationship stands'.[106] Unfortunately the RBA never did take this concern further and reveal to Bannon its disquiet over Clark and the SBSA's structure and lending.

It took the RBA until 1987 before it used its powers to try and pull the SBSA in line with its prudential standards. In November 1987 the RBA threatened to block the SBSA's overseas expansion. The RBA had requested that the SBSA meet these guidelines as far back as May 1985 without any substantial compliance. But by

1987, with the management desperate to receive approval to invest in New York, the SBSA agreed to comply with the guidelines.

The RBA minutes recorded that the 'SBSA (or at least its Managing Director) has been grudging in accepting our prudential requirements. I think we should make it clear that our support of applications by SBSA to establish operations [in New York] is not given lightly – that we should be satisfied that SBSA does co-operate with us in giving effect to our banking and prudential policies'.[107] As the Auditor-General contended, the change in attitude by the SBSA to comply with the rules, was only because the 'bank needed the Reserve Bank endorsement in order to open a New York office'.[108]

Similarly, it seems that the SBSA only complied with the RBA's capital adequacy ratio (a form of liquidity control) when the RBA indicated it would withhold its endorsement for the State Bank to establish a New York branch. Even then, the RBA noted that the State Bank was 'the last bank to comply with the RBA's capital adequacy requirements'.[109]

In March 1986 the RBA requested that the SBSA conform to its capital adequacy requirement but management did not present this matter to the board until December 1987.[110] It again seems no coincidence that the management sought board consent just after the RBA reminded it of its power to veto the State Bank's overseas activities. The board agreed to this request but was not provided by management with the history of the disputes between the RBA and the SBSA over this matter. The failure to do so, in the opinion of the Auditor-General, was at best 'seriously inept' and showed that the Managing Director 'at least tacitly, misled the board'.[111]

A similar stand-off occurred between the RBA and the SBSA over the requirements regarding large credit exposures. Under RBA rules, the SBSA was obliged to inform it in advance of any exposure that was unduly large – notably exposures above 10 per cent of shareholder funds and, in particular, any undertaking which would breach 30 per cent of shareholder funds.[112] These rules, the SBSA argued, cut directly across the bank's claim that it had a comparative advantage in the speed of its decision making. When the RBA wrote to the SBSA informing them that, for prudential reasons, the SBSA should notify them, in advance, of any large exposure which went beyond the 30 per cent limit, Matthews replied that the SBSA found this unacceptable. He wrote that:

> Since the merger, State Bank has been structured to respond very quickly to requests for funding arrangements. Where necessary, we are able to process an application, including consideration by the board of directors, within 24 hours. As a result of this level of service, the bank has been able to gain a competitive advantage on several occasions. We would not like to see this comparative advantage eroded.[113]

Given that this statement came at the time that Clark was admitting to the RBA that the SBSA did not have the depth of staff nor the systems to handle rapid growth, Matthews' statement reads as one that, at least, misunderstood the misunderstood the RBA's concerns.

RBA and the Equiticorp Company

A clear example of the bank's different approach to that of the RBA is in the case of Equiticorp.[114] In June 1987, following an approach from Equiticorp, the SBSA lifted its exposure to that company from $50 million to $250 million. Matthews telephoned the RBA informing it of the transaction. The Reserve Bank calculated that this transaction went against its prudential guidelines, putting the exposure at 60 per cent of the SBSA's capital and 'counselled strongly against SBSA committing itself to the transaction'.[115]

The RBA diary note of the telephone conversation listed four reasons why it opposed the deal, these being: the exposure was 'too large'; it came on top of the fact that the SBSA had already 'several commitments in excess of 30 percent of capital'; the SBSA's claim that it had a 'selling down arrangement' was in the opinion of the RBA not likely to lessen the bank's commitment and that Clark was on the Equiticorp board, and the RBA was concerned that there was a potential conflict of interest. This concern prompted the RBA to note that it 'was not possible to ignore the association of the Managing Director of SBSA with the client'.[116]

Expressed simply, the SBSA management and board disregarded the RBA's counsel and went ahead with the transaction with Equiticorp. The RBA, however, did not let the matter rest. The Reserve Bank Governor wrote to the Chair of the board, Lew Barrett, expressing 'disappointment' that the SBSA had not adopted the RBA's counsel, concluding his letter with the poignant and pointed comment that

> in the last resort, you are not obliged to accept our advice on prudential matters. I should say, however, that had a bank that is subject to the Banking Act put to us a proposal of a similar nature and scale, we would have used such powers as we have to oppose it very strongly.[117]

Chairman Barrett replied to the RBA that in the SBSA's view the exposure to Equiticorp was not a full exposure but merely an 'underwrite' that could be sold down.[118] In the Auditor-General's view this claim 'does not stand close scrutiny'[119] and reflected badly on both Barrett and the board's ability to challenge the claims of management or to realise that the management was 'obstructing communication between the Reserve Bank and the board'.[120] That is, the Reserve Bank had raised, with the management, its concerns over Equiticorp before the SBSA made its offer but this counsel was not referred to the board until after the 'round robin' approval process. When the Reserve Bank subsequently wrote to the Chair of the board, Lew Barrett, raising its objections, the board did not seem to show concern at previously being kept in the dark over Equiticorp, rather the board endorsed the decision of the management to lend to Equiticorp.[121] By doing so it sent a clear signal to the RBA that the board was prepared to side, uncritically, with management and against the Reserve Bank's advice.

A $2 million weekend

The neglect of RBA advice was seemingly general within the bank. For instance, in December 1987 Equiticorp (re)approached the SBSA for another loan. Masters recalls how Ottaway came into his office on Friday 11 December asking the question: 'How would you like to earn fees of two million dollars over the weekend?',[122] to which he got an enthusiastic affirmative reply. On Monday 14

December 1987 the board was approached via a telephone ring around seeking approval of a $200 million exposure to Equiticorp. It needs to be remembered that at the time Equiticorp was a New Zealand company heavily involved in share market speculation and the approach was made to the SBSA only two months after the 1987 share market crash which had devastated both Australian and New Zealand corporate stocks.

Ottaway and Masters in their weekend's work, in MacPherson's opinion, had so structured the loan (in the form of a 'put option') to get around, at least in the first instance, 'Reserve Bank prudential recommendations'.[123] The loan was around 50 per cent of SBSA capital, thereby over-stepping the 30 per cent Reserve Bank guidelines. The SBSA went to the trouble of seeking legal advice so as to ascertain whether the 'put option' was a loan. The legal advice indicated that the 'put option' was in effect a loan, placing the State Bank 'at substantial risk'.[124] Notwithstanding this advice and the RBA's previous warning over the SBSA dealing with Equiticorp, the board approved the loan in January 1988.[125]

The State Bank, however, overlooked the fact that it was obliged to supply a quarterly return to the RBA listing its large exposures. When the RBA did eventually receive the bank's return it promptly telephoned Matthews wanting to know to whom the large exposure listed on the return was made. Once pressed, Matthews admitted that the loan was to Equititcorp but implied that this was merely the resurrection of the old loan, whereas it was in fact a new loan. By doing so, as the Auditor-General noted, Matthews 'misled' the Reserve Bank.[126] The fact that the SBSA made this second transaction in the manner it did, as MacPherson noted, showed the 'derisive way' in which the SBSA regarded the RBA's prudential supervision.[127] This contributed to the board not fully appreciating that it was entering into a major transaction with a company of which Clark was 'holding a directorship'.[128]

This misjudgement had long term repercussions for the bank as the final volume of the Royal Commission noted the board and BFC acted inappropriately in regard to Equiticorp. The report said that Clark's role was at least 'suspicious' and the 'suspicion was that he did play a role in the transaction',[129] a suspicion which Judge Perry said was proven and Clark was ordered to pay $81.2 million damages to the SBSA for the losses incurred by the bank in regard to Equiticorp.[130] Likewise, the board of directors was found to be negligent not following up its own recommendation of obtaining an outside evaluation of the Equiticorp offer. The board was obliged to pay compensation for this error of judgement, compensation which was basically covered by the board's indemnity insurance policy. Initially Clark sought protection behind a family trust from paying any of the damages Undeterred by this tactic the Liberal government pursued Clark challenging this defense. In February 1998 an agreement was struck between Clark's wife and the Olsen Government whereby Mrs (Micaele) Clark would pay $1.5 million in total damages.[131] With legal costs deducted the final payment was only $800,000.[132]

Ignoring the warnings

The Auditor-General was critical of the board for not controlling the management after they had received signs from the RBA that it was concerned over the SBSA's lending. MacPherson observed that, 'the directors did receive warning signs which should have prompted them to adopt a more assertive position'.[133] The Auditor-General pointedly singled out Clark and Matthews for his harshest criticism, saying their 'failure to properly appreciate the significance of the Reserve Bank messages, demonstrates, in my opinion, an inexcusable lack of competence'.[134] He added that Clark and Matthews, along with other senior executives, 'seem to have been incapable of communicating in terms other than that characterised by circumlocution and euphemism', using 'verbiage calculated to conceal and suppress, rather than to expose and elucidate'.[135] Of the Managing Director, the Auditor-General said, that Clark 'failed to adequately discharge his responsibilities' and that his 'disdain' for the RBA adversely affected the rest of the officers, and it is 'difficult to resist the inference that Mr Clark's view of the State Bank's relationship with the Reserve Bank permeated through most of the State Bank's senior management level'.[136] MacPherson added that the failure of senior management to appreciate the genuine concerns of the RBA was an 'important shortcoming', and that 'ultimately it is management's shortcomings which are critical causes of the State Bank's financial difficulties.'[137]

For its part the Reserve Bank had by 1989 come to realise that the SBSA had serious management deficiencies, was adopting a high risk strategy and finally that the bank had grown at an abnormally fast rate. The RBA's approach was to consult with the management, trying to ascertain whether the managers were reporting its concerns to the board. However, as the Auditor-General commented, it was evident that the Reserve Bank had genuine disquiet over the SBSA's prudential management as early as 1986 and each subsequent year should have reinforced this concern.[138] The RBA did not, however, take its misgivings to the Premier but rather dealt only with the bank. By not doing so it gave Bannon the impression that the RBA was satisfied with the bank. Even if the RBA had consulted with the Premier nothing may have come of this – but according to John Bannon he would have taken their concerns seriously:

> So at no time did I have any doubts that the Reserve Bank was enforcing the same requirements and the State Bank providing the same information as any of the other majors. It came as a revelation of the Royal Commission, where first I knew there had in fact been fracas and information withheld and things of that kind and that's one area I would have been absolutely livid. I know this is one area, because I placed such weight on it.[139]

The private auditors

> Auditors also deserve a special mention. If the audit profession cannot function any more usefully than it did in Australia in the 1980s then it might as well be abolished. As almost every auditor named in this book has since been the subject of a large lawsuit it is unfortunately risky to say much more. Hopefully, the lawsuits against auditors and their insurers will improve the diligence of the profession in future (Trevor Sykes, *The Bold Riders*).[140]

In keeping with Bannon's strategy of ensuring that the establishment of the SBSA was politically uncontroversial he decided to appoint private auditors to audit the bank and the BFC, rather than the Auditor-General, saying:

> The accounts of the bank were to be audited by external auditors, even though the bank as a statutory authority would ordinarily have had its account audited by the Auditor General. I saw this as a signal to the commercial world that the State Bank business was to be assessed in the same way as other business, by those most skilled in auditing the accounts of commercial businesses and not subject to the criticism that auditing was 'in house'. While this possible criticism misunderstands the statutory role and independence of the Auditor General, the use of private sector auditors was seen as avoiding any adverse perceptions in the market place.[141]

In contrast to the usual method of auditing public sector enterprises through the Auditor-General, whose reports on the enterprises are tabled in the parliament, the SBSA was to be audited as if it was a private sector entity but, in MacPherson's judgement, was not subject to the Companies Code. The lack of public accountability to the parliament suited the bank, which wanted to be independent from the government, just as it also matched the parliament's new-found faith in the accountability of the market. But with the SBSA not being accountable to the parliament it was the taxpayers who were thereby placed at a disadvantage.

In placing the SBSA in the orbit of private sector auditors, both the government and the opposition were complicity eroding the responsibility of the parliament over public enterprises – an erosion which deeply concerned many public officials. For intstance, in his 1989 report to parliament, the previous Auditor-General Tom Sheridan was concerned that public accountability was being dramatically eroded and this was undermining 'the cornerstone of the Westminster System'.[142] He wrote prophetically that 'there is a growing tendency for some public sector activities to become removed from parliamentary scrutiny (and the accountability process), despite the fact that public funds are involved or that a contingent liability rests with the government, either directly or indirectly, through guarantees it has given.[143] Sheridan explicitly highlighted his statement with the observation that 'if (as is the case in some public sector enterprises) the Auditor-General is not the appointed auditor of those subsidiary bodies then the financial accountability chain of the Westminster System is broken. This applies also where a government chooses to appoint a private sector auditor, rather than the Auditor-General, as the appointed auditor of a public enterprise'.[144]

Under the State Bank Act, the private auditors were given the task of attesting whether the bank's accounts were properly drawn up so that, on an annual basis, they gave a true and accurate picture of the income and expenditure of the bank, that the balance sheet presented was a true and accurate picture of the bank's affairs, and that the accounting records were properly kept and tested for defects or irregularities. Concomitantly, under the Act, the Auditor-General's role was relegated to that of investigating the bank only when something went wrong.

The SBSA's accounts were audited by Peat, Marwick, Mitchell & Co. (now known as KPMG Peat Marwick) and those of BFC and its subsidiaries were audited by Price Waterhouse. Following the collapse of the bank these two auditing firms came under the public spotlight. In evaluating the external auditors the Auditor-General did not re-audit the books; instead he sought to test whether the auditing processes conducted by Peat, Marwick, Mitchell and Co. and Price Waterhouse were consistent with the standard professional practices of auditors. In essence, the test was whether the audits were conducted in accordance with a professional norm, based on the ordinary standard of skill, diligence, care, accuracy and recourse to action which auditors are expected to take so as to match their professional standing. He concluded that in regard to the annual accounts of 1987–88, 1988–89 and 1989–90, the standard in some regards was not met and as a consequence the auditors might be held liable for their attesting to accounts which, in terms of the norm, were not a true and accurate picture of the bank's financial position.[145]

Naturally, as both firm's professional standing was at stake and there was possibility that the auditors might be held liable for these alleged short-comings, the matter did not rest there. The auditors provided the Royal Commission with their own expert advice countering that of the experts advising the Auditor-General. In due course, Royal Commissioner Mansfield decided to pass on to a legal task force the issue of whether there was negligence on the part of the auditors, to see whether a case could be mounted against them. The lawyers then advised the Brown government on the matter and as a consequence Attorney General Griffin took out civil action in the Supreme Court for a blanket claim of $4 billion for the losses incurred by the bank, a case which the auditors contested. Both auditing firms reached an out of court settlement in September 1997 for $120 million, which it is speculated came from the auditors' indemnity insurance.[146]

The SBSA was established on the basis of building on the past while transforming the focus of the bank to that of a corporate entity. But the drive to corporate banking soon overwhelmed the retail lending processes of the old bank. The growth of corporate loans, however, was until too late never matched by the creation of systems of prudential control. Rather, such systems were a hindrance to the growth strategy of the management and to the remuneration procedures within the bank.

In the end the drive was to lend and few within the bank were given the power or support to look after the shop. Instead when a system seemed to be established it was soon swamped by the sheer volume of the lending or was revolutionised to match some new management fad. The whole internal process of asset and liability management became dominated by its inability to catch up with the speed and quantity of corporate loans being made.

Outside the bank the over-lapping controls were collectively ineffective in preventing the disaster from occurring. The Treasurer and Treasury did not have the expertise or the parliamentary backing to challenge the SBSA. Rather, both relied upon the assurances emanating from the bank. For his part, Premier Bannon was ever cognisant of the political imperative not to be seen as interfering in the SBSA or to be regarded as keeping a watching brief on it. Such a position had a certain political logic to it but as will become evident this was a weakness in commercial legal terms, where he was legally responsible to protect the tax payer guarantee of the bank's capital. This weakness was highlighted by Commissioner Jacobs in his investigation. Bannon relied on the board and to an extent the external auditors to oversee the bank but in the end neither gave him warnings of the bank's internal failings until it was far too late. In regard to the RBA, it did not go beyond its informal charter of overseeing the bank on a voluntary basis and did not warn the Premier of its concerns. Finally, the private sector auditors, in the opinion of Auditor-General MacPherson, were on some specific issues not adequately assessing the bank in terms of the standard auditing procedures of the day.

As the next chapter will show, the bank was ever keen to keep up the appearance that it was the most successful bank in Australia in the 1980s. Such a representation, however, merely confirmed how far it had changed from its ancestral roots in the old State Bank and the Savings Bank of South Australia.

8

Keeping up appearances

From the outside the SBSA presented an image of continuity with its predecessors, the Savings Bank of South Australia and the old State Bank of South Australia, while simultaneously subverting that tradition. In its advertising and annual reports the SBSA spoke of building on the past, yet the cautious loans for housing and land was being swamped by aggressive corporate lending. The past retained its prominence in advertising for housing loans in South Australia, although the images it evoked were selectively middle class buyers of heritage houses in gentrified Adelaide suburbs rather than concessional home buyers in working class suburbs. The SBSA, nevertheless, remained prominent in funding local events (e.g. John Martin's Chrstmas Pageant) and sporting teams and appeared to be carrying on the tradition of the merged banks. Yet by 1986 it was a corporate bank taking high risk loans around the world without the wherewithal to know the extent of its lending let alone whether it was taking too high a risk.

The new State Bank building: a monument to global success
Earlier in our tale, we noted the pride taken in the building of the Savings Bank's head office. To recall this past, it is important to remember the difference in cultures. On 2 February 1943 His Excellency, Governor Sir Malcolm Barclay-Harvey, opened the new Savings Bank office in King William Street. The opening ceremony was austere, befitting the dark days of World War II. The Trustees took great pride in its modern structure of steel frame and reinforced concrete. Ninety two percent of the material for the building was Australian and most was from South Australia.[1]

In November 1985 the SBSA board decided to develop a multi-storey building, to tower over the Adelaide skyline as a symbol of the new corporate and global image of the bank. The board looked for a symbol to celebrate its success as the fastest growing bank in Australia. Its new headquarters was planned to be a landmark for the future. To this end land was acquired which abutted the 1943 Savings Bank premises in Currie Street. The design of the new building was to be functionally modern while it was intended that the structure would stand in stark contrast to the past. With the Savings Bank playing only a niche role in local banks, the new bank would tower over the Adelaide city as a symbolic reference to the SBSA's prominent position in the State's economy. The board was told that the intention behind the design was to make the building attractive to 'high quality tenants and prove to be a focal point in the City of Adelaide'.[2] The design and outward appearance of the building were of functional dullness, implying that the State Bank's success came from its clinging to its conservative past. Its size and visual prominence were to imply something different – that the bank was a global entity.

The State Bank Tower was heralded as combining 'heritage and modern architecture'.[3] The heritage was, however, over-powered by the sheer size of the new tower, where the past lost its meaning as it was overtaken by the bank's new-found corporate identity. The old entrance to the Savings Bank remained, as did the retail ground floor counters, serving retail customers, yet these seemed to take on the appearance of an artefact of the bygone era of banking, where thrift and savings were the dominant philosophy. The lending chamber was like some historic reconstruction, set against the modernist tower where the corporate business and major decisions were now being made. In many ways the Savings Bank, with its polished wood and sombre toned fittings, became like a museum piece of what the bank was like when time passed it by, and had little relevance to the new bank.

It was not to be in the wood panelled past where the senior managers were to set up their corporate business but in the shimmering interior of the new tower. The Managing Director presided from a plush suite, with the finest wines (chosen by Max Schubert of Grange Hermitage fame) ready at hand and the customary paintings on the walls, chosen (in Gordon Gekko style) for their market value and impact. This was Clark's inner sanctum where only the anointed could enter and join his 'doing the deal' team. It was here the million dollar cheques were handed over and where the celebrations for capturing corporate clients were held.

The top floor became the realm of the Managing Director, on the floor below him was BFC, and below them the merchant banking arm, Ayres Finnis. There was a layer of corporate banking separating the executives from the rest of the retail bankers. It became a barrier separating the new from the old.

In justifying the new building to the parsimonious Premier, the SBSA Board initially indicated to Bannon that these plush executive offices were for renting to high profile corporate clients which the bank said was essential to cover the cost of the building. Nevertheless, when the building was completed these floors became the bank's head office. The change, according to Tim Marcus Clark, was forced on him and the board: 'I had originally intended to remain in 97 King William Street, but our directors consider that Level 30 is an outstanding floor in Adelaide's premier building that will prove ideal headquarters for State Bank, well into the future.'[4] However, the size of the new building and readiness of Clark to take up his residence on the top floors belied the image of a reluctant and modest executive, forced against his will upward to the new exclusive surrounds.

The new philosophy
In November 1985 when the bank decided to create its headquarters it wanted to make a statement by the sheer size of the building. The aim was that it would tower over the central business district. However, this concept ran into planning restrictions and public criticism that its size went against the city's heritage plan. What was of concern to local planners and historians was that the bank was seeking a special privilege to override Adelaide planning regulations to build six storeys above the height restrictions. The tower thus became a touchstone for Clark's philosophy that Adelaide was being held back by an anti-development mentality.[5] Clark took it on himself to openly lambast the South Australian heritage lobby saying the choice was between their backwardness and modernisation.[6] He argued

that the choice for Adelaide was 'develop or decay', contending that South Australia needed 'prime development' to promote overall 'property development'.[7] Addressing a Liberal Party luncheon in January 1988, Clark said that:

> Investors had shied away from South Australia, with their cash and plans firmly in tow, because negative influences had made it hard to do business. Many in this city and this State do not like change. They would like to keep things as they are, but attempts to maintain the status quo will end only in decay and stagnation. If developers decide to undertake a major project in Adelaide or try to change any part of the existing framework, they are immediately pounced upon. Adelaide cannot have development and conservation as exclusive and separate concepts.[8]

The building became something of a test of this philosophy. It was equally based on the perception that the building was to make a statement and therefore be attractive to corporate clients. To attract corporate clients the bank asserted it was necessary to capture a potential window of opportunity in the commercial rental markets. It was anticipated that if the new tower could be built quickly then the top floors could be let to these clients before they were lured to other premises. By early 1986 Premier Bannon was won over to the State Bank's claim that the building had to be rushed through the planning process so that it would be commercially viable.[9] With the perception that the project had to be built quickly, the government 'fast tracked' the development, therein by-passing the planning laws.[10]

The Premier and perceptions

Nevertheless, from the outset Premier Bannon had misgivings about the State Bank Tower. In March 1986 the Premier wrote to Managing Director Clark questioning him as to why he had not been fully informed of the board's decision to go ahead with the building. He began his letter with the caveat that, 'Consistent with the commercial thrust of the bank, it is not my intention to raise any objection to the proposal, subject to the planning/regulatory aspects which are under examination and subject to some points which I wish to make concerning the framework within which this proposal has been developed and will be implemented … I note that your 'media release' took place one day after the date of your letter to me and on the same day as that letter reached my Department'.[11]

The first point Bannon was making was merely over the matter of courtesy in that he was not given adequate consultation or significant warning of the SBSA's decision which caught the Premier unawares and politically exposed. The second point of concern to Premier Bannon was the impact of the development on the bank's profits and subsequently on the contribution the SBSA would make to the State. Thirdly, he wanted the bank to consult with the South Australian Government Financing Authority (SAFA) as to what would be the best method to finance the project. Finally, Premier Bannon asked the bank to consider how the financing of the project inter-meshed with the investments of other public financial institutions. On this Bannon wrote that:

> We have a number of public sector organisations within the State in the business of long term investment, including the SGIC, the Superannuation Fund

Investment Trust [SASFIT], SAFA, the bank and potentially the Workers Compensation Board. The question of whether, and if so how, this activity needs to be coordinated is clearly important. I have asked the Treasury to put this issue to study and would expect officers of the Department to be in touch with the bank as the study progresses'.[12]

Clark replied that he felt the bank had given the government sufficient warning and that rather than being the SBSA's problem it was Bannon's fault as in his absence there seemed no clear line of command for communication between the bank and the government. Clark then said that the bank's investment in the Centre would not 'reduce the flow of funds to the Treasury of taxation and dividends'. Clark agreed that there should be consultation over 'major projects on a "whole of state" basis', which side-stepped the issue of the SBSA not seeing itself, or being in practice, part of the State's public financial structure.[13] Clark concluded his letter with the following sentence 'We note your comments concerning co-ordination, and will await further advices from Treasury'.[14]

Having sent a message of reassurance to the Treasurer, as the Auditor-General noted, the issue was then ignored by Clark and the bank. MacPherson could find no reference to consultation between the Treasury and the bank on this topic following this exchange of letters.[15] Rather, it would seem that the inquiry from the Premier over the funding of the new State Bank Centre resulted in the decision of the board to ensure that the project was funded via an off-balance sheet company, Kabani Pty Ltd, so as to keep the issue within the bank itself and outside Treasury scrutiny on this arrangement. Royal Commissioner Jacobs noted that 'pressure from the Government' over the project was undoubtedly a factor in the decision to fund the centre off-balance sheet.[16]

The initial funding for the project came from the Bank of Tokyo, with all interest capitalised until the building was completed. The finance was then transferred through Kabani and parcelled out to Lonsby Westpac for 60 per cent, the Commonwealth Bank for 30 per cent and Beneficial Finance Corporation for 10 per cent.[17] The building was let through two other off-balance sheet companies, Ollago Pty Ltd and Bulwark Pty Ltd. The Auditor-General was highly critical of the running of these latter companies, especially as they did not prepare financial statements in the specified time for the years 1986, 1987 and 1988 as laid down by the Companies Code. In the end, this matter was referred to the Australian Securities Commission for investigation but no action was taken as it was outside the five year prescribed limitation period.[18] The point is that the SBSA ignored the request by the Premier to join in with the other public financial authorities in South Australia. Instead the SBSA kept the whole financing to itself and carried out its business in a manner which was at best irregular. This approach was a far cry from that adopted in 1943 when the Savings Bank prided itself as a local institution committed to the state, morality and Empire.

In-house development
In keeping with Tim Marcus Clark's bold style of management, he decided to build the new premises using in-house staff, despite the fact that none had the experience to handle such a large development. Clark appointed Peter Rumbelow as administrative co-ordinator of the project. Rumbelow had not worked on a major project

and his only experience in commercial construction was in the building of some regional bank branches. The fast tracking of the project meant that decisions were made under pressure. As the Auditor-General observed, the initial claim of a 'window of opportunity' to obtain commercial tenants so as to 'fast-track' the deal, through the planning process was open to question when it was made in 1986 and soon proved illusory.[19]

The Auditor-General noted that the narrow time-frame for the project combined with Rumbelow's lack of experience placed him in a compromised position as he was so reliant on the advice of the construction firm:

> In my opinion, notwithstanding the evidence that the consultants endeavoured to give their best advice to Mr. Rumbelow, the fact remains that Mr Rumbelow should not have been the bank's representative in the project. From the very nature of such a project, the consultants may have been involved in conflicts of interest from time to time ... Not only should the bank not have allowed Mr Rumbelow, with his lack of experience in this complex area, to make important decisions on its behalf, but the respective responsibilities of the consultants should have been more clearly defined.[20]

In the Auditor-General's view, the State Bank Centre was an example of poor management decisions, beginning with Clark's delegation of the project to a dedicated, hard working but inexperienced officer, Rumbelow and the financing of the project by an off-balance sheet company to prevent scrutiny of the management by the government. In contrast, Commissioner Jacobs reduced the issue of the building to the Premier's supposed drive for revenue. For Commissioner Jacobs, the dispute between the SBSA and the Premier was an example of the Treasurer not intervening because he was only concerned with the 'profit' transfer to Treasury and therefore failed to scrutinise the bank and the building of the new head office.[21] This is, however, only one of the inter-changes between Premier Bannon and the bank. There is something more revealing in this exchange than government revenue.

The other interpretation is that the Premier was unable to bring the SBSA into the public sector and coordinate the State's public finances. Instead he was prepared to accept the perception that the SBSA was building a tower for commercial purposes. When this became questionable the Premier offered a mild rebuke but when challenged kept his owned counsel and moved on to other matters. The Premier was following his standard procedure of 'satisficing', that is, keeping many people satisfied as a symbol of good government. Moreover, as Commissioner Jacobs noted, the blow-out in the cost of the building and the use of off-balance sheet arrangements as well as the blow out in costs by over 50 per cent was kept from Premier Bannon. These arrangements and expenditure did not appear in the SBSA's financial statements from 1986 to 1990.[22]

Jacobs comments that the failure of Clark and Barrett to inform Premier Bannon of the escalation in the State Centre Project costs was a deliberate deception. If Bannon had known, according to Jacobs, he may have 'lost faith in the bank.'[23] Jacobs adds that 'one cannot avoid the strong suspicion that the Treasurer wasn't told this information because it was bad news, and neither the bank nor the Director wanted him to have cause to question his trust in them'.[24]

The State Bank Centre example revealed that the management were given tasks beyond their experience. The cost of the construction blew out from $85 million in 1985 to $122.50 million by July 1988.[25] Yet rather than take stock the board decided not to disclose this information to the Bannon government. At the time the SBSA was conducting this slight of hand it was offering subsidy packages to attract clients to the building, which in turn increased the debt to the bank to over $152 million.[26] In 1988, the bank estimated the value of the building at $237 million. In 1997 it was sold for $62 million, bringing the loss to the taxpayers of a minimum of $85 million over the initial costs of construction.[27]

The financial miscalculations over the new head office also show how the board was ever ready to support its management and to close ranks over internal financial arrangements. The board went along with the management's suggestions, without questioning in depth the costs. This reliance on management was never more evident than with the bank's largest loss, that of the REMM–Myer complex. The board supported the management's plan to be involved in a prestigious and prominent project in the heart of Adelaide without due consideration of the risks involved in the project.

REMM–MYER

At the 28 July 1988 State Bank Board meeting, the directors were informed by management of the blow-out in the cost of constructing the State Bank Centre, from $82 to $120 million. At the same meeting, the directors approved a management proposal to finance a shopping complex for Myer Stores Ltd in the Rundle Mall. The proposal had been approved the day before at a three hour meeting of the Lending Credit Committee. The financing of the deal was complex, but in essence the SBSA was to be the lead financier, initially on 'bridging finance', of the development, and then the loan syndicate among other banks. The SBSA Board was putting at risk $120 million in the first stage of the funding, to facilitate the developer, REMM, to pay out the existing mortgages and to commence the development. But the first stage led indubitably to the second where the bank was to underwrite the project, anticipated to be syndicated, for another $330 million. The proposal estimated that the completion value of the Myer Complex would be around $553.1 million and the development costs to be around $450 million to $490 million. From the outset the project had received considerable media attention and anticipation had grown that there was to be a major new development in Adelaide's premier shopping precinct.

Of the project, Bannon commented that while it was important to the government, he contended that he had made it clear that the bank alone should determine the commercial viability of the investment:

> ... Tim forcefully said they would make up their own minds and I believed that it was the credit committee that would consider it and then the board would consider it. In early July [1988] when I was walking with him through Victoria Square and I was aware that the State Bank was considering being involved, I recall I said to Mr Clark that the project had attracted a lot of attention and it would be pity if it did not go ahead in such a key area of Adelaide ... I said I would like the bank to examine the matter seriously, but I made it plain that I did not expect the bank to get involved if it was not a sound commercial

transaction from the bank's point of view. My recollection is that Mr Clark agreed.[28]

Similarly, the Department of State Development, headed by Dr Lindner, was keen to facilitate the project, if for no other reason than to quell criticisms of the department's economic role.[29] Similarly, Lord Mayor Steve Condous (who was later to be elected to the House of Assembly for the Liberal Party) was a keen advocate for the REMM-Myer project as a stimulus for shopping in the city centre. Equally, the head of the Department of Premier and Cabinet, Bruce Guerin was keen 'to make sure the development happens, provided it was commercial to do so'.[30]

In May 1988 the REMM group acquired the site using a letter of credit of $40 million as part of a stand-by facility, backed by a put option of $43.14 million for the Myer Brisbane site. At that stage the ANZ Capital Market Corporation led the financing of the proposal. In June 1988 the ANZ group, because of changes to the tax laws, withdrew from the project, leaving REMM in a position of exposure[31]. In the month that followed this withdrawal, Chief Project Manager, Peter Mullins prepared the proposal to finance the project. It was his proposal that the board agreed to on 28 July 1988.

The idea for the REMM–Myer shopping complex was imported from the United States. The concept behind it was for the Myer Centre to dominate the city shopping precinct. The design of the new Centre was meant to attract attention. The Emeritus Director of the Art Gallery of South Australia Daniel Thomas, said the building was:

> not bad for the neo-heritage 1990s. The Myer Centre's animation, its bright colour – green and gold, with flashy red neon trim – is a marvellous climax to the anything-goes mood of a good shopping mall. It plays exuberantly off its friendly, elegant enemy David Jones next door. It glitters down lanes from the sober-sides corporate stock-exchange district. It's a good neighbour, a generous contributor to that shoppers' delight of a century earlier, the Adelaide Arcade.[32]

Peter Mullins's proposal contained two critical elements, the first was the staging of the project, the second was the guarantees being requested by Myer Stores Ltd to ensure the completion of the project.

Stage One was basically the acquisition of existing mortgages and the demolition of the site. Stage Two involved the construction of a department store, office block, tavern, amusement arcade and multiple shops. In regard to the guarantee this involved a tripartite arrangement between REMM as the developer, Myer Stores Ltd as the major leesee and the SBSA as lead financier. The arrangement invoved Myer Stores Ltd signing a 75 year lease in return for a guarantee that the project would be completed. Additionally, as an inducement for Myer Stores Ltd to relocate, REMM underwrote the profits of the retailer between 1988 and 1989 to the limit of $27 million. Myer Store Ltd was also to be compensated if there were delays to the project.

At the time of the signing of stage one, the financing of this major project was finely balanced at best, it would bring marginal return to the bank, at worst, the endeavour could result in large losses for the SBSA, with no escape clause for the bank[33]. In the view of the Auditor-General the initial proposal by the Chief Project Manager, Mullins, was so ill-considered as to be 'dangerous' and the losses were likely to be 'substantial'.[34] The Auditor-General considered that the board, once having made the first imprudent decision, was then obliged to continue to meet the costs of the project and accept the loss.[35]

This view was concurred with by Commissioner Jacobs who said that the board's decision on 28 July 1998 to undertake the project was 'unsafe'.[36] He added that a 'moderately careful study of the document' prepared by Mullins for the board would have shown that the proposal was of high risk and that the decision to approve the funding was not made on 'valid commercial grounds'.[37]

From the outset, there were constant delays in commencing the construction. In November 1988 Stage One had not commenced due to the reluctance of tenants to vacate, and to owners of adjoining sites refusing to consent to any interference with their rights. There is a certain irony in that a 'neo-heritage' shopping centre, based on an American concept of shopping and amusement, was situated in the heart of an old 'English/Adelaide establishment', where the Liberal Party headquarters sat side by side with medical specialists and where the Englishness of the Adelaide Club matched its sturdy neighbours. The old was not going to give way easily to the new. While these protracted negotiations with the adjoining interests were going on the REMM group was using up its Stage One capital to dig a large hole in the centre of their demolition site. There was no turning back now. No government would see a hole in the centre of its prime shopping centre remaining for very long – especially not if it came close to an election and the SBSA was unable to syndicate the loan.

While the demolition was delayed concern also reverberated within the SBSA over syndicating the loan. By April 1989 no syndicate had been created and the repeated delays to the project made the financial market jittery investing in the project. The SBSA had no alternative but to continue its 'bridging finance' arrangements to meet the capital demands for the development. In June 1989 the board was faced again with the irreversible logic of its initial decision, and of continuing its commitments. The board agreed to borrow another $190 million to support the project. This decision, as the Auditor-General noted, meant that the likely overall debt for building the Centre was between $550 and $580 million.[38] In short, the bank within nine months of agreeing to lead the syndicate, was now tied to the construction of the centre for Myer even though the bank would probably make a loss.

In September 1989, Mullins presented to the board a new proposal for a joint venture with REMM to complete the centre by March 1991, with the proviso that should REMM not meet its obligations by 31 March 1992 then total ownership would fall to the bank. The anticipated debt was then envisaged to be $575 million. An independent assessor, of Colliers International, estimated the value of the project at completion to be $557 million.[39] At the 28 September 1989 board meeting the directors had little option but to approve the new arrangements. Again in October and November 1989 the board was confronted with the problem that no financial syndicate had been formed and the 'bridging finance' arrangements had to be extended.

By January 1990 'bridging finance' had been extended to $300 million and consequently the bank's exposure was raised by another $70 million.[40] To syndicate the loan the SBSA made the concession to the effect that should there be a loss from the project then the SBSA would pay the syndicated members before the State Bank itself. Moreover, the SBSA was still obligated to Myer Stores Ltd to the complete the development. Compounding the continual financial difficulties with the project were construction dilemmas with Stage Two.

On the building site there was a series of industrial disputes. The REMM group was now under enormous pressure to complete the project as quickly as possible. The company was discovering, however, that the successful tactics it had used in Brisbane, notably of using preferred subcontractors, and selective union agreements, were causing disharmony. Equally, the unions, knowing that the bank was financing the deal and that there was little other building work in South Australia, were not above placing bans on the site to gain concessions from REMM. The State Bank then approached Premier Bannon to intercede, on its behalf, with the unions but this proved to no avail.[41]

By April 1990 'bridging finance' had risen to $335 million.[42] Just as the development seemed to be making headway inclement weather resulted in further delays. In October 1990 the board was faced once again with increasing its financial exposure and had to add another $45 million to the finance burden of the project.[43] By December 1990, the full costs of completing the Centre had blown-out to $744 million and this exceeded the Reserve Bank prudential limits for any single project.[44] The board had, however, no option but to again agree to increase its financing to $398 million.[45]

Then the effect of the decline in the property market was brought starkly home to the board in February 1991 when it was reported that the annual rental for the Myer Complex was likely to be $28.5 million compared to $38.5 million in the original estimate.[46] On 17 January 1991 the board was informed that a possible loss to the bank was now $249 million and this was without even calculating the fees to be paid on the capitalisation of the debt.[47]

When the REMM-Myer Complex was completed in 1991, the total liability to the bank was over $900 million. In 1996 the Myer Complex was sold for $152 million which meant that the loss was over $750 million for the taxpayers. The SBSA's largest loss was brought about by a board being prepared to make an ill-judged decision to support a dangerous proposal from the management for an open-ended guarantee to build a prominent shopping centre.

Interpretation one: it's the management's fault
In sum, the decision of 28 July 1988 to approve financing the REMM–Myer Complex in the end cost the taxpayers in excess of $750 million. For the Auditor-General the fault lay with the initial decision by Mullins, which failed to balance out the risk against the possible profit. For the Auditor-General, lending officer Mullins, the Managing Director, the Lending Credit Committee and the board should all have recognised the weakness in the project and the high risk entailed in the initial proposal and all should have rejected it.

Interpretation two: it's the Premier's fault
Commissioner Jacobs considered that the initial decision was irresponsible and not made for sound commercial reasons. This led him to see the decision within his larger scenario of a flawed relationship between the bank, its board and the

Premier. In short, in Commissioner Jacobs' view the decision was made for political and not commercial reasons:

> The bank, as on previous occasions was seeking to please the Government: the management was bending over backwards to present material in a way that aimed at a favourable outcome in order to fulfil Government hopes. The board was anxious to please the Government to the extent that it almost suspended commercial responsibility in supporting a project that was demonstrably too finely balanced to be safe and sound.[48]

Jacobs, with typical rhetorical flair, but with a sharp judicial sting in his tone aimed at Bannon, commented that the board 'passed the ultimate responsibility to the Treasurer himself, and the Treasurer, still living in splendid indifference to other evidence that the bank's commercial judgement was questionable and very likely flawed, himself put the final and vital seal on the financial package by authorising and approving the participation of SAFA'.[49]

In contrast to Jacobs, the Auditor-General regarded the SAFA funding as of only minor interest. The board agreed to this funding in only broad terms and was not in the same range as the initial decision to fund Stage One.[50] The Auditor-General concurred with Commissioner Jacobs that 'there was external pressure on the bank, and notably on Mr Mullins to see the project proceed'.[51] The Auditor-General was highly critical of the initial proposal and more importantly of both the Lending Credit Committee and the board for not exercising commercial judgement in regard to Mullins's initial proposal.[52] In short, once the board had agreed to the Mullins proposal, the role of the government, including the SAFA put option, was secondary.[53]

Interpretation three: shared blame
Jacobs was to moderate his position somewhat in his second report. In this report he directed his judgement towards the board arguing that it had a responsibility to resist any pressures from the outside. Jacobs wrote that:

> The haste in which the proposal was presented, and the lack of any real opportunity to examine its complexity and weigh up the 'pros and cons' suggests that prudence yielded to the Bank's desire to be seen as a major player in the 'big league'.[54]

In the final Royal Commission report, Commissioner Mansfield brought together both Jacobs's judicial interpretation with that of MacPherson's causative interpretation. He placed the onus on the board for the losses over REMM. Mansfield found that while the board was aware of the government's interest in the project that its members were still able and did act independently in making an 'uncommercial transaction'.[55] Commissioner Mansfield found that the proposal was warranting careful re-appraisal by Lending Credit Committee and the board because in the final analysis, at best, the complex was going to produce marginal profit at a very high level of risk.[56]

Mansfield recommended further investigation into why the proposal was approved by the board (Bakewell, Barrett, Byrne, Clark, Hartley, Nankerville,

Searcy and Summers) and why the Lending Credit Committee (Masters, Matthews, Wright and Mallett) had recommended the REMM facility to the board. He also recommended Chief Manager Corporate Banking, Mullins, be investigated for negligence of due care.[57] Given the number of individuals involved in the project, the complexity of its funding and the series of errors made by the management and the board, the external pressures on the bank, statutory legal limitation,and the contested nature of negligence and due care legal cases, no charges were laid.

In summary of the REMM-Myer case study the point at issue for this book is not that of apportioning the blame rather it is merely to emphasise how distinct were the decisions made by the SBSA managers and board from those of their predecessors. In the old banks a proposal to lead finance such a venture as the REMM-Myer Centre would not have arisen let alone be agreed to. There was clearly a culture transformation, which had occured within the SBSA, it is probably best summed up by the comment, which Stephen Paddison had allegedly made over the REMM-Myer decision, that we have just 'bet the Bank on this one'.[58]

Adsteam

A similar sense of cultural revolution within the SBSA can be attested in its dealings with the Adelaide Steamship Company (Adsteam). In June 1984 the SBSA advanced $10 million to Adsteam, and by 1990 the SBSA's exposure to Adsteam had risen to $456 million.[59] Adsteam was an Adelaide based company and could therefore be seen as conforming to the bank's charter of promoting the 'balanced development of the state'. Most of the company's assets, however, were outside of South Australia. Moreover, Adsteam had built an empire on debt financing, provided freely by the banks.

Adsteam was headed by the entrepreneur, John Spalvins, who was lauded in the media for his adventurous takeover tactics. He was both an Adelaide and a national corporate hero. When he married Cecily Rymill, Spalvins entered into one of Adelaide's major establishment families. He scoffed, however, at suggestions that his success had anything do with his class connections. Rather he said his rise to corporate prominence was due to positive thinking: 'It's all in the state of mind, like the share market', adding that 'one of the joys of this country is the equal opportunity'.[60] Spalvins was a strong supporter of the philosophy of self interest, notably in terms of corporate executives being granted the right to become owners of the firm they managed.[61]

Spalvins devised an ingenious take-over strategy whereby Adsteam would acquire less than 50 per cent of any firm it acquired. The acquired firm would then buy shares in Adsteam, so it became difficult for the market to know who owned whom. In brief, the strategy was to partly take-over firms but not consolidate them into the Adsteam group. The part purchase arrangement was also a defensive tactic used by Adsteam against entrepreneurs seeking to take-over the group. The tactic involved the financial structuring of the group as if they were separate but linked entities under the Adsteam flag. Yet their borrowings were inter-connected so that the security of the loans depended upon the share market accepting that the companies were un-consolidated. The danger was that should the market lose faith in Adsteam, it would lead to a collapse of faith and financial support for all entities in the Adsteam stable. For instance, the retailer David Jones Ltd, having been partly bought by Adsteam, bought Adsteam shares and when the value of David Jones

Ltd fell so did that of Adsteam until the debt structure was all that was left and the banks were then left holding worthless 'negative pledges' from Adsteam. At its peak the Adsteam stable controlled, but technically did not own, assets of $11 billion with annual sales of around $12 billion.

The Adsteam stable survived the share market crash of October 1987. But in 1990, after an ambitious bid to take over the firm, Industrial Equity Ltd, owned by another corporate raider, Sir Ron Brierley, the share market turned against the group as a whole. As a counter-attack to the takeover bid, Brierley had launched a scathing criticism of the financial structure and viability of the Adsteam group, which struck a chord with market analysts. In mid 1990 the share price of the group fell dramatically, prompting the lenders to re-evaluate their loans. The individual firms in the group found that they could not obtain credit and could not sell sufficient assets, in a depressed market, to meet their debt obligations. In December 1990, banks with liabilities to Adsteam, led by the ANZ, Westpac, the National, the Commonwealth Bank, and the Bank of America, obliged Adsteam to restructure and re-schedule its finances. At that time 109 banks had exposure to the Adsteam stable with the SBSA being the fifth largest lender.[62] The SBSA to its credit had been one of the first banks of the 109 to recognise in late 1989 that Adsteam was vulnerable and to close down it lines of credit, notably in refusing to enter into any more 'negative pledge' arrangements. A decision, unfortunately for the taxpayers, was taken too late to protect the bank's money.

'Negative pledges' to a 'blue chip' company

The SBSA's involvement with Adsteam began almost immediately upon the formation of the SBSA. In June 1984, the SBSA granted Adsteam a credit facility of $10 million.[63] The bank, under the false assumption that Adsteam was 'as good as a blue chip' company, relaxed its prudential requirements, lending to Adsteam on an unsecured basis, taking 'negative pledges' as guarantee on loans.[64] Negative pledges became an 'in' concept in banking in the 1980s, whereby a company would pledge not to sell off assets as a form of security for a loan. This tactic worked only so long as its pledge assets were of value and the company remained solvent. For the SBSA the danger with Adsteam was that each company was backed by a 'negative pledge' against shares of another in the stable, so that a cumulative fall in the price of any or all of the Adsteam group would mean that there could be a cumulative series of unsecured loans.[65] Moreover, because of its ever-evolving credit management system the SBSA never knew its total exposure to the Adsteam stable nor did it ever conduct a review of its total loans to Adsteam before it was too late. It was then left with unsecured or poorly backed loans.[66]

Additionally, by not aggregating the total exposure of the bank to Adsteam it was implicitly avoiding its prudential limit to the consolidated group. For example, at its peak in December 1989 the bank's total exposure to Adsteam was $559 million, which was $253 million in excess of its prudential limit.[67] In its desire to lend to Adsteam the bank was quite willing to assume, following the other major banks, that if a corporation was in the Adsteam stable it was 'blue chip' and prudential standards could be lowered. Similarly, when it suited it, the State Bank justified a loan to an Adsteam subsidiary on a non-aggregated basis. In other words, the desire was to lend to the group as a whole into one of its entity companies. In short, the SBSA was all too ready to acquiesce to Adsteam demands no matter the banking logic. This was also evident in the State Bank's failure to challenge Adsteam's refusal to provide cash flow forecasts and budget information when making a loan.[68] In general, loans made to Adsteam were unsecured, backed mostly by 'negative pledges'. Additionally, the loans to Adsteam were based on the assumption that security was the 'first recourse' should the loan fail. An assumption criticised by the Auditor-General who argued that the bank erroneously believed that the 'first recourse' was against the shares or property of the borrower and not 'the borrower and the borrower's income'.[69] He commented that best practice is for the lender to regard 'the liquidation of security as his last recourse rather than his first recourse'.[70]

'Round robin' approvals

The method of lending was characterised by making quick decisions, so as to beat the competition, to meet the requests of Adsteam. In his investigation of the loans to Adsteam, MacPherson found that many loans were made practically on the day of request, sometimes at inquorate meetings, on the basis of a 'round robin' ring around of the directors. Round robins were used to get an indication of the directors' intentions in regard to any Adsteam loan and then in principle an approval could be made of the loan.[71] Moreover, there were instances where the round robin approvals were not confirmed at board meetings.[72]

For instance, when the bank increased its exposure to one of the Adsteam stable, Industrial Equity, on 8 October 1987 for $80 million, this was approved using a 'round robin' of telephone calls to directors, which was then agreed to by the board on 13 October 1987. By then, MacPherson contends that, Industrial Equity had already received the money.[73] Similarly, on 23 March 1988, the bank approved a loan to Adsteam for $35 million on inadequate information a day before it was presented to the board.[74] Again on 11 and 12 May 1988 the directors approved a loan to an Adsteam stable company, Buckley & Nunn, for $115 million via a 'round robin' telephone link before a full board meeting perused the loan. In the Auditor-General's view Adsteam was notified of the approval of this loan on 13 May 1988 and yet the board did not meet until 26 May 1988.[75]

The 'round robin' process prevented the directors having the opportunity to collectively evaluate the loan. By allowing this practice to become a norm in regard to substantial loans to Adsteam, the directors, in the Auditor-General's view, were failing in their prudential duty of controlling the business of the bank.[76] The board was but sharing in the belief of the managers and other banks that Adsteam was as safe as a 'blue chip' company and did not need to be scrutinised as rigorously as non-'blue-chip' companies. In regard to Adsteam, the Auditor-General considered that the transactions were not adequately and properly supervised, directed or controlled by the Board of Directors.[77]

The SBSA's exposure to Adsteam had began at $10 million in 1984 rising to $100 million by 1986 and was $110 million at the time of the share market crash of October 1987. The State Bank's exposure then tripled to be $330 million in 1988. This is a startling rise given that Adsteam's security was based on pledges against the value of the shares in the stable as the 'first recourse'. In 1989 the SBSA's exposure to the stable rose to $559 million, it was then that the bank decided that the Adsteam stable was overly exposed and began to reduce its own vulnerability down to $3128 million. It stood at this level when in 1990 the share market lost faith in Spalvins's strategy and the banks then stepped in to salvage what they could from all of their 'negative pledges'. Again Adsteam was a case where the culture inside the bank and that outside coalesced in a disastrous manner for the taxpayers. In sum, the SBSA was to lose $83.4 million on its Adsteam exposure.[78]

Pegasus
The final case study in how the SBSA's culture had been transformed from its historic roots involves that of that of BFC and a thoroughbred race-horsing company called Pegasus. As was mentioned in the first half of the book, the old State Bank had lent to a similar type of leasing company with great success. In the following case the lending was to lead to tragic results. It all began in December 1985 when Pegasus Leasing, headed by the prominent Adelaide pastoralist Alistair McGregor, approached Beneficial Finance proposing a joint venture for the purpose of leasing thoroughbred racehorses. At that time McGregor, a prominent rural identity, needed capital due both to personal and business reasons. McGregor was a former member of the Australian Wool Board, a member of the International Wool Secretariat, a former Chairman of the Australian Breeding Co-operative, a former deputy Chair of the South Australian Jockey Club and a member of the Adelaide Club. A joint venture company, Pegasus Leasing Pty Ltd (at the time with receivables of $5.5 million) was formed between McGregor and BFC, and between 1985 and 31 December 1987 leased racehorses.[79] Due to its poor performances and bad debts the nominee company was wound up in December 1987. At the time, BFC's joint venture committee recommended that no new Pegasus joint venture be formed.

However, under the instigation of the head of BFC, John Baker, on January 1 1988, a more substantial Pegasus Leasing joint venture was born. It had two related companies, the joint venture firm Pegasus Leasing and a company effectively controlled by McGregor, Pegasus Security. Pegasus Leasing commenced business with assets of less than $1 million, and via unsecured loans, rose to $62 million by June 1989, at this point its liabilities exceeding its assets.[80] Despite the fact that it had traded unprofitably and was in debt BFC kept lending to Pegasus and by December 1990 its liabilities had risen to over $100 million. In December 1990 Pegasus Security went into receivership and Pegasus Leasing was fully absorbed into BFC with unsecured loans of $97.9 million.[81] At 31 January 1991 BFC's losses on Pegasus Leasing were around $40 to $46 million and from Pegasus Security another $7.1 million.[82]

In its short existence Pegasus Leasing became a highly diverse company. It was engaged in speculating on Aboriginal art works, on a United Kingdom laundry business, an insurance brokerage firm, a debt factoring business to the crash repair industry, and owning a warehouse in Adelaide. Its basic business, nevertheless, was the bloodstock leasing of racehorses. In brief, the joint venture provided loans, in the form of finance leases over thoroughbred horses, which were used by the lessee-borrowers for racing and breeding, with the horses providing security for the loan.[83] The intention was that the joint venture would receive its profits in respect of leases in the form of the difference between the interest rate it charged on the leases and the interest rate it held on its loan from BFC. The critical factors were, on the one side, the level of interest rates and on the other side, the availability and market value for the thoroughbreds, and their success rate in winning prize money. As well there was the cost of the upkeep of the thoroughbreds and their continued good health. Expressed simply, this was a high risk business.

The joint venture brought together McGregor's blood stock expertise with Beneficial Finance's financial resources. In 1985 McGregor was interested in gaining control of Pegasus Securities, a company he had formed with a number of Adelaide businessmen. Baker and his deputy Reichart, along with one of the senior managers, Mr Martin, and one of its directors, Mr Williams, all shared an interest in race-horses (it is worth noting that Mr Williams declared his conflict of interest and took no part in deliberations when Pegasus Leasing was considered).[84] Likewise, it should be noted that Commissioner Jacobs declared his minor interest in a syndicate connected to McGregor. The bringing together of McGregor's expertise with BFC's money had a synergism as the thoroughbred racehorse business was booming, with prices for horses rising faster than the rate of inflation.

The idea behind the leasing arrangement was very much part of the 1980s pursuit of assets which were out-stripping high interest rates. According to MacPherson, the problem with the BFC arrangement with McGregor was that he did not have the assets to cover the loans should the market for race-horses fall.[85] That is, as the Auditor-General noted, McGregor had nowhere near the assets to cover BFC's exposure of $111 million.[86] He added that what BFC was doing was bankrolling 'a small entrepreneur operating in a niche financial market that Beneficial Finance perceived could, with financial support, build a profitable and successful business. It would bear most of the financial cost of failure'.[87]

In August 1989 Baker had become concerned at the size of BFC's exposure to Pegasus Leasing and sought to take it off-balance sheet and transfer a portion of it to the SBSA. Pegasus Leasing was in debt to Beneficial to the amount of $62 million and to an off-balance sheet company, Kabani, for another $20 million.[88] It was then decided to divide up this loan even further by shifting another $20 million off-balance by transferring it through a Reverse Principal and Agency Agreement to the SBSA. But, in what Auditor-General MacPherson calls [Monty] 'Pythonesque' meetings, no one could identify which bit of the $62 million pie was to be the $20 million portion to be held by the SBSA, nor what a Reverse Principal Agency Agreement might mean in regard to the loans.[89]

By 30 June 1990 Pegasus Leasing had total assets of over $100 million but it was deeply in debt. This state of affairs, according to the Auditor-General, had been caused, on the one hand, by Pegasus Leasing's poor administration which had not kept pace with the diversity of its assets growth. On the other hand, the debt crisis could be said to be caused by the ready supply of capital from BFC without adequate supervision. Rather, in MacPherson's opinion, BFC 'relied on Pegasus Securities staff, and particularly Mr McGregor, to conduct the business'.[90] During 1990 the management of the State Bank was so worried about Beneficial Finance that it directed one of the senior executives, Michael Hamilton, to carry out an investigation into the subsidiary.

The outcome of this inquiry was that in August 1990 pressure was placed on Baker to resign and he was soon followed by his deputy Reichart. With Baker and Reichart's departure the BFC Board in October 1999 sought to exercise more control over Pegasus Leasing and a review of Pegasus' 1,200 clients was made and pressure was placed on McGregor for BFC to take full control of the venture. McGregor resisted this move, and according to the record of the meeting he claimed he had only given 'his personal and corporate guarantees in August 1990 only because he was assured that the wind down of the operations would not be so precipitous as to adversely affect his interests'.[91] McGregor added that legally the joint venture required a three months' notification of intention before the venture could be terminated.

The tactic bought McGregor time but luck was against him. With the onset of the recession the thoroughbred race horse market declined dramatically, due in part to a lack of capital and in part to the response of breeders to the boom which had flooded the market with horses, many poorly bred. In addition, one of McGregor's major competitors had failed, which only added to the surplus of horses on the market. As a consequence, in 1990 the value of horses at yearling sales fell by rates of 30 to 40 per cent and brood mares by 90 per cent.[92] The fall in prices left the bloodstock syndicates without working capital and horses that had devalued in price. As Colin Hayes who had trained horses for McGregor noted, 'people were buying yearlings for half a million dollars two years ago which are worth nothing now. But they are still paying interest on their borrowings'.[93]

In November 1990 BFC devised an action plan by which it sought to engage McGregor in running down the joint venture. According to the Auditor-General McGregor was, however, reluctant to go down this path. He had built up the syndicates and realised that if the companies were placed in receivership the horses would not cover the debts owed by him and the syndicate members and therefore he would have to meet the debts from his and his associates' assets. Given the circles McGregor had moved in this meant material losses by many prominent people, notably from his family and his friends. As Mr McEwin, one of his staff at Pegasus Leasing commented, 'anyone seeing the register [of Pegasus Leasing] would have recognised at least 70 per cent of the names, a number of them had been knighted'.[94]

At a meeting held on 7 December 1990 between BFC and McGregor to review the financial position of Pegasus Leasing and Pegasus Securities, Mr McGregor advised the BFC officials that he required finance of about $1 million or he would be obliged to place Pegasus Securities in receivership. He left the meeting without his request being granted. On 10 December BFC transferred the files of Pegasus Leasing to Beneficial's premises and a number of Pegasus staff were retrenched. On 11 December 1990 Mr McGregor took his own life.[95]

On 24 December Pegasus Security was placed into receivership and by then Pegasus Leasing was fully absorbed into the SBSA. The bank began to run down the company by selling off assets, principally the horses. As the SBSA's director of banking at that time, Stephen Paddison, bluntly expressed it, 'the money to Pegasus Leasing is out there sitting on the backs of some horses'.[96] The bank then pursued McGregor's estate and his clients' assets. This understandably raised criticisms from his widow, particularly when she discovered that 'the State Bank were let into the house while I was out and did an inventory of the contents'.[97]

In 1992, the SBSA was still pursuing its losses and was accused in State Parliament by opposition leader, Dean Brown, of 'threatening to bankrupt each of the partners'.[98] The then Treasurer, Frank Blevins, defended the bank, commenting that the SBSA was 'acting in a top commercial way and was doing nothing that Westpac, ANZ or any other banks that are having difficulties are not doing'.[99]

Nevertheless, there was a sense of injustice felt by many pursued for their debts, since BFC had provided what they saw as an openline of credit.

The Auditor-General considered that the whole joint venture process in BFC was fundamentally flawed. He wrote that:

> In my opinion, the fundamental failing of Management of Beneficial Finance was to fail to recognise the deficiencies in the joint venture strategy. Reliance upon the experience and expertise of a joint venture partner within that partner's business experience is one thing. To provide that partner with almost unlimited finance, enabling it to expand and grow the business beyond the limits imposed by normal commercial constraints, is an invitation to disaster. For this failing, the managing director of Beneficial Finance, Mr Baker must accept the heaviest blame.[100]

Similarly, MacPherson was highly critical of Baker's role in the Pegasus arrangements. He claimed that Baker displayed 'a dangerous disdain for the professional judgement of others'.[101] The Auditor-General added that Baker's attitude to formal procedures was 'unsatisfactory' for a Senior Manager.[102] The Auditor-General added that the inadequate monitoring of Pegasus by BFC might have been caused by a conflict of interest, saying that:

> In my opinion, finance transactions between a company and its directors and senior employees involve issues of propriety and sensitivity. It is important that prudent policies governing such transactions are established and strictly enforced. I am of the opinion in relation to Pegasus Leasing joint venture, such policies were not established and, as a result, that the directors of Beneficial Finance did not monitor and control financial transactions between Mr Baker and officers of Beneficial Finance who entered into financial dealings with the joint venture had potential conflict of interest. Given that ordinary formalities which should have been observed with all transaction were not always carried out in transactions between Pegasus Leasing and the related parties, ... I consider that in relation to financial dealings with related parties, directors of Beneficial Finance and officers of both Beneficial Finance and Pegasus Leasing who were responsible for the administration of the affairs of the joint venture failed adequately or properly to supervise, direct, and control, the operations, affairs and transactions of respectively Beneficial Finance and of Pegasus Leasing.[103]

In sum, the Pegasus Securities began as a risk venture in a climate of high inflation where profits were to be made on the prediction that inflated prices would continue. From the outset the enterprise was high risk in a competitive niche market of thoroughbred race-horses. By the end of 1987 it was clear that Pegasus Leasing was not performing well, yet a new joint venture agreement with Pegasus Leasing was signed. It was this agreement which saw BFC and then the SBSA's exposure rising to $97.7 million with an estimated loss of around $50 million.[104] The venture was typical of the decade of the 1980s, where high levels of both interest rates and inflation increased the risk in corporate endeavours.

To reiterate, it is not the object of this book to criticise individuals for making decisions which were typical of that period. While the Auditor-General is forthright in his disapproval of the methods used by Baker and Reichart, it needs to be remembered that they were following the market trends of the 1980s. With the benefit of hindsight we can now see that many bankers in this period took too higher risks without due care to the interests of their shareholders.

In a final chapter to this sorry episode, Baker was pursued by the government and an out of court settlement was made in February 1999 with Mr Baker paying $25,000 as settlement of the damages case against him.[105] In defending the out of court settlement, Attorney-General Trevor Griffin said the case against John Baker, in regard to a conflict of interest over the 1989 Lameroo Lake venture in which BFC made losses of over $4.3 million, had 'significant evidentiary problems'.[106] Griffin noted that Baker had 'cooperated with the South Australian Asset Management Corporation, that is the remnants of the State Bank, in its efforts to make other recoveries as a result of the collapse of the State Bank.'[107] He added that the costs incurred in pursuing Baker over the Lameroo Lake matter 'is something like $136,000' and 'if we had gone to trial, the estimated cost was a further $70,000.'[108] In explaining the $25,000 settlement the Attorney-General said that 'before the media becomes too rampant about that figure when compared with the amount that was originally claimed, that on all the advice that I received that was a fair figure.'[109] The implicit point in the Attorney-General's statement is that the media was reflecting the public mood to blame somebody but that every individual has the right to be treated fairly before the law.

The examples in this chapter show how the culture which permeated society in the 1980s became imbedded into the bank, where the driving force within the bank was to make loans. The desire to lend was made possible by the government guarantee which allowed the bank to borrow money to fund the loans in the cases discussed in this chapter, the State Bank Centre, the REMM–Myer Complex, Adsteam and Pegasus. In all four cases the decisions to go ahead were driven by the culture of the period. The debts left by these deals then had to be picked up by the taxpayers. It was this culture – a far cry from the thrift morality upon which the Savings Bank was founded, and the over-arching board control of the old State Bank – which destroyed the bank.

9

Welcome to the circus

When Premier Bannon announced on 10 February 1991 that the taxpayers were bailing out the State Bank of South Australia (SBSA) to the amount of $970 million (rising to $3.1 billion) he also reported that, in accordance with the State Bank Act, the Auditor-General was to investigate the reasons for the bank's losses. Such an inquiry was to be conducted in private, although its findings would be made public. The media, the opposition and the Australian Democrats became restless and began to beat their respective drums for a public inquiry into the SBSA's debacle, threatening to put up their own tent obliging the government to participate or be ridiculed in their absence.[1] When the parliament met on Tuesday 12 February, Bannon was 'trapped' into calling a Royal Commission which he announced at a press conference called by the media.[2]

The government appointed flamboyant, recently retired judge Sam Jacobs as ring master and he, appropriately, had his tent erected outside the stock exchange building, in the heart of town. The season of performances was set to last just 12 months, but the deadline was repeatedly extended and lasted for 31. The critical phase of the Commission was its second year, when it turned more blatantly from inquisitorial to accusatorial, and moved towards its star act, Premier John Bannon. The media began to build up the expectation that Bannon would, and in fact had to, prove his innocence or be condemned. Bannon, weighed down by the bank's losses and by the discipline of the Commission, went through his routine without convincing either the Commission or the media that his act was one of high innocence. When the Royal Commissioner dismantled his tent, representation and reality had become one, the accused found guilty as charged by the media, and politically paraded as some sort of freak that was best removed from the public eye.[3]

After the shock of such a show, the rest of the performances seemed an anticlimax, yet there were even greater horrors to be had for those few, those hardy few, who were prepared to stay around for the main event. The Auditor-General revealed a grotesque inner world, where bankers believed the market was truth and played a game of dare to win, with public money, and lost.[4] The rules of the game were set by the host, Tim Marcus Clark, and the idea was to beat your opponent to the client and, at any price, make a deal. The game was licensed by the Federal and State Labor governments, who fully supported this deregulated financial circus, and shared with the bankers the belief that the market contained an inner essence that was of benefit not just to the players but to the paying public and the nation. Even spectacular spills and self destruction by the fire-eating bankers did not deter the backers of this greatest show on earth. Rather, we now find it showing in all parts of the globe, where agents think there is a public prepared to pay the price of entry.

Having assisted Bannon into the vanishing box the media was not prepared to have him magically reappear at the end of the show. Instead they took the Auditor-General's findings as a sideshow, reminded the audience not to forget what they had seen under the big top, in particular, that it was the Labor government which was 'milking the bank for political advantage and profit and ignoring mounting, incontrovertible, evidence of impeding disaster that should have been obvious'.[5] When the Auditor-General presented his second set of reports on BFC and the external auditors, showing that the fire-eaters were not just living dangerously but that they were endangering the public, the media took up the call for a refund and for the spectacle of these performers going to prison.

With Bannon banished and the Auditor-General's tent taking over the limelight, Commissioner Jacobs stepped down and was replaced by the counsel assisting the Commission, John Mansfield. Mansfield's task was to bring the curtain down on the dual shows by incorporating the findings of the Auditor-General's inquiry into the Royal Commission. In his report, made public on 7 September 1993, Commissioner Mansfield drew a careful distinction between performances which were, in legal terms, showing 'conflict of interest' and those acts which revealed 'gross negligence' that it would be legally feasible to seek a refund.[6] Mansfield found that while Bannon had made mistakes in his actions there was no 'wilful neglect' on his part, and therefore he was not liable for the loss. However, he proposed that most of the directors and some of the managers should be investigated further, by two legal task forces, so that criminal or civil court prosecutions might be mounted in regard to 'negligence' and/or a 'conflict of interest' with the aim of getting a modicum of the money back for the owners of the bank.

The media, having joined in the clamour for the circus, then turned on it, saying it was an inappropriate conveyance for (political) justice. The media's concern, as articulated by the daily paper, was that the Arnold government might just dodge the electoral car careering towards it, and therefore the Commission would have been a waste of money. The total cost of the Royal Commission and the Auditor-General's inquiry was $34.81 million of which $19.43 million was legal costs. The *Advertiser* editorialised that:

> A phalanx of lawyers has been enriched, not much light has been shed, what remains is the prospect of a series of civil actions and the general caveat that there should be a lot more prudence. There were monumental blunders. There were extraordinary events and attitudes within the publicly accountable bank, exacerbated by gross political incompetence. It did not stop with the sacrificial lamb Mr Bannon has become. The Royal Commission ends with a whimper. In a sense that is appropriate as it was the wrong vehicle for the inquiry.[7]

The *Advertiser* need not have feared that the desire for political justice would not be fulfilled. The Royal Commission gave the Leader of the Opposition, Dean Brown, a passport to an electoral landslide.

A grim sideshow

The State Bank Royal Commission was regarded as the big top where the players in the SBSA saga could strut their stuff inside the discipline of a judicial discourse. The Auditor-General's inquiry was, however, a grimmer affair, held behind closed doors, where the bankers and directors were challenged by administrative and financial discourses and were shown up for a series of alleged failings. The reportage on the Royal Commission was constructed along court room lines but underpinned by a media conviction that Bannon had to prove why he was not guilty as charged. The State Bank debacle itself, let alone the Commission, had ended Bannon's career on the political stage. Nothing was going to save him from slipping from prominence to obscurity (in reality, to the obscurity of a postgraduate student, sweeping the historical records on federation). Nevertheless, the fall of Bannon was vigorously sought by the media and he became the symbol for the bank's debt crisis. By usurping the Auditor-General's report, the Royal Commissioner had reduced the lessons of the bank's fall to the personality of the Premier and not to the globalisation of the bank and the cultural transformation that had occurred within the bank to make it a global market player.

The displacement of the Auditor-General's report was achieved both by the Commissioner producing a stand-alone, first report, six months ahead of the Auditor-General's report, and by the representation of the Commission's first report as the dominant truth on the bank's fall. Equally, this displacement was facilitated by the legal delays to the Auditor-General's inquiry, caused by MacPherson being led by the directors and managers into a hall of mirrors, known as 'natural justice', from which he had to be rescued by the parliament.[8] There were six legal challenges to the Auditor-General's inquiry on the grounds of 'natural justice' and 'procedural fairness', which so delayed MacPherson's inquiry as to dislocate it from the Royal Commission, a dislocation which was to the legal advantage of the managers and directors of the bank. The Commissioner's guilty verdict relegated the Auditor-General's findings to the dustbin of history and turned the dual investigation into one of entertainment, devoid of the class denouement so evident in the Auditor-General's findings. So let the circus begin.

Under the big top

While the Auditor-General's investigation became caught up in the hurdy-gurdy of the courts, the Royal Commission became the biggest show in town. The Commission's daily schedule slotted into the evening news bulletins and current affairs shows and gave the journalists ample time to construct a story for the *Advertiser* the next morning. The Commission had all the trappings of a court room carnival with only the one mask, that of the personification of innocence, being worn.[9] Given how prominent a part the SBSA had played in Adelaide's business and legal life it was hard for the players not to be both actors in, and interested spectators of, the proceedings. The confusede relationship between spectacle and reality was reinforced by the local ABC '7.30 Report', who hired look-a-like actors to re-stage the Royal Commission hearing in court-room mode.[10]

From its outset, however, this circus struggled for a purpose, principally because the Commission was playing a joint role to that of the Auditor-General's investigation. The Auditor-General was investigating what went wrong and why, while the Commission examined the public relationship between the bank and the government. The mutually compatible reports were to be interdependent and this can explain, in part, why the Commissioner decided to start his investigation from the bottom and move in a coronial fashion from the SBSA's birth, in 1984 to its terminal illness in 1991. When the Commission began with the 'tent peggers', who put the merger together, and then moved to the backstage managers, the Commission could be seen as operating in a linear and logical manner. It could also be seen as merely meandering along, waiting for the Auditor-General to give it a light to shine on the star performers. The assembled QCs, nevertheless, did not take the proceedings as a warm-up for the main acts. Instead they juggled points of law, tossing loaded barbs at one another and the witnesses and displayed the cross examinational dexterity that had given them their silken reputations.

Eventually, Commissioner Jacobs, as ring master, became tired of all this over-acting and set rules for the legal players. When the witnesses did appear, senior counsel assisting the Commission took them painstakingly through their prepared statements, seeking to conjure from the witnesses a legal refutation. He was then followed by the QCs representing the interested parties, whose cross examinations were notable for their one dimensional performances. Under this adversarial discourse no one was going to make a confession, or rescue another who had fallen by the financial wayside, as such actions would be like red meat to the waiting legal lions, hungry for a juicy cross-examination.[11] As such, the Commission's circus was spectacularly dull, unless you were paid to keep a score card on the deflection of blame or for those afflicted aficionados who desperately hung out for the occasional witticisms from the bench. Not that the Commission was meant for public consumption. For a start there was limited room for the spectators of this show, and symbolically the seats for the public were placed behind those of the media. When the Commission wandered through the bit players, these seats remained practically empty. The public kept up with the Commission through the media, and for the public the media's dramatisation of this circus replaced the real thing and became the entertainment itself.

By the time the Auditor-General's findings were due to be delivered to the Commission, the hearing had only heard from 11 witnesses, only one of whom, Stephen Paddison, could be said to be a major player. The witnesses gave the appearance of being burdened by the discipline of the Commission. The proceedings appeared to have much motion but no momentum. How much the Commission had struggled for a sense of direction can be seen by the fact that a middle manager, Chris Guille, spent 31 hours in the witness box trying to explain the intricacies of international exchange to an incredulous Commissioner and an ever dwindling public.[12] Then the unexpected happened, the Auditor-General reported to the Attorney-General that given the practical and legal difficulties he was facing he would not be able to report by September and needed an extension of time,[13] an exercise he repeated in March the following year. The Commissioner then successfully applied to the Attorney-General to have his terms of reference altered so that he could report separately from the Auditor-General.

When the Commission recommenced in April 1992, following Commissioner Jacobs' coronary operation, it had a new and dangerous life. The safety net of the Auditor-General's inquiry had been removed and any slip on the high wire of cross examination could now be fatal. Those appearing before the Commission knew the enhanced danger, as did the media – which also saw it as an opportunity to pour kerosene onto the fire burning under Premier Bannon. In other words, a cursory glance at the media would see that the focus of guilt had narrowed from that of blaming all the players to allowing Bannon to take the rap for the whole show. The reversal of proof so characteristic of royal commissions was now sutured into the media's reading of each piece of evidence in terms of whether it proved Bannon's guilt.[14]

The pressure on Bannon to prove his innocence intensified as the hearing moved towards the appearance of its star act. Bannon was preceded by Tim Marcus Clark and then the last Chair of the board, David Simmons. Clark's plea was that, as a contracted employee, he relied on others and that, in any case, he operated democratically and not as others claimed as an 'autocrat'.[15] His defence was that he delegated lending responsibility downward to the managers, supervisory power sideways to his deputy, Matthews, strategic direction upward to the board, and accountability outward to the Premier. He pointed out the instances where Bannon had approached the bank over interest rates prior to three elections, implying that this was the rule rather than the exception. Like witnesses before him, Clark retreated to the mantra of 'I can't recall' (made notorious by United States President Ronald Reagan before the Iran–Contragate hearings) when confronted by inquisitive or even innocuous cross-examination.

At the end of Clark's appearance before the Commission, even the media was surprised at how tame was the cross-examination of this witness by the legal lions.[16] The restraint of the QCs is understandable in terms of their realisation that if the star act was to take the blame for the failure of the whole show, their clients would be better off. The Chair of the board followed this logic to its extreme. David Simmons argued that the bank was driven from outside by the government. He claimed the capital funding of the bank was at a rate disadvantageous to the bank and to the benefit of the South Australian Financial Authority (SAFA). Consequently, as the bank had to obtain expensive capital it had to take high risks so as to pay the interest on this capital and to meet the demands for profit from the Treasury. Needless to say, Simmons was herein offering the Commissioner a motive to attribute fault to the government in order to deflect it from himself and the board.

Simmons' appearance under the spotlight was accompanied by the revelation that he kept extensive diary accounts of his meetings, which were then requested and sanitised by the Commission.[17] They were read by the media as incontestably truthful accounts of his meetings with Clark and Bannon. The diaries were accompanied by shock horror revelations in the media. More pointedly expressed, the diaries were selectively used to show how Bannon was the voice of authority in the interchanges between Simmons, Clark and Bannon. They were also used to personalise the power brokers and to stress the point that Bannon had used his position of power to pressure the bank to hold down interests rates and how Clark went 'berserk' over such a request, implying to the reader that the Managing Director was a volatile individual.[18] When the media began to use the diaries as a factual basis for making accusations against the bank, the media's lawyers were kept very busy. The media then saw the diaries as perhaps only a certain construction of the truth, the truth as perceived from the point of view of the author.

The stage was now set for Bannon's star performance before the Commission. When Bannon took the stand for a marathon stint, the back stalls were full and there was even a queue to see him perform his escapology. The media coverage made it clear that it was Bannon who was on trial and it was up to him to prove his innocence.[19] Bannon saw it differently, and performed as if the Commission was roped off from its representation. He reiterated his position that the bank was 'at arm's length' from the government, that he had 'confidence' in the board which he 'felt had a degree of skill' and 'business acumen' and that Clark 'always had an answer to any doubts.[20] In practice, he said, 'I saw the bank running itself'.[21] Bannon's nine day performance was restrained yet forthright in the defence of his position. That was the rub. The performance was not being judged as mere evidence but as the accused failing to blow away the cloud of guilt that hung over the stage. His act was covered in accusatorial smoke and weighed down by the discipline of the hearing and by his belief that the Commission was going to live up to a legal ideal of impartially evaluating the evidence and presented in a measured tone.[22]

The final act of the Royal Commission was the submissions from the counsels representing the interested parties. Cathy Branson for the bank blamed the board. Michael Abbott for the board, called her 'sanctimonious' and in the next breath said the directors 'did all that could be expected of them'. He said the board, however, was too reliant on the 'charismatic' but enigmatic Clark and blamed Bannon for not strengthening the board and monitoring the bank. Tim Anderson, for the Managing Director, said his client worked 'diligently and tirelessly' for the bank but in hindsight his judgement was 'flawed'. Robert Lawson, for the leader of the opposition, focused on Bannon, saying that either his claim of 'hands off' the bank was refuted by the evidence on his approaches to the bank over interest rates, or that 'he was so hands off' in general that this 'was beyond the spectrum of legitimate policy' as set out in the Act.[23] John Doyle QC, for the government, said the bank was a commercial entity, 'autonomous' from the government, and that, in contrast to what the directors claimed, the bank was not milked by the government, instead, it received favourable treatment in terms of its capital and did not meet the accepted industry standard of a 15 per cent return on capital to the owners.[24]

While they were pulling down the scaffolding from the Commission and selling off the seats, the Auditor-General's inquiry was still entrapped in a Supreme Court maze of mirrors, where lawyers, acting for a number of the directors and senior bankers, continually challenged the procedures adopted by MacPherson. When he changed his procedures to meet their demands, they changed their demands for new procedures and demanded all the material he had used in reaching his interim findings. It seemed as if MacPherson would never escape from this reflection of natural justice and in despair he cried out to the Attorney-General for help.

In the meantime, Jacobs decided to publish his interim findings, accompanied by all the fanfare of a media lock up, live crosses to the 'jury room', where the journalists gave their verdict on the report, then to the parliament, for door-stop interviews, and finally, the obligatory photograph of the Commissioner in front of transcripts of the hearings. The media heralded the Commissioner's verdict in a triumphant tone: guilty as charged, they cried. The *Advertiser* led its front page with the dramatic banner heading 'Judgement Day', followed by the sub-headline, 'Labor in crisis'. Just in case the reader might miss the point, there was a front page editorial in black border, editorialising that: 'The Arnold government is morally obliged to resign on the strength of the alarming findings. Labor deserves, and can expect a savage repudiation at the next election'.[25] Articles in the paper then listed Jacobs' damning criticisms of Bannon as the 'facts' supporting its opinion. Bannon, the journalists reported, was 'dazzled by Clark', had a 'myopic' vision of the bank, failed to react to the 'plethora of signs of impending doom', had a 'complacent acceptance of the bank's optimistic but rather glib assurances', and failed to change his hands off policy 'almost to the bitter end'.[26]

Commissioner Jacobs' first report was written in the form of an authoritative author leading the reader to an incontrovertible conclusion. Jacobs begins his report by addressing the reader saying his tome is like a 'whodunit' where the prologue gives it all away.[27] In the prologue Jacobs constructs his judgement around a legal proof based on sound commercial law that the Act gave the Premier the power and the responsibility to control the bank. Bannon did not protect the taxpayers as was, in Jacobs's reasoning, his responsibility. Instead, Bannon was prepared to try and influence the bank, while proclaiming in public that he was adhering to an 'arm's length' approach. Jacobs says that 'from the very beginning there was from time to time Government involvement and influence in the policy and decisions of the bank'.[28] He added that the government 'on some occasions sought to derive political advantage from such involvement'.[29] Equally, while Bannon had power to intervene he did not 'exercise' this power 'effectively', rather he failed to strengthen the board or to listen to the warning signs over the Managing Director.[30]

Moreover, Bannon acquiesced in the bank's growth for the 'parochial' reason of promoting the bank as the 'flagship' for the State.[31] Further, according to Jacobs, the bank was driven to grow from outside by its capital needs being met by SAFA on terms 'more advantageous to SAFA than the bank', and the interest paid on the capital 'was instrumental in the development by the bank of a profit enhancement culture without sufficient regard to, or compliance with, accepted criteria of performance, ie. profitability'.[32] Additionally, the Treasurer always granted approval to any of the bank's acquisitions that were sought from him. From 1987 onward, Jacobs noted, it should have been 'apparent to the board that the bank might be facing serious financial difficulties in the immediate and foreseeable future' but neither the 'board of the bank nor Treasury took any effective steps to monitor or control the growth of the bank'; instead the Treasurer negligently did not control the bank's growth or address the mismatch between its growth and profitability or even act on the advice of his Economic Adviser that the bank needed to be investigated'.[33]

Jacobs applies a legal analysis based on commercial law to argue that Bannon had the responsibility to act as guarantee of the bank. In this Jacobs perceptively applied his legal mind to the judicial logic of the SBSA Act. However, Jacobs, perhaps due to his ill-health or to the disjunction between his first report and that of the Auditor-General's report tends to embellish his findings in such a manner that it only fueled the media's narrative of Bannon's guilt.

Jacobs's 'whodunit' is constructed on the pillars of empiricism and legal positivism. Empiricism is embedded in the construction of the report, in the form of chapters based on financial years, that lead the reader to the conclusion that the SBSA's irresponsible growth was tied incontrovertibly with Bannon's failure to monitor or stop the SBSA's dangerous lending. Positivism as expressed in the form of setting up the narrative around legal truths, principally, in the construction of a series of refutations of Bannon's claim of a 'hands off' approach to the bank and a formalistic reading of the Act, regarding its powers as implied duties on Bannon to monitor and control directly the bank. He wrote that Bannon was so 'dazzled' by Clark and the bank's apparent success that he could not see the danger signs.[34] By 1988, Jacobs commented, 'the evolving drama of the bank's affairs was approaching its climax. The scene had been set. The denouement would come later. In the meantime the Treasurer maintained the same dramatic persona, and adhered to the script which he had set, so that the 'march of folly continued inexorably'.[35] Bannon meets Macbeth, the Renaissance popes, George III and Richard Nixon.

Just in case the reader missed the march of guilt, Jacobs reiterated his verdict in the conclusion. He wrote that, 'it is impossible to ignore the criticism in the report of the role played by the then Treasurer, Mr Bannon, but it would be a fundamental error to assess that role without also examining the role of Under Treasurer and his officers, of SAFA, of the board and Mr Clark, and of the Reserve Bank. None of these escape criticism, and sometimes severe criticism'.[36] Then Jacobs put in the legal rub, saying that Bannon claimed that he was 'let down' by those he placed trust in. However, the 'compelling evidence' is that 'they were no longer deserving of such confidence'.[37] Jacobs then dismissed the claims that the financial events of the 1980s or financial deregulation could be regarded as causes of the bank's fall. Using the evidence of the 'independent', 'expert witness', Professor Tom Valentine, to bolster his argument, he argued that the economic events of the 1980s and financial deregulation was known to those in the industry and that it was not market failure but the fault of the directors, the board, the Treasury and especially the Treasurer for not heeding the market's warning signs.[38]

To find Bannon guilty, however, Jacobs had to deal with the public's perception that Tim Marcus Clark, as Managing Director, might have something to do with the bank's collapse. Here Jacobs' legal reasoning was ingenious for he suspended judgement on Clark and the board to his second report which appeared at a critical distance from the interim report, and, then he attributed to Clark an implied diminished responsibility. Following Clark's counsel Tim Anderson QC, the Commissioner depicted Clark as having a flawed personality, being someone who was overly committed to the bank, 'his bank', a man with 'enormous drive and entrepreneurial flair who, although personally ambitious was more ambitious for the bank'.[39] His commitment to the bank and his aggressive drive and his 'blind optimism' was however, 'unrealistic', so unreal that it indicated that Clark was impetuous and that he had to be controlled. That is, here was a person clearly in need of (parental) guidance which was not given by Bannon. Rather, Bannon was 'dazzled' by this (child-like) banker.

The second report
In the five months between the first report and the second Bannon resigned from the political stage. Jacobs then published his second report on the board and the management of the bank. The report came out three weeks before that of the Auditor-General's, stealing its limelight. In his second report, Jacobs lambasted the board members for their lack of prudence saying that collectively the board seldom seemed able or willing to 'grasp the nettle or crack the whip'.[40] Jacobs then

reminded the readers of his previous guilty verdict, saying, in effect, that it was the government that appointed the board, and that it was the government which refused to strengthen it, and that the board's reluctance to stand up to management or to the Managing Director was explicable in terms of Bannon's supposed 'enthusiastic public support' for Clark. He said that it was an 'inescapable inference that the very close rapport and confidence that was known to exist between Mr Clark and Mr Bannon, and which Mr Bannon had publicly proclaimed, was a very strong influence on the board in its conduct of the bank's affairs'.[41] Similarly, the Commissioner castigated Clark for failing to discharge his duties and control management and the bank's growth and then adds the mitigating factor that 'the bank's expansion was uncritically approved by the Treasurer'.[42]

The media did not miss the double-edged nature of Jacobs' second report. In particular, the *Advertiser* headed its front page with the bold claim, 'Criminal charges vow' and highlighted how the board 'capitulated' to Clark, how Clark in turn was 'contemptuous of the board' and how the management was 'gung ho' and 'reckless'.[43] Then in a front page article its political editor, Nick Cater, stressed that if the board was 'meekly compliant' it was 'the Government's responsibility to change it'. Again taking his lead from the tenor of the report, Cater drew the fishy analogy: 'Leaving the goldfish to baby sit the children does not remove the duty of parental responsibility'.[44] The editorial takes up this theme with vigour, if for no other reason than it was the week of the 1993 Federal election, saying that, 'Although Mr Jacobs identifies complacency and lack of professionalism by the board, and a deliberate inclination by bank management to mislead the government and Parliament, he makes it clear that Bannon and his government were the direct beneficiaries of a mistaken and self interested reading of the State Bank Act which led to a hands off policy but a hands-out-for-the-profits mentality'.[45] The paper's attention then began to shift to the question of whether criminal charges would be laid against those in the bank who so 'recklessly' lent public money. This question had to wait, however, for the Auditor-General's Report which was made public on 31 March 1993.

In search of cause and effect
The Auditor-General's first report, of twelve volumes, was based on two forms of causation. The first MacPherson called 'scientific', the second he termed legal, in the sense of 'the real and effective cause of the losses', that is, 'who or what was really to blame for the losses?'[46] He then concluded that in purely scientific terms financial deregulation and the economic events of the 1980s were contributory causes for the financial position of the SBSA as at 10 February 1991. Nevertheless, for him, the real and effective causes of the SBSA's losses were to be found in the failure of the bank and the bank group (including BFC), in the face of changing economic times and deregulation, to adopt 'sound policies and practices which were calculated to protect it from any reasonably foreseeable economic downturn'.[47] MacPherson then set out to show how the SBSA grew so fast that it never put in place systems to protect itself, rather its growth was of a high-risk kind – driven by its 'entrepreneurial', 'aggressive' and 'autocratic' Chief Executive Officer.[48] He argued that Clark was able to globalise and expand the bank's assets because 'there was nothing to stand in his way' – 'deregulation opened up new

markets', there was no 'formal supervision by the Reserve Bank', even what there was Clark 'chafed' at. Moreover, Clark dominated the board which too often acquiesced in the demands of the managers to lend, so as to grow, and, finally, 'there was no share price to worry about'.[49]

According to MacPherson, Clark introduced a market culture where the bank was inspired to beat the opposition to a client and 'doing the deal and doing it quickly',[50] then, in turn, inflating the profit margin on the deal, by up-front fees, so that each year the imperative was to do more deals, just to stand still. It was the excesses of the 1980s at its worst, conducted by a State Bank guaranteed by the people of South Australia'.[51] In this process not just the culture of the bank was transformed but also the direction of lending, which shifted from a bank serving the South Australian housing market and local producers, to one that was predominantly a corporate bank, where two-thirds of its assets were outside the State.[52]

In other words, when the local parochial SBSA was pushed into the global financial market by its management and board it was sucked into the vortex of global corporate banking and disappeared under its depths. It was also able to be devoured because Treasurer Keating had removed the regulations and because the Federal Labor government (uncritically) and the Bannon government (with criticisms) supported deregulation and the globalisation of the Australian economy. It was a globalisation that was instituted without the realisation that there was no effective means of controlling the excesses of the market players. It was only after the speculative disasters of the 1980s which affected both public and private banks that the Reserve Bank's powers to monitor banking were enhanced.

In this deregulatory vacuum, Clark wrought his cultural revolution onto a bank which found it so difficult to manage its growth, that it literally never knew what its liabilities were at any one time. MacPherson was most damning of Clark for his failure to take due care of the bank's assets and liability management or to convey accurately to the board the parlous condition of the bank's supervisory systems. He said of Clark that he 'failed to adequately or properly supervise, direct and control the operations, affairs and transactions of the bank, and that he failed to provide the board with information that was timely, reliable and adequate.'[53]

For MacPherson, the 'tragedy' was that the board 'did not call a halt to the growth that it did not understand'.[54] He added that a 'reasonably prudent board – whatever its skills – would have done much more than the board did'.[55] He commented that a little bit of 'commonsense' would not have gone astray on the board. 'To be blunt', MacPherson wrote, 'there is nothing esoteric about asking questions, seeking information, demanding explanations and extracting further details. There is nothing unduly burdensome in expecting each director, to the best of his or her ability, to insist on understanding what was laid before them, even at the risk of becoming unpopular. Both the law, and a basic sense of duty and responsibility, demand it'.[56]

It is clear from the above that MacPherson's list of causes for the bank's disastrous losses and his apportioning of the blame are in tension with Jacobs's legal reasoning. For the Commissioner, it was Bannon who was legally responsible for the losses; for MacPherson it was Clark and his team which caused the losses. In particular, for MacPherson, it was Clark and his management team and the board, in general, that were at fault.

The media not only did not point out the different forms of enquiry between the two reports but relegated MacPherson's report to secondary importance, as a sideshow to Jacobs's big top truth. When the Auditor-General's findings were released they were overshadowed by the (beat-up) coverage of a gun siege/terror at a local high school.[57] The *Advertiser* led its coverage with MacPherson's recommendations for further legal investigations into the possibility of prosecutions being launched against Clark and the directors. Political reporter Nick Cater again reiterated his position (and that of the paper) that the Royal Commission's First Report was the truth on what went wrong and that it was the tactic of the Arnold government to 'shift the blame' away from Bannon and the Labor government.[58] An editorial reaffirmed the political view, that the readers should remember 'what the Bannon government was doing' while all this mismanagement was going on 'Mr Jacobs tells us that it was milking the bank for political advantage and profit and ignoring mounting, incontrovertible evidence of impending disaster that should have been obvious'.[59]

The final act
The displacement of the Auditor-General's findings had one more act to be played out. The Auditor-General's second series of reports (one confidential and six public volumes) targeted BFC and the external auditors for criticisms. He pointed out that BFC represented only 13 per cent of the SBSA Group's assets but represented around 43 per cent of the Group's total loan losses.[60] As for the external auditors, MacPherson found that there were instances where the respective auditing of the bank, in terms of industry standards, both 'inappropriate and inadequate'.[61] He recommended that further legal investigations be carried out to ascertain whether the auditors were financially liable for their mistakes.[62] The *Advertiser* clung desperately to its political line that: 'The Auditor-General's condemnation of managers of millions of dollars who "speculated widely" is an appalling indictment of a government which should have acted. A government which did nothing until it was far too late. It's time for that government to go'.[63]

It was left to John Mansfield to bring the two inquiries together in the final Royal Commission report. In doing so, Mansfield focused on the legal basis for mounting prosecutions against members of the board and some of the managers, whose decisions could provide the basis for either civil or criminal prosecutions so as to get some of the money back. The *Advertiser* headed its coverage of the report with the front page editorial saying: 'Bannon cleared of wilful neglect: Clark should be prosecuted' and went on to say 'at the end of the huge expense and distraction of the Royal Commission and parallel Auditor-General's inquiry, South Australia has not been provided with an anatomy of what went wrong, who did it, why, when, where and for how much. It has been on the receiving end of millions of words of legalistic argument leading inevitably to legalistic conclusions'.[64]

It was only when the Arnold government fell through the electoral safety net at the 1993 election that the *Advertiser* could turn its attention to the pursuit of Tim Marcus Clark and the litigation against the other directors. At the same time, the paper gave its full support to the Brown government's drive to globalise the state's economy, through the sale of its public assets to overseas interests. The lessons of the cultural transformation and globalisation of a public institution, the SBSA, as outlined in the Auditor-General's inquiry, were conjured away, to reappear in the form of lessons about political mismanagement and the need to sell off public assets. In this feat of illusion, the extensive literature on the dangers of financial deregulation take flight like pigeons, escaping from under a magician's cape.[65] The judicial reduction of the bank's demise to personal mistakes legitimises the sale of the bank and other public assets at an intensified rate, while simultaneously conjuring away criticism of the globalisation of the local economy.[66]

The two reports, to a greater and a lesser extent, discuss the bank's debt crisis in legal and personal/political terms, thereby allowing the economy and the market to remain as implied truths and leaving the present to be lived as if the past has no lessons to tell about the instability of global capitalism. The structural logic of the financial market, to conquer and destroy, is matched by the cultural logic of representing this as progress, and the problems of the 1980s in South Australia as but a personal fall from the highwire of political life. The narratives of the past, that can reflect on the future, become unfashionable to contemplate and we are condemned to the market as an unquestioned truth.

A eulogy to public banking

On 11 March 1998 there was a celebration of the 150th year of operation of the Savings Bank of South Australia. The Advance Bank/St. George Group, through its subsidiary Bank SA, sponsored a lift out section of the *Advertiser* with the heading 'Thanks SA', which said that 'the bank [SBSA] did suffer at the beginning of this decade – as a result of a departure from normal core business. However, subsequently it has consolidated as the leading bank in SA, with around 600,000 customers, and is proudly part of the fifth largest banking group in Australia' (*Advertiser*, 11 March 1998). The advertising campaign copied that of the Savings Bank 125th anniversary in 1973, where babies born on 11 March were presented with cheques from the bank by prominent sportsmen.

There was a series of ironies here. The old State Bank had disappeared from the picture, even though it would have been 100 years old in 1996. The 'bad bank' was still in operation, chasing the lenders of the reckless loans to obtain money back for the taxpayers. The Savings Bank no longer can provide 50 per cent of its profits to the State in revenue to the Treasury. Rather the Savings Bank in its supposed new guise as Bank SA supplies a steady stream of dividends to its interstate parent from its business in South Australia. There is no money provided in concessional loans for public enterprises or for housing and rural producers, additionally, annual sponsorship of community groups, sporting and cultural events had remained but at a significantly lower proportion than in the past. In celebrating the proud history of public banking in South Australia, the Bank SA campaign had an echo of the campaigns of 1898, 1923, 1948 and 1973. Yet this effort at celebrating the history of the Savings Bank, no matter its noble intentions, seemed not to have captured the place of public banking in South Australia. Hopefully, this book fills in some of that absence by showing how the past does weigh heavily on the present.

One only needs to step back and think how banking has changed over the last ten years at the branch level to recognise what has been lost. At the start of the 1980s the branches were mini-banks in themselves and were able to handle nearly all the requests at the local level. The bank managers knew their customers and in turn the customers knew who to approach to ask for a loan. Additionally, the local branches were the basis for training the workforce, notably the men, from the teller to the loan manager to the branch manager. By the end of the 1980s all this had changed. The local branch had become a glorified cash shop devoid of the traditional banking meaning and it is the automatic teller to which we now turn to access our savings. Banks moreover, no longer uphold or instil the morality of thrift, rather it is credit to which banks extol as a philosophy for their customers. A philosophy which enhances their profits but one that disturbs many who can remember the virtues of saving.

The tale ends
Now we come to the end of the tale. In the telling, there have been many tales, some impressive in their moral tone of the dangers of lending in a pervasive culture of acquisition. Others show how the inward-looking modernism of the 1950s and 1960s set the conditions for the takeover of the new bank in the 1980s. Paternalism, patriarchy and authoritarianism were transformed into autocracy and the promotion of individual self-interest where women were still outsiders in a man's world of banking. It is also a tale of how women were held up as the model for thrift in the Savings Bank only to be disregarded when they sought to foster good house-keeping within the SBSA.

In telling this tale of the rise of two public banks and their fall when they merged there were many contesting interpretations seeking to find a receptive audience. This was never more obvious than in regard to what went wrong with the SBSA. Commissioner Jacobs depicted his tale in terms that were highly critical of Premier Bannon – a judgment which was echoed in the media. In contrast, Auditor-General MacPherson regarded Tim Marcus Clark as the 'growth hormone' within the SBSA that destroyed the plant that was the SBSA. This book borrows from both of these interpretations, without necessarily agreeing with either. It has concluded with an explanation of how the bank became dislocated from the past as it slipped into a global era. It is a tale which stands as a metaphor for the political economy of South Australia in particular: inward-looking capitalism became global overnight, and in doing so destroyed both the good and the bad of the past.

In the end, the State Bank of South Australia was privatised with the public paying for its losses and the private buyer gaining from its profits. This is as clear a case of the socialisation of debt and privatisation of profit as one is likely to see, a tale where the 1980s re-lives the history of the 1890s, but as a blank parody. From the 1890s financial crises public banking in South Australia was born and flourished, from the 1980s crises public banking disappeared.

Notes

Chapter 1

1. Bataille, G., *The Accursed Share: An Essay on General Economy*, New York, Zone Books, 1991, p. 124.
2. Savings Bank of South Australia, History and Progress, 1848–1985, published by authority of the Board of Trustees, 1982, p. 7.
3. Butlin, S.J., 'The Beginning of Savings Banks in Australia', *Royal Australian History Society Journal*, vol. xxxiv, 1982, pp. 1–46.
4. Savings Bank of South Australia, *History and Progress, 1848–1928*, p. 8.
5. Bataille, G., *The Accursed Share*, 1991, p. 136.
6. Savings Bank of South Australia, *History and Progress 1848–1928*, p.9.
7. Ewens, L.J., *The South Australian Savings Bank, The Story of the Pioneer Savings Bank 1841–1848*, (together with an Appreciation of its Secretary John Wotherspoon), Adelaide, Pioneers' Association of SA (ND).
8. Savings Bank of South Australia, *History and Progress, 1848–1928*, p.13.
9. ibid. p.13.
10. Savings Bank of South Australia, *A Short Review of Fifty Years, 1848 to 1898*, Report to the Board of Trustees, 1898, p. 1.
11. Savings Bank of South Australia, Mortgage Loans and Lending 1848–1956.
12. ibid.
13. ibid.
14. ibid.
15. Early Documents Relating to the Foundation of the Bank (Series 1A), *A Handbook for Bank Clerks*, Section edition, 1888.
16. Savings Bank of South Australia, Mortgage Loans and Lending 1848–1956.
17. ibid.
18. Savings Bank of South Australia *History and Progress, 1848–1928*, p. 41. Savings Bank of South Australia, Board of Trustees, 2 September 1852, 1 February 1853, January 1854. In a publication celebrating the Savings Bank of South Australia it was recorded in somewhat whimsical fashion that, 'in 1856 the era of railway development opened in South Australia when the first steam train ran from Adelaide to Port Adelaide. To mitigate the danger of railway travel, passengers were advised to journey by day rather than by night and to resist the impulse to leap from the train while it was going'. Savings Bank of South Australia, *Highlights from History 1848–1948*, issued by the bank on the occasion of its Centenary, 11 March 1947.
19. Gobbett, D., 'The Financial System', in K. Sheridan (ed.), *The State as Developer, Public Enterprise in South Australia*, Adelaide, Wakefield Press, 1986, p. 156.
20. Shann E., *An Economic History of Australia*, London, Methuen, 1930; J.B. Hirst, *Adelaide and the Country from first Settlement in 1788, to the Commonwealth in 1901*, Melbourne, Macmillan, 1965; T.A. Coghlan, *Labour and Industry in Australia*, Oxford University Press, 1918, Part V, Chapter ix, (reprint 1965); W.A. Sinclair, 'Urban boom in Nineteenth – Century Australia, Adelaide and Melbourne', in *Journal of the History Society of South Australia*, 10, 1982 and W.A. Sinclair, 'Gross Domestic Product in South Australia, 1861 – 1938', Flinders Working Papers in Economic History, Adelaide, Flinders University Press, 1982, E. Richards, 'South Australia and the Great Crash of 1893', in S. Brugger (ed.), *South Australia in the 1890s*, Adelaide, Constitutional Museum, 1983, E.A. Boehm, *Prosperity and Repression in Australia 1887–1897*, Oxford University Press, 1971, chapters 8 and 10.
21. Savings Bank of South Australia, 'A Short Review of Fifty Years 1848 to 1898', Memo to the Board of Trustees, 1898.
22. ibid.
23. Richards, E., 'South Australia and the Great Crash of 1893' in Brugger, 1983.
24. Boehm, *Property and Depression in Australia, 1887–1897*, Ch. 10.
25. R.M. Gibbs, *Bulls, Bears and Wildcats, A Centenary History of the Stock Exchange of Adelaide*, Adelaide, Peacock Publications, 1988, p. 31.
26. Hirst, *Adelaide and the Country 1870–1917*.

27. Whitelock, D., *Adelaide: A Sense of Difference, from Colony to Jubilee*, Adelaide, Savvos Publications, 1985, p. 114.
28. Lamshed, M. *The South Australian Story*, Adelaide, Advertiser Publishing, 1958.
29. Sykes, T., *Two Centuries of Panic: A History of Corporate Collapse in Australia*, Sydney, Allen & Unwin, 1988, p. 124.
30. Gibbs, *Bulls, Bears and Wildcats*, 1988 p. 31.
31. Sykes, *Two Centuries of Panic*, 1988, p. 135; M. Cannon, *The Land Boomers*, Melbourne University Press, 1976.
32. Savings Bank of South Australia, Minutes of the Board of Trustees, 16 April, 1886 see also the *Register*, 14, 15, 16 April 1886.
33. Savings Bank of South Australia, Minutes of the Board of Trustees, July, 1886.
34. Blainey, G. and Hutton, *Gold and Paper: A history of the National Bank of Australia*, South Melbourne, Macmillan, 1983, p. 70.
35. Savings Bank of South Australia, Annual Reports, 1882, 1886, 1889, 1898. See also the *Observer*, 28 July 1888; *Express*, 3 August 1888, pp. 2–4.
36. State Bank Royal Commission, Parliamentary Papers, South Australian Parliament, 1888.
37. Gibbs, *Bulls, Bears and Wildcats*, 1988, p. 90.
38. Cannon, *The Land Boomers*, 1976, p. 135; T. Sykes, *Two Centuries of Panic*, 1988, p. 150.
39. Gibbs, *Bulls, Bears and Wildcats*, 1988, p. 90.
40. ibid. p. 94; T. Sykes, *Two Centuries of Panic*, 1988, p. 186.
41. Wadham, E.J., 'The Political Career of C.C. Kingston', Department of History, M.A. Thesis, University of Adelaide, 1953; C. Campbell, 'C.C. Kingston Radical Liberal and Democrat', Department of History, B.A. Thesis, University of Adelaide, 1976.
42. South Australian Parliamentary Debates House of Assembly, (SAPD HA), 20 November, 1894, p. 2411.
43. SAPD HA, 20 November, 1984, p. 2412.
44. ibid. p. 2409.
45. ibid. p. 2409.
46. Savings Bank of South Australia, Minutes of the Board of Trustees, 23 November, 1894 (serves 4).
47. ibid.
48. Gibbs, *Bulls, Bears and Wildcats*, 1988, p. 114.
49. *The Register*, 13 November, pp. 6, 20 November 1894, pp. 2–9. Also the *Register*, 5 August 1894, pp. 43, 13 February 1895, pp. 6, 24 August 1895, p. 6.
50. *The Advertiser*, 13 November, 20 November p. 13, 1894. See also 29 November, 1894, p. 24 and see the *Advertiser*, 17 September, 1895, p. 4 and 4 October 1895, pp. 4–5.
51. Savings Bank of South Australia, Minutes of the Board of Trustees, 9 August, 1895.
52. ibid.
53. SAPD HA 9 October, 1895, p. 1714.
54. ibid. p. 1715.
55. ibid. p. 1715.
56. ibid. p. 1715.
57. SAPD HA 6 November 1895, p. 2086.
58. ibid. p. 2086.
59. State Bank of South Australia Minutes, 1896–1923.
60. ibid.
61. ibid.
62. ibid.
63. SAPD HA, 4 November, 1896, p. 673.
64. ibid. p. 673.
65. ibid. p. 674.
66. ibid. p. 310.
67. Ledgers, Advances to Settlers Act 1912–1978, but includes the loans under the State Advances Act 1895. The loans examples given here are from the first entries in 1896.

Chapter 2

1. Savings Bank of South Australia *History and Progress, 1848–1928*, p. 35.
2. ibid. pp. 54–58.
3. ibid. pp. 54–60.
4. ibid. p. 42.
5. SAPD Legislative Council (LC) 22 October 1907, p. 344.
6. ibid. p. 357.
7. ibid. p. 357.
8. Savings Bank of South Australia *History and Progress, 1848–1928*, p. 42.
9. ibid. pp. 40–41.
10. Manning, G.H. and Haydon Manning, *Worth Fighting For: Work and Industrial Relations in Banking Industry in South Australia*, Adelaide, Australian Bank Employers Union, South Australia and Northern Territory, 1989, p. 51.
11. ibid. p. 24.
12. Garnaut, C. 'Remodelling a Model: the Thousand Homes Scheme in Colonel Light Gardens' *Journal of the Historical Society of South Australia*, No. 23, 1995 pp. 5–36. See also Royal Commission on the Thousand Homes Contract, House of Assembly Parliamentary Papers, Adelaide, 1925.
13. SAPD HA, 20 August 1924, p. 308.
14. Garnaut, 'Remodelling a Model', 1995, p. 16; and State Bank of South Australia, Minutes of the Board of Directors, January, February, March 1924.
15. Report of the Royal Commission, 1925, p. 36.
16. Garnaut, 'Remodelling a Model', 1995, p. 17, see also 'Builders Grievances – State Bank and Soldiers' Home' *Observer*, 2 June 1923, 'Housing the People', *News*, April 1924.
17. SAPD HA 25 August 1925, p. 565.
18. SAPD HA 27 August 1928, p. 619.
19. SAPD HA 15 September 1925, p. 747.
20. ibid. p. 748.
21. State Bank of South Australia, Report of the Board of Management, 1926.
22. State Bank of South Australia, Report of the Board of Management, 1927.
23. State Bank of South Australia, Report of the Board of Management, 1926.
24. State Bank of South Australia Minutes 1926–1984, now cited as State Bank of South Australia, Report of the Board of Management, 1926.
25. State Bank of South Australia, Report of the Board of Management, 1926.
26. State Bank of South Australia, Report of the Board of Management, 1933.
27. State Bank of South Australia, Report of the Board of Management, 1938; see also Marsden, S. *Business, Charity and Sentiment, The South Australian Housing Trust 1936–1986*, Adelaide, Wakefield Press, 1986, pp. 2–14.
28. State Bank of South Australia, Report of the Board of Management, 1932.
29. State Bank of South Australia, Report of the Board of Management, 1933.
30. State Bank of South Australia, Report of the Board of Management, 1942.
31. Bromhill, R., *Unemployed workers; a social history of the Great Depression in Adelaide*, St. Lucia Queensland University Press, 1978, pp. 124–125.
32. *Advertiser*, 14 August 1936.
33. ibid.
34. ibid.
35. ibid.
36. ibid.
37. ibid.
38. State Bank of South Australia, Report of the Board of Management, 1932.
39. ibid.
40. State Bank of South Australia, Report of the Board of Management, 1931.
41. ibid.

42. ibid.
43. State Bank of South Australia, Report of the Board of Management, 1932.
44. State Bank of South Australia, Report of the Board of Management, 1933.
45. State Bank of South Australia, Report of the Board of Management, 1936.
46. ibid.
47. ibid.
48. ibid.
49. State Bank of South Australia, Report of the Board of Management, 1934.
50. State Bank of South Australia, Report of the Board of Management, 1936.
51. ibid.
52. ibid.
53. State Bank of South Australia, Report of the Board of Management, 1937.
54. State Bank of South Australia, Report of the Board of Management, 1940.
55. State Bank of South Australia, Report of the Board of Management, 1942.
56. State Bank of South Australia, Report of the Board of Management, 1941.
57. ibid.
58. ibid.
59. State Bank of South Australia, Report of the Board of Management, 1942.
60. ibid.
61. State Bank of South Australia, Report of the Board of Management, 1945.
62. ibid.
63. Playford, T. *Advertiser*, 26 February 1944.
64. State Bank of South Australia, Report of the Board of Management, 1947.
65. ibid.
66. *Advertiser*, 13 June 1945.
67. State Bank of South Australia, Report of the Board of Management, 1948.
68. ibid.
69. State Bank of South Australia, Report of the Board of Management, 1949.
70. ibid.
71. ibid.
72. State Bank of South Australia, Report of the Board of Management, 1950.
73. Gobbett, 'The Financial System', 1986, p. 158.
74. Depression years of the 1930s, Savings Bank of South Australia, Board of Trustees, Report to the Board, Some Considerations Effecting the Volume of Reports and Withdrawals, May 1931.
75. ibid.
76. ibid.
77. ibid.
78. ibid.
79. ibid.
80. Report by the Secretary, Mr. T.J.M. Linn, of the Bank's Mortgage Securities, to the Board of Trustees, 7 March 1935.
81. Depression years of the 1930s, Savings Bank of South Australia, Board of Trustees, Report to the Board, Some Considerations Effecting the Volume of Deposits and Withdrawals, May 1931.
82. ibid.
83. Depression years of the 1930s, Report by the Secretary, Mr. T.J.M. Linn, of the Bank's Mortgage Securities, to the Board of Trustees, 7 March 1935.
84. ibid.
85. Depression years of the 1930s, Mortgage Loan Interest, 31 August 1935.
86. ibid; see also Depression Period 1930–1938, by the Acting Manager R.J. Pedler, 29 September 1938.
87. Depression years of the 1930s, Report by the Secretary, Mr. T.J.M. Linn, of the Bank's Mortgage Securities, to the Board of Trustees, 7 March 1935.
88. ibid.

89. ibid.
90. Dignum, A.C. Dignum Report on Mortgages to the First Annual Managers Conference, Savings Bank of South Australia, 29 January 1936.
91. ibid.
92. Minutes of the Board of Trustees, Savings Bank of South Australia, Sub-Committee for Interest Arrears, July 1931.
93. ibid.
94. ibid.
95. Minutes of the Board of Trustees, Savings Bank of South Australia, Sub-Committee for Interest Arrears, July 1935.
96. ibid.
97. Minutes of the Board of Trustees, Savings Bank of South Australia, Sub-Committee for Interest Arrears, July 1936.
98. ibid.
99. ibid.
100. Minutes of the Board of Trustees, Savings Bank of South Australia, Sub-Committee for Interest Arrears, July 1940.
101. ibid.
102. ibid.
103. ibid.
104. ibid.
105. Caire, H.M., 'The Bank as Landlord' discussion paper presented at the Savings Bank of South Australia, Proceedings of the Third Conference of Senior Officers and Branch Managers, 29 and 31 January 1938.
106. ibid.
107. ibid.
108. ibid.
109. ibid.
110. Savings Bank of South Australia, Minutes of the Board of Trustees, 27 January 1936.
111. Savings Bank of South Australia, Minutes of the Board of Trustees, 18 December 1936.
112. Savings Bank of South Australia, Minutes of the Board of Trustees, 23 December, 1938, file number 33676.
113. Minutes of the Board of Trustees, Special Board Minutes 270, May 1934.
114. ibid.
115. Matthew, J.E., *The Commonwealth Banking Corporation, Its Background, History and Present Operations*, Sydney, Australia, 1980, p.43.
116. Minutes of the Board of Trustees, Special Minutes, 270, 272, 278, containing copies of letters between Chairman of the Commonwealth Bank, Claude Reading and Premier Butler, filed under May 1934 file.
117. ibid.
118. ibid.
119. Minutes of the Board of Trustees, Board Memo, summarising the proceedings of the Conference from Mr Caire to Chairman Rundle, 11 November 1941, filed under 36941.
120. ibid.
121. ibid.
122. ibid.
123. ibid.
124. Minutes of the Board of Trustees, Board Minutes, 15 October 1942, file number 37929.
125. Minutes of the Board of Trustees, Board Minutes, 23 March 1943.
126. Savings Bank of South Australia, *Our Century: Savings Bank of South Australia 1848–1948*, published by the bank, 1948, p. 138.
127. *Our Century*, 1948, p. 108.
128. ibid. p. 111.
129. Minutes of the Board of Trustees, 19 February 1942, file no. 37258.

130. ibid.
131. ibid.
132. *Our Century*, 1984, p. 57.
133. ibid.
134. Minutes of the Board of Trustees, 12 October 1943, file number 38897.
135. ibid.
136. Stretton, H. *Ideas for Australian Cities*, 2nd ed. Melbourne, Georgian House, 1975, pp. 131–174.
137. *Workers Weekly Herald*, Friday 19 September 1941.
138. Minutes of the Board of Trustees, Letter from General Manager Pedler to Premier Playford, 15 September 1941.
139. Minutes of the Board of Trustees, Letter from Premier Playford to General Manager Pedler, 16 September 1941.
140. ibid.
141. Minutes of the Board of Trustees, General Manager Pedler's memo to the Board of Trustees, 7 October 1941.
142. Board Minutes, 21 June 1943, file no. 38609A.
143. Minutes of the Board of Trustees, Letter from the Treasurer to the Board, filed in Special Minutes, 38705, 28 July 1943.
144. Minutes of the Board of Trustees, 8 August 1943, file number 39664.
145. Minutes of the Board of Trustees, 15 August 1943, file number 39666.
146. Minutes of the Board of Trustees, 9 December, 1943, Special Minute 632.
147. Minutes of the Board of Trustees, 5 August 1943, file number 39669.
148. Minutes of the Board of Trustees, 9 December 1943, Special minutes, 632.
149. Minutes of the Board of Trustees, 17 December 1943, Special Minute 639.
150. Minutes of the Board of Trustees, 17 December 1943, Special Minute 639.
151. Minutes of the Board of Trustees, 12 February 1944.
152. ibid.
153. Minutes of the Board of Trustees, 29 June 1945, file number 40539.
154. Minutes of the Board of Trustees, 7 September 1945, file number 40672.
155. Minutes of the Board of Trustees, 14 September 1945, file number 40774 and 40896.
156. Minutes of the Board of Trustees, 14 September 1945, file number 40595.
157. ibid.
158. Minutes of the Board of Trustees, 13 November 1945, file number 40598.
159. Minutes of the Board of Trustees, 21 December 1945, file number 41085.
160. Caire, H.M. 'Recent Developments in the Mortgage Lending Field', Proceedings of the Fifth Conference of Senior Officers and Managers at Branches held at Head Office, 26 and 28 January 1946.
161. 'Recent Developments', January 1946.
162. ibid.
163. Minutes of the Board of Trustees, 3 October 1943, file number 39802.
164. Draft Letter to Depositors, 9 August 1944, filed in papers relating to Minutes of the Board of Trustees, 8 August 1944, file number 39644.
165. Minutes of the Board of Trustees, 8 August 1944, file number 39644.
166. ibid.
167. George, G. The Bank's Public Relations in The Fifth Conference of Senior Officers and Managers at Branches, 26 & 28 January 1946.
168. Minutes of the Board of Trustees, 8 August 1944, file number 39644.
169. The Bank's Public Relations, 26 & 28 January 1946.
170. Minutes of the Board of Trustees, 14 December 1944, file number 39983.
171. Minutes of the Board of Trustees, 15 March 1945.
172. Minutes of the Board of Trustees, Special Minute 658, 15 March 1945.
173. Minutes of the Board of Trustees, 6 April, 16 March corresponded in Special Minute 660.
174. ibid.

175. ibid.
176. ibid.
177. Minutes of the Board of Trustees, 6 June 1945 corresponded in Special Minute 660.
178. ibid.
179. Minutes of the Board of Trustees, 14 June 1945 corresponded in Special Minute 671.
180. ibid.
181. Minutes of the Board of Trustees, 14 June 1945 corresponded in Special Minute 680.
182. Minutes of the Board of Trustees, 14 June 1945 corresponded in Special Minute 671.
183. Minutes of the Board of Trustees, Letter to Premier Playford filed with Board Minutes 14 June 1945, Special Minutes.
184. SAPD HA 9 October, 1945, p. 445.
185. ibid. p. 445.
186. ibid. p. 460.
187. ibid. p. 460.
188. ibid. p. 460.
189. ibid. p. 461.
190. SAPD HA 9 October, 1945, p. 461.
191. SAPD LC, 26 October 1945.
192. Minutes of the Board of Trustees, 2 November 1945 see Special Minutes 682.
193. Minutes of the Board of Trustees, 6 November 1945 see Special Minutes 658–687.
194. Pedler, R.J.H. concluding remarks to The Sixth Conference of Senior Officers and Managers and Branches, 25 & 27 January 1947.
195. ibid.
196. Minutes of the Board of Trustees, 8 October 1946, file number 41947, 41903, 44267 and 41947.
197. Minutes of the Board of Trustees, 2 November 1945, file number 40919.
198. ibid.
199. Minutes of the Board of Trustees, 2 June 1974, file number 17667.
200. Minutes of the Board of Trustees, 22 January 1946.
201. Minutes of the Board of Trustees, 1 March 1948, see Special File on the Bank's centennial celebration.
202. *Advertiser*, 11 March 1948.
203. *Advertiser*, 12 March 1948.
204. ibid.
205. *Advertiser*, 15 March 1948.
206. Minutes of the Board of Trustees, 18 May 1945, file number 40421.
207. ibid.
208. Minutes of the Board of Trustees, 3 July 1945, file number 40556.
209. ibid.
210. ibid.
211. Minutes of the Board of Trustees, 24 August 1945, file number 40714.
212. Minutes of the Board of Trustees, 15 March 1946, file number 41364.
213. Minutes of the Board of Trustees, 26 April 1946, file number 40715.
214. ibid.
215. ibid.
216. ibid.
217. ibid.
218. Minutes of the Board of Trustees, 6 February 1946, file number 41436.
219. Minutes of the Board of Trustees, 9 April 1946 file number 41496.
220. ibid.
221. ibid.
222. Letter from Mr Linn to Mr Caire filed under Board Minutes, 5 April 1946 file number 41436.
223. Report from Mr George to Mr Caire, Assistant Federal Manager, 23 January 1946, Minutes of the Board of Trustees, 12 April 1941, file number 41456.

224. Minutes of the Board of Trustees, 12 April 1946, file number 41456.
225. ibid.
226. ibid.
227. Letter from General Manager Pedler to the Treasurer, 20 June 1946, as reply from the Treasurer to the General Manager 15 July 1946, filed under Minutes of the Board of Trustees, 6 August 1946, file number 41789.
228. Minutes of the Board of Trustees, 24 January 1947, file number 42249 and 42259.
229. Letter from Mr Barratt from the Australian Bank Official's Association, 1 November 1949, to General Manager of the Savings Bank, considered by Lew Hunkin Chairman of the Board of Trustees, Minutes of the Board of Trustees, 3 November 1949, file number 45652.
230. Legal opinion from Messrs Baker, McEwin, Millhouse and Wright on 23 November 1949, Minutes of the Board of Trustees, 1 December 1949, file number 45789.
231. Minutes of the Board of Trustees, 1 December 1949, file number 45789.
232. Minutes of the Board of Trustees, 9 July 1946, file number 41700, 41282 and 41848.
233. Minutes of the Board of Trustees, 12 January 1950, file number 45857, 45812 and 45652.
234. Minutes of the Board of Trustees, 30 July 1953, file number 50317.
235. Manning, *Worth Fighting For*, 1989, p. 172.
236. Manning, *Worth Fighting For*, 1989, pp. 172–175.

Chapter 3

1. State Bank of South Australia, Branch Manager's Report on Renmark Branch, 1927.
2. ibid.
3. ibid.
4. ibid.
5. ibid.
6. State Bank of South Australia, Branch Manager's Report on Renmark Branch, 1928.
7. State Bank of South Australia, Branch Manager's Report on Renmark Branch, 1929.
8. ibid.
9. Correspondence between Manager Chapman and General Manager 12 May 1930, 17 May 1930, 30 June 1930 and 14 November 1930, accompanying the State Bank of South Australia, Branch Manager's Report on Renmark Branch, 1929.
10. State Bank of South Australia, Branch Manager's Report on Renmark Branch, 1930.
11. ibid.
12. ibid.
13. ibid.
14. ibid.
15. ibid.
16. State Bank of South Australia, Branch Manager's Report on Renmark Branch, 1931.
17. ibid.
18. State Bank of South Australia, Branch Manager's Report on Renmark Branch, 1932.
19. ibid.
20. ibid.
21. State Bank of South Australia, Branch Manager's Report on Renmark Branch, 1932.
22. State Bank of South Australia, Branch Manager's Report on Renmark Branch, 1933.
23. ibid.
24. State Bank of South Australia, Branch Manager's Report on Renmark Branch, 1934.
25. State Bank of South Australia, Branch Manager's Report on Renmark Branch, 1935.
26. State Bank of South Australia, Branch Manager's Report on Renmark Branch, 1936.
27. ibid.
28. State Bank of South Australia, Branch Manager's Report on Renmark Branch, 1937.
29. State Bank of South Australia, Branch Manager's Report on Renmark Branch, 1939.
30. State Bank of South Australia, Branch Manager's Report on Renmark Branch, 1940.

31. State Bank of South Australia, Branch Manager's Report on Renmark Branch, 1942.
32. State Bank of South Australia, Branch Manager's Report on Renmark Branch, 1945.
33. ibid.
34. ibid.
35. ibid.
36. ibid.
37. ibid.
38. State Bank of South Australia, Branch Manager's Report on Renmark Branch, 1947.
39. ibid.
40. State Bank of South Australia, Branch Manager's Report on Renmark Branch, 1948.
41. ibid.
42. ibid.
43. State Bank of South Australia, Branch Manager's Report on Renmark Branch, 1950.
44. ibid.
45. State Bank of South Australia, Branch Manager's Report on Renmark Branch, 1953.
46. ibid.
47. ibid.
48. ibid.
49. State Bank of South Australia, Branch Manager's Report on Renmark Branch, 1965.
50. ibid.
51. State Bank of South Australia, Branch Manager's Report on Renmark Branch, 1968.
52. ibid.
53. State Bank of South Australia, Branch Manager's Report Kimba Branch, 30 June 1927.
54. ibid.
55. State Bank of South Australia, Branch Manager's Report Kimba Branch, 30 June 1928.
56. ibid.
57. ibid.
58. ibid.
59. Letter from General Manager Warren to Mr Matthews attached to Managers Report Kimba Board, 30 June 1928.
60. State Bank of South Australia, Branch Manager's Report Kimba Board, 30 June 1929.
61. ibid.
62. ibid.
63. ibid.
64. Letter from General Manager Warren to Mr Matthew as accompanying the Managers Report Kimba Branch, 30 June 1930.
65. State Bank of South Australia, Branch Manager's Report Kimba Board, 30 June 1930.
66. Telegram from Matthew to the General Manager attached to the Manager's Report Kimba Branch, 30 June 1930.
67. State Bank of South Australia, Branch Manager's Report Kimba Board, 30 June 1930.
68. ibid.
69. ibid.
70. ibid.
71. ibid.
72. ibid.
73. ibid.
74. ibid.
75. State Bank of South Australia, Branch Manager's Report Kimba Board, 30 June 1932.
76. ibid.
77. ibid.
78. State Bank of South Australia, Branch Manager's Report Kimba Board, 30 June 1933.
79. ibid.
80. ibid.
81. State Bank of South Australia, Branch Manager's Report Kimba Board, 30 June 1934.
82. State Bank of South Australia, Branch Manager's Report Kimba Board, 30 June 1935.

83. ibid.
84. State Bank of South Australia, Branch Manager's Report Kimba Board, 1936.
85. ibid.
86. State Bank of South Australia, Branch Manager's Report Kimba Board, 1939.
87. ibid.
88. State Bank of South Australia, Branch Manager's Report Kimba Board, 1946.
89. State Bank of South Australia, Branch Manager's Report Kimba Board, 1941.
90. ibid.
91. Correspondence from Manager Fewster to the Manager State Bank of South Australia, accompanying the Manager's Report Kimba Branch, 30 June 1941.
92. ibid.
93. ibid.
94. State Bank of South Australia, Branch Manager's Report Kimba Branch, 1942.
95. ibid.
96. State Bank of South Australia, Branch Manager's Report Kimba Branch, 1943.
97. ibid.
98. State Bank of South Australia, Branch Manager's Report Kimba Branch, 1945.
99. ibid.
100. State Bank of South Australia, Branch Manager's Report Kimba Branch, 1946.
101. State Bank of South Australia, Branch Manager's Report Kimba Branch, 1947.
102. State Bank of South Australia, Branch Manager's Report Kimba Branch, 1948.
103. State Bank of South Australia, Branch Manager's Report Kimba Branch, 1949.
104. ibid.
105. State Bank of South Australia, Branch Manager's Report Kimba Branch, 1950.
106. ibid.
107. ibid.
108. State Bank of South Australia, Branch Manager's Report Kimba Branch, 1951.
109. ibid.
110. ibid.
111. State Bank of South Australia, Branch Manager's Report Kimba Branch, 1954.
112. State Bank of South Australia, Branch Manager's Report Kimba Branch, 1955.
113. State Bank of South Australia, Branch Manager's Report Kimba Branch, 1956.
114. State Bank of South Australia, Branch Manager's Report Kimba Branch, 1959.
115. ibid.
116. ibid.
117. State Bank of South Australia, Branch Manager's Report Kimba Branch, 1961.
118. ibid.
119. ibid.
120. ibid.
121. State Bank of South Australia, Branch Manager's Report Kimba Branch, 1962.
122. ibid.
123. ibid.
124. State Bank of South Australia, Branch Manager's Report Kimba Branch, 1964.
125. ibid.
126. ibid.
127. ibid.
128. State Bank of South Australia, Branch Manager's Report Kimba Branch, 1965.
129. State Bank of South Australia, Branch Manager's Report Kimba Branch, 1966.
130. State Bank of South Australia, Branch Manager's Report Kimba Branch, 1967.
131. State Bank of South Australia, Branch Manager's Report Kimba Branch, 1968.
132. ibid.
133. ibid.
134. ibid.
135. State Bank of South Australia, Branch Manager's Report Kimba Branch, 1969.
136. ibid.

137. ibid.
138. State Bank of South Australia, Branch Manager's Report Kimba Branch, 1970–1974.
139. State Bank of South Australia, Branch Manager's Report Kimba Branch, 1974.
140. ibid.
141. State Bank of South Australia, Branch Manager's Report Yacka Branch, 1928.
142. ibid.
143. State Bank of South Australia, Branch Manager's Report Yacka Branch, 1929.
144. ibid.
145. State Bank of South Australia, Branch Manager's Report Yacka Branch, 1930.
146. ibid.
147. ibid.
148. State Bank of South Australia, Branch Manager's Report Yacka Branch, 1931.
149. State Bank of South Australia, Branch Manager's Report Yacka Branch, 1933.
150. State Bank of South Australia, Branch Manager's Report Yacka Branch, 1937.
151. ibid.
152. State Bank of South Australia, Branch Manager's Report Yacka Branch, 1941.
153. State Bank of South Australia, Branch Manager's Report Yacka Branch, 1945.
154. ibid.
155. State Bank of South Australia, Branch Manager's Report Yacka Branch, 1954.
156. State Bank of South Australia, Branch Manager's Report Yacka Branch, 1961.
157. ibid.
158. State Bank of South Australia, Branch Manager's Report Yacka Branch, 1967.
159. ibid.
160. ibid.
161. State Bank of South Australia, Branch Manager's Report Yacka Branch, 1969.
162. State Bank of South Australia, Branch Manager's Report Yacka Branch, 1974.
163. State Bank of South Australia, Branch Manager's Report Millicent Branch, 1950.
164. State Bank of South Australia, Branch Manager's Report Millicent Branch, 1961.
165. ibid.
166. ibid.
167. State Bank of South Australia, Branch Manager's Report Millicent Branch, 1962.
168. ibid.
169. ibid.
170. State Bank of South Australia, Branch Manager's Report Millicent Branch, 1963.
171. ibid.
172. State Bank of South Australia, Branch Manager's Report Millicent Branch, 1964.
173. ibid.
174. ibid.
175. State Bank of South Australia, Branch Manager's Report Millicent Branch, 1965.
176. ibid.
177. State Bank of South Australia, Branch Manager's Report Millicent Branch, 1966.
178. State Bank of South Australia, Branch Manager's Report Millicent Branch, 1965.
179. State Bank of South Australia, Branch Manager's Report Millicent Branch, 1966.
180. ibid.
181. State Bank of South Australia, Branch Manager's Report Millicent Branch, 1967.
182. ibid.
183. ibid.
184. State Bank of South Australia, Branch Manager's Report Millicent Branch, 1969.
185. ibid.
186. State Bank of South Australia, Branch Manager's Report Millicent Branch, 1971.
187. ibid.
188. State Bank of South Australia, Branch Manager's Report Millicent Branch, 1974.
189. ibid.
190. State Bank of South Australia, Branch Manager's Report Southern Branch, 1961.
191. ibid.

192. ibid.
193. ibid.
194. ibid.
195. ibid.
196. State Bank of South Australia, Branch Manager's Report Southern Branch, 1962.
197. ibid.
198. ibid.
199. ibid.
200. ibid.
201. ibid.
202. State Bank of South Australia, Branch Manager's Report Southern Branch, 1964.
203. ibid.
204. ibid.
205. ibid.
206. State Bank of South Australia, Branch Manager's Report Southern Branch, 1965.
207. ibid.
208. ibid.
209. State Bank of South Australia, Branch Manager's Report Southern Branch, 1966.
210. ibid.
211. ibid.
212. ibid.
213. ibid.
214. ibid.
215. State Bank of South Australia, Branch Manager's Report Southern Branch, 1972.
216. State Bank of South Australia, Branch Manager's Report Southern Branch, 1975.
217. ibid.
218. ibid.
219. ibid.
220. State Bank of South Australia, Branch Manager's Report Southern Branch, 1977.
221. State Bank of South Australia, Branch Manager's Report Southern Branch, 1979.
222. State Bank of South Australia, Branch Manager's Report Southern Branch, 1980.
223. ibid.
224. ibid.
225. State Bank of South Australia, Branch Manager's Report Southern Branch, 1982.
226. ibid.
227. ibid.
228. As reported in the *Advertiser*, 9 July 1946.
229. *Advertiser*, 9 July 1946, and *Advertiser*, 23 August 1946.
230. Mr Cilento's correspondence to the General Manager table Savings Bank of South Australia, Minutes of the Board, 10 August 1950, file numbers 46583, 46660, 467550.
231. Savings Bank of South Australia, Minutes of the Board of Trustees, 10 August 1950.
232. ibid.
233. ibid.
234. ibid.
235. ibid.
236. Savings Bank of South Australia, Minutes of the Board of Trustees 5 October 1950, file number 46587, 44605 and 46755.
237. ibid.
238. Savings Bank of South Australia, Minutes of the Board of Trustees 31 October 1965.
239. Savings Bank of South Australia Annual Report, 30 June 1954.
240. *Advertiser*, 5 August 1955.
241. Savings Bank of South Australia Annual Report, 30 June 1955.
242. Ferrier, P.L. 'The Depositor – our Bread and Butter' (Acting Public Relations Officer, 2, Proceedings of the Eighth Conference of Senior Officers and Managers of Branches, 30 January, 1 February, 1954.

243. ibid.
244. Savings Bank of South Australia Annual Report, 1966, 1970, 1984.
245. *Sunday Mail*, 3 December 1955.
246. Letter from Mr Marshall to Mr Caire 29 August 1961, reply 1 September September 1961 accompanying, Savings Bank of South Australia, Minutes of the Board of Trustees, 1 September 1961 file numbers: 60558, 60567, 60611, 60633, 60698, 60723, 60744, and 60844.
247. Minutes of the Board of Trustees, 1 September 1961.
248. ibid.
249. ibid.
250. Minutes of the Board of Trustees, 10 May 1962 file number 616361.
251. ibid.
252. ibid.
253. Minutes of the Board of Trustees, 12 April 1962, and see Board Minutes, 10 May 1962, file number 616361 and Annual Report of the Savings Bank of South Australia, 1966.
254. Savings Bank of South Australia Press Release, 22 December 1955 as cited on Radio 5DN and in the *News*, 23 December 1955.
255. *News*, 23 December 1955.
256. Lamshed, M. *The South Australian Story*, Advertiser Publications, 1955.
257. ibid.
258. Savings Bank of South Australia Annual Report, 30 June 1957.
259. ibid.
260. ibid.
261. See correspondence from Premier Playford to General Manager Mr Caire and Under Treasurer Seaman Minute No 559 to Premier Playford, 14 October 1961 file number 60611.
262. Minute Number 559, 14 October 1961.
263. ibid.
264. SAPD HA 7 October 1961, as tabled with Board Minutes, 14 October 1961.
265. Minutes of the Board of Trustees, 26 October 1961 file number 60844.
266. Minutes of the Board of Trustees, 26 October 1961.
267. ibid.
268. Letter from Chairman Hunter to Premier Playford, Board Minutes, 26 October 1961, file number 60844.
269. Minutes of the Board of Trustees, 16 November 1961, file number 60518.
270. ibid.
271. Minutes of the Board of Trustees, 7 December 1961, file number 60744.
272. Minutes of the Board of Trustees, 7 December 1961, file number 60844.
273. Minutes of the Board of Trustees, 19 April 1962, file number 60518.
274. ibid.
275. Minutes of the Board of Trustees, 19 September 1962, file number 61894.
276. ibid.
277. See the exchange of correspondence between the ABA and General Manager Cilento on the following dates; 25 May 1962, 23 August 1962, 10 September 1962, 13 September 1962, 1 October 1982, 9 November 1962.
278. Minutes of the Board of Trustees, 1 October 1962.
279. Speech by Hon. Sir Lyell McEwin SAPD, LL, 9 October 1962 tabled at Board Minutes, 9 October 1962, file number 62085.
280. Board Minutes, 8 January 1963, file number 62272.
281. Board Minutes, 3 May 1962, file number 61328 .
282. Savings Bank of South Australia Annual Report, 30 June 1962.
283. Minutes of the Board of Trustees, 3 May 1961 file number 61390.
284. Minutes of the Board of Trustees, 1 July 1961.
285. Minutes of the Board of Trustees, 16 December 1961, file number 60960.
286. Minutes of the Board of Trustees, 24 May 1962, file number 61400.

287. ibid.
288. Minutes of the Board of Trustees, 19 July 1962, file number 61615.
289. ibid.
290. ibid.
291. Minutes of the Board of Trustees, 7 August 1962.
292. ibid.
293. Minutes of the Board of Trustees Savings Bank of South Australia, Sub-Committee for Interest Arrears, 30 June 1961.
294. ibid.
295. ibid.
296. ibid.
297. ibid.
298. ibid.
299. ibid.
300. ibid.
301. ibid.
302. ibid.
303. ibid.
304. ibid.
305. Minutes of the Boad of Trustees Savings Bank of South Australia, Sub-Committee for Interest Arrears, 30 June 1962.
306. ibid.
307. ibid.
308. ibid.
309. ibid.
310. Minutes of the Board of Trustees, 3 February 1963, file number 62402.
311. ibid.
312. *Advertiser*, 3 March 1965.
313. ibid.
314. ibid; see also *News,* 3 March 1965.
315. *Advertiser*, 3 March 1965.
316. ibid.
317. ibid.
318. ibid.
319. ibid.
320. ibid.
321. ibid.
322. Letter from the Savings Bank of South Australia General Manager to his counterpart in the State Bank, 2 April 1965 held in Special Files in operation with the State Bank, file numbers 74802, 76129, 76165.
323. *Advertiser*, 31 August 1967.
324. *Advertiser*, 20 September 1967.
325. Letter from Chairman Hunkins to Treasurer Pearson, 11 July 1968, file number 69980, 69943.
326. Minutes of the Board of Trustees, 31 October 1968, file number 70273.
327. ibid.
328. ibid.
329. Minutes of the Board of Trustees, 30 November 1968, file number 69833B.
330. Minutes of the Board of Trustees, 7 November 1968, file number 70300.
331. Letter 12 December 1968 filed with Minutes of the Board of Trustees, 30 November 1968, file number 69833B.
332. Treasurer Pearson's 7th December 1968 letter contained in file accompanying Minutes of the Board of Trustees, 21 August 1969.
333. Minutes of the Board of Trustees, 20 November 1969, file number 71708.
334. ibid.

335. ibid.
336. Minutes of the Board of Trustees, 20 November 1969, file number 71708.
337. ibid.
338. ibid.
339. Savings Bank of South Australia Annual Report, 30 June 1968.
340. Reproduced in Savings Bank of South Australia Annual Report, 30 June 1968.
341. ibid.
342. Minutes of the Board of Trustees, 5 December 1960 file number 70392.
343. ibid.
344. ibid.
345. Minutes of the Board of Trustees, 19 December 1968, file number 703892.
346. ibid.
347. Freeman's letter t the General Manager, 20 January 1972, file number 74356.
348. Minutes of the Board of Trustees, 20 January 1972, file number 74356.
349. ibid.
350. ibid.
351. Board Minutes, 4 March 1976.
352. Savings Bank of South Australia Annual Report 1970.

Chapter 4

1. Savings Bank of South Australia, Minutes of the Board of Trustees, 10 September 1971, file number 73900.
2. Letter from Premier Dunstan, accompanying Board Minutes, 10 September 1971, file number 73900.
3. Minutes of the Board of Trustees, 18 November 1971, file number 74212.
4. ibid.
5. ibid.
6. SAPD LC, 17 November 1971 p. 3090.
7. SAPD LC, 17 November 1971 p. 3094.
8. SAPD LC, 17 November 1971 p. 3091.
9. SAPD LC, 17 November 1971 p. 3092.
10. ibid.
11. Minutes of the Board of Trustees, 18 November 1971, file number 74121.
12. Minutes of the Board of Trustees, 20 December 1971, file number 74239.
13. ibid.
14. Premier Dunstan's letter to Chairman Hunkin, 3 February 1972, tabled in Minutes of the Board of Trustees, 13 February 1972, file number 74761.
15. Minutes of the Board of Trustees, 25 May 1972, file number 74802.
16. ibid.
17. Letter from Chairman Jeffrey the Premier, 23 May 1973; Minutes of the Board of Trustees, 25 May 1972, file number 75715.
18. Minutes of the Board of Trustees, 25 May 1972, file number 75715.
19. Letter of reply from Premier Dunstan to Chairman Jeffrey 18 April 1973; Minutes of the Board of Trustees, 25 May 1972 file number 74802.
20. Minutes of the Board of Trustees, 25 May 1972, file number 74802.
21. Minutes of the Board of Trustees, 25 October 1973, file number 768267A.
22. ibid.
23. Minutes of the Board of Trustees, 3 June 1971, file number 73504.
24. ibid.
25. ibid.
26. ibid.
27. ibid.

28. Correspondence from the ABOA to the General Manager, 2 July 1971, 22 July 1971; Minutes of the Board of Trustees, 22 July 1971, file number 73688.
29. Minutes of the Board of Trustees, 22 July 1971, file number 73688.
30. ibid.
31. ibid.
32. Letter from J Sanders, Federal Secretary ABOA to the General Manager, 2 August 1971, Minutes of the Board of Trustees, 15 August 1971.
33. Minutes of the Board of Trustees, 15 August 1971, file number 73504.
34. ibid.
35. ibid.
36. ibid.
37. ibid.
38. ibid.
39. Manning, *Worth Fighting For*, 1989, pp. 175–181.
40. Minutes of the Board of Trustees, 9 September 1971, file number 73877.
41. Letter from Staff Inspector to General Manager, 5 May 1972; file number 74773.
42. ibid.
43. ibid.
44. Minutes of the Board of Trustees, 8 February 1973, file number 75779.
45. ibid.
46. Minutes of the Board of Trustees, 29 March 1973, file number 75981.
47. ibid.
48. Correspondence filed under Minutes of the Board of Trustees, 12 April 1973, file number 760331.
49. Minutes of the Board of Trustees, 12 April 1973, 76033.
50. ibid.
51. ibid.
52. ibid.
53. State Bank of South Australia, Annual Report 30 June 1974.
54. ibid.
55. SAPD HA, 30 October 1973, p. 1283.
56. SAPD HA, 9 October 1973, p. 1393.
57. SAPD HA, 9 October 1973, p. 1395.
58. Report of Sir Walter Scott and Sir John Marks, hereafter titled the Marks and Scott Report, 19 September 1975.
59. Marks and Scott Report, 19 September 1975.
60. ibid.
61. ibid.
62. Co-operation with the State Bank, Letter from Sir Walter Scott and Sir John Marks to Premier Dunstan 24 July 1975.
63. ibid.
64. ibid.
65. SAPD HA, 19 August 1975.
66. ibid.
67. Minutes of the Board of Trustees, 30 October 1975 file number 79832.
68. ibid.
69. SAPD HA, 17 October 1973, p. 1287.
70. Minutes of the Board of Trustees, 7 January 1976, p. 79545.
71. Letter from the General Manager Mr. Shepperd to Premier Dunstan, 19 September 1974.
72. Bob Bakewell memo to Mr. Shepperd, 12 February 1976.
73. Shepperd's memo to Mr. Bakewell, 4 March 1976.
74. General Manager Shepperd's memo to the Savings Bank Trustees, 12 March 1976.
75. ibid.
76. General Manager Shepperd's memo to the Savings Bank Trustees, 12 March 1976.

77. SAPD HA, 19 February 1976, p. 2185.
78. ibid.
79. ibid.
80. ibid.
81. ibid.
82. SAPD HA, 10 February 1976, p. 2187.
83. ibid, p. 2191.
84. *Advertiser*, editorial, 11 February 1976.
85. Don Dunstan, Chifley Memorial Lecture, University of Melbourne, cited in the *Bulletin*, 31 July 1970.
86. *Bulletin*, 31 July 1970.
87. Letter of cooperation between the two boards, 18 March 1976.
88. Minutes of the Board of Trustees, 10 June 1976, file number 80138.
89. ibid.
90. ibid.
91. Minutes of the Board of Trustees, 7 January 1977, file number 81391.
92. ibid.
93. ibid.
94. ibid.
95. General Manager's memo to the Board of Trustees, 13 March 1977, filed under CM4.
96. Minutes of the Board of Trustees, 12 February 1978, file number 82388.
97. Minutes of the Board of Trustees, 16 March 1978, file number 82484.
98. ibid.
99. Savings Bank of South Australia Annual Report, 30 June 1978.
100. ibid.
101. State Bank of South Australia Minutes, 1926–1984, 21 December 1976.
102. ibid.
103. ibid.
104. ibid.
105. ibid.
106. ibid.
107. SAPD HA, 29 November 1977, p. 1082.
108. ibid, p. 1087.
109. ibid, p. 1087.
110. SAPD LC, 29 November 1977, p. 1087.
111. ibid, p. 1245.
112. SAPD HA, 7 December 1977, p. 1282.
113. SAPD HA, 8 December 1977, p. 1313.
114. Minutes of the Board of Trustees, 16 October 1978.
115. Correspondence between Shroder Narling & Co Ltd on a Contingency Proposal, 5 August 1979 to the Board of the Bank of Adelaide.
116. Sykes, T. *Two Centuries of Panic*, Young N., *Figuratively Speaking*.
117. The Reserve Bank was keen to protect its interests and put pressure on the Bank of Adelaide Board to make a deal with the merger shareholders to seek the bank. At the meeting held at the Reserve Bank offices in Adelaide, Sunday 23 September 1979, present were Premier Tonkin, Under Treasurer Ron Barnes, Assistant Under Treasurer Basil Kidd, Governor Reserve Bank of Australia, H.W. Knight Deputy Governor D. Sanders and Chairman of the Participating Banks in the loan Consortium R.J. White. Governor Knight from the outset 'made it clear that he would be very frank in disclosing information of a highly confidential and sensitive nature to achieve our objective'. He said that 'the eyes of the world are now on us', 'we have not had a bank collapse for nearly 50 years', however the 'Bank of Adelaide and its subsidiary savings bank are basically good business but F.C.A. has been allowed to grow roughly to an equal size and its current problems are therefore beyond the capacity of the bank'. In response, Premier Tonkin 'outlined his serious concern that the developing lobby will

be able to carry the day at the shareholders' meeting.' The Reserve Bank governor suggested that 'the best course of action, within the bounds of propriety, was seen to be to encourage a favourable vote at the shareholders' meeting'. As the Reserve Bank could not be seen to make a public stance, it was best that the 'major shareholders', the AMP and John Martins, declare their intentions to support the ANZ offer. (Minutes of the confidential meeting between the Reserve Bank and Premier Tonkin, Sunday 23 September 1979.)

118. *Advertiser,* 16 October 1979 the *News,* 15 October 1979.
119. P.P. McGuiness, 'How Harry Knight buried bank inquiry in words' *National Times*, 17 November 1975.
120. *Advertiser*, 20 November 1979.
121. State Bank of South Australia Minutes, 1926–1984, 15 January 1980.
122. ibid.
123. ibid.
124. ibid.
125. ibid.
126. State Bank of South Australia Minutes, 1926–1984, 1 March 1980.
127. State Bank of South Australia Minutes, 1926–1984, 1 April 1980.
128. ibid.
129. ibid.
130. ibid.
131. ibid.
132. State Bank of South Australia Minutes, 1926–1984, 3 July 1980.
133. ibid.
134. State Bank of South Australia Minutes, 1926–1984, 23 October 1979.
135. ibid.
136. ibid.
137. ibid.
138. State Bank of South Australia Minutes, 1926–1984, 17 December 1980.
139. ibid.
140. ibid.
141. ibid.
142. State Bank of South Australia Minutes, 1926–1984, 3 July 1980.
143. State Bank of South Australia Minutes, 1926–1984, August 1980.
144. ibid.
145. ibid.
146. ibid.
147. Memo from the Attorney General to the State Bank Board of Management, 23 February 1981.
148. Correspondence between Premier Tonkin and Chairman Barrett, 10 December 1980.
149. Correspondence between solicitor McEwin and Johnson and the Savings Bank General Manager, 18 November 1980.
150. Acting General Manager K. Matthews memo 'Some Aspects of Recent Performance', March 1981.
151. ibid.
152. ibid.
153. Letter from Acting General Manager K. Matthews to Premier Tonkin, filed with Board Minutes, 26 March 1981, file number 85906.
154. Minutes of the Board of Trustees, 26 March, file number 85900.
155. Premier Tonkins letter filed with Minutes of the Board of Trustees, 13 August 1981.
156. Minutes of the Board of Trustees, 5 November 1981, file number 86449A.
157. Correspondence between Chairman Barrett and Premier Tonkin, 4 January 1982.
158. Correspondence over the amendments between General Manager Simmons to Under Treasurer R.D. Barnes, 22 January 1982.
159. SAPD HA, 13 November 1981, p. 1864.

160. ibid, p. 1864.
161. ibid, p. 1864.
162. Correspondence between General Manager Simmons and Premier Tonkin, May 1982. See also Strategic Development Plan by General Manager Simmons, May 1982.

Chapter 5

1. SAPD HA 19 November 1981, p. 2091.
2. SAPD HA 3 March 1981, p. 3292.
3. SAPD LL 2 June 1981, p. 4218.
4. Interview with the Author, 15 February 1994.
5. Bannon, J. Australian Labor Party Economic Statement, May 1982.
6. ibid.
7. ibid.
8. Interview with the Author, 15 February 1994.
9. Badcock, B. 'Was the South Australian Labor Party Struck down by a Bus?', *Politics*, 17, 1, May 1982.
10. Hasluck, N. *Offcuts, from a Legal Literacy Life*, 1993, Nedlands, Univ. of Western Australia Press, p. 26.
11. Bannon, J. 'Overcoming the Unintended Consequences of Federation', *Australian Journal of Public Administration*, Vol. 46, No. 1, pp. 1–9.
12. Letter from Mr Seaman, Chair of the State Bank (1896) to Premier Bannon, 9 February 1983.
13. State Bank of South Australia (1896), Final Report, 30 June 1983.
14. ibid.
15. ibid.
16. State Bank of South Australia (1984) First Annual Report, 30 June 1984.
17. ibid.
18. Kowalick, I. transcript to the State Bank Royal Commission, Justice S. Jacobs, 1993 SBSA RC, 1993.
19. MAG minutes, tabled at RC into SBSA, 1993.
20. SAPD HA, 29 November 1983, p. 2034.
21. ibid, p. 2031.
22. ibid, p. 2056.
23. ibid, p. 2057.
24. ibid, p. 2036.
25. ibid, p. 2057.
26. ibid, p. 2449.
27. ibid, p. 2449.
28. State Bank of South Australia (1984) Annual Report 30 June 1988.
29. ibid.
30. ibid.
31. Kowalick, transcript to the RC into the SBSA, 1993.
32. SAPD HA 29 November 1983, p. 2058.
33. Interview with the author, 15 February 1994.
34. SAPD HA 29 November, 1983, p. 2035.
35. ibid, p. 2056.
36. Interview with the Author, 15 February 1994.
37. ibid.
38. Baudrillard, J. 'Simulacra and Simulations' in Jean Baudrillard *Selected Writings*, edited with an Introduction by Mark Poster, Stanford University Press, 1988, p. 182.
39. RC into SBSA, final report (3), presented by J.R. Mansfield QC,. September 1993, p. 237.
40. RC into SBSA, first report, presented by Honourable S.J. Jacobs AOQC, November 1992, p. 89.

41. RC into the SBSA, 1 1992, p. 121.
42. ibid, p. 293.
43. ibid, p. 293.
44. RC into SBSA, 3, 1993, p. 240.
45. Interview with the author, 15 February, 1994.
46. Bannon, J. submission to the RC into the SBSA.
47. SAPD HA, 29 November 1983 p. 2060.
48. ibid, p. 2060.
49. ibid, p. 2060.
50. ibid, p. 2060.
51. ibid, p. 2060.
52. SAPD LC, 7 December 1983, p. 2451.
53. ibid, p. 2451.
54. ibid, p. 2451.
55. AGR into SBSA 1993, 6–95.
56. ibid, 6 , 95.
57. ibid, 6, 93.
58. ibid, 6, 93.
59. RC into SBSA, 1992, p. 21.
60. ibid, p. 69.
61. AGR into SBSA, 1993, pp. 3, 22.
62. Interview with the Author, 15 February 1994.
63. Simon, H.A. *Administrative Behaviour: a study of decision making process in administrative organisation*, 2nd. edn, New York, Macmillan, 1957.
64. Interview with the Author, 15 February 1994.
65. Barnes, V. *South Australian Biographies*, Blue Book of South Australia, Netley, Griffin Press, 1980, p.100.
66. *Advertiser*, 2 October 1991.
67. Clark, T.M. evidence given to the House of Representatives, Standing Committee on Finance and Public Administration, Adelaide, Friday 27 September 1991, p. 3772.
68. Abbott, M. QC, in House of Representatives, Standing Committee on Finance and Public Administration, Adelaide, Friday 27 September, 1991, p. 3796.
69. *Advertiser*, 21 February 1991.
70. *Advertiser*, 7 July 1991.
71. *Advertiser*, 15 February 1991.
72. *Advertiser*, 14 October 1992.
73. *Advertiser*, 7 August 1991.
74. ibid.
75. ibid.
76. AGR into SBSA 1993, p. 1, 25.
77. ibid, pp. 1, 25.
78. ibid, pp. 1, 21.
79. Simmon's submission to the RC into SBSA, 1992.
80. Abbott, M. QC, submission on behalf of the Board of Directors, RC into SBSA, 1993.
81. Simmons' submission to the RC into SBSA, 1992.
82. Grossman, L. *It's a Sin, Essays on Post Modern Politics of Culture*, Sydney, Sydney University Press, 1988, p. 32.
83. Interview with the Author, 15 February 1994.
84. Bannon, J. submission to the RC into SBSA, 1992.
85. Searcy, evidence to RC into SBSA, 1992.
86. Interview with the Author, 15 February 1994.
87. ibid.
88. RC into SBSA Volume 2 1993, p. 19.
89. ibid, p. 21.
90. AGR into SBSA 1993, pp. 10, 21.

91. ibid, pp. 10, 21.
92. *Advertiser*, 16 February 1991; *News* 28 February 1991; *Advertiser*, 23 November 1997.
93. *Advertiser*, 16 February, 1991.
94. *Advertiser*, 17 February 1991.
95. AGR into SBSA, 1993, pp. 21–18.
96. ibid, pp. 21–16.
97. ibid, pp. 21–16.
98. Interview with the Author, 15 February 1994.
99. *News*, 20 October, 1987.
100. *News*, 19 February 1988.
101. Interview with the Author, 15 February 1994.
102. ibid.

Chapter 6

1. Tim Marcus Clark, promotional talk 'State Bank of South Australia in the State of South Australia', April 1985.
2. ibid.
3. ibid.
4. State Bank of South Australia, First Annual Report, 30 June 1984.
5. ibid.
6. ibid.
7. Report of the Auditor-General on an Investigation into the State Bank of South Australia, Adelaide, State Print, 1993 (hereafter AGR, 1993).
8. AGR into SBSA 1993, pp. 2–15.
9. ibid, 1–23.
10. ibid, pp. 1–47.
11. ibid, pp. 1–27.
12. Paddison, S. Evidence to House of Representative Standing Committee on Finance and Public Administration, 30 April,. 1991, p. 1510.
13. *Asia Banking*, 1 May 1987.
14. AGR into SBSA, 1993, pp. 1–47.
15. ibid, pp. 4, 46.
16. ibid, pp. 4, 46.
17. ibid, pp. 3, 23.
18. ibid, pp. 3, 23.
19. ibid, pp. 1, 24.
20. ibid, pp. 4, 46.
21. ibid, pp. 4, 46.
22. ibid, pp. 3, 23.
23. ibid, pp. 3, 23.
24. ibid, pp. 3, 23.
25. ibid, pp. 3, 22.
26. ibid, pp. 3, 22.
27. ibid, pp. 3, 21.
28. ibid, pp. 3, 21.
29. ibid pp. 3, 22.
30. ibid, pp. 3, 22.
31. ibid, pp. 3, 21.
32. ibid, pp. 3, 22.
33. ibid, pp. 3, 25.
34. ibid, pp. 3, 21.
35. ibid, pp. 3, 26.
36. ibid, pp. 1, 23.

37. ibid, pp. 4, 6.
38. ibid, pp. 4, 6.
39. ibid, pp. 4, 6.
40. ibid, pp. 4, 6.
41. ibid, pp. 5, 30.
42. ibid, pp. 2, 16.
43. ibid, pp. 5, 30.
44. ibid, pp. 3, 20.
45. ibid, pp. 1, 64.
46. ibid, pp. 5, 42.
47. ibid, pp. 5, 42.
48. ibid, pp. 5, 41.
49. ibid, pp. 5, 42.
50. ibid, pp. 5, 42.
51. ibid, pp. 5, 42.
52. ibid, pp. 1, 77.
53. ibid, pp. 5, 42.
54. ibid, pp. 5, 33.
55. ibid, pp. 5, 36.
56. ibid, pp. 1, 47.
57. ibid, pp. 5, 42.
58. ibid, pp. 5, 34.
59. ibid, pp. 19, 62.
60. ibid, pp. 19, 62.
61. ibid, pp. 19, 62.
62. ibid, pp. 19, 62; see also M. Stutchbury, *Boom to Bust: the recession Australia had to have?* North Sydney, Financial Review Press, 1991, p. 8.
63. ibid, pp. 19, 63.
64. ibid, pp. 19, 62.
65. ibid, pp. 19, 62.
66. AGR into SBSA, 1992, p. 36.
67. AGR into SBSA, 1993, pp. 19, 66 and AGR into SBSA, 1993, p. 1.
68. ibid, pp. 19, 96.
69. ibid, pp. 9, 54.
70. ibid, pp. 19, 55.
71. ibid, pp. 19, 56.
72. RC into SBSA, 1, 1992, p. 135.
73. RC into SBSA, 2, 1993, p. 48.
74. ibid, p. 45.
75. ibid, p. 47.
76. ibid, pp. 19, 98.
77. ibid, pp. 19, 97.
78. ibid, pp. 19, 99.
79. ibid, pp. 19, 78.
80. ibid, pp. 19, 99.
81. ibid, pp. 19, 118.
82. *Advertiser*, 13 March 1991.
83. AGR into SBSA, 1993, pp. 19, 29.
84. ibid, pp. 19, 62.
85. ibid, pp. 27, 15.
86. ibid, pp. 27, 16.
87. ibid, pp. 27, 15.
88. ibid, pp. 27, 15.
89. ibid, pp. 27, 16.
90. ibid, pp. 27, 13.

91. ibid, pp. 27, 15.
92. ibid, pp. 27, 17.
93. ibid, pp. 27, 17.
94. ibid, pp. 27, 17.
95. ibid, pp. 27, 16.
96. ibid, pp. 27, 16.
97. ibid, pp. 27, 16.
98. ibid, pp. 27, 16.
99. ibid, pp. 27, 19.
100. ibid, pp. 27, 20.
101. ibid, pp. 27, 24.
102. ibid, pp. 27, 24.
103. ibid, pp. 27, 25.
104. ibid, pp. 27, 19.
105. ibid, pp. 27, 23.
106. ibid, pp. 27, 23.
107. ibid, pp. 27, 23.
108. ibid, pp. 27, 27.
109. ibid, pp. 27.
110. ibid, pp. 27, 28.
111. ibid, pp. 27, 28.
112. ibid, pp. 27, 29.

Chapter 7

1. AGR into SBSA, 1993, pp. 1, 43.
2. ibid, pp. 1, 23.
3. ibid, pp. 20, 37.
4. ibid, pp. 1, 24.
5. ibid, pp.1, 21.
6. ibid, pp.20, 31.
7. ibid, pp.1, 47.
8. ibid, pp.1, 97.
9. ibid, pp.1, 97.
10. ibid, pp.20, 17.
11. ibid, pp.20, 31.
12. ibid, pp.20, 31.
13. ibid, pp.20, 37.
14. ibid, pp.20, 44.
15. ibid, pp.20, 44.
16. ibid, pp.20, 31.
17. ibid, pp.20, 91.
18. Peters, T. and Waterman, R. *In Search of Excellence*, Sun Tzu, trans T. Cleary, *The Art of War*, Boston, Random House, 1988.
19. Ward. P, 'Bonfire of the Vanities', *Australian*, 19 September 1993, p. 4.
20. AGR into SBSA, 1993, pp. 20, 18.
21. ibid, pp. 20, 18.
22. ibid, pp. 20, 25.
23. ibid, pp. 20, 14.
24. ibid, pp. 20, 21.
25. ibid, pp. 20, 21.
26. ibid, pp. 20, 21.
27. ibid, pp. 20, 18.
28. ibid, pp. 20, 22.

29. ibid, pp. 20, 59.
30. ibid, pp. 20, 41.
31. ibid, pp. 20, 37.
32. ibid, pp. 20, 46.
33. ibid, pp. 20, 47.
34. ibid, pp. 1, 98.
35. ibid, pp. 20, 32.
36. ibid, pp. 20, 124.
37. ibid, pp. 19, 143.
38. ibid, pp. 19, 142.
39. ibid, pp. 19, 143.
40. RC into SBSA, 3, 1993, p. 13.
41. AGR into SBSA, 1993, pp. 20, 38.
42. ibid, pp. 20, 38.
43. AGR into SBSA, 1993, pp. 1, 43.
44. ibid, pp. 1, 43.
45. Clark, T.M. Submission to the RC into SBSA, 1992.
46. ibid.
47. AGR into SBSA, 1993, pp. 8, 19.
48. ibid, pp. 8, 44.
49. AGR into SBSA, 1993, pp. 8, 44–45.
50. ibid, pp. 8, 45.
51. ibid, pp. 8, 45.
52. ibid, pp. 7, 15.
53. ibid, pp. 7, 15.
54. ibid, pp. 7, 15.
55. ibid, pp. 7, 15.
56. ibid, pp. 7, 17.
57. ibid, pp. 7, 19.
58. ibid, pp. 7, 20.
59. ibid, pp. 7, 22.
60. ibid, pp. 7, 25.
61. ibid, pp. 7, 27.
62. ibid, pp. 7, 28.
63. ibid, pp. 7, 80.
64. ibid, pp. 7, 80.
65. ibid, pp. 7, 80.
66. ibid, pp. 23, 39.
67. ibid, pp. 23, 39.
68. ibid, pp. 23, 39.
69. ibid, pp. 23, 39.
70. ibid, pp. 7, 126.
71. ibid, pp. 7, 126.
72. ibid, pp. 7, 127.
73. ibid, pp. 7, 145.
74. ibid, pp. 7, 150.
75. ibid, pp. 7, 151.
76. ibid, pp. 7, 152.
77. ibid, pp. 7, 160.
78. ibid, pp. 7, 162.
79. ibid, pp. 8, 153.
80. ibid, pp. 7, 144.
81. ibid, pp. 7, 145.
82. ibid, pp. 7, 135.
83. ibid, pp. 7, 135.

84. ibid, pp. 1, 46.
85. ibid, pp. 7, 135.
86. ibid, pp. 8, 23.
87. ibid, pp. 8, 23.
88. ibid, pp. 1, 28.
89. ibid, pp. 7, 138.
90. ibid, pp. 8, 26.
91. ibid, pp. 8, 26.
92. ibid, pp.8, 34.
93. Bannon, submission to RC into SBSA, 1992.
94. Kowalick, I., House of Representatives Standing Committee on Finance and Public Administration, 30 April 1991, p. 1560.
95. AGR into SBSA, 1993, pp. 15–22.
96. ibid, pp. 15, 88.
97. ibid, pp. 15, 34.
98. ibid, pp. 15, 81.
99. ibid, pp. 15, 36.
100. ibid, pp. 15, 75.
101. ibid, pp. 15, 34.
102. ibid, pp. 15, 144.
103. ibid, pp. 15, 144.
104. ibid, pp. 15, 148.
105. ibid, pp. 15, 149.
106. ibid, pp. 15, 150.
107. ibid, pp. 15, 51.
108. ibid, pp. 15, 79.
109. ibid, pp. 15, 180.
110. ibid, pp. 15, 73.
111. ibid, pp. 15, 74.
112. ibid, pp. 15, 83.
113. ibid, pp. 15, 84.
114. ibid, pp. 1, 77.
115. ibid, pp. 15, 85.
116. ibid, pp. 15, 86.
117. ibid, pp. 15, 82.
118. ibid, pp. 15, 89.
119. ibid, pp. 15, 89.
120. ibid, pp. 15, 89.
121. ibid, pp. 15, 91.
122. ibid, pp. 15, 99.
123. ibid, pp. 15, 101.
124. ibid, pp. 15, 102.
125. ibid, pp. 15, 102.
126. ibid, pp. 15, 111.
127. ibid, pp. 15, 112.
128. ibid, pp. 15, 112.
129. ibid, pp. 15, 160.
130. ibid, pp. 15, 160.
131. *Advertiser*, 6 March 1999 and 30 April 1999.
132. *Advertiser*, 30 April 1999.
133. AGR into SBSA, 1993, pp. 15, 184.
134. AGR into SBSA, 1993, pp. 15, 184.
135. ibid, pp. 15, 188.
136. ibid, pp. 15, 182.
137. ibid, pp. 15, 183.

138. ibid, pp. 15, 111.
139. Interview with the Author, 15 February 1994.
140. Sykes, T., *The Bold Rider, Behind Australia's Corporate Collapses*, St Leonards, Allen & Unwin, 1994, p. 576.
141. Pierpoint' making a comment on the failure of Peat Marwick Mitchell and Company to notice any irregularities in the accounts of the Bank of Adelaide, the *Bulletin*, 29 May 1979.
142. Bannon, J., submission to RC into SBSA, 1997.
143. Sheridan, T. (Auditor-General), Auditor-General's Report to the Parliament, 30 June 1989.
144. ibid.
145. RC into SBSA, 3, 1993., p. 200.
146. ibid. p. 225 and *Advertiser*, 6 March 1999.

Chapter 8

1. Savings Bank of South Australia, *Our Century: A History of the First Hundred Years of the Savings Bank of South Australia, 1848–1948*, published by the bank, 1984, p. 59.
2. ibid, p. 59.
3. Feature article appearing in the *Journal of British Fire Service Association*, November 1987.
4. Clark, T.M., Letter to State Bank of South Australia Customers, 8 November, 1988.
5. Clark, T.M., *Australian*, 29 August 1987.
6. ibid.
7. Clark, T.M., *Advertiser*, 29 August 1987.
8. *Advertiser*, 14 January 1988.
9. AGR into SBSA, 1993, pp. 24, 9.
10. ibid, pp.1, 112.
11. AGR into SBSA, 1993, pp. 24, 15.
12. ibid, pp. 24, 16.
13. ibid, pp. 24, 17.
14. ibid, pp. 24, 17.
15. ibid, pp. 24, 17.
16. RC into SBSA, 1, 1992, p. 84.
17. AGR into SBSA, 1993, pp. 24, 28.
18. ibid, pp. 24, 41.
19. RC into SBSA, 1, 1992, p. 83.
20. ibid, p. 187.
21. ibid, p. 187.
22. ibid, p. 187.
23. ibid, p. 187.
24. ibid, p. 187.
25. AGR into SBSA, 1993, pp. 24, 23.
26. ibid, pp. 24, 23.
27. ibid, pp. 24, 31.
28. Bannon, J., submission to the RC into SBSA, 1, 1992.
29. RC into SBSA, 1, 1992, p. 189.
30. ibid, p. 189.
31. AGR into SBSA, 1, 1992, pp. 14, 19.
32. Thomas, D. *Adelaide Review*, March, 1994.
33. AGR into SBSA, 1993, pp. 14, 13.
34. ibid, pp. 14, 51.
35. ibid, pp. 14, 52.
36. RC into SBSA, 1992, p. 198.

37. ibid, p. 198.
38. AGR into SBSA, 1993, pp. 14, 17.
39. ibid, pp. 14, 21.
40. ibid, pp. 14, 25.
41. ibid, pp. 14, 26.
42. ibid, pp. 14, 26.
43. ibid, pp. 14, 28.
44. ibid, pp. 14, 29.
45. ibid, pp. 14, 29.
46. ibid, pp. 14, 30.
47. RC into SBSA, 1993, pp. 14, 31.
48. ibid, p. 202.
49. ibid, p. 202.
50. AGR into SBSA, 1993, pp. 14, 31.
51. ibid, pp. 14, 34.
52. ibid, pp. 14, 36.
53. ibid, pp. 14, 37.
54. RC into SBSA, p. 88.
55. RC into SBSA, 3, 1993, p. 99.
56. ibid, p. 99.
57. ibid, p. 102.
58. ibid, p.88.
59. AGR into SBSA, 1993, pp. 9, 115.
60. *Australian Financial Review*, 13 November 1987.
61. ibid.
62. AGR into SBSA, 1993, pp. 9, 8.
63. ibid, pp. 1, 115.
64. ibid, 1993, pp. 9, 38.
65. ibid, pp. 9, 38.
66. ibid, pp. 9, 40.
67. ibid, pp. 9, 36.
68. ibid, pp. 9, 68.
69. ibid, pp. 9, 69.
70. ibid, pp. 9, 42.
71. ibid, pp. 9, 70.
72. ibid, pp. 9, 71.
73. ibid, pp. 9, 70.
74. ibid, pp. 9, 19.
75. ibid, pp. 9, 72.
76. ibid, pp. 9, 76.
77. ibid, pp. 9, 76.
78. *Australian Financial Review*, 1 April, 1993.
79. AGR into SBSA, 1993, pp. 27, 48.
80. ibid, pp. 33, 46.
81. ibid, p. 191.
82. ibid, pp. 33, 5.
83. AGR into SBSA, 1993, pp. 33, 19.
84. RC into SBSA, 3, 1993, p. 194; *Advertiser*, 9 December 1991; *Advertiser*, 24 February, 1991.
85. AGR into SBSA, 1993, pp. 33, 11.
86. ibid, pp. 33, 11.
87. ibid, pp. 33, 11.
88. ibid, pp. 33, 42.
89. ibid, pp. 33, 42.
90. ibid, pp. 33, 47.

91. ibid, pp. 33, 54.
92. ibid, pp. 33, 57.
93. *Advertiser*, 13 December 1990.
94. *Advertiser*, July 1992.
95. AGR into SBSA, 1993, pp. 33, 54.
96. *Advertiser*, 4 January 1991.
97. *Advertiser*, 22 May 1991.
98. *Advertiser*, 10 October 1992.
99. ibid.
100. AGR into SBSA, 1993, pp. 33, 65.
101. ibid, pp. 33, 28.
102. ibid, pp. 33, 28.
103. ibid, pp. 33, 61.
104. ibid, pp. 33, 13.
105. *Advertiser*, 6 March 1999.
106. SAPD HA, 2 March 1999, p. 759.
107. ibid, p. 759.
108. ibid, p. 760.
109. ibid, p. 761.

Chapter 9

A version of this chapter first appeared in the journal *Policy, Organisation and Society*, Summer 1997, pp. 125–149, and is reproduced here with permission of the editors.

1. Bannon, J., Interview with the Author, 15 February 194.
2. See Baudrillard, J., 'Simulacra and Simulations', in Jean Baudrillard, *Selected Writings*, edited by Mark Poster, Stanford University Press, 1988, pp. 119–149; Postman, N. and Powers, S. *How to Watch TV news*, New York, Penguin, 1992; McRobbie, A, *Postmodernism and Popular Culture*, London, Routledge, 1999, pp. 16–19; Atheide, P.L., and Snow, R.P. *Media Worlds in post-journalism era*, New York, Aldine de Gruyter, 1991.
3. AGR into SBSA, 1993, 1, 20–24.
4. *Advertiser*, April 1991; see also Kenny, C. *A State of Denial*, Adelaide, Wakefield Press, 1998; Peachman, A. (ed) *Westminster Inc, A survey of three states in the 1980s*, Annadale, Federation Press, 1995.
5. RC into SBSA, 3, 1993, pp. 31–49.
6. *Advertiser*, 7 September 1993.
7. AGR into SBSA, 1993, pp;. 1–13 to 1–18.
8. Bhaktin, M., *Rabelais and his World*, Cambridge; Kristeva, J., *The Kristeva Reader*, edited by Toril Moi, Oxford, Basil Blackwell, 1986.
9. Baudrillard, pp. 119–149; see also McNoir, B. *News and Journalism in the UK*, London, Routledge 1998; Postman, N. and Powers, J. *How to Watch TV News*, London, Methuen, 1982, Snow, R.P. *Creating Media Culture*, California, Sage, 1983.
10. On legal discourse see G. Turkel, 'Michel Foucault: Law Power and Knowledge' *Journal of Law and Society*, U17, 2, Summer 1990, pp. 170–194; L. Sackett, 'A post-modern panopticon – the Royal Commission into Aboriginal Deaths in Custody', in *Journal of Social Issues*, V. 28, 3. 1993, pp. 228–244 .
11. Baudrillard, J. *The Transparency of Evil: Essays on Extreme Phenomena*, tr. J, Benedict, London, Verso, 1993; Helen Grace 'Business, Pleasure, Narrative: The Folktale in our times', in R. Diprose and R. Ferrell, *Cartographies: Post-structuralism and the Mapping of Bodies and Spaces*, North Sydney, Allen & Unwin, 191, p. 119.

12. At an Australian Institute of Public Administration Conference, in Adelaide, titled the 'Truth of the Matter,' 28 May 1993; Ken MacPherson spoke scathingly of how witnesses could not find time, in their all-so-busy schedules, to appear before him and of how some witnesses had the audacity to use coffee breaks to walk out (mid cross-examination), with their counsel in tow, obliging him to subpoena them for another appearance. At one level this is a comedy of errors at another its a tragedy played out at public expense.
13. The *Advertiser* had set a team to report on the Royal Commission and the issues that arose from it and around it, the team was headed by their senior political journalist, Nick Cater. Cater constructed each witness who appeared before the Commission around the peg of Bannon's need to prove his innocence and this view predominated throughout the second phase of the Commission. An indication of Cater's political line is to be found in a piece he wrote on the eve of Bannon's appearance before the commission, where he commented that, 'The length of the Premier's arm has been the dominating issue in the Commission so far as it has examined the relationship between the Government and the bank in the lead up to the Bank's collapse in February 1991'. *Advertiser*, Tuesday 11 August, 1992, p. 13. For other examples of 'trial by media' see Nick Cater, 'Bannon told of Concerns' *Advertiser*, 14 May 1992; 'Faithful servant throws mean punch at master', *Advertiser*, 30 May 1992; 'Porky-pie a vital question unlikely to be answered', *Advertiser*, 4 July 1992; 'Dancing Around the Issue', *Advertiser*, 21 August 1992.
14. *Advertiser*, 2 July 1992, p. 3.
15. *Advertiser*, 4 July, 1992.
16. These diaries were linked to claims made by the *Advertiser*'s investigative journalist, David Hallenby, that 'a source close to the Auditor-General's inquiry' had leaked to Hallenby that the investigation had uncovered 'criminal activity' on an 'incredible scale' within the SBSA, see Hallenby, the *Advertiser*, 7 July, 1992. When the Auditor-General's report was published these allegations evaporated and the *Advertiser* settled out of court for an alleged amount of $300,000 to the SBSA.
17. *Advertiser*, 10 July 1992.
18. *Advertiser*, 11 August 1992.
19. Bannon, J., Transcript to RC into SBSA, 11 August, 1992, pp. 14212–14213.
20. Bannon, J., Transcript to RC into SBSA, 11 August, 1992, pp.14292.
21. On the debates on the construction of legal truths and on legal positivism see C. Douzinas, R. Warrington and S. McVeigh, *Postmodern Jurisprudence, The law of text in the text of law*, London: Routledge, 1991 pp. 21–24; P. Goodrich, *Legal Discourse*, London: MacMillan, 1987; F. Burton and P. Carlen, *Official Discourse*, London : Routledge & Kegan Paul, 1979, pp 60–71; and J.Brumer, 'Psychology, morality, and the Law', in D.N. Robinson, *Social Discourse and Moral Judgement*, California: Academic Press, 1992, pp.99–112.
22. Lawson, R. QC, submission to RC into SBSA, 1992. Lawson was later to be elected to the Legislative Council for the Liberal Party.
23. Doyle, J. QC, submission to the RC into SBSA, 1992.
24. *Advertiser*, 18 November 1992.
25. ibid.
26. Jacobs writes that: 'In detective fiction, one usually has to read to the end of the narrated investigation to discover 'who did it' ... Occasionally, however, the author foreshadows the end of the story in a prologue: accordingly the substance of the present chapter is devoted to summary of the conclusions of the Commission with respect to a number of important issues touching the relationship of the bank to the Government and the nature and adequacy of communication pursuant to that relationship. Most of the conclusions will be clarified and sometimes further explained or expanded in subsequent chapters of this report'. Royal Commission, First Report, November 1992, p. 18.
27. RC into SBSA, 1992, p. 19.

28. ibid, p. 19.
29. ibid, p. 19.
30. ibid, p. 22.
31. ibid, p. 21.
32. ibid, pp. 22–23.
33. ibid, p. 172.
34. On the populist thesis of reducing leaders and their followers/governments to a 'march of folly' see, B. Tuchman, *The March of Folly, from Troy to Vietnam*, London: M. Joseph, 1984.
35. RC into SBSA, 1992, p. 389.
36. ibid, p. 389.
37. ibid, p. 389.
38. ibid, p. 391.
39. ibid, p. 2.
40. ibid, pp. 16–21.
41. ibid, p. 23.
42. *Advertiser*, 10 March 1993.
43. ibid.
44. ibid.
45. AGR into SBSA, 1993, pp. 1–19.
46. ibid, pp. 1–20.
47. ibid, pp. 1–23.
48. ibid, pp. 1–23.
49. ibid, pp. 1, 24.
50. ibid, pp. 1, 24.
51. ibid, pp. 1, 23.
52. ibid, pp. 1, 26.
53. ibid, pp. 1, 22.
54. ibid, pp. 1, 24.
55. ibid, pp. 1, 39.
56. ibid, pp. 1, 39.
57. *Advertiser*, 1 April 1993.
58. ibid.
59. AGR into SBSA, 1993, pp. 27, 43.
60. *Australian Financial Review*, 1 July 1993.
61. ibid.
62. *Advertiser*, 1 July, 1993.
63. *Advertiser*, 6 September, 1993.
64. The literature on the adverse affects of the globalisation of national economies and on their foreign exchange and financial systems is wide, a sample of this literature is: 'Fear of Finance', the *Economist*, September 19 1992; P.G. Cerny, 'Patterns of Financial Globalisation: Financial Market Structure and the Problem of Governance', *Contemporary Trends In Financial Globalisation Conference*, ISA, Washington, 28 March–1 April 1994; M. Moran, 'The State and the Financial Services Revolution: A Comparative Analysis', *Western European Politics*, v.17, 3, pp. 158–178; P. England, 'Financial Deregulation in Sweden', *European Economic Review*, 34, 1990, pp. 385–393; S. Strange, 'Finance, Information and Power', *Review of International Studies*, 16, 1990, pp. 259–274; S. Strange, *Casino Capitalism*; New York,: Blackwell, 1986; F. Block, *The Origins of International Economic Disorder: a study of the United States international monetary policy from World War 2 to the present*, Berkeley: Univ. of California Press, 1977. It is also possible to see the instability of the global financial system in the collapse of particular financial institutions – see J. R. Bath, *The Great Savings and Loans Debacle*, Washington: AIE press, 1991; H. Armstrong and D. Gross, *Tricontinental, The rise and fall of a merchant bank*, Melbourne University Press, 1995; and Sykes,*The Bold Riders*.

65. As would be apparent, I hope, by now, I am arguing that Commissions on their own cannot facilitate ideological closures – rather it is their representation in the media that is critical in the construction of any commission's ideological affect. There is some discussion of commissions as ideological exercises see for instance, Burton and Carlen, *Official Discourse*; B. Wynne, *Rationality and Ritual, The Windscale Inquiry and Nuclear Decisions in Britain*, St Ives: British Society for the History of Science, 1982; P. Sheriff, 'State Theory, Social Sciences, and Government Commissions', *American Behavioural Scientists*, 26, 5, 1983, pp. 669–80; A. Ashforth, 'Reckoning Schemes of Legitimation: On Commissions of Inquiry as Power/Knowledge Forms', *Journal of Historical Sociology*, v.3, 1, 1987; and see P. Weller (eds), *Royal Commissions and the Making of Public Policy*, Melbourne: MacMillan, 1994.
66. Jameson, F., *Postmodernism or the Cultural Logic of Late Capitalism*, London, Verso 1991, p. 20

Select bibliography

Books and Journal Articles

Achebe, C. *Things Fall Apart*, London, Heinemann, 1958.

Armstrong, H. and Gross, D. *Tricontinental, The rise and fall of a merchant bank*, Melbourne University Press, 1995.

Ashforth, A. 'Reckoning Schemes of Legitimation: On Commissions of Inquiry as Power/Knowledge Forms', *Journal of Historical Sociology*, v.3, 1, 1987.

Atheide, P.L. and Snow, R.P. *Media Worlds in a Post-Journalism Era*, New York, Aldine de Gruyter, 1991.

Badcock, B. 'Was the South Australian Labor Party Struck Down by a Bus?',*Politics*, v.17, 1, May 1982.

Bannon, J. 'Overcoming the Unintended Consequences of Federation', *Australian Journal of Public Administration*, v.46, no.1, pp.1–9.

Barnes, V. *South Australian Biographies*, Blue Book of South Australia, Netley, Griffin Press, 1980.

Bataille. G. *The Accursed Share: An Essay on General Economy*, New York, Zone Books, 1991.

Bath. J.R. *The Great Savings and Loans Debacle*, Washington, AIE press, 1991.

Baudrillard, J. 'Simulacra and Simulations' in *Jean Baudrillard Selected Writings*, ed. Mark Poster, Stanford University Press, 1988.

Baudrillard, J. *The Transparency of Evil: Essays on Extreme Phenomena*, tr. J, Benedict, London, Verso, 1993.

Bhaktin, M. *Rabelais and his World*, trans. H. Iswolsky, Cambridge, Mass., 1968.

Blainey, G. and Hutton, *Gold and Paper: A history of the National Bank of Australia*, Melbourne, Macmillan, 1983.

Block, F. *The Origins of International Economic Disorder: A study of the United States international monetary policy from World War 2 to the present*, Berkeley: Univ. of California Press, 1977.

Boehm, E.A. *Prosperity and Depression in Australia 1887–1897*, Oxford University Press, 1971.

Broomhill, R, *Unemployed workers; a social history of the Great Depression in Adelaide*, St. Lucia, Queensland University Press, 1978.

Brugger, S. (ed.), *South Australia in the 1890s*, Adelaide, Constitutional Museum, 1983.

Brumer, J. 'Psychology, morality, and the Law', in D.N. Robinson, *Social Discourse and Moral Judgement*, California, Academic Press, 1992, pp.99–112.

Burton F. and Carlen, P. *Official Discourse*, London, Routledge & Kegan Paul, 1979.

Butlin, S.J. 'The Beginning of Savings Banks in Australia', *Royal Australian History Society Journal*, vol. xxxiv, 1982, pp.1–46.

Campbell, C. 'C.C. Kingston Radical Liberal and Democrat', Department of History, B.A. Thesis, University of Adelaide, 1976.

Cerny, P.G. 'Patterns of Financial Globalisation: Financial Market Structure and the Problem of Governance', *Contemporary Trends In Financial Globalisation Conference*, ISA, Washington, 1994.

Coghlan, T.A. *Labour and Industry in Australia*, Oxford University Press, 1918, Part V, Chapter ix, (reprint 1965).

Comans, J.G. 'The Irvine Memorial Lecture: The Appointment of Judges to Royal Commission of Inquiry', *Australian Law Journal*, no.57, 1979, p.159.

Diprose, R. and R. Ferrell, *Cartographies: Post-structuralism and the Mapping of Bodies and Spaces*, North Sydney, Allen & Unwin, 1991, pp.113–126.

Douzinas C., Warrington, R. and McVeigh, S. *Postmodern Jurisprudence, The law of text in the text of law*, London, Routledge, 1991.

Dunstan, D. 'Who Runs South Australia?', Chifley Memorial Lecture, University of Melbourne, cited in the *Bulletin*, 31 July 1970.

Dunstan, D. *Felicia: the political memoirs of Don Dunstan*, Melbourne, Macmillan, 1981.

England, P. 'Financial Deregulation in Sweden', *European Economic Review*, 34, 1990, pp.385–393.

Ewens, L.J. *The South Australian Savings Bank, The Story of the Pioneer Savings Bank 1841–1848*, (together with an Appreciation of its Secretary John Wotherspoon), Adelaide, Pioneers' Association of SA, (ND).

Fitzpatrick, B., 'On Royal Commissions', *Civil Liberties*, 2, July 1954, pp.1–4.

Foucault, M. *Discipline and Punish, The Birth of the Prison*, trans. A. Sheridan, Middlesex, Penguin, 1975.

Foucault, M. 'On Power' in Michel Foucault, *Politics, Philosophy, Culture Interviews and other Writings 1977-1984* ed. L. Kritzman, New York, 1988.

Garnaut, C. 'Remodelling a Model: the Thousand Homes Scheme in Colonel Light Gardens' *Journal of the Historical Society of South Australia*, no.23, 1995, pp.5–36.

Gibbs, R.M. *Bulls, Bears and Wildcats, A Centenary History of the Stock Exchange of Adelaide*, Adelaide, Peacock Publications, 1988.

Goodrich, P. *Legal Discourse: Studies in linguistics, rhetoric and legal analysis*, London, MacMillan, 1987.

Grace, H. 'Business, Pleasure, Narrative: The Folktale in our times', in R. Diprose and R. Ferrell, *Cartographies: Post-structuralism and the Mapping of Bodies and Spaces*, North Sydney, Allen & Unwin, 1991, pp. 113–126.

Green, R. and Genoff, R. *Making the Future Work: Crisis and Change in the South Australian Economy*, St. Leonards, Allen & Unwin, 1993.

Grossman, L. *It's a Sin, Essays on Post Modern Politics of Culture*, Sydney University Press, 1988.

Hasluck, N. *Offcuts, from a Legal Literary Life*, Nedlands, University of Western Australia Press, 1993.

Hirst, J.B. *Adelaide and the Country from first Settlement in 1788, to the Commonwealth in 1901*, Melbourne, Macmillan, 1965.

Jameson, F. *Postmodernism or the Cultural Logic of Late Capitalism*, London, Verso, 1991.

Kenny, C. *A State of Denial*, Adelaide, Wakefield Press, 1998.

Kristeva, J. *The Kristeva Reader*, edited by Toril Moi, Oxford, Basil, Blackwell 1986.

Lamshed, M. *The South Australian Story*, Adelaide, Advertiser Publishing, 1958.

Lyotard, J.F. *The Postmodern Condition: A Report on Knowledge*, trans, G. Bennington and B. Massumi, Minneapolis, University of Minnesota Press, 1993.

McCarthy, G. 'At Arm's Length the Premier and the Banker' paper presented to the Australasian Political Science Association Conference, Brisbane, 17–19 July 1991.

McCarthy, G., 'Private Culture, Public Loss', in Green, R. and Genoff, R. *Making the Future Work: Crisis and Change in the South Australian Economy*, St. Leonards, Allen & Unwin, 1993, pp.95–113.

McCarthy, G. and Taylor, D., 'The Politics of the Float: Paul Keating and the Deregulation of the Australian Exchange Rate', *Australian Journal of Politics and History*, v.41, no.2, 1995, pp.219–239.

Macfarlane, I. 'Money Credit and the Demand for Debt', *Reserve Bank of Australia Bulletin*, May, 1989.
Macfarlane, I. 'Credit and Debt, Part II', *Reserve Bank of Australia Bulletin*, May 1990.
Manning, G.H. and Haydon Manning, *Worth Fighting For: Work and Industrial Relations in the Banking Industry in South Australia*, Adelaide, Australian Bank Employers Union, South Australia and Northern Territory, 1989.
Marsden, S. *Business, Charity and Sentiment, The South Australian Housing Trust 1936-1986*, Adelaide, Wakefield Press, 1986.
Matthew, J.E. *The Commonwealth Banking Corporation: Its Background, History and Present Operations*, Sydney, Australia, 1980.
McGuiness, P.P. 'How Harry Knight buried bank inquiry in words' *National Times*, 17 November 1975.
McNoir, B. *News and Journalism in the UK*, London, Routledge 1998.
McRobbie, A, *Postmodernism and Popular Culture*, London, Routledge, 1999.
Moran, M. 'The State and the Financial Services Revolution: A Comparative Analysis', *Western European Politics*, v.17, 3, pp.158–178.
Peachman, A. (ed) *Westminster Inc, A Survey of three states in the 1980s*, Annadale, Federation Press, 1995.
Peters, T. and Waterman, R. *In Search of Excellence: lessons from America's best-run companies*, Sydney, Harper & Row, 1982.
Phillips, M.J., 'Some Lessons for the Eighties', *Reserve Bank of Australia Bulletin*, November, 1990.
Postman, N. and Powers, S. *How to Watch TV News*, New York, Penguin, 1992.
Richards, E. 'South Australia and the Great Crash of 1893', in S. Brugger (ed.), *South Australia in the 1890s*, Adelaide, Constitutional Museum, 1983, pp.261–277.
Sackett, L. 'A post-modern panopticon, the Royal Commission into Aboriginal Deaths in Custody', *Journal of Social Issues*, v.28, 3, 1993. pp.228–244.
Sackville, R. 'Royal Commissions in Australia What Price Truth?' *Current Affairs Bulletin*, no.60, v.12, 1984, pp.3–13.
Said, E.W. *Culture and Imperialism*, London, Routledge, 1978.
Savings Bank of South Australia, *Highlights from History 1848-1948*, issued by the Savings Bank of South Australia on the occasion of its Centenary, 11 March 1947.
Sawer, G. 'Should Judges sit on Royal Commissions?' *Nation*, no.40, 1960, pp.7–8.
Shann E. *An Economic History of Australia*, London, Methuen, 1930.
Sheriff, P. 'State Theory, Social Sciences, and Government Commissions', *American Behavioural Scientists*, 26, 5, 1983, pp.669–80.
Simon, H.A. *Administrative Behaviour: a study of decision-making process in administrative organisation*, 2nd. edn, New York, Macmillan, 1957.
Sinclair, W.A. 'Urban boom in Nineteenth-Century Australia, Adelaide and Melbourne', in *Journal of the History Society of South Australia*, 10, 1982, pp.3–15
Sinclair, W.A. *Gross Domestic Product in South Australia, 1861-1938*, Flinders Working Papers in Economic History, Adelaide, Flinders University Press, 1982,
Snow, R.P. *Creating Media Culture*, California, Sage 1983.
Strange, S. *Casino Capitalism*, New York, Blackwell, 1986.
Strange, S. 'Finance, Information and Power', *Review of International Studies*, 16, 1990, pp 259–274.
Stretton, H. *Ideas for Australian Cities*, 2nd ed. Melbourne, Georgian House, 1975.

Stutchbury, M. *Boom to Bust: the recession Australia had to have?* North Sydney, Financial Review Press, 1991.
Sun Tzu, *The Art of War*, trans T. Cleary, Boston, Random House, 1988.
Sykes, T. *The Bold Rider, Behind Australia's Corporate Collapses*, Sydney, Allen & Unwin, 1994.
Sykes, T. *Two Centuries of Panic: A History of Corporate Collapse in Australia*, Sydney, Allen & Unwin, 1988.
Thomas, D. 'Constructing Adelaide - the top ten buildings', *Adelaide Review*, March 1994, pp.12–13.
Tuchman, B. *The March of Folly, from Troy to Vietnam*, London, M. Joseph, 1984.
Turkel, G. 'Michel Foucault: Law Power and Knowledge' *Journal of Law and Society*, v.17, 2, Summer, 1990, pp.170–194.
Wadham, E.J. 'The Political Career of C.C. Kingston', Department of History, M.A. Thesis, University of Adelaide, 1953.
Ward, P. 'Bonfire of the Vanities', *Australian*, 19 September, 1993, p.4.
Weller, P. (eds) *Royal Commissions and the Making of Public Policy*, Melbourne, MacMillan, 1994.
Whitelock, D. *Adelaide: A Sense of Difference, from Colony to Jubilee*, Adelaide, Savvos Publications, 1985.
Wynne, B. *Rationality and Ritual, The Windscale Inquiry and Nuclear Decisions in Britain*, Chalfont St Ives, British Society for the History of Science, 1982.

Official Reports, Submissions, Interviews, and Bank Records

Abbott, M. QC, Address to House of Representatives, Standing Committee on Finance and Public Administration, Adelaide, Friday 27 September, 1991.
Abbott, M. QC, Submission on behalf of the Board of Directors, Royal Commission into State Bank of South Australia, 1993.
Bannon, J. *Australian Labor Party Economic Statement*, May 1982.
Bannon, J, Australian Labor Party Launch, November 1982.
Bannon, J. Submission to the Royal Commission into the State Bank of South Australia, Adelaide, 1992.
Bannon, J. Interview with the Author, 15 February 1994.
Caire, H.M. 'Recent Developments in the Mortgage Lending Field', Proceedings of the Fifth Conference of Senior Officers and Branch Managers, held at Head Office, 26 and 28 January 1946, Adelaide, Savings Bank of South Australia.
Caire, H.M. 'The Bank as Landlord' discussion paper presented at the Savings Bank of South Australia, Proceedings of the Third Conference of Senior Officers and Branch Managers, held at Head Office, 29 and 31 January 1938, Adelaide, Savings Bank of South Australia.
Clark, T.M. Evidence given to the House of Representatives, Standing Committee on Finance and Public Administration, Adelaide, Friday 27 September 1991. Canberra, Australian Government Publishing Services, 1991.
Clark, T.M. Letter to State Bank of South Australia Customers, 8 November, 1988.
Clark, T.M. Submission to the Royal Commission into State Bank of South Australia, Adelaide, 1992.
Dignum, A.C. Dignum Report on Mortgages to the First Annual Managers Conference, Savings Bank of South Australia, 29 January 1936.

George, G. 'The Bank's Public Relations' in The Fifth Conference of Senior Officers and Branch Managers at Branches, held at Head Office, 26 & 28 January 1946. Adelaide, Savings Bank of South Australia.

Jacobs, S.R. AO, QC, First Report into the State Bank of South Australia, November 1992, Adelaide, State Print, 1992.

Jacobs, S.R. AO, QC, Second Report into the State Bank of South Australia, March 1993, Adelaide, State Print, 1993.

Keating, P. Interview with the Author, 11 September, 1990.

Kowalick, I. House of Representatives Standing Committee on Finance and Public Administration, Adelaide, 30 April, 1991. Canberra, Australian Government Publishing Services, 1991.

Kowalick, I. Transcript of the State Bank Royal Commission into the State Bank of South Australia, Adelaide, 1992.

Lawson, R. QC, Submission to Royal Commission into State Bank of South Australia, Adelaide, 1992.

Linn, M.T.J. Report by the Secretary of the Bank's Mortgage Securities, to the Board of Trustees, 7 March 1935, Adelaide, Savings Bank of South Australia records.

MacPherson, K.I. Report of the Auditor-General on an Investigation into the State Bank of South Australia, Volumes 1 to XVI, Adelaide, State Print, 1993.

Mansfield, J.R. QC, State Bank of South Australia Final Report (3) Adelaide, State Print, 1993.

Matthews, K. 'Some Aspects of Recent Performance', Memorandum, March 1981, Adelaide, Savings Bank of South Australia records.

Paddison, S. Evidence to House of Representative Standing Committee on Finance and Public Administration, Adelaide 30 April 1991, Canberra, Australian Government Publishing Service.

Royal Commission on the Thousand Homes Contract, House of Assembly Parliamentary Papers, Adelaide, State Print, 1925.

Savings Bank of South Australia, History and Progress, 1848–1928, Board of Trustees, Adelaide, 1928.

Savings Bank of South Australia, A Short Review of Fifty Years 1848 to 1898, SBSA, Adelaide, 1898.

Savings Bank of South Australia, Board of Trustees, Report to the Board, 'Some Considerations Effecting the Volume of Reports and Withdrawals', May 1931, Adelaide, Savings Bank of South Australia records.

Savings Bank of South Australia, Early Documents Relating to the Foundation of the Bank (Series 1A), 'Handbook for Bank Tellers', second edition, 1888, Savings Bank of South Australia records.

Savings Bank of South Australia, Minutes of the Board of the Trustees, Adelaide, Savings Bank of South Australia records.

Savings Bank of South Australia, Depression Years of the 1930s, Adelaide, Savings Bank of South Australia records.

Savings Bank of South Australia Sub-Committee for Interest Arrears, accompanying Minutes of the Board of Trustees, Adelaide, Savings Bank of South Australia records.

Savings Bank of South Australia, Co-operation with the State Bank 1930–1984, Adelaide, Savings Bank of South Australia records.

Savings Bank of South Australia, Pre-Merger Documents 1983–1984, Adelaide, Savings Bank of South Australia records.

Savings Bank of South Australia, Merger -Progress to Date, Adelaide, 1983–1984, Savings Bank of South Australia records.

Savings Bank of South Australia, Mortgage Loans and Lending, 1848–1984, Adelaide, Savings Bank of South Australia records.

Savings Bank of South Australia, *Our Century: A History of the First Hundred Years of the Savings Bank of South Australia*, 1848–1948, published by the bank, 1948.

Scott, W. (Sir), Marks, J. (Sir), 'Marks and Scott Report', Adelaide, 19 September 1975.

Searcy, R.P. Evidence to Royal Commission into State Bank of South Australia, Adelaide, State Print, 1992.

Sheridan, T. Auditor General's Report to the Parliament, 30 June 1989, Adelaide, State Print, 1989.

Simmons, D.W. Submission to the Royal Commission into State Bank of South Australia, Adelaide, 1992.

State Bank of South Australia, Ledgers Advance to Settlers Act 1912–1978, Adelaide, State Bank of South Australia records.

State Bank of South Australia, Manager's Report Kimba Branch, 30 June 1927–1974, Adelaide, State Bank of South Australia records.

State Bank of South Australia, Manager's Report Millicent Branch, 30 June 1950–1974, Adelaide, State Bank of South Australia records.

State Bank of South Australia, Manager's Report on Renmark Branch, 30 June 1927–1974 Adelaide, State Bank of South Australia records.

State Bank of South Australia, Manager's Report Yacka Branch, 30 June 1928–1974, Adelaide, State Bank of South Australia records.

State Bank of South Australia, Manager's Report Southern Branch, 30 June 1961–1982, Adelaide, State Bank of South Australia records.

State Bank of South Australia, Report of the Board of Management 1926–1984, Adelaide, State Bank of South Australia records.

State Bank of South Australia Minutes 1926–1984, Adelaide, State Bank of South Australia records.

State Bank of South Australia Report of the Board of Management, Adelaide, State Bank of South Australia records.

State Bank of South Australia Managers Report 1926–1984, Adelaide, State Bank of South Australia records.

State Bank of South Australia, Lending – Adelaide Office, Adelaide, 1966–1984, State Bank of South Australia records.

State Branch of South Australia Minutes 1895–1926, Adelaide, State Bank of South Australia records.

State Bank Royal Commission, Parliamentary Papers, South Australian Parliament, State Print, 1888.

Index

Abbott, Michael (QC) 140, 143, 218
Addison, H M 18
Adelaide Land Investment Company 12
Adelaide Steamship Company 180, 205–8
Advance Bank xiv, 225
Alfred, Duke of Edinburgh 10
Allen, W 5
Anderson, Tim 218, 220
Anthony, Ernest 26
ANZ Bank 80, 115–6, 152, 154, 201, 206, 210
Archibald, William 17
Australian Bankers Association 85
Ayers, Sir Henry 12, 16
Baker, Mr 166, 209, 211
Baker, McEwin, Millhouse and Wright (Messrs.) 54,
Bakewell, Robert 49, 109–111, 113, 141
Bank of Adelaide x, 69, 80, 89, 111, 115–6
Bank of New South Wales 3, 15, 80–1
Bank of South Australia (1837) 3, 14
Bank of Tokyo 198
Bank SA (1994) xiv, 12
Bannon, John (Premier) ix, x, 121, 125–138, 144, 146–7, 149, 163, 186, 191–3, 197, 200, 213, 217–224
Barclay-Harvey, Sir Charles Malcolm 40, 195
Barnes, R D 128
Barrett, Lew 49, 94, 119, 128, 138, 145–6, 149, 164, 189, 199
Barwell, Sir Henry 25
Basedow, P 12
Bastyan, Sir Eric 85
Beaumont-Smith, G 77
Becker, Heini 114
Beneficial Finance Corporation xiv, 113, 128, 139, 149, 159–61, 165–7, 192, 198, 208, 210–2, 223
Bishop, Sir William 49, 109
Blevins, Frank 210
Boland, K J 99
Bonython, J 103
Bradman, Sir Donald 94

Branson, Cathy 218
Brierley, Sir Ron 206
Brown, Dean 121, 138, 210, 214
BT Corporate Finance 136
Butler (Premier) 37–9
Byrne, Molly 139
Byrnes, P E 128
Caire, H M 36, 38, 43, 52, 80
Cairs, Mr 69
Campbell, A 16
Castine, John William 15–19
Cater, Nick 221–3
Catt, Alfred 17
Chapman, A D 57–9
Chappel, Ian
Chifley, Ben (Prime Minister) 38, 44, 46
Cilento, A W W 49, 77–8
Clark, Tim Marcus x, 132, 139, 142–8, 149–52, 157, 164, 168–80, 182, 184–8, 190–2, 196–7, 217–24
Colonial Office vii, 4
Colton, John 6, 12, 16
Commercial Bank of Australia 11, 12, 64–5, 81
Commonwealth Bank of Australia 37, 79–80, 120, 152, 154, 155, 198, 206
Condous, Steve (Lord Mayor) 201
Coombs, H C 85
Corcoran, Des 111, 115–6
Corporation of Adelaide 4
Crimes, Ernie 109–110
Crooks, Alexander 11
Cudmore, C R 47
Cumming, P 5
Curtin (Prime Minister) 38–9
Dashwood, Captain G F 5
Davenport, S 5
Davenport, Sir Samuel 11
Davis, Leigh 129–130, 135
De Garis, Ren 125
Denny, William 24
Dignum 33
Dittman 76

Downer, Sir John 16
Doyle, John (QC) 218
Dumas, Lloyd 44
Duncan, Peter 127
Dunford, J R 113
Dunstan, Don (Premier) ix, 83, 90, 96–115
Dutton, F S 5
Dyer, G J 68
Eastick, Bruce 103–4
Electricity Trust of South Australia 86, 92, 112
Elizabeth II, Queen 79
Equiticorp 139, 145, 189
Everard, William 12
Ewens, L T 69
Farquhar, Mr 67
Fenner, Charles 49
Ferrier, P L 79
Fewster, J G 66
Finance Corporation of Australia x
Financial Corporation of Australia 115
Finnis, Ayers 180
Finniss, B T (Premier) 5, 9
Fisher, James Hurtle (Resident Commissioner) 4, 9,
Fisher, Joseph 16
Flaxman, C 5
Foreman, Audrey 53
Foster (Judge) 50–1
Fraser, R A 67
Fray, Manager 76
Freburg, Henry 24
Freeman, Eric 94, 102
Galloway, F A 65, 69
Gardiner, G V and F J 34*
Gawler (Governor) 4
George, Gordon 50
Gibson, Milne 58
Giffen, Mr 70
Gilbert, William 7, 16
Giles, Clement 15
Glyde, S D 11
Graves, T 16
Grey (Governor) 4
Griffin, Trevor 212
Group Asset Management Division xiv, 158
Guerin, Bruce 128, 201

Guille, Chris 164, 216
Gunn, John (Premier) 25
Hall, Steele 90, 103
Hancock, Keith 128, 138, 145, 149
Hardy, A 12, 16
Harrison, Sir James 94
Hartley, Rod 141, 143
Hasluck, Nicholas 127
Hawker, A S (Lord Mayor) 40
Hawkins, Allan 139, 145
Hazel, Jim 180
Hector, John 5
Hill, Murray 98, 114
Hindmarsh, John (Governor) vii, 6
Hogben 44
Holder (Treasurer) vii, 14–19
Howard, John 121
Howells, E R 108, 113
Hunkin, Len 49, 83, 90, 94, 97
Huntley, G 49, 98
Hunwick, L V 91
Hurford, Chris 94
Inglis, G 18
J P Morgan (merchant bank) 157, 159, 178
Jacobs, Samuel (Royal Commissioner) 132–3, 136, 144, 163–4, 193, 199, 204, 214, 216, 219–20
Jeffrey, G H P 4, 98–9, 109
Jeffries (Attorney-General) 26, 44
Johnson, J A 18
Johnston, Elliott 116
Keating, Paul 173, 222
Kerr, Warren 44
Kingston, Charles 14
Kneebone, A F 113
Kneebone, Henry 25
Knowles, George 45
Kowalick, Ian 128, 131
Lacey, Mr 26
Lawson, Robert 218
Ligertwood, G C (QC) 41, 44–6, 50
Linn, Tom 31
Lyons, J A 37
McEwin, A G 128
McEwin, Sir Lyell 85
McGregor, Alistair 208–10
McInnes, John 26

McLeay (Lord Mayor) 49
MacPherson, John 17
MacPherson, Kenneth (Auditor-General) 136, 164, 166, 171–4, 176–9, 182–92, 198, 203, 207–12, 214–8, 221–3
Mallett, Trevor 164, 176, 180
Mansfield, John (Royal Commissioner) 133, 136, 193, 204, 214
Marks, Sir John 104
Marshall, H 80
Masters, Mr 52, 190
Matthews, Ken 63, 120, 164, 181, 187, 191, 217
Meeking, Julie 180–1
Menzies, Robert (Prime Minister) 79
Merger Advisory Group 127–134, 145, 151
Millhouse, Robin 90, 108
Milne, R L 8, 12, 16
Montefiore, J 5
Moray Parks Fruit Company 58, 62
Mullins, Peter 201–5
Mundy, A M (Colonial Secretary) 5
Murray, D 12
Nankerville, Bill 139
Napier, Sir Mellis 50
National Australia Bank 3, 14, 81, 152, 154, 206
National Cash Register Company 78
Neuenkirchen, Manager 45, 49
Newoly E S 61
Norrie, Sir Willoughby 50
O'Halloran, Captain W L 5
O'Loghlin, J 16
O'Loughlin, M F (Justice) 128, 145
Oliphant, Sir Mark 102
Olsen, John 129, 132, 135, 138, 147
Ottaway, Graham 176–9
Paddison, Stephen 174–6, 181, 205, 210, 216
Peacock, W 5
Pearson (Treasurer) 90–1
Peat, Marwick, Mitchell and Co. (KPMG Marwick) 192
Pedler, R J H 44, 48, 53
Pegasus Leasing 208–11
Perkins, Professor 18
Phillipps, Sir W Herbert 30, 33
Pinsch, Carl 13

Playford, Sir Thomas (Premier) 29, 38–42, 45, 47, 50, 69, 78, 83–4, 103
Plunkett, Nell 53
Price Waterhouse 192
Reading, Claude 38
Reichart, Erich 166–7, 209
REMM–Myer 200–5
Renmark Fruit Growers Co-op Ltd. 60–1
Reserve Bank of Australia 81, 85, 88–9, 130, 159–61, 163, 171, 186–91, 222
Richards, Robert 26, 47, 50
Richardson, W 43
Riding, Manager 74–5
Riverland Fruit Producers Co-operative 118–9
Roake, L E 62
Robe, F H (Lieutenant Governor) vii, 4
Robertson, Brian 117
Rowed 70
Rumbelow, Peter 198–9
Rundle, J C 35, 37, 39, 41, 47–50
Rymill, Cecil 205
Rymill, Sir Arthur 98, 111, 114, 116
SA Fishermen's Co-op 74–6, 118
Savings Bank of New South Wales 37
Savings Bank of South Australia (1848) vii, 5–16, 21–3, 30, 39–56, 77–95, 96–122
Scott, Alan 116
Scott, Henry 12
Scott, Sir Walter 104
Seaman, G F 69, 83–4, 100, 108, 113
Searcy, Rob 138, 144
Shepherd, A G 109
Sheppard, S 18
Sheridan, Tom 192
Simmons, David 136, 139, 143, 146, 217
Simmons, Don 139
Simmons, P J 121, 128
Smith, E T 16
Smith, Keith 139
South Australian Company 3, 14
South Australian Government Financing Authority 197–8, 219
South Australian Housing Trust 86, 88, 92, 112
South Australian State Treasury 156–7, 171, 199

Spalvins, John 205
Spence, J B 18
Stanton S 18
State Bank Centre 195–6, 199–200
State Bank of New South Wales 155
State Bank of South Australia (1896) vii, 18–20, 21–30, 96–122
   Kimba Branch 62–70
   Millicent Branch 72–4
   Renmark Branch 57–62
   Southern Branch 74–7
   Yacka Branch 70–1
State Bank of South Australia (1984) x–xiv, 149–212
   Cayman Island sub-branch 163
   New York Office 163
State Bank of Victoria 154, 155
State Government Insurance Commission 96, 197
Story, C R 97
Summers, Tony 140
Sumner, Chris (Attorney-General) 129–130, 135
Sun, Chin Wing 181
Sutton, Charles 42
Symons, C J 18

Taggart, Steve 181–2
Taulaks, R B 59–60
Taylor, J C 72, 89
Taylor, Norman 44, 49, 52
Thomas, Daniel 201
Thompson, A B 69
Timms, Joseph 24
Todd, Charles 21
Tonkin, David 110–4, 116, 119–122
Torrens, Robert 13
Town and Country Bank 11
Union Bank 14
Union Mining Company 6
Walker, C A D 91
Walsh, Frank 89
Warren, Edgar 19, 66
Watts, Captain J 5
West, 81
Westpac Banking Corporation 152, 154, 206, 210
Wiling, Ruth 53
Williams, Mr 209
Wilson, J P 22
Wilton, J H 91
Wotherspoon 5
Young, Norma 116